P9-CMF-899

rup.

THE CHRIST OF HISTORY
AND OF EXPERIENCE

PRINTED BY MORRISON AND GIBB LIMITED,

FOR

T. & T. CLARK, EDINBURGH.

LONDON : SIMPKIN, MARSHALL, HAMILTON, KENT, AND CO. LIMITED.
NEW YORK : CHARLES SCRIBNER'S SONS.
TORONTO : THE WILLARD TRACT DEPOSITORY.

Jesus Christ

THE
CHRIST OF HISTORY

AND OF

EXPERIENCE

BEING THE KERR LECTURES FOR 1897

BY

REV. DAVID W. FORREST, M.A.

WELLINGTON CHURCH, GLASGOW

EDINBURGH

T. & T. CLARK, 38 GEORGE STREET

1897

31057

232 P
F77 c

Given by Dr. Leahy

The Rights of Translation and of Reproduction are Reserved.

THE KERR LECTURESHIP.

◆

THE "KERR LECTURESHIP" was founded by the TRUSTEES of the late Miss JOAN KERR, of Sanquhar, under her Deed of Settlement, and formally adopted by the United Presbyterian Synod in May 1886. In the following year, May 1887, provisions and conditions of the Lectureship, as finally adjusted, were adopted by the Synod, and embodied in a Memorandum, printed in the Appendix to the Synod Minutes, p. 489. From these the following excerpts are here given :—

II. The amount to be invested shall be £3000.

III. The object of the Lectureship is the promotion of the study of Scientific Theology in the United Presbyterian Church.

The Lectures shall be upon some such subjects as the following, viz. :—

    A. Historic Theology—

        (1) Biblical Theology, (2) History of Doctrine, (3) Patristics, with special reference to the significance and authority of the first three centuries.

    B. Systematic Theology—

        (1) Christian Doctrine—(a) Philosophy of Religion, (b) Comparative Theology, (c) Anthropology, (d) Christology, (e) Soteriology, (f) Eschatology.

        (2) Christian Ethics—(a) Doctrine of Sin, (b) Individual and Social Ethics, (c) The Sacraments, (d) The Place of Art in Religious Life and Worship.

Farther, the Committee of Selection shall from time to time, as they think fit, appoint as the subject of the Lectures any important Phases of Modern Religious Thought or Scientific Theories in their bearing upon Evangelical Theology. The Committee may also appoint a subject connected with the practical work of the Ministry as subject of Lecture, but in no case shall this be admissible more than once in every five appointments.

IV. The appointments to this Lectureship shall be made in the first instance from among the Licentiates or Ministers of the United Presbyterian Church of Scotland, of whom no one shall be eligible, who, when the appoint-

v

ment falls to be made, shall have been licensed for more than twenty-five years, and who is not a graduate of a British University, preferential regard being had to those who have for some time been connected with a Continental University.

V. Appointments to this Lectureship not subject to the conditions in Section IV. may also from time to time, at the discretion of the Committee, be made from among eminent members of the Ministry of any of the Nonconformist Churches of Great Britain and Ireland, America, and the Colonies, or of the Protestant Evangelical Churches of the Continent.

VI. The Lecturer shall hold the appointment for three years.

VIII. The Lectures shall be published at the Lecturer's own expense within one year after their delivery.

IX. The Lectures shall be delivered to the students of the United Presbyterian Hall.

XII. The Public shall be admitted to the Lectures.

PREFACE.

———◆———

THESE Lectures on the relation between the Historical
and the Spiritual in Christianity were delivered, on
the Kerr Foundation, to the students of the United
Presbyterian College, Edinburgh, in January and Feb-
ruary of this year. They are now published substantially in the form in which they were delivered, with
the inclusion of passages then omitted for want of
time. Some points which did not admit of more than
a general reference in the Lectures will be found more
fully discussed in the appended Notes. While I have
endeavoured throughout the volume to acknowledge
my obligations, I am conscious that there is an indebtedness both to persons and to books, of which
no adequate acknowledgment is possible.

My sincere thanks are due to the Rev. John
Hutchison, D.D., Bonnington, Edinburgh, and John
Hutchison, Esq., LL.D., Glasgow, for their kindness in
reading the proofs; and to the Rev. Professor Orr, D.D.,
Edinburgh, for valuable counsel and suggestion. I have
also been assisted by the Rev. George M'Arthur, M.A.,
in the preparation of the Index.

D. W. F.

GLASGOW, *October* 1897.

vii

" Ego sum primus et novissimus, et vivus, et fui mortuus, et ecce sum vivens in saecula saeculorum."—REV. i. 17, 18.

"Vita manifestata est, et vidimus."—I JOHN i. 2.

CONTENTS.

———✦———

LECTURE I.

THE UNIQUENESS OF CHRIST'S MORAL SELF-CONSCIOUSNESS.

ix

LECTURE II.

CHRIST'S SELF-CONSCIOUSNESS AS INTERPRETED BY HIS CLAIMS.

LECTURE III.

*THE GROWTH OF CHRIST'S SELF-CONSCIOUSNESS,
AND THE METHOD OF HIS SELF-MANIFESTATION.
JESUS AND THE TWELVE*

Contents

LECTURE IV.

THE TRANSITION FROM THE HISTORICAL TO THE SPIRITUAL CHRIST.

LECTURE V.

THE PERSON OF CHRIST AND HIS REVELATION OF THE GODHEAD.

Contents

LECTURE VI.

THE OBJECTIVE ELEMENT IN THE REDEMPTIVE WORK OF CHRIST.

LECTURE VII.

THE NEW LIFE IN CHRIST AND THE CONDITIONS OF ITS REALISATION.

LECTURE VIII.

THE RELATION OF THE SPIRITUAL TO THE HISTORICAL IN CHRISTIAN FAITH.

LECTURE IX.

THE CONDITIONS OF THE FINAL JUDGMENT—IS FAITH IN CHRIST NECESSARILY CONSCIOUS?

b

NOTES TO THE LECTURES.

——◆——

LECTURE I.

LECTURE II.

LECTURE III.

LECTURE IV.

LECTURE I.

THE UNIQUENESS OF CHRIST'S MORAL SELF-CONSCIOUSNESS.

Synopsis.

The two elements in Christian Faith : historical and spiritual.
Their alleged incongruity.
Purpose and plan of the present Course of Lectures.

Dual character of the moral consciousness.
Development of the moral Ideal in Judaism.
This Ideal accepted, but further enriched, by Christ.
His conception of God and man, as Father and son, involved the 'infinite nature' of Duty.
Relation of Duty to Immortality.
Finality of Christ's moral Ideal.

Christ devoid of an element universally present in man's religious life : His moral consciousness single, not dual.
Why the testimony of the Gospels and Epistles on this point is irresistible.
Christ's abstention from " common prayer."
The *positive* implications of 'sinlessness' : Christ unhaunted by misgivings for the 'might-have-been.'
The objections made to His conduct in special instances : why futile.

Dr. Martineau's denial that Christ constitutes a separate moral type : its untenableness.
Natural evolution fails to account for Christ alike in connection with (1) what precedes Him, and (2) what follows Him. The latter failure fatal.

Though a unique type, He is essentially a *human* type, of goodness : bears the developing mark of humanity.

LECTURE I.

THE UNIQUENESS OF CHRIST'S MORAL
SELF-CONSCIOUSNESS.

IT is a distinctive mark of the Christian religion that it blends together inseparably the historical and the spiritual. It claims to be based on a supreme historic Personality, who not only proclaimed the highest truths of God's holiness and love, but who realised in His own character all that God demands of man as His child, and thus broke the sad immemorial traditions of human sin, and offered up in suffering and in death a stainless life, which God crowned by a triumphant resurrection. It claims, moreover, that He who manifested this character took up such a position relatively to other men, and so emphasised the importance of His own personality, as could only be justified on the assumption that He was God manifest in flesh, and that His human life was but the means whereby He took the manhood into God, and so became the beginning of a new spiritual experience in humanity. But the bare acceptance of these truths does not constitute faith. The belief that Jesus lived, died, and rose, or that He came into the world to achieve the blessing of man's deliverance, is one thing; belief *in* Him is another, and implies the formation of a fellowship in which Christ is to us as individuals all that God can be.

3

Clearly such a faith, which is a spiritual act, has its roots in history, and that in two ways. First, our conception of what Christ is as the indwelling life of the Church and of the individual soul, derives its content from His earthly character and work. Secondly, He Himself possesses His present power to deliver and renew us only because He was once a sharer in the moral struggle of our race, and came forth from it victorious. It was by virtue of His own human triumph that He acquired, as the Lord of humanity, the capacity and the right to be the guarantee of ours. Hence, while Christianity professes to be adapted to all times and conditions as an immediate reality in experience, it is yet anchored to one particular epoch and to a special personality in the past. For this reason it seems to some to consist of two incompatible parts joined together with untempered mortar. On the one hand, they say, it does justice to the religious instinct which tells us that faith means an immediate communion of the soul with God; and, on the other, it perverts the nature of this communion by making it include a certain intellectual attitude to a historical event. It therefore unwarrantably seeks to shut out from this true fellowship with God, which is the deepest necessity of the heart, all who, in the difficult sphere of historical investigation, arrive at conclusions which it disapproves. By this binding together of spiritual experience with matters of opinion whose right determination involves profound philosophical problems and the delicate weighing of testimony, a twofold evil results. Many scientific and cultured minds are regarded as irreligious merely because they will not be guilty of intellectual dishonesty; while

the untrained masses are called upon in the name of
faith to give adhesion to asserted facts which they have
no capacity of verifying.[1]

Now Christianity took its rise, not in an abstract
conception of what ought to be, but in the recognition
of what had been. The faith in a living Christ, in
whom alone the power of our sonship to God is restored,
was not the product of an idealising imagination, but
the conviction to which men felt themselves impelled by
the facts of Christ's earthly life, and the spiritual experiences which it awaked in them. My purpose in these
lectures is to discuss the relations between the historical
and spiritual in Christianity with special reference to
their alleged incongruity. The argument is necessarily
a gradual and cumulative one. In the present lecture
I shall try to show that the moral self-consciousness of
Jesus was incontestably of such a character as makes it
impossible to account for Him by any theory of normal
development, and in the next that His self-consciousness, as interpreted by the claims He made, implies His
eternal or transcendent Sonship. In the third lecture I
shall deal with the growth of this self-consciousness, and
then with the method which He adopted in His self-
manifestation to men as the incarnate Son. Under the
latter head I hope to show that Teaching formed but one
of the media in this manifestation, and that the selection

---

[1] "It is by no means," says Professor T. H. Green, "a piece of mere intellectual wantonness to disturb the faithful in that theory of their faith which
they have come to think inseparable from faith itself, to inquire whether faith,
as a spiritual state, is necessarily dependent on assent to those propositions concerning ostensible matters of fact which form the basis of theological dogma.
Such inquiry is necessary for the vindication of faith itself, and even for its
presentation in its properly scriptural character." — *Miscellaneous Works*,
p. 266.

of a special circle of associates, like the twelve disciples, was necessary for the reception or recognition of such a revelation of personality.   The fourth lecture will treat of the Resurrection as the transition point from the historical to the spiritual.   I shall there discuss the question of the Christophanies, and endeavour to prove that they present just those characteristics which were required to verify to the disciples, not only the persistency and continuity of Christ's life after death, but its transformation, the entrance of His total personality into a higher and permanent mode of existence.   The fifth lecture will deal with the view of Christ's person and of the Godhead to which His earthly life as interpreted by the Resurrection and by Christian experience inevitably leads.   In this connection I shall treat of the Christology of the apostles, and of the true nature, as it appears to me, of the decisions of the great Church Councils, and the degree in which modern Kenotic theories tend to modify or elucidate them.   The sixth lecture will be a discussion of the Objective element in the work of Christ relative to human redemption, and specially of its relation to the receptivity of the individual soul.   In the seventh I shall speak of the new life of sonship which Christ mediates, of the Church as the home in which it is fostered, and of Humanity as the total sphere in which alone it realises itself.   In the eighth lecture I shall endeavour to show that the union of the historical with the spiritual in the Christian Faith does not make of it an incongruous amalgam, that the same union pervades the entire moral life of man, and that the historical element in Christianity is of such a nature as renders it capable of exceptional verification.   The final lecture will deal with the problem, how far the view of Christianity which I have presented is reconcilable with the undoubted fact that a moral character of peculiar excellence and attractiveness is often possessed by those who reject the historic faith of the Church. Or, to put the matter briefly, Is faith in Christ necessarily conscious?

I start, then, with the moral self-consciousness of Jesus as constituting a unique type of human personality.

When we begin our resolves for a better life our idea of the aim to be reached is usually comparatively simple. We are conscious of some glaring faults in certain departments of our conduct, such as physical self-indulgence, or hastiness of temper, or inconsiderateness towards others. We set ourselves to amend these; and just in proportion as we succeed, new lines of duty and self-denial unfold themselves. Quite possibly we may disregard them, and make no effort to remove the further defects that have been disclosed to us; but that is not because we have achieved our end and remain placidly content with the result, but because we are weary of the continual struggle. We may refuse to respond to the fresh claims made upon us, but none the less we know they exist; and by impatiently turning away from them we surrender the possibility of moral progress. If, on the other hand, we acknowledge their authority, and address ourselves to meet them, they but prove to mark another stage in an endless journey. Nay, more than that; for advance in the moral life is not properly represented by a direct ascent towards some final height, where the lower points are wholly overpassed. There is in it, not only a heightening, but a deepening and widening, of the entire conception of duty. As one phase or

capacity of our being leads to another, so it is in turn
reacted upon; and the successes that we gain in any
part of our character are not final, relieving us of all
struggle or concern regarding it. The real goal which
is set before us, and the attainment of which alone
satisfies, is not any single supreme point, but the complete harmony of an infinitely complex nature. The
richer a man's spiritual life becomes, the clearer is his
conception of this complexity, of the numberless factors
whose right relation to each other constitutes human
goodness. Hence it is that his self-consciousness bears
a dual witness. At the same moment that it encourages
him by the assurance of his progress and growth in
moral power, it alarms and depresses him by testifying
to the widening of the gulf that separates him from
his ideal. The same experience that declares his increasing unity with God emphasises his divergence
from Him.

Sometimes this strange and abiding antinomy in
human character is described as if it implied that the
better one is, the worse he feels himself to be. But
that is not quite the case. The saint who has, through
the efforts of long years, attained a conspicuous strength
and nobleness, knows very well that he is better than
before; that he has rid himself of obstructions and
weaknesses that hampered his being and obscured his
vision. He feels that he has been moving forward and
upward; he is under no delusion of retrogression; but
he is more overwhelmed than of old by the distance that
stretches between him and the end of his endeavour,
not because the distance is greater, but because formerly
he did not realise how great it was. The increase of

moral power which he has gained by resistance to one form of evil is, as it were, more than counterbalanced by the increased sense of obligation which that moral power has given him.   The conflict deepens and broadens, and seems to lose itself in an almost inextricable confusion.   It is this fact which accounts for the unspeakable self-abasement of devout souls.   There is nothing unreal in their cry of self-loathing when they confess themselves the chief of sinners.   That confession, notwithstanding its form, does not involve a comparison of their own condition before God with that of others,— a comparison for which, as they would be the first to admit, they have not, and cannot have, the requisite knowledge.   It is not a phrase to be interpreted by the rules of logic; it is the language of a heart so keenly alive to the incalculable claims that remain to be fulfilled, that it can only prostrate itself before the Holiest. Such a one may have reached heights which previously he never hoped to scale,—which then, indeed, he could not even descry,—but the sense of achievement which this experience has brought is almost overborne and swallowed up by his new consciousness of the altitudes that tower above him.   The problem is further from solution than ever, because it is not the same problem to which he addressed himself at the first.   It has opened out into far-reaching meanings, the very terms of which he can hardly comprehend.   The more he succeeds in acquiring self-denial, generosity, purity of heart, the more utterly hopeless does the quest appear to him.

It may be said that this description of the dual witness of our moral consciousness does not apply to humanity universally ; that Aristotle, for example, in his

"Ethics," sets forth the high-minded man[1] as the loftiest type of character; and the high-minded man is he who, possessing a rare degree of merit, values himself as he deserves. But everything depends on the standard by which men try themselves. A proud self-content, as in Pharisaism, is perfectly natural to those for whom the religious life consists of a definite round of ritual observances. If we believe that duty can be thus summed up, the fulfilment of it becomes a very practicable thing. If, again, we travel beyond this travesty of religion to the experience of those who, like the Greeks, had some true conception of moral obligations to others, yet for whom these obligations were still limited and calculable, then though there may remain elements of self-dissatisfaction in a good man's view of his conduct, he will not be increasingly overwhelmed by the thought of an impossible task. The Greek idea of virtue was essentially æsthetic. It demanded, above all, balance and proportion in the character. Human qualities were for it measurable things, like the parts of a work of art, and forming together in their mutual relation a complete ¬d compact whole. We feel at once how inadequate suc.. a view is. It is not merely that we differ from it, but we cannot by any stretch of imagination conceive of ourselves as holding it. It is an outworn conception of the ideal of conduct, to which there was no possible return when once the vision of the Infinite Holiness dawned upon humanity. "We needs must love the highest when we see it."[2]

The Jewish race was the means of revealing to the

---

[1] μεγαλόψυχος, *Eth. Nicom.* 4. 3, 3 sq.
[2] See Note 1, p. 381, "The Greek and Christian Ideals of Conduct."

world the absoluteness and endlessness of human obligation. The revelation was a gradual process; but the
root-idea from which the perfect flower grew is already
expressed by the great prophets of the eighth century.
Their protests against a ceremonial worship; their declaration that God demanded mercy rather than sacrifice;
that, as the Holy One, He could be satisfied with nothing
but a spiritual worship and an ethical service,—implied
an infinite element in the relation which the soul sustained towards Him. "Woe is me," cries Isaiah,
smitten with the vision of the intolerable brightness,
"for I am undone; because I am a man of unclean lips:
for mine eyes have seen the King, the Lord of Hosts."[1]
This consciousness of unspeakable guilt before the Infinite was only possible to one who had at least the dim
consciousness of an infinite nature within himself to
which he had not been loyal.

But though the sense of an immeasurable responsibility is present in Hosea and Isaiah, it is not so much
that of the individual as of the member of a sacred community.[2] They lived in the marvellous historic life of
the chosen race, and almost merged themselves in it.
Their duty consisted in remaining true to the heritage
of their fathers, and transmitting it undimmed to their
children, that the generation to come might praise the
Lord. While, therefore, they held that Jehovah was no
sectional deity, but the God of the whole earth, yet in

[1] Isa. vi. 5.
[2] Speaking of Hosea, Prof. Kirkpatrick says, "Israel is treated as an
individual, as possessing a solidarity and continuity of life, as responsible for
its actions. Jehovah's covenant is with the nation, not, primarily, with the
individuals of the nation. It is in the later prophets that the doctrine of personal responsibility begins to appear, which is fully developed in the New
Testament."—*Doctrine of the Prophets*, p. 129.

their noblest hope of the future they never conceived of Him as the God of other races and tribes in the same way as He was the God of the Jews. Israel remained still His peculiar people. The heathen nations would submit to His authority, and come to worship at Zion. But their position would be one of subjection. They would show forth His glory by doing homage to His power, but not by entering into that direct relation of loving obedience sustained by the children of Abraham. Just because Isaiah and Micah could not rise to the *universality* of man's obligation to God, they failed to realise the depth of its *individual* content. That which was deepest in their religious consciousness was associated, not with the essential characteristic of humanity, but with the special gifts conferred upon Israel. And though in the course of time the moral conception, which was the heart of the matter, necessarily broke through the inadequate form in which it clothed itself, yet so long as this national restriction lasted it obscured the full value of the single soul to God.

The deliverance of the prophetic thought from its limitations came in the only possible way,—through the teaching of events that lowered the national pride. It was on the eve of that destruction of the Jewish state which he perceived to be inevitable, that Jeremiah spoke of a time when God would write His new covenant on men's hearts, and all should know Him from the least to the greatest.[1]   It was during the bitterness of the Exile that Ezekiel dwelt so strenuously on the absolutely personal character of righteousness, "The soul that sinneth, it shall die,"[2] and that the Second Isaiah beheld

[1] Jer. xxxi. 31–34, cf. 29, 30.   [2] Ezek. xviii. 20.

in the future the participation of all nations in the salvation of God as their common strength and joy.[1] Jewish particularism was being purged out by disaster, and the true service of God disclosed in its universal and individual greatness.[2] On the individual side the ultimate expression to which Judaism attained is found in those Psalms which belong probably to the time of the Persian and Greek domination. Conscious of the glorious past of Israel, and humiliated by her present debasement, the psalmist is thrown back upon himself, and holds his lonely colloquy with his God.[3] The absence of the outward divine witness in a holy nation does not destroy his religious faith, it intensifies it; revealing to him the abysmal deeps of his own personality and the mysterious reality and riches of the divine fellowship. It is this detachment from external conditions which gives the Psalms their permanent value as the utterance of a soul deserted or despised of men, but full face with God.

A well-known epigram[4] declares that there are two facts in history which astonish us,—that Shakespeare was born an Englishman, and that Jesus Christ was born a Jew. But the contrast of Christ with Judaism lies on the surface: His affinity with it is central. He came in the line of the Jewish prophets and psalmists. He both absorbed and purified their ideals. It might seem as if

---

[1] Isa. lx.

[2] "Israel on the way to Exile is on the way to become Israel after the Spirit." G. A. Smith, *Book of Isaiah*, vol. ii. p. 29.

[3] See Pfleiderer, *Philosophy and Development of Religion*, vol. ii. pp. 57, 58.

[4] The epigram, I think, is Heine's, but I cannot recall the precise reference. See, however, his *Shakespeare's Mädchen und Frauen* (edit. 1839), p. 1, where the same contrast is treated with incisive irony.

their conception of human obligation in the service of
the Holy One could not be surpassed in depth and keenness.   Yet while He accepted it, He gave it a fuller and
richer significance by the higher revelation He made of
God's character as the Father.   The psalmist had said,
" Like as a father pitieth his children, so the Lord
pitieth them that fear Him."   Jesus said in effect, " The
Father pitieth all souls that He hath made, because they
are His children.   He maketh His sun to rise on the
evil and on the good."   This beneficence to just and
unjust alike was the proof, not of God's moral indifference,
but of His measureless longsuffering and His passion to
redeem.   Just as He was mindful of those who feared
Him, and did not cast them off in their times of faithlessness ; so He did not withdraw, even from those who
feared Him not, the influences and beseechings of His
grace.   God was no more, as of old, fundamentally the
Holy One who was also good ; but essentially He was
the perfect Love, which is perfect Holiness and something
more, holiness with an inner necessity of self-communication.   The intimacy of this Fatherly relation in which
God stood to man not only added a darker hue to each
transgression, but enlarged the range of the service which
man as son owed to God.   It drove him to a keener
self-searching, because it awoke in him the consciousness
of a more blessed destiny.   So long as holiness is for us
the final determinative quality in God, our conception of
likeness to Him is apt to assume somewhat of a negative
character.   Goodness means then individual severance
from evil, and tends to grow self-centred.   But when we
see that the determinative quality in God is love, our
duty to Him is transformed into a positive and endless

service. His unceasing self-communication by which He deals with men as they are, only in reference to what they ought to be and may yet become, constitutes the law, as it is the basis and inspiration, of our obedience. We can rest in nothing short of that perfection which is already complete in Him.

Very closely allied to this thought of the moral value of the individual to God is the idea of his immortality. Christ's argument for the continued personal existence of the patriarchs rests upon this ground, that the fellowship into which God entered with Abraham, Isaac, and Jacob was the expression of His eternal love, and made them partakers of His eternity. A communion like this is "not born for death." But the more profound and penetrating it is, the more complete God's self-impartation and man's capacity of receiving it, so much the more clearly is man bound up with the abidingness of God. If his immortality is involved in his power of knowing God as the Holy and Merciful One, it becomes doubly sure when God's fellowship with him has the personal significance, the specific moral content, implied in Fatherhood and Sonship. The recognition of it is not an inference from that fellowship : it is a realisation of what the fellowship means. In a remarkable passage Mr. Frederic Myers has told us how one day at Cambridge, when walking with George Eliot in the Fellows' Garden at Trinity, " she, stirred somewhat beyond her wont, and taking as her text the three words which have been used so often as the inspiring trumpet-calls of men—the words, *God*, *Immortality*, *Duty*—pronounced with terrible earnestness, how inconceivable was the *first*, how unbelievable the *second*,

and yet how peremptory and absolute the *third*."[1]
The idea of the infinite nature of duty, which is
the dominant principle of religious Positivism, is the
distinct creation of Christianity; and it certainly could
never have attained its present range and intensity had
it not been indissolubly associated with the other two
infinites which George Eliot rejected, the infinite life of
God in which we share, and the endlessness of our communion with Him. It is a shallow misconception to
think that immortality has rather a quantitative than a
qualitative worth, that the longer or shorter existence of
the individual does not affect his essential value as a
moral being. There are cases, and this is one of them,
where quantity, continuity, *does* emphatically determine
our estimate of the quality. If a man is convinced that
the duty which he owes to others operates but for a
season, that the character which he has painfully built
up in moral strength and attractiveness will soon cease
as a personal force, that whatever influence may flow
from him after death, a final arrest is put on his own
spiritual growth, then Duty can very seldom have for
him the range or imperativeness which would attach to
it, if he realised that every present fidelity and failure
had a permanent effect in moulding the service he will
render to God in the measureless future. If, as with
George Eliot, this sense of the infinite nature of duty
remains as keen as in a Christian saint, it becomes an
oppressive weight. Divorced from its concomitant
truths of God and immortality, it leads to a weary
and pathetic striving after an ever-vanishing ideal, for
the attainment of which the soul has neither the support

[1] *Essays: Modern*, p. 269.

of an infinite love in its struggle, nor time to complete
its work.[1]

What concerns us here, however, is not so much that
the conception of duty as an infinite thing suffers a
certain depreciation when severed from the sanctions and
inspirations through which it rose, as that it has become
in one form or other an inherent principle of modern
thought and action.   The standard of obligation may, as
with the Christian, be found in the perfection of God, or,
as with the Positivist, in the constitution of human nature
itself; but in both cases the demand which it makes of
them, the law which it prescribes, " Die to self, that you
may live," is infinite.   Their moral consciousness inevitably bears a double witness.   The more it assures them
of an increasing harmony with the ideal of self-sacrifice,
the more it accentuates their divergence from it.   *The
harmony and the divergence are two permanent sides of the
one spiritual experience.*   Yet He who has awaked men
to this ideal, and for whom it existed in its ultimate and
most imperative form, had the sense of harmony *without*
the divergence; that is, He was free from an element
which exists universally in the religious life, and through
which that life, as we know it, is built up.   What, then,
are the grounds which render it impossible for us to
doubt that Jesus actually possessed this unique characteristic ?

In such an inquiry we are, of course, not entitled to
presuppose the inspiration of the four Gospels.   We have
to deal with them simply as accounts, professing to be
historical, of the acts and words of Jesus, and to treat

---

[1] See Note 2, p. 383, "The Consequence of divorcing Duty from
Immortality."

2

them as any other documents of the same class. Leaving
aside the Fourth Gospel for the present and dealing only
with the Synoptics, there is a general consensus of
critical opinion that to a large degree they are drawn
from two common sources, one a narrative of the *Acts* of
Jesus, more or less similar to Mark's Gospel; the other
a collection of His *Sayings*, written probably by the
Apostle Matthew, and forming the basis of the canonical
Gospel bearing his name.[1]   These were not in any sense
a complete record, and various additional incidents and
utterances seem to have been preserved either orally or
in written form. This is practically implied by the
statement of Luke in his preface, that he found many
narratives in existence regarding Christ's life. His
Gospel itself contains miracles, parables, and sayings
which have no parallel in the first two Gospels,[2] and
which probably had some other origin than the two
sources mentioned above. He claims to trace the course
of events accurately from the very first by a careful
examination of all his available materials. The differences between the Synoptics, so manifest and so remarkable, have been explained by some critics[3] as owing to
the diverse sources from which they drew; and by others[4]

---

[1] See Beyschlag, *N.T. Theology*, vol. i. pp. 29-31 ; Bruce, *Kingdom of
God*, pp. 1-4.

[2] Whether the First or the Third Gospel presents the more primitive
version is a question which will probably never be finally decided. As it has
to be determined by internal evidence, the " personal equation " must always
enter into the critical verdict. In different passages the balance seems to
incline now to the one Gospel, now to the other. Luke certainly connects
the sayings of Christ much more accurately than Matthew with the incidents
out of which they sprang ; but his arrangement of the incidents themselves
pays little regard to chronological order. Cf. Lightfoot, *Biblical Essays*,
p. 180 ; Bruce, *Kingdom of God*, pp. 9-14.

[3] Weizsäcker.   [4] Bruce.

as partly due to the Evangelists themselves, to their individual characteristics, and the special purpose they had in view. But in whatever particulars they vary, they are absolutely uniform in their picture of Christ's moral self-witness. They portray Him as confessing ignorance,[1] as overwhelmed with grief, as wrestling in prayer. The reality of His humanity, His utter dependence on the Father, His obedience to a Will above His own, these are set forth with the greatest emphasis through all the variety of His experience. But the note of contrition which ever belongs to the saintly soul is in His case wholly absent. Yet, according to all human analogy, it ought to have been more pronounced in Him than in others. As He surpassed all in His sense of nearness to God, so He ought to have surpassed them in the depth of His humiliations.

We have to remember that the question here is not regarding a particular incident or isolated saying of Christ which might have passed unobserved, or at least been speedily forgotten. A single moral fault committed by a hitherto stainless soul, if we can imagine that, alters its entire relation to God. Penitence, however true, will not restore its stainlessness: *that* is gone for ever. It can no longer take up the attitude of unbroken fellowship and loyalty. Even if it could maintain its fidelity henceforth, it could never rid itself of the dark memory, but must perpetually approach the Father as one conscious of a great failure and pleading an unmerited mercy. But such future fidelity is impos-

---

[1] Mark xiii. 32. There can be little doubt that the parallel passage in Matthew (xxiv. 36) also contains the words οὐδὲ ὁ υἱός. See Westcott and Hort, *n.* ; Gore, *Dissertations*, p. 84, *n.*

sible. The moral nature is a unity; and the spirit of selfishness or revolt out of which the one sin sprang tends to repeat itself, and leaves no portion of the inward life untouched. In a deep sense, " he that offends in one point is guilty of all." The consciousness of unworthiness is thus not an occasional, but an abiding element in character. It penetrates and colours all thought and feeling. Therefore, if it belonged to Christ, it must have continually manifested itself, and become an inseparable part of the impression He produced. But such a supposition is utterly contradicted by the whole presentation given us in the first three Gospels, by Christ's references to Himself as the Founder of the new kingdom of God, by His attitude to those who acknowledged their sinfulness before Him, by His conduct at the Last Supper. It had evidently not a fragment of support in the very varied sources known to the Synoptic writers, and what they did find there constitutes an emphatic refutation of it.

Now the Synoptic account, so far as it bears on the question of Christ's moral self-revelation, has a direct truthfulness, and a coherence and unity of impression, wholly unaccountable unless it be substantially a reproduction of the statements and belief of the twelve disciples themselves. But we have other means of knowing what that belief was. Peter in his First Epistle speaks of the death of Christ as of a lamb without blemish and without spot,[1] and says that He died[2] for sins once, the righteous for the unrighteous, that He

---

[1] Chap. i. 19.

[2] ἀπέθανεν, not ἔπαθεν. See Westcott and Hort ; Johnstone, *Comm. on First Ep. of Peter*, p. xviii.

might bring us to God. The Fourth Gospel[1] and the First Epistle of John are penetrated with the same conception of " Jesus Christ the righteous," and whatever theory be entertained regarding the actual authorship of both as they now stand, they could never have borne the name of the son of Zebedee in the early Church, unless they represented his view on such a primary point as the moral nature and lordship of Jesus. It is, moreover, absolutely certain from the undisputed Epistles of Paul that the first apostles were unanimous on this point. With regard to many subjects, he had to contend with them ; on this, he had only to repeat and endorse their testimony. It was a fundamental article of the Church's creed, laid down by those who had been the associates of Jesus in His earthly life. Their verdict cannot be explained away by saying that they were no authorities on the *inner* life of Jesus, that they could only testify to what they saw and heard, and that their witness counts for no more than the declaration that *they* found no fault in Him. It counts for a great deal more. To argue thus is to ignore the specific characteristic of His relation to them. In all His intercourse He was dealing with their spiritual life, leading them to deeper thoughts of God and of what they ought to be to Him, impressing upon them with irresistible power the need of absolute reality and veracity of character. Not merely His words, but His very presence probed their hearts and made sincerity for them the first of moral duties. Yet He so

[1] That the Fourth Gospel depicts the sinless self-consciousness of Jesus requires no argument ; and the Synoptic testimony is adequate of itself. I have felt it better, therefore, to reserve the problem of the Fourth Gospel till the next lecture, because the Johannine presentation of the self-witness of Jesus differs in some measure from the Synoptic.

bore Himself at every stage as to convey to them the
inevitable conviction of His sinlessness.   If there was *any*
suppression of truth in this, it was not incidental, but
constant and uniform.   He maintained this air of moral
supremacy and isolation most markedly in those great
moments when He lifted them into the closest communion with God, when He spoke most solemnly of
Himself and the mission entrusted to Him by the
Father.   Can it be rationally supposed that He who has
branded hypocrisy as the most odious of sins, could
have committed it in its most awful form?   He, if any
man, had "truth in the inward parts," and was driven
by the necessity of His being so to act that others to
whom He was constantly revealing Himself should not
cherish any untrue idea of His character.   Therefore
the testimony of the apostles is no external thing.   Being
founded on Christ's self-manifestation it really touches
the inmost quality of His life.

There is one fact in His self-manifestation which in
this connection demands special reference.   He never
united with the disciples in prayer.   This abstention is
a matter of primary significance, for it severs Him from
all other religious teachers and prophets.   With them,
fellowship in devotion has ever been a chief means
whereby they have led their followers into the secret
places of the Divine.   It is first of all a need of their
personal life, and keeps the heart fresh in humility and
brotherly love.   Without it, their own vision of God
would become blurred.   So also it binds to them the
hearts of others whom they are seeking to guide and
uplift, by the sense that it imparts of a common experience of struggle and aspiration.   The leader may have

far surpassed his followers, but he has travelled by the
same road, and has not yet reached the goal. His loftier
attainment is thus not an oppression and a despair, but
an inspiration. Christ emphatically recognised the value
of united prayer for the soul's quickening and refresh-
ment. "I say unto you, If two of you shall agree on
earth as touching anything that they shall ask, it shall be
done for them of My Father which is in heaven. For
where two or three are gathered together in My name,
there am I in the midst of them."[1] But there is not the
slightest indication, either in the Synoptics or in John,
that He observed it. At the Transfiguration, Luke tells
us, "He took Peter and John and James, and went up
into a mountain to pray. And, as He prayed, the
fashion of His countenance was altered." The disciples
had fallen into a state of deep depression in consequence
of the declaration of His approaching death; Jesus was
anxious to raise them from their dangerous stupor. In
order to do this, says Godet, He took them to the mount
"to pray with them, knowing by experience the influence
a sojourn upon some height has upon the soul."[2] But
the Evangelist does not say that our Lord went up to
pray "with them." He went up *to pray*, to pour out His
heart to the Eternal Father. It was nightfall, and the
disciples, having engaged in their own evening devotions,
had lain down to sleep. But still their Master was wrapt
in a divine communion, and *as He continued praying*, the
Transfiguration came to Him. The brightness of the

---

[1] Matt. xviii. 19, 20.

[2] *Comment. on St. Luke, in loc.* So Weiss, "They could not have
beheld this vision, if Jesus had not allowed them to participate in His life of
prayer, and if He had not prayed with and for them, in order to strengthen
their weak faith."—*Life of Christ*, vol. iii. p. 99, *n*.

light that clothed Him awoke the sleeping apostles.
The encouragement imparted to them in their dejection
sprang, not from their prayers with Him, but from the
revelation that came to them through His prayer.

Consider, too, what is implied in such an account as
this: "It came to pass, as He was praying in a certain
place, that when He ceased, one of His disciples said
unto Him, Lord, teach us to pray, as John also taught
his disciples. And He said unto them, When ye pray,
say, Father, hallowed be Thy name."[1] Professor Bruce[2]
argues that this request implies that Jesus practised
family prayer as the head of a household, and that it
was the impressiveness of His social prayers which made
the disciples conscious of the feeble, vague, stammering
words in which they uttered their wants to God, and
led them to long for His instruction and guidance. But
is it not precisely the opposite inference which should
be drawn? Either these social prayers which He is
supposed to have daily offered were practically identical
with the prayer which He now prescribed,—in which
case the disciples already knew how He meant them to
approach God,—or they differed, as I hope to show
they must have done, in one central point, in which case
they would have been an inadequate expression of the
disciples' needs. Jesus was evidently in the habit of
passing up into special personal communion with God,
even when others stood by His side. "It came to pass
as He was *alone* praying, His disciples were with Him,

---

[1] Luke xi. 1 (R.V.). This is Luke's form of the Lord's Prayer: the
longer form is in Matthew. Here, as usual, Luke gives the historic setting;
but it is not so certain that his version of the words is the more accurate.
Cf. Meyer, *St. Matthew*; Godet, and Plummer, *St. Luke, in loc.*

[2] Bruce, *The Training of the Twelve*, p. 51.

and He asked them, Who do the multitudes say that I
am?"[1]   These seasons, when the Master was with them
and yet withdrawn from them into an inward fellowship,
"had always a peculiar solemnity for those that surrounded Him."[2]   They bore home to the disciples the
secret of His life, the elevation and strength that flow
from prayer; and it was only natural that, seeing the
inspiration which it brought Him in every crisis of His
experience, they should long to enter more fully into its
blessedness. "Lord, teach us to pray. And He said,
When *ye* pray, say . . ." It was *their* prayer, not His.
And why not His? Because it had in the heart of it a
petition which He could never utter: "Forgive us our
sins; for we also forgive every one that is indebted to us."
Yet that petition was indispensable for them. Every
prayer of theirs had to contain an element of confession
before it could be acceptable to the Father. Even when
it consisted chiefly of adoration or supplication, it must
be permeated by the feeling of unworthiness. They
could only draw near to God aright as penitents, acknowledging mercies which they had not deserved, imploring
a grace which they had often despised. This undertone
of shortcoming was to be the note of their devotion;
and it had no place in His. Hence, if Jesus practised
family prayer, as the head of a household, either it contained, or it did not contain, the element of confession.
If it did, it gave the disciples a false impression of *His*
character; if it did not, it led to a false idea of *their
own*. In either case, it would have lessened that conviction of His peculiar and unshared relation to God
which all other phases of His conduct tended to produce.

[1] Luke ix. 18.   [2] Godet.

This incident is almost in itself decisive. But it does not stand alone; it is in harmony with the entire picture of Christ as given in the Gospels. In taking leave of His followers, He abstains from that form of farewell which religious teachers in all ages have observed. We recognise the "touch of nature" when St. Paul, after his address to the Ephesian elders, who feared they should see his face no more, kneeled down and prayed with them all.[1] How better could he part with them than at the "feet of God"? But Christ's last prayer[2] was a prayer not *with* them, but *for* them; and in its references to Himself, when His whole life lay in the past, is absolutely free from those experiences of remembered fault which give to all our devotion its sharpest cry, "I have glorified Thee on the earth; I have finished the work which Thou gavest Me to do." There is not a whisper of contrition; only the spirit of a perfect confidence, and the ring of an assured triumph. The best of men hopes to enter heaven but as a humble penitent; Jesus enters it as a conqueror.

The Synoptics and the Fourth Gospel are here at one. They all speak of His prayers, and even record for us some of the words He used in His thanksgivings, supplications, and intercessions; but uniformly represent Him as solitary in His devotion, in circumstances where all human analogy and the very needs of the soul itself would lead us to expect a fellowship. How could they possibly omit all allusion to what, if it occurred at all, must have been a part of His daily intercourse with His followers, and the recollection of which would be specially treasured? It is not one passage here or there that

[1] Acts xx. 36.   [2] John xvii.

compels this conclusion regarding Him; it is the tenor
and cast of the narrative as a whole.   There is but one
explanation of so strange an isolation.   Jesus showed
His true humanity in this, that prayer was as necessary
for Him as for others; and the fact that He never
observed it in a social form is one of the many proofs
that He was conscious of standing in a relation of moral
rectitude towards the Father attained by none other of
the sons of men.[1]

The full significance of such a consciousness on His
part is apt to be lost by us from the negative shape in
which we express it.   The word *sinlessness* suggests at
first rather the absence of defect than the presence of an
active and pervading holiness.   But negative though its
form be, its content is supremely positive.   In ordinary
usage we divide sins into those of commission and of
omission.   Our duty is violated, not only by acts of sheer
wrong-doing, but also by leaving out of our life that
which God meant to be there.   It is in this latter aspect
that the sense of sin overwhelms us with an infinite
oppressiveness.   The lie which we are tempted to tell
is a definite thing : we are, as it were, brought face to
face with it.   Whether we yield or resist, we feel that we
can in a manner estimate the character of the fault.[2]
But the helpful service which we might have rendered,

---

[1] See Note 3, p. 385, " The Prayers of Christ."

[2] We cannot, indeed, measure our total responsibility, even in telling a
single falsehood ; for our blameworthiness can only be fully judged by reference to the backgrounds of our character and our whole past relation to the
moral possibilities of our life.   But there is a definite calculable fact in the
foreground, whereas the omitted duties of self-sacrifice have frequently no
foreground at all.   They may have never entered into our consciousness.   We
are only sure that we have been guilty of such, but cannot tell what or how
great they are.

but neglected, belongs to the incalculable. We have
no standard of measurement here, and are carried far
into the unconscious backgrounds of our life. We have,
for example, a certain piece of work to do, and we do
it; but can we ever say we have done it fully? How
many elements enter into its right performance? Even
if we accomplish it to the best of our ability, is that
ability all that it might have been? Have our habits
in the past preserved and matured for us the best
energies of body and mind, the finest perceptions of the
soul?

> " Our deeds still travel with us from afar,
>   And what we have been makes us what we are."

We know with absolute certainty that there have been
times when moods of self-indulgence or evil temper have
possessed us, and that they have now become interwoven
with an inextricable series of experiences. The wilfulness of yesterday may be repented of, and that repentance
may be the means of opening to us wonderful visions of
God's law or love; but whatever it does for us, it does
not bring us just the strength that would have come
from obedience to what God originally demanded of us.
That demand of His we know to be the ultimate test of
our duty, and no mystery attaching to the spiritual
blessing that occasionally comes through revulsion from
past misdoing can blind us to that fact.

As every act is thus the expression of a moral
being, which has been created by all former fidelities and
failures, it involves in itself an endless complexity of
elements. We cannot say of any service we perform
that it is what it should have been. I may strive in
the most unselfish way to help some distressed soul; I

may act up to my knowledge and do the best I can for
him; but my knowledge of spiritual needs has been
coloured by my past imperfect practice. To what extent
it has been impaired it is impossible for me to estimate.
This incapacity to realise the degree of our shortcoming
is one of the heaviest burdens of the spiritual life. Nor
is there any escape from it; it grows heavier with every
advance in spirituality.

We see, then, how immensely positive Christ's consciousness of sinlessness is. It is the affirmation of His
fulfilment, in all its details, of the ideal of life prescribed
by the Father. He is touched by no such hesitancies
as are inevitable in *our* dealings with others. When
He lays upon the young ruler a command of obedience
so testing that the latter goes away sorrowful, His love
for the young soul in its struggle opens up no question
in His mind as to the wisdom of so severe an injunction.
That is the doubt that haunts us when we have spoken
some unpalatable truth, and found our remonstrance un-
availing. Have we not gone too far? Was this not a
case where gentleness and encouragement might have
succeeded? And so we are tossed about by endless and
indefinable regrets. Jesus has the clear assurance that
He is not in any way responsible for " the great refusal."
He denounces the Pharisees in terms of exceptional
sternness, and has no misgivings—just what the earnest
and pure soul cannot get rid of—lest disappointment or
anger may have given a keener edge to His words, or
caused needless offence to some simple heart. Yet those
personal problems bearing on our right relation to others
which *we* feel we never solve, and, at the most, make
only distant approximations towards solving, were surely

peculiarly subtle and complicated in Christ's case, from what He professed to be and do. He had to relate His new doctrine to the beliefs and customs of an established faith, to pronounce judgment on the most sacred traditions, to retain, reject, transform, and to bear home His message to those whose hearts and minds were saturated with the faith which He came at once to supersede and to complete. He had also so to act Himself that His life should be a guarantee and proof of the truth He declared, which was peculiarly bound up with His own personality. It was a work which, from the normal point of view, teemed with searching perplexities as to what it was necessary to declare at any period and what to withhold, in the interest of the message itself and the varied characters with which He had to deal. The strenuous moral enthusiast or the aspiring saint tends, in spite of himself, to constant introspection. It is the accompaniment of his spiritual honesty. He may be quite aware that it has an unhealthy side, but a keen self-examination is his only preservative against a possible self-deception.[1] This kind of self-criticism has no place in Jesus. His life is woven in one piece. The dominant feeling that it leaves with us is that of wholeness, of unity. The parts and stages of it blend into each other, not from a consciously-planned scheme, but from the natural unfolding of an inner necessity. *Vestigia nulla retrorsum.* He comes to each new duty untrammelled by any rebuking memories, and the problems of casuistry have no meaning for Him. In all the diversity of His relations with men He addresses each with the same unwavering note of authority. That He

[1] See Note 4, p. 386, "The 'morbidity' of Self-examination."

is able to do so implies at the very least that He is
conscious He has never deflected at any point from
the line prescribed, has taken each stage as it came, and
got out of it all that the Father meant Him to get; and
so He confronts the present with an undimmed confidence.   It is not the victory of a soul that selects
carefully from conflicting courses, but of one that walks
right onward in the security of a divine communion.

Thus He who has widened to infinity the bounds of
personal obligation, and intensified in men the abiding
sense of lost opportunities and dishonoured ideals, Himself retains the unclouded serenity which is the " bright
consummate flower" of self-realisation.   This is not a
difference of attainment in goodness ; it is a different
type of moral character, another order of humanity.

Attempts, indeed, have been made to dispute the
perfect holiness of Jesus by challenging His conduct in
particular instances.   It has been said that in His boy-
hood He displays a want of filial obedience ; that when
He drives the buyers and sellers out of the Temple He
exhibits an excess of passion ; that in the deliverance
of the Gadarene demoniac He unwarrantably destroys
the property of others ; that He treats the Syro-Phœn-
ician woman with a harshness that suggests contempt.
It is not needful to dwell on these objections.[1]   They
largely rest on an abstract treatment of certain elements
in the case, and a misappreciation of the spiritual issues
involved.   Any slight difficulty that remains, as Godet
points out, springs from our ignorance, in part, of the
precise circumstances which determined Jesus' action.
But the real and final answer is that He stood self-

---

[1] For a detailed discussion, see Godet, *Defence of the Faith*, pp. 193–200.

vindicated; that the memory of these incidents brought
Him no tremor of regret in later hours. This cannot
be explained by any lower ideals or lack of moral self-
knowledge on His part; and if He followed unperturbed
a course which at all perplexes us, it was because His
clearer vision perceived facts which lie beyond our range.

There is only one instance of this kind which merits
any special examination. It is that wherein Jesus, in
His conversation with the young man who asked how to
attain eternal life, refuses to be called " Good." [1] " There
is none good but One, that is, God." What Jesus rejects
here is the epithet as applied by the ruler, which in his
lips was a title of conventional courtesy. It had no
moral depth or inwardness. Jesus will not have the
holiest terms thus cheapened, and restores to the word its
true content by reminding him that there is only one
Being absolutely good, and that all goodness in men
flows from Him. He Himself as man is not good in the
absolute sense, as God is, but draws His goodness from
a complete dependence on the Father. Of this human
perfection there is no repudiation in Christ's words, for
the ruler did not believe He possessed it. There is only
a refusal to accept the designation when it was not
bestowed on right grounds. Some have interpreted the
passage as if it meant, " Only God is good, but you do
not recognise Me as God; therefore you ought not to
call Me good." This seems to me less likely for many

---

[1] τί με λέγεις ἀγαθόν ; This is the true reading, as given in Mark and
Luke.   Matthew's version, as it is now accepted, " Why askest thou Me
concerning that which is good ? " is apparently a modification, arising from the
fear of inferences hostile to the purity of Jesus.   Meyer, *Comm. on St. Matt.*
xix. 17; Godet, *Comm. on St. Luke* xviii. 18.   Cf. Gore, *Bampton Lectures*,
pp. 13, 198 ; and *Dissertations*, p. 96, *n.*

reasons.[1]   But whatever view is taken, the only *im-*
possible interpretation is that which represents Jesus as
on this sole occasion disowning a perfection which His
entire life before and after shows that He claimed.

Dr. Martineau, while not disputing the stainlessness
of Jesus, refuses to admit that He constitutes a solitary
type.   " Those," he says, " who shrink from recognising
in Christ a human impersonation of Divine character
often press upon us the question, whether, then, we are
to regard Him as a unique being, differing not in
degree only, but also in kind, from the just and wise and
saintly of every age.   I answer by a parable : he that
always hits the mark does not differ in kind from those
whom he surpasses ; yet if all others fall short of this,
he is unique.   In truth, the whole antithesis between
degree and kind, borrowed from natural history and
becoming ever fainter even there, is absolutely empty
and unmeaning when transferred to the sphere of moral
life.   The differences of which the conscience takes
cognisance lie entirely among the inner springs of action,
as ranged upon a progressive scale of relative excellence :
and thus admitting of comparison and depending on it,
can never be anything else but matters of gradation and
intensity.   To speak of them as belonging to distinct
categories or orders of being, is to declare them incom-
mensurable, subject to no common measure, and therefore to deny any universal moral law. . . . We can
neither deny to faithful, heroic, and holy men, to a
Socrates, a Marcus Aurelius, a Blaise Pascal, an approach

---

[1] Can it be thought that Jesus regarded it as possible for the ruler to
recognise His essential divine Sonship, when even the apostles did not fully
realise it during His earthly life ? (see below, pp. 69, 131-4).   Besides, the
term " God " in the absolute sense is applicable only to the Father.

3

to Christ upon the same line, nor claim for Him any
pre-eminence that removes them from His fellowship.
But neither can we speak otherwise of God Himself.
He also, with all the infinitude of His perfections, is still
but the Father of Spirits, and on the side of moral goodness differing from His children only in degree." [1]

Surely there is here a great confusion of idea.   It is
unquestionable that moral qualities—justice, love, pity—
mean the same thing in us and in God : otherwise there
could not be one moral universe.   To say this is one
thing, but it is quite another to say that moral *personality*
is the same in both, or that any advance in goodness will
bring us nearer to the self-consciousness of the Absolutely Holy.   The difference between Him and us is not
one of " gradation " or " intensity," but of essential moral
characteristic.   It is a great gulf fixed.   No comparison
can be instituted between us upon a progressive scale
of relative excellence.   So also as regards Jesus.   His
goodness, indeed, was not like the Father's, original,
self-contained ; but human, derivative, sustained by the
constant reception of the Spirit bestowed from above.
Yet, though human, its distinction from the goodness of
other men was not that of the greater from the less.   It
is never possible for the best of men to feel that he
absolutely hits the white even in his noblest act, because
of the ineradicable sense that his past shortcomings may
in an incalculable way have altered his course or blurred
his vision.   If we are to keep to Dr. Martineau's inappropriate   quantitative   simile,   and   represent   the
maximum as one hundred points, which Jesus makes,
then, instead of others making seventy or eighty, and

[1] *Hours of Thought*, vol. ii. 217–219.

thus only falling relatively short, they do not even make one point, never do anything with the same feeling that He consistently had of a duty perfectly fulfilled. Therefore His whole moral achievement is typically apart from theirs.[1]

It is this isolation of Jesus, relatively to the future as well as to the past of humanity, that renders Him doubly inexplicable on any purely naturalistic theory of development. The early Hebrew religion, for example, had very likely for its background, as critical research declares, the elemental nature-religions of the Semitic pastoral peoples, was intermingled with prevailing superstitions, and adopted during its course, as raw material, popular customs, festivals, and legends. The God of Israel had at first, we are told, the same tribal character and relation as the deities of the neighbouring nations, and faith in Him did not exclude polytheism. This may be so, but no one has ever been able to explain by natural and normal causes how it was that, while the religions of the other Semitic tribes continued merely local, sensuous, and hardly ethical, that of Israel rose to the apprehension of a holy personal God who stands above nature. It is not enough to say, Evolution.

---

[1] Dr. Martineau departs, however, in his latest book, *Seat of Authority*, from this representation of Jesus as actually stainless, and falls back on the exploded interpretation of the words used by Jesus to the ruler. "This condition, 'without sin,' is not to be pressed out of its relative significance for every growing mind into a rigid dogmatic absolutism ; it tells simply the impression of His life upon its witnesses, without contradicting the self-judgment which felt hurt by the epithet 'Good';" and he speaks of Jesus' "susceptibility to possible repentance and consciousness of something short of 'Good'" (p. 651). Though this view is, as has been shown, incompatible with the facts in their totality, it has more self-consistency with his general position than the attempt made in the *Hours of Thought* to retain the old Socinian idea of Jesus' sinlessness, while denying that He constitutes a separate moral type.

What were the factors in the development, operating within this one little section of the Semitic race, whereby it alone gradually advanced till it reached this lofty spiritual faith, while all its neighbours wallowed in the slough of naturalism? Schultz tells us, after the most exhaustive analysis, that no mere historical explanation can account for it, or make it more than partially intelligible; that "it can be explained only by revelation, that is, by the fact that God raised up for this people men whose natural susceptibilities to moral and religious truth, developed by the course of their inner and outer lives, enabled them to understand intuitively the will of the self-communicating and redeeming God regarding men, and to possess the religious truth which maketh free, not as a result of human wisdom and intellectual labour, but as a power pressing in on the soul with irresistible might."[1]

Precisely: there were historical conditions and historical laws at work; but something else was at work also, a spiritual factor not hitherto existing in human experience, but blending in this development with what was present already, and producing in the Hebrew nation a unique spiritual result. Regarded *sub specie æternitatis* it was itself natural, part of the ultimate order of the spiritual universe; but it was no more evolved from the forces and conditions previously operating in humanity than the animal is evolved from the inorganic.

Yet, just as the animal stage when once reached is kept, so this new spiritual factor having once entered humanity remained there, continued to operate and

[1] *O. T. Theology*, vol. i. 54.

unfold itself in ever greater measure. The divine communion into which the Jews were raised formed the starting-point for a fuller vision of God in future generations. It became an abiding element in the further development of the race. With Jesus it is just the reverse. The new factor whose presence is attested by His moral nature has in no subsequent case created a similar result. If His personality represents a new stage in man's consciousness of God, it is a stage which closes with Himself. He has no more been reproduced in Christendom than He was anticipated in Judaism. There is a double break in the continuity. Naturalistic evolution fails to account for Him alike in connection with what precedes and with what follows Him, and it is the latter failure which is fatal.

Sometimes we conceal this from ourselves by thinking of Jesus as occupying a similar position in the religious sphere to that which Shakespeare holds in the intellectual. Evolution, we are reminded, is not at all inconsistent with the appearance of outstanding personalities, to which subsequent ages present no parallel. But the genius that belongs to certain men in different departments of life,— in war, in statesmanship, in poetry,—and by which they soar above their contemporaries and their successors, is simply the intensification of a gift or gifts possessed by others. Their superiority is one of degree. Christ's is one of *kind*. Neither in Socrates nor in Pascal is there the slightest resemblance to the *quality* of moral nature that Jesus exhibited. Those who have most absorbed His spirit, and who, on the principle of development, ought certainly to show some sign of approximation to Him, realise most keenly that no comparison can ever be instituted between Him and them " upon a progressive scale of relative excellence." They attain His peace, but it is not theirs, as it is His, through direct fellowship with God ; it is mediated by Him. And in them it is not, as in Him, at present realised ; it is implicit, the beginning and pledge of a complete victory, whose time is not yet. Nor, when that time comes, in the mystery of the Here-after, is their experience one with His. The conscious-ness of those who have been washed from their sins will be eternally different from that of Him who, through all His earthly years, remained undefiled. The prodigal may traverse the distance that separates him from the saint, but no conceivable spiritual progress can bring the sinful soul to the consciousness of sinlessness. Of that consciousness we may say, *Nascitur, non fit.* It must exist from the beginning ; when lost, it cannot be regained.[1]

While Jesus thus presents a unique type of goodness, yet it is essentially a *human* type. There are some who argue that because He lacks one element everywhere present in humanity, He really falls out of its fellowship, and ceases to be the brother of men. But sin is not an inherent characteristic of human nature ; it is an intrusion. *De facto*, it is universal ; *de jure*, it has no title to be there. From the verdict of conscience on this matter there is no appeal. We may be unable to understand the conditions under which a sinless soul develops, because we cannot get away from the shadow cast by our own experience. It is through erring and repenting that *we* pass into a nobler life, and a fuller vision of the divine ; yet there is never any acquiescence in the fault

[1] See Note 5, p. 388, "Christ and Evolution."

as a blessed thing in itself, or as anything but an alien
element in our humanity.   What we recognise as indispensable to a life of goodness truly human is, that it
should be teachable, receptive, advancing ; that it should
deepen and enlarge with every fresh form of experience
and unfolding of circumstance.   The life of God is
eternally complete, and His holiness incapable of increase.
He is the First and the Last.   But Christ's life on earth
had the developing mark of humanity.   It passed through
many stages, and " learned obedience " in each.   He
increased in wisdom, taking " possession, in the name of
His Father, of the several domains of human life as they
opened one after another before Him."   The family in
Nazareth, the Jewish nation, mankind, these in succession appealed to Him as spheres of service.   Nor was
He educated merely by receptivity, but by resistance.
Though for the most part His moral life seems to unfold
itself calmly, it had its crises of self-searching and trial.
The suggestions which are, no doubt, pictorially treated
in the Synoptic account of the Temptation imply just
such a conflict as would naturally arise at the beginning
of a career like His.   His alarm at Peter's suggestion
that He should not tread the path of suffering, and the
quick emphasis of His rebuke, betray what Dr. A. B.
Davidson does not scruple to call ' His weakest point '—
regret that He cannot save from pain the hearts that
loved Him.[1]   And the scene which all subsequent ages
have designated " the Agony " tells of a spiritual struggle
in the depths of His being.   Now, God cannot be tempted
with evil ; but here is One who felt the attractions of
friendship, the bitterness of desertion ; whose heart

[1] *Hebrews*, p. 108.

glowed with unaffected wonder at the faith of the
centurion, and burned with indignation at the shameless
hypocrisy which condemned in others what it tolerated
in itself; and who yet so carried Himself through all
these shifting emotions of the soul that they not only
never impaired the balance of His moral nature, but
left Him the richer and stronger for each experience.
Temptation, indeed, to such a One had a character to us
unimaginable, for He knew nothing of those surging
evil influences out of far-back hours which do so much to
undermine our resisting power and half paralyse our
hopefulness.   But none the less is the goodness which is
thus built up emphatically human.   It is daily nourished
from hidden sources in the fellowship of the Father, and
grows in strength by growing in dependence and surrender.   Christ's freedom from stain or shortcoming is
not the destruction of His humanity, but its completion.

LECTURE II.

CHRIST'S SELF-CONSCIOUSNESS AS
INTERPRETED BY HIS CLAIMS.

SYNOPSIS.

Christ's moral self-consciousness—the fundamental fact.
Just because unique, the interpretation of it must come from Himself.
    1. His finality as a Teacher of God's will.
    2. His decisive pronouncements on *individual* character.
    3. Makes attachment to Himself imperative.
    4. Claims to be the final Arbiter of human destinies.
The self-assertion of Jesus incompatible with normal human goodness: His
    example in this respect cannot be imitated.

" The Son of Man ": its double reference to service and lordship.
" The Son " of the Father.
His consciousness of Sonship involves a transcendent element in His being.
It is not created by His consciousness of Messiahship, but underlies and
    determines it.

The Fourth Gospel in substantial harmony with the Synoptics on the two
    main points :
    1. His relation to men.
    2. His relation to the Father.
The Sayings as to His pre-existence.

The Johannine authorship.
Difficulty regarding the Discourses, though sometimes exaggerated, yet a real
    one.
The author of the Fourth Gospel not, like Luke, a compiler, but a reproducer
    from his own experience.
Reads the beginning of Jesus' ministry in the light of the end.
The Synoptics and the Fourth Gospel as historical documents.

LECTURE II.

CHRIST'S SELF-CONSCIOUSNESS AS INTERPRETED BY
HIS CLAIMS.

THE unique character of Christ's moral self-consciousness
is the fundamental fact regarding Him. The discussion
of it is not complicated by the problems that arise in
connection with His teaching. The religious doctrines
or ideas of a great teacher have to be placed historically
in order to determine their comparative originality, and
the quality and value of the contribution he has made to
the spiritual knowledge of humanity. Still more, the
investigation of their truth or accuracy is not a little
affected by questions of local or temporal colouring.
How far was the speaker influenced by inherited traditions, or by his environment? What deductions on
these grounds have to be made from his doctrine, so as
to reach what is permanent and universal in it? These
questions have a peculiar emphasis in Christ's case, just
because He so clearly entered into a line of spiritual
succession, and affiliated Himself to the instructions and
prophecies of an older time. The complexity that thus
arises, so far, at least, as it affects the central articles of
His teaching, is not, as I hope to show later, so great as
has been frequently affirmed. But it exists, and it is
therefore of primary moment that we have something

43

which is not open to minute disputation, which does not rest on isolated phrases or acts, but which is involved in any rendering we give to the life of Jesus that does adequate or approximate justice to the facts. We may, of course, *a priori* rule out the possibility of such an isolated phenomenon as a moral consciousness of unbroken harmony with God ; but to do so is neither criticism nor common sense. It is not to interpret facts, but to deny them or pass them by. Treat the records as you may, no hypothesis of modification, omission, or insertion will ever eliminate this distinctive quality from Christ's character, without destroying the verisimilitude of the portraiture.

But Christ's moral self-consciousness is fundamental for another reason. Religion is not a theory, but an experience. To use the words of Amiel, it is a " life, mystical in its root and practical in its fruits, a communion with God, a calm and deep enthusiasm, a love which radiates, a force which acts, a happiness which over-flows." [1] Its aim is not to speak great things of God, and of what He is or can be to His children; it is to make these things a reality within the soul. This is the object of all religious leaders and reformers; they call men to enter into this blessedness, and they join the company of seeking and aspiring hearts. But is the goal they make for more than a glorious but unattainable dream ? They have themselves no inward witness of personal triumph, manifesting itself in ways by which their followers can be assured that the hope *does* translate itself into fact. With them it is still an aspiration ; with Christ it is a possession. Therefore His message has

[1] *Journal*, vol. i. 224.

behind it the guarantee that He knows the way to the
secret places of an unfathomable peace.　It is obvious
that, standing apart as He does in His spiritual achievement, it is not possible for us to interpret and explain
Him, as we may explain others.　We have no analogies
of experience to apply.　We can neither tell how such a
lonely consciousness could have grown up, nor what it
means for our life, now that it is there before us.　*He
must interpret Himself;* show us by the attitude He
takes up, in His words and deeds and unexpected
silences, why He is there, and what His relation to us is.
We can see, indeed, that in some respects[1] He has realised
the very ideal of humanity which we cherish and long to
reach ; but He has not reached it along our lines, and so
the inspiration of His life is enfeebled by a doubt.　What
further significance He has for humanity as a pledge of
spiritual power or joy, can only be known through His
self-manifestation.

That self-manifestation takes many forms, and
naturally the first aspect in which we have to consider
it is the exceptional position which He assumes as a
teacher of God's will, relatively to the past of Judaism.
It is perfectly plain that the law and the prophets possessed for Him a divine authority.　While He strenuously
repudiated the Rabbinic rules and glosses as the commandments of men, yet what was known as the Mosaic
code, even in its ritual part had for Him its place in the
order of God's revelation.　There is one saying of His
in which this view is affirmed with the strongest emphasis,
" Verily I say unto you, Till heaven and earth pass away,

---

[1] That there were other qualities in His character not belonging to a purely
human ideal, see below, pp. 55–60.

one jot or one tittle shall in no wise pass from the law
till all things be accomplished."[1]   The genuineness of
these words has been challenged, but upon purely
arbitrary and *a priori* grounds.   The connection in
which they appear shows that He attributes permanence,
not to the literal form, but to the inner content of the
commandments of the law; because He regards the least
of them as having a value as the symbol of a spiritual
truth, which alone would abide.[2]   In the deepest sense
He claims, not to destroy, but to fulfil them.   Yet how
free is His handling of those very commandments, notwithstanding their historic sacredness.   He reserves to
Himself the title of pronouncing what their essential
meaning is, of translating them from the imperfection of
the letter into the fulness of the divine intention.   It is
He who decides what shall disappear and what remain.
He endorses, modifies, abrogates, and yet at the same
time insists that the principles which He lays down
cannot in their turn be abrogated.   He is never confused or uncertain amid all the multiplicity of details in
the Jewish law; each falls into its place, and He passes
judgment on it with the accent of absolute assurance,
"Verily I say unto you."   It is not the tone of one who
believes, but of one who *knows*; who shares the full
thought of God towards man, and therefore speaks truths
which no time can supersede.   The "authority" which
even at an early stage[3] of His ministry the people felt
to attach to His teaching, sprang, not merely from the
self-witnessing character of the message, but from the

[1] Matt. v. 18.
[2] Beyschlag, *N.T. Theology*, vol. i. pp. 110, 111; Bruce, *Kingdom of God*, pp. 64–67.
[3] Mark i. 22.

transparent confidence with which He delivered it. And
He adopts the same attitude towards the prophets as
towards the law. In His parable of the Husbandmen,
they are but *servants* whom God has sent; He is the
Son; and so God's final appeal to His people. He
comes in a long succession of messengers, but He does
not so much belong to it as conclude and complete it.
When we remember the reverence which all pious Jews
had for the great souls raised up in old times to be God's
spokesmen, we can understand the strength of inward
evidence which led Jesus to assert for Himself so supreme
a place and function. I am not here dealing with the
question whether He claimed to fulfil or realise in His
own person and life the demands and hopes of Jewish
law and prophecy, but with the finality which He
assumes to belong to His *teaching* about God : and this
assumption involves the consciousness, not only of a
unique relation towards God, but of a vocation towards
Humanity, which admits of no parallel or repetition.

Quite as remarkable is the decisiveness with which
Jesus pronounces upon the characters of *individuals*.
He never once stands puzzled and helpless, as we continually do, before the problems presented by other lives.
He seizes the solution by instinct, and issues a command
of personal duty as if there were no protest or appeal
possible. And He is always doing it; not on supreme
occasions only, or in seasons of special illumination
such as visit the noblest souls at times. All hours are
the same for Him. His insight does not come from His
being exalted above Himself : it is His normal gift. It
is no surer in crises that might have been anticipated by
ordinary foresight than in moments of surprise. At each

step men press forward with cries for help or guidance,
with captious queries or objections; and His replies are
not so much the answer to an appeal as the reading
of a life.   He disposes of them; enjoins upon one immediate surrender, " Follow Me," but forbids another who
desired to follow Him, and charges him to return to his
home and friends.[1]   That Jesus should *constantly* deliver
such personal verdicts, to the extent of imposing the
most testing sacrifices on reluctant or half-reluctant souls,
is simply inconceivable, unless He bore the indisputable
consciousness of being called to this unique task and of
possessing for it unique powers.[2]   Sometimes this extraordinary note of authority is lost or dulled for us by the
graciousness which we also feel to pervade His intercourse with men.   But there is no incompatibility between
them.   The grace lay in the whole character and purpose
of His message, but the authority belonged to Him as
the one bearer of it, without whom it would have had no
meaning at all.   To forget this is to commit the same
mistake as is done by those who turn Christ's brotherliness into a friendly geniality, and pass by the moral
strenuousness and sternness which lies at the heart of
His Gospel, and is the indispensable prerequisite of its
restorative power.

This assumption of a title to dispose of others is still
more visible when He passes judgment on their moral
state before God.   Again and again He declares to
them the forgiveness of their sins.   Here, too, it is of
the essence of the matter that He is dealing with individuals.   For there is a sense in which His Church

[1] Luke ix. 57–62, viii. 38, 39.   See latter part of Note 13, p. 398.
[2] Cf. Denney, *Studies in Theology*, p. 29.

claims the right of pronouncing absolution to the penitent.
But she does not decide absolutely who the penitent are,
in this case or in that.   An earnest Christian may indeed
in the name of Christ feel warranted in assuring a
troubled and humble soul that God's pardon rests upon it.
But he does this because of the indications which he thinks
he finds of true repentance; it is an inference, amounting
it may be to high probability, but at the best to no more
than moral certainty.   Moreover, he does not reach this
conviction immediately: it forms itself gradually, as the
facts of the character he is judging unfold themselves:
and no matter how sincere the repentance appears to be
in the first agony of awakened guilt and sorrow, he has
to wait till it seems to prove itself genuine by subsequent
amendment and consecration.   But Jesus speaks the
word of absolution at once, to those who have never
crossed His path before: to those in whose case there
were no indubitable signs, recognised by others, of a true
penitence: and He speaks it, not with moral, but with
absolute certainty.   " Thy sins are forgiven;" "thy faith
hath saved thee."[1]   This, if it is anything, is substantially
a claim to read the heart, to proclaim God's estimate of
the character, as it can only be done by Him who alone
truly knows the Father and the Father's thoughts of His
children.[2]

In the case of the paralytic, Christ defends Himself
from the charge of blasphemy in pronouncing forgiveness,
by replying to the objectors, " Whether is easier to say
to the sick of the palsy, Thy sins are forgiven, or to say,
Arise, and take up thy bed and walk?   But that ye may
know that the Son of Man hath authority on earth to

---

[1] Matt. ix. 2 ; Luke vii. 50.   [2] Cf. Matt. xi. 27.

4

forgive sins, He saith to the sick of the palsy, Arise, take
up thy bed and go unto thy house." [1]   Dr. Martineau
renders the meaning thus: "*Sins in heaven* (*i.e.* in their
spiritual aspect), whose moral heinousness, relative to the
secret conscience, is measurable only to the Searcher of
hearts, are certainly reserved for the mercy of God alone.
But *sins on earth*, in their temporal expression by visita-
tions of incapacity and suffering, He has from of old
permitted His human prophets to remit; and when such
a Son of Man takes pity on a stricken brother, what
matters it whether he goes up to the sentence and pronounces it thus far reduced, saying, ' Herein, the sin is
forgiven,' or whether he goes down to the prison doors,
and opening them bids the captive ' Arise, and go to his
house'?" [2]   What, then, did Christ's absolution refer to?
What was the *spiritual* benefit bestowed by His pardon?
If He in no way conveyed to the paralytic the assurance
of the Divine favour, then the remission was not of the
sin, but merely of its temporal expression in suffering.
Would Christ have alarmed the suspicions of the scribes
and incurred the charge of blasphemy, when He intended
by the phrase " Thy sins are forgiven thee" to say
nothing more than that He had authority to cure, which
was not in question?   Manifestly He meant something
very real as regards the man's own sense of guilt.   The
phrase " on earth" does not belong to sins, but to the
forgiveness of them, or the authority to forgive them: [3]
and even if it were otherwise, surely it is a grotesque
view which by contrasting " sins on earth" with " sins in
heaven" would empty the phrase " sins on earth" of all

[1] Matt. ix. 4–6.   [2] *Seat of Authority*, p. 345, *n.*
[3] Meyer, *Comm. in loc.*

its spiritual content. What meaning would then attach
to Christ's similar declaration of pardon in the case of
one like the "woman of the city," where no remission
took place of the "temporal expression" or penalty of
the sin?

Professor Bruce, on the other hand, regards Christ's
claim to forgive as directed against Pharisaic notions.
"The Pharisees viewed God's relation to sin from the
side of His majesty; Jesus, on the contrary, viewed it
from the side of His grace. God, He says to His
critics, is not such as you imagine—severe, slow to forgive, and jealous of His prerogative; He is good and
ready to forgive, and has no desire to monopolise the
privilege of forgiving. He is willing that it should be
exercised by all on earth in whom dwells His own spirit;
and My right to forgive rests on this, that I am a sympathetic friend of the sinful, full of the grace and charity
of heaven."[1] What is here said of the spirit of Christ's
judgment is said admirably. But is there anything in
the Synoptic account which remotely suggests that Jesus
is speaking as a type of spiritual humanity, and vindi-
cating, not only for Himself, but for all who may share
His sympathetic spirit, a title to pronounce forgiveness?
Is it not clear that He takes the scribes' question as
referring to Himself alone, from the way in which He
seeks to prove to them *His* right to pronounce forgiveness "by visibly demonstrating His right to pronounce
upon the man another Divine blessing"[2]? From such
an argument we may at least draw the inference that He
affirms His authority to be as complete and as excep-

---

[1] *Kingdom of God*, p. 174.
[2] Wendt, *Teaching of Jesus*, vol. i. 211, *n.*

tional in the spiritual sphere as He shows it to be in the
natural. The central significance of Christ's answer lies,
not in His possession of a quality which He shares with
others, and which it is their duty to strive to attain,
but in the peculiar title possessed by Himself alone to
pronounce forgiveness of sins. Nor does history or
experience teach us that any of His followers, however
truly they may cherish His spirit, approach His confident
assurance in pronouncing forgiveness on individuals, any
more than they approach His consciousness of unbroken
harmony with God. Whatever meaning be attributed
here to the term " Son of Man," it cannot be divested of
a uniquely personal reference. The best comment on
Christ's words is that of Bengel, " Cœlestem ortum hic
sermo sapit."

Again, He makes loyalty and attachment to Himself
the first duty of man, and the condition of the spiritual
blessing He has come to proclaim : " He that loveth
father or mother more than Me is not worthy of Me."[1]
" Whosoever shall lose his life for My sake and the
Gospel's shall save it."[2] Some have argued that in thus
conjoining His own name with His Gospel, He indicates
clearly enough that it is the Gospel or message which is
the real object of attachment for men, and that the
reference to Himself is a personification, meaning only
that He is the bearer of it. But His relation to His
message is not of this accidental character. His right
to declare it is based on a unique personality, on His
separate and unshared consciousness of communion with
the Father : it is a function belonging essentially to Him
and no other. And this very consciousness of His forms,

[1] Matt. x. 37.   [2] Mark viii. 35.

so to speak, the heart of the message.   For His preaching from beginning to end is a proclamation of salvation.
It is not simply a doctrine of a higher and more penetrating righteousness than that taught in the Old Testament.   That in itself, however emphatic as a revelation
of the holiness without which no man can see the Lord,
would be a sentence of despair.   But Christ's message is
a word of emancipation : it is a doctrine of grace, which
at once includes and fulfils the new demand of an inner
and complete righteousness.   It can only be this, if it
contains a spiritual dynamic, whereby the oppressed
heart is quickened and renewed, and feels within it the
promise and potency of the perfect service of God.   And
Christ pledges this power to men in His Gospel, because
He is not only conscious that He possesses it as no one
else does, but that it belongs to Him supremely to
mediate it to others.   Thus His message is not something
which can be severed from His personality.   When so
divorced, it loses its innermost characteristic.   The conduct of those who sought His help, and to whom He
says so often, " Thy faith hath saved thee," is, as has
been well said,[1] at bottom a faith in Christ; nor does
the elementary conception they had of their relation to
Him alter the fact that it was just this trustful attachment to Himself that He recognised and rewarded.
It constituted the medium through which alone the
victorious spiritual strength which dwelt in Him became
the guarantee of their triumph.

The assumption of such a supremacy in the spiritual
world cannot be an incidental or temporary thing.   He
who is indispensable in one case is necessary in all.   If

[1] Beyschlag, *N. T. Theology*, vol. i. p. 143.

He is entitled to stand between God and *any* soul, and
insist that He alone can mediate to it Divine fellowship
and peace, it must be on the ground of an inherent right
which makes Him the Lord of *all* souls.   It is only when
we realise what is here involved that we cease to be
astonished at His startling claim to be the final Judge of
men and Arbiter of their destinies.   Whatever pictorial
elements exist in the eschatology of the Gospels, there
can be no doubt that for Jesus there was a point in the
future when the significance of the world's history shall
be laid bare and a seal set on the moral value of each
human life.   That day will be pre-eminently the day of
revelation, the bringing to light of the secret realities
that make men what they are ; and Christ tells us that
He is the Revealer.   It is *His* presence that will
illuminate and interpret each character to itself; it is
His estimate that will decide the issue.   Nor is this a
claim put forth by Him merely on a single occasion or
in doubtful terms of imagery ; it is reiterated in various
forms but with unvarying emphasis.   Whenever He
speaks of the Future Judgment, He Himself occupies the
central place.   In that day He shall say to those who
falsely called Him Lord, Lord, " I never knew you."
" The Son of Man shall come in the glory of His Father,
and then shall He render unto every man according to
his deeds."   That He should be ashamed of men in that
day, will be their sufficient condemnation.   He shall
open and close the door of the eternal marriage feast.
" He shall sit on the throne of His glory, and before Him
shall be gathered all the Gentiles ; and He shall separate
them one from another."[1]   We are not here discussing

[1] Matt. vii. 22, 23, xvi. 27 ; Mark viii. 38 ; Matt. xxv. 10, 12, 31, 32.

the moral possibility or rationality of the ultimate separation of souls, nor the principle that determines and
vindicates acceptance or rejection.[1]   What we are dealing
with at present is simply the *fact* of such a Judgment
as indubitably testified by Christ, and the light thrown
upon the uniqueness of His personality by the confident
assertion that it is His alone to test and to arbitrate.
Professor Seeley[2] does not exaggerate when he declares
that to deny that Christ claimed the office of Judge of
mankind is possible only to those who altogether deny
the credibility of the Gospels.   For not only is the fact
attested by numerous sayings that have every conceivable mark of genuineness, but it is in line with those
other characteristics we have discussed; with Christ's
finality as the Revealer of God to men, with His assumption of the right to control the ordering of their
lives, to forgive them in God's name, to be the one
Mediator to them of divine life and peace.   The universality of relationship and authority, which is asserted by
His claim to be the Judge of all human souls,[3] is present
as truly, though implicitly, in each of these demands.
They are but different expressions of a Personality which
in every phase of its self-manifestation struck the same
dominant note; nor is the imperiousness less in the
sphere of grace than of judgment.   He who is the First,
as alone able to mediate the divine life to men, cannot
but be the Last as the arbiter of their fitness for the
final Kingdom.

These supreme offices, so multiform and pervasive,

---

[1] See Lecture IX.

[2] *Ecce Homo*, p. 39.

[3] On Wendt's view of the sectional character of Christ's Judgment, see
below, p. 345, *n.*

which Christ assigns to Himself cannot be explained
away by any Oriental figurativeness in the phraseology.
They involve an attitude of soul towards God and man
which would be incompatible with veracity in any other
than He.   They rise naturally out of a background of
consciousness which is not itself normal; and therefore
the attempt to eliminate them does not leave us in His
case a simple ideal type of human goodness.   He is
penetrated with a profound sense of His own greatness,
and He constantly shows it.   He upbraids the Jews with
their demand for a sign accrediting His mission, in sad
contrast to the Queen of the South who eagerly listened
to the wisdom of Solomon; "and, behold, a greater than
Solomon is here."   And again, "I say unto you that
One greater than the Temple is here."[1]   Or take the
questions which He addressed to the disciples near
Cæsarea Philippi—"Who do men say that I am?"
—"Who do *ye* say that I am?"   Do not these words
suggest to us a somewhat disagreeable self-consciousness,
an eager desire for personal recognition?   Is there any
feeling which is more fatal than this to what we regard

---

[1] Matt. xii. 42, 47.   Cf. xxvi. 11, "Ye have the poor always with you;
but *Me* ye have not always."   "The life of Jesus Himself," says T. H. Green,
"was, if the expression may be allowed, an absolutely original one. . . .
Whether Son of God or Son of Man, He was so by a direct title of His own,
not, as His followers were, by a mediated heritage.   As the Jews said of Him,
'He bare record of Himself.'"   *Works*, vol. iii. p. 167.   Dr. Martineau
recognises (*Seat of Authority*, pp. 581, 582) that expressions of self-assertion,
like those quoted above, blend very ill with the highest kind of goodness that
is merely human; and so he attributes them, not to Jesus, but to the retro-
spective interpretation of the Church.   This reading back must have been
pretty thorough, for the same note of intense self-consciousness permeates the
entire story, and is present in incident as well as phrase.   If Jesus never
assumed this tone at all, one can only say that the early Church achieved a
miracle of verisimilitude in its reconstruction of His life.   "Credat Judæus
Apella."

as the noblest character?   There are qualities such as
hypocrisy, altogether irreconcilable with virtue, destructive of it in every sense ; there are others, and obtrusive
self-appreciation is one, irreconcilable with the *highest*
virtue.   We are thrilled by Danton's cry—" Que mon
nom soit flétri; que la France soit libre "; *let my name
be blighted ; let France be free* [1]—because it strikes the
note of self-forgetfulness.   Whether genuine for him or
not, we say, ' That is the tone in which men should
speak; this indifference to the personal interest, this
absorption in the service of a cause.'   And so we love
to see a great man as the final shadows deepen upon
him, rise above the natural longing for a secure place in
men's hearts, and commit himself and his work calmly
to the keeping and appointment of God.   Wordsworth,
who with all his genius and lofty consecration was only
too conscious of the value of his message for humanity,
passes at last into this higher mood.   " It is indeed a
deep satisfaction," he writes near the close of life, " to
hope and believe that my poetry will be, while it lasts, a
help to the cause of virtue and truth, especially among
the young.   As to myself, it seems now of little moment
how long I may be remembered.   When a man pushes
off in his little boat into the great seas of Infinity and
Eternity, it surely signifies little how long he is kept in
sight by watchers from the shore." [2]   He is as deeply
persuaded as ever that he has been entrusted with the
utterance of truths which fortify and wisely chasten the
spirits of men ; but he does not think that his utterance
of them is indispensable to their power and prevalence,

---

[1] See Carlyle, *French Revolution*, vol. iii. p. 115.
[2] F. W. H. Myers, *Wordsworth*, p. 182.

still less that they will be lost unless identified with his personality.

How widely apart and alien is Christ's manner of thought. At the departing hour He observes a farewell feast with the disciples, and in the most solemn form charges them to continue the observance as a commemoration of Himself and His relation to them. " Do this in remembrance of Me." [1] Doubtless it is by fellowship with a person, not by the acceptance of principles, that the spiritual nature is regenerated and built up; and to allow those who have been a living embodiment of high moral power to fall into oblivion, is to reject a chief means of grace. So it may be said, Christ's words are but an application of this law. Yes, but it is the application of it to Himself which makes all the difference. It might be necessary for the welfare of the disciples that they should remember Him. It was quite another thing for *Him* to insist on this necessity. He does not in the least disguise that He wants men to form judgments on Him, but it is not for His sake, but for their own. That they should think rightly of Him was a matter, in His view, of essential moment for their deepest life before God.[2] We talk too easily of Christ

[1] Luke xxii. 19. Luke alone among the Synoptics gives these words, which Paul's account (1 Cor. xi. 24, 25) also contains. As they are wanting in Matthew and Mark, it is held by many that they were not spoken by Jesus at the Last Supper. But see, on the other hand, Beyschlag, *N.T. Theology*, i. 177, and Godet, *St. Luke, in loc.* That Christ meant the observance to be perpetual is beyond question. " There can be no doubt," says Dr. Bruce, "that a rite, capable of giving symbolic utterance to so much meaning, was intended to be repeated. . . . To perform so pathetic an act once was to make it a standing institution" (*Kingdom of God*, p. 251). That Jesus performed it *at all* is the significant thing as a revelation of His self-consciousness.

[2] See Note 6, p. 391, " Dean Stanley on Christ's self-suppression."

as our great Example.   The peculiarity of His attitude is that *it cannot be imitated*.   Here is a note we cannot sound.   It is as if He said, I am first: there is no second.

Nor is this all.   When we demand self-forgetfulness as the condition of goodness, we are but echoing Christ's words.   It is He who has made this demand imperative in us.   Yet He points to Himself as an instance of self-suppression at the very time when He is authoritatively affirming His own pre-eminence.   " Take My yoke upon you, and learn of Me; *for* I am meek and lowly in heart." [1] He forbids His disciples to accept titles of honour, to be called Rabbi or Master; " for One is your Master, even the Christ." [2]   What an assumption lies here.   Surely a strange way of recommending lowliness, in the tones of absoluteness and autocracy.   Humanity is pretty well agreed that there are few things more offensive than the humility that dwells upon its own excellence.   It is also pretty well agreed that the life of Jesus is the supreme ideal of human character   When we put these two facts together, and consider that He whom men take as the loftiest moral type of the race emphasised His own lowliness and self - sacrifice, we feel that there were elements in Him that cannot possibly blend in a merely human consciousness, and that irresistibly suggest a

[1] Matt. xi. 29.   Dr. Bruce (*With Open Face*, p. 146) argues as against Dr. Martineau, that the words, " I am meek," etc., are "not self-eulogy, but self-description.   They describe a *mood*, rather than lay claim to a *virtue*." I confess they seem to me to express not a passing mood, but a permanent characteristic of the consciousness of Jesus.   Nor even as the utterance of a mood do they strike one as harmonising with the *normal* ideal of humanity.

[2] Matt. xxiii. 8, 10.   The phrase "even the Christ" occurs only in the 10th verse.   It is an interpolation in the 8th, though plainly implied.   Bruce, *Kingdom of God*, pp. 153, 154.

higher Being and a unique function to mankind. Thus the special claims which He makes are not an aggravation of the problem which His character presents : they are in a very real sense an alleviation, for they offer an explanation of the existence in Humanity of a moral consciousness which without them would be inexplicable.

It is by keeping these facts in view that we can alone hope to understand the name, Son of Man, by which He loved to designate Himself.[1] A favourite rendering is that which represents it as Christ's description of His intense brotherliness and nearness to men, the lowliness of His spirit, the weakness and privation of His lot. An argument for this is drawn from the use of the phrase in Ezekiel. The designation, " Thou Son of Man," by which every commission the prophet receives from God is introduced, sets forth, we are told,[2] his profound sense of the nothingness of the human agent, when called to be the organ of a divine intent, so that he is emptied of all semblance of dignity and pride, can only yield himself to be disposed of by the hand of God, and move with lowly and equal sympathy among the brotherhood of mankind. Dr. Martineau gets rid of all the passages that speak definitely of the coming glory [3]

---

[1] " It appears more than fifty times, without reckoning the parallel passages ; and there can be the less doubt of its originality that it is found only in His mouth, and not applied to Him by others."—Beyschlag, *N. T. Theology*, vol. i. p. 60.

[2] Martineau, *Seat of Authority*, pp. 337, 338.

[3] Even the saying, " The foxes have holes, and the birds of the air have nests; but the Son of Man hath not where to lay His head " (Luke ix. 58), which Dr. Martineau (*Seat of Authority*, p. 338) takes as the typical expression of the lowliness connoted by the name, and which he uses to discredit the idea of authority or glory as also designated by it, practically derives all its point from the contrast it involves between an *implied* dignity and a *visible* humiliation. On Dr. Martineau's rendering the whole thing is reduced to a tautology :

of the Son of Man by boldly discarding them as un-historical, and attributing them to the later consciousness of the Church which had come to believe in Jesus as Messiah. It was a reading back into the past from the standpoint of a faith attained only a generation after-wards. But why in that case did the Church not put the direct claim to be Messiah into the lips of Jesus? why did it wrap up His Messianic dignity in an enig-matic name? If it be said, because it could not exhibit Him "as habitually employing a name which He care-fully avoided; and so the Messianic feeling had to embody itself in some other term which could find a sanction in His own practice," then the argument really comes to this, that the Church had *so much* regard for the facts of Jesus' life that it would not attribute to Him a title which He had never assumed,[1] but also *so little* regard for them that it actually took another title and filled it with a meaning just the opposite of what He intended. Surely the care with which it portrays Jesus' slowness in assuming the name of Messiah is some guarantee that, if it so frequently represents Him as employing the other name of Son of Man with a con-notation of dignity and sovereignty, it is because it is not creating or reading back, but recording.

It is simply inconceivable that the name which Jesus chooses as the best designation of His person and work

---

"The sympathetic and lowly man has a lowly lot." Other passages also, as, *e.g.*, "The Son of Man is come to seek and to save that which was lost," or, "The Son of Man came not to be ministered unto, but to minister," lose half their force if there be no similar contrast implied, and the predicate only repeats or unfolds the content of the subject.

[1] On Dr. Martineau's impossible theory that Jesus never claimed to be the Messiah, see Lecture III. p. 93, and Note 19, p. 409.

should signify merely His abasement, His equal sympathy with others, and thus be in direct antagonism to the whole impression of sovereignty which His bearing made, and was intended to make, upon men. If He wished them to understand by His employment of the phrase " Son of Man " that He stood upon the common level, but with an intenser feeling than that possessed by any other of brotherliness, meekness, and readiness to serve, then how came He to act constantly in a manner so wholly contrary to this? What meant His revision and supersession of the Mosaic law, His sovereign tone in commanding obedience and forgiving sin? If His conduct conveyed, as it did even in its most gracious aspects, a sense of His aloofness, supremacy, and right to reign, it is quite certain that this and no other would be the view taken by those who heard Him, of His own thought concerning Himself; and they would not err in so doing, if we are to allow to Him the most elementary self-consistency.

There would, further, have been something peculiarly unhappy in the selection of the name as a mere synonym for lowliness. It would then have contradicted and defeated its own object; for it inevitably suggested the great vision of Daniel, who saw " coming with the clouds of heaven One like unto a Son of Man," to whom was given " dominion, glory, and a kingdom, that all the peoples, nations, and languages should serve Him : and His dominion is an everlasting dominion." [1] That this was an allusion which it carried, and was intended by Jesus to carry, is not only probable but certain from the words which He uses at His trial in His reply to the

[1] Dan. vii. 13, 14.

High Priest's question,[1] and which, according to the triple Synoptic account, He had previously employed in His discourse on the Last Things.[2] "Ye shall see the Son of Man sitting at the right hand of power, and coming in the clouds of heaven." Mr. Carpenter, who admits this to be a genuine saying of Jesus, denies that it has any personal reference to Him. Daniel's vision, he argues plausibly enough, is simply a picture of the establishment of the kingdom given to the saints of the Most High. The mysterious figure is a symbol, like the lion, the bear, and the leopard, which represented the great Gentile empires. But it is nobler than they; it wears a human form, and stands for other qualities than those of bestial appetite and worldly might. "The majestic personage to whom the perpetual sovereignty over all the world is assigned is the purified Israel, who will rise into glory and receive the obedience of all worldly powers."[3] And Mr. Carpenter holds that Jesus uses the phrase in this imaginative sense as a symbol of the triumph of God's people. "Why," he asks, "should it have a personal application on His lips which it has not in the Book of Daniel?"[4] For the simple reason that this symbolic interpretation is wholly inadmissible in other places where the name is found, and where nothing but a reference to Himself will even make sense of the passage. "The Son of Man came eating and drinking"; "the Son of Man hath not where to lay His head"; "the Son of Man came not to be ministered unto, but to minister." It would be preposterous to suppose that

[1] Matt. xxvi. 64.
[2] Matt. xvi. 27 ; Mark xiii. 26 ; Luke xxi. 27.
[3] J. Estlin Carpenter, *The Synoptic Gospels*, p. 104.
[4] *Ibid.* p. 247.

Jesus employed the word in two senses, now as an impersonal symbol, now as a personal designation. So there is only one way for Mr. Carpenter out of the difficulty; and he takes the leap. He denies the genuineness of these latter and personal passages as they stand. But this is to repudiate what is almost universally accepted even by his own school.[1] Moreover, the words of Jesus at His trial on which Mr. Carpenter relies are not, even in themselves, capable of a merely symbolic or ideal sense. In reply to the question, " Art Thou the Christ, the Son of the Blessed?" He answers, " I am: and ye shall see the Son of Man sitting at the right hand of power."[2] There would be no point in the reply unless it had a note of self-reference and self-vindication.[3]

---

[1] Mr. Carpenter's interpretation of the phrases I have quoted and of others similar to them is the *ne plus ultra* of improbable exegesis. *Ibid.* pp. 381–386. It is curious that Dr. Martineau and Mr. Carpenter, who take substantially the same theological attitude, should be so utterly divergent in their rendering of Jesus' use of the term " Son of Man." In the view of the latter it is a symbol of the future glory of God's people, and has no personal reference. In that of the former it is essentially personal, and describes, not the glory of Christ, but the lowliness and sympathy of His character. The expressions that are historical to the one are repudiated by the other as the creation of an after-time. They pretty well refute each other's negations.

[2] Mark xiv. 61, 62.

[3] While it is true that the passages in the Gospels where " Son of Man " occurs are all so penetrated with Messianic meaning that Messiah might just as well be substituted for it (Beyschlag), yet this identification was not as clear to the Jews as to us. " Son of Man " was in their minds an indeterminate conception, with divergent associations drawn from Ezekiel and from Daniel. Whether they interpreted the language of the latter as symbolic or personal may be open to question ; but, as it undoubtedly conveyed the idea of supreme power and triumph, they found it somewhat bewildering to reconcile this thought with the sympathy and humility which were suggested by the name in other prophetic utterances, and which were so plainly characteristics of Jesus Himself. Hence, though on His lips it was a designation of the Messiah, it was a *veiled* designation ; and purposely so, as enabling Him on account of its diverse meanings or allusions to introduce gradually into the minds of His disciples the new and deeper conception of Messiahship which

There is thus embedded in the name a consciousness on the part of Jesus of a kingdom which He came to establish, and of which He is the Head. But He is the Head of it in virtue of being the Son of Man; in virtue, that is, of qualities that are truly human, tenderness, sympathy, generosity, as opposed to the irrational authority and brute force of heathen kingdoms. Hence He frequently introduces the term in connection with abasement and self-surrender, not as indicating that He has no authority, but as descriptive of the character of that authority, and the means whereby it has become His. He attains and perpetuates His lordship through service, and His lordship is such as none other can share, because His service is such as none other can render.[1] This is the only interpretation that will suit the diverse passages, which associate the name both with glory and with humiliation. It resolves their apparent contradiction, because it implies that the two contrasted ideas are only abstract opposites, and that they are in reality the two phases of an essential unity. "Whosoever of you will be the chiefest, shall be servant of all." This dual experience is a characteristic of the kingdom itself; it belongs to the members as well as to the Head. But it belongs to Him in a sense supreme and solitary:

alone He had come to realise. The parts of the Book of Enoch in which the Messiah is termed Son of Man are perhaps post-Christian. Stanton, *Jewish and Christian Messiah*, p. 59 ff.; Drummond, *Jewish Messiah*, pp. 48–73. On the other hand, Charles, *Book of Enoch*, pp. 30, 314–317, Thomson, *Books which influenced our Lord*, pp. 407–410, and Briggs, *Messiah of the Gospels*, p. 25, assign a pre-Christian date. "Our Lord always takes for granted," says Dr. Thomson, "that His auditors knew that He designated Himself as Messiah by this title." If this be so, how comes it that Jesus, who from the first called Himself the Son of Man, treats Peter's confession of His Messiahship as a newly-revealed truth of unspeakable moment?

[1] Mark x. 43–45.

5

He can dwell upon His self-sacrifice without loss of humility, not only because it has a height and a depth which they can neither approach nor measure, but because it has a quality in it different from theirs. That He is capable of this self-sacrifice, whereby He is indeed the servant of all, and so the lord of all, inevitably involves the wonderfulness of the " self" that makes it, and we ought not to suffer the vagueness attaching to the name " Son of Man " to hide this from us. When Meyer says, " He who among mere men calls Himself the Son of Man, *means thereby* to declare that His human existence is something miraculous, a form of existence which is not original to Him," he lays himself open to Beyschlag's [1] criticism, that Jesus could not be guilty of the parodox of employing a term which identified Him with men, when He intended to convey by it a meaning precisely the opposite. But it is rather the form of Meyer's exposition that is at fault, than the underlying idea. Certainly the primary emphasis lies on the *human* character of the work which Jesus came to do; but just as certainly He who alone stands in this universal relation to humanity cannot be merely a member of it.

What, then, was the mysterious background in His being which rendered such a universal relation possible? It was the consciousness of His divine Sonship, " All things are delivered unto Me of My Father: and no man knoweth the Son, save the Father; neither knoweth any man the Father, save the Son, and he to whomsoever the Son willeth to reveal Him." [2] Consider what the knowledge of the Father here means. It is not an intellectual quality, the understanding of His will; it is the fulfil-

---

[1] *N. T. Theology*, vol. i. p. 61.   [2] Matt. xi. 27 ; Luke x. 22.

ment of His will, through obedience and fellowship.
All moral knowledge comes through experience and life,
and if the right life is not there, right knowledge is impossible. Hence men cannot truly know God till they
become like Him, till they enter into union with Him
through the possession of His Spirit. It is thus that
the word is used in the Fourth Gospel, " This is life
eternal, that they should know Thee the only true God,
and Him whom Thou didst send, even Jesus Christ."
Jesus takes His stand between the Father and all men.
It is through Him that true sonship is born in them and
sustained. He possesses it and imparts it. He cannot
impart to others His *individual*[1] sense of perfect unity
with God ; but He claims to be able to restore them to
harmony with the Father, to a true filial spirit. This
mediation of His is not a temporary stage, but a permanent condition of their development and progressive
knowledge of the Father's life. His consciousness of
Sonship is closely associated with His redeeming work,
with His unreserved consecration of Himself in the world
to the Father's will. The conviction that as the Son He
alone knows the Father, leads immediately to the other
thought, that He is the intermediary of this knowledge
to all others ; " to whomsoever the Son willeth to reveal
Him." Hence it is specially emphasised at the Baptism,
when He was entering on His mission, and at the
Transfiguration, when the great turning-point of the
mission had been reached, and the shadows of the end
began to fall. It is penetrated and filled with a spiritual
and practical content. But this content—the absolute
knowledge of the Father, and the adequacy to impart

[1] See *ante*, pp. 37-8.

the Father's life—was so transcendent in Jesus, that we are compelled to believe that such a relation of perfect love between the Father and Him who knew Himself to be the Son, had not its birth in time; that it was an eternal reality which only received a special expression under human conditions in the life of Jesus. When speaking of the Last Things, He intimates how in one point these human conditions exercise a limiting effect on a relationship which is yet represented as supreme above all comparison. "Of that day or that hour knoweth no one, not even the angels in heaven, *neither the Son*, but the Father." [1]

It is true, indeed, that the name Son of God is in the Old Testament applied to Israel, and in particular to the Theocratic King,[2] who is to be God's "firstborn, higher than the kings of the earth." [3] It denotes there simply that His people and their sovereign are the peculiar object of God's favour, and chosen by Him for an exceptional mission. But this usage throws not the least light on the meaning of the Sonship claimed by Jesus, which has to be interpreted by reference to Himself and the connection in which He employs it. Consequently it avails little to ask what the name imports on the lips of those who apply it to Him, such as the Centurion and the High Priest.[4] In all probability it is with them but an intensification of the Old Testament idea of pre-eminent nearness to God or selection for a high function of service. Nay, even the fact that Jesus, according to Matthew, accepts the designation from Peter, "Thou art the Christ, the Son

[1] See *ante*, p. 19, *n.*   [2] Ps. ii. 7.
[3] Ps. lxxxix. 27.   [4] Matt. xxvii. 54, xxvi. 63.

of the living God," [1] does not prove that for Peter
it had the same significance as for Himself.   The
apostle at that stage could have had no such conception
of Christ's Deity as he afterwards attained.   But Jesus
welcomes his confession, not because it is adequate, but
because it is at least the beginning of a true recognition.
When Beyschlag says that " in thus accepting a name
which was current among the people, He can have
attached to it no new and unheard-of meaning," [2] he
must have forgotten that Jesus also endorses the title
of Messiah ascribed to Him, even though it did *not*
mean for Peter what it meant for Him.   Half the work
of Jesus was just the filling of terms commonly used
with a richer content.   This applies, above all, to His
own unshared consciousness of Sonship.   That Sonship
for Him was unique, not merely because it was capable
of receiving and responding to the full loving purpose of
the Father, but because it lay at the basis of all sonship
in others, and therefore had a universal meaning for the
race.   That is the explanation He Himself gives of
those characteristics of autocracy, of self-assertive
humility, which are so utterly bewildering in so self-
sacrificing a soul.

Many have endeavoured to represent these claims
as implying, not His Deity, but simply His Messiahship.
Sharing as He did, it is said, the religious traditions of
His race, He felt Himself called of God by indisputable
inward witness to be the Messiah, the fulfiller of all the
best hopes of the past.   No doubt He read these hopes

---

[1] Mark has only, " Thou art the Christ," viii. 29.   Luke has " the Christ
of God," ix. 20.

[2] *N. T. Theology*, vol. i. p. 69.

in a more spiritual sense than was ever hitherto con-
ceived; He altered the character of the Messiah's work;
He eliminated some elements and introduced others.
But still the relation in which the Messiah stood to
God remained for Him unchanged. The Jews never
expected the "Anointed One" to be Himself divine.
However supreme His function in the realisation of
God's purpose, and separated though He was by an
impassable gulf from that of all other servants of the
Lord, He was still only God's messenger. When Jesus,
then, assumes exceptional prerogatives in commanding
loyalty to Himself, and in mediating as the Son between
all men and the Father, He is not disclosing His own
inner nature as divine, or at all intending to suggest
such a thought; He is merely speaking in an official
sense as the Unique One appointed by God to be the
promised deliverer. It is the expression of His historic
consciousness of Messiahship.

But it requires little argument to show that the
change, which all must admit in Jesus' idea of the quality
and significance of the Messiah's mission, necessitates a
change in His idea of the Messiah Himself. It might
well be that that mission, as viewed by the Jews, did not
involve in their minds a divine nature for its accomplishment, and yet that the mission as reconstrued by Jesus
did so. The Messianic hope of the Jews varied greatly
from age to age; it is a vague picture which floats and
wavers on the horizon. But certain particulars remain
more or less distinctly present. 1. The Messiah was to
be in an altogether special sense God's minister. He
would be the perfect realisation of the theocratic king.
He would stand in a peculiar relationship of union with,

and dependence upon, Jehovah.   The stamp of God's authority would be visibly upon Him ; the favour of God would be manifestly with Him.   2. In Him the heart's yearnings would find absolute satisfaction.   Prophets and righteous kings only pointed to and typified Him. But when He came, men would " not look for another." The long vista of expectation was closed with His form. 3. He would not only be the culmination and completion of Israel's desire and blessedness ; He would be supreme over all nations of the earth.   Sometimes these nations were represented as coming to Jerusalem to render a willing homage ;   at other times as alien and reluctant, and crushed by the Messiah as the vicegerent of the true God.   In one form or other His supremacy would be complete.[1]

If that was the floating historic idea of the Messiah, what new elements did Jesus introduce into it ?   He denationalised the whole conception, and so spiritualised it.   The kingdom of God, as He viewed it, was a kingdom which men entered one by one, not merely as Jews, but as men whose hearts turned to Him as the deliverer.   Their fitness for it was inward and spiritual ; and this fitness sprang from a right relation to Himself. Therefore His power had to extend to the deepest life of the soul, to its inmost struggles and temptations.   The Messiah's salvation of His people had now to be wrought out, not by His external interposition in their behalf, but by His identification with them.   His lowliness and suffering, which seemed at first the negation of His

---

[1] Stanton, *Jewish and Christian Messiah*, pp. 146–149 ; cf. Drummond, *Jewish Messiah*, pp. 388–390.   A clear and succinct account of the growth of the Messianic Hope in the Old Testament is given by Stanton in the *Cambridge Companion to the Bible*, pp. 120–123.

authority, were the very means by which it was created
and maintained.   They emphasised the spiritual nature
of His own victory over the world, and therefore the
spiritual nature of the victory that He secured for others.
The deliverance became theirs, not by His action
independently of their own, but through their personal
receptivity as individuals to the life which centred in
Him.   It was just because He could thus be to the
individual what God alone can be, that He could declare
Himself the ultimate Judge of both quick and dead.
This was a function which the Jews never assigned to
the Messiah.[1]   He was, indeed, to pronounce judgment
on the Gentile nations by shattering the world-dominion
of the heathen, and so opening up the way for the
Messianic kingdom upon earth.   But the final and
eternal verdict on men's characters was reserved for God
Himself.   Jesus, in ascribing this office to Himself,
distinctly lays claim to an inalienable prerogative of
Deity.   It may be a question whether even the hopes
attaching themselves to the old Messianic idea could have
been in any real manner fulfilled by One who was not
divine.   If he were to be the full satisfaction of the
heart's desire, to bring inward righteousness as well as
outward prosperity and peace, it is hard to conceive how
this mission could be discharged by any creature of God,
no matter how exalted.[2]   But, in arguing thus, we are
apt to import into the Jewish idea an individualism which
belongs to a later time.   The thought of personal
responsibility was not yet denuded of its national

[1] *Jewish and Christian Messiah*, pp. 140, 291 ; Drummond, *Jewish Messiah*, p. 390.   Cf. Charles' view, *Book of Enoch*, pp. 125-129, 315.

[2] See Gore, *Dissertations*, p. 17, *n.* 8.

reference. But we may fairly say that the " prophetic soul dreaming on things to come" spoke more wisely than it knew, and conjured up visions which we can now see to be unattainable, unless under conditions which could not then be forecast.

What we have to do with, then, is not the Messiah as expected by Israel, but the Messiah as conceived by Jesus. When the external elements of deliverance were purged out, and the sphere of redemption transferred from the nation to the single soul, it was morally impossible for Him to retain for Himself the former solitary and supreme authority of the Messiah, unless He had the witness in Himself that He possessed the divine power of searching, moulding, and judging human hearts. It is an entire misconception to suppose that Jesus attained first to the official consciousness of Messiahship, and then, in the light of that, arrived at the personal consciousness of His Sonship to the Father. If we can say that the one preceded the other, it was the personal which gave birth to the official, not *vice versâ* ; or rather, as they probably arose in close association with each other, the personal lay at the basis of the official, and implied it : certainly it could never have been created by it. Jesus felt that He, and He alone, realised in Himself what was yet to be realised in the people ; and this consciousness of His own Sonship in the fullest sense, awaked the Messianic consciousness that only through Him all the individuals of the nation could become really the children of God.[1]

In this discussion I have for obvious reasons confined myself to the Synoptics. Is the representation which is

[1] Weiss, *Life of Christ*, vol. i. p. 303, *n.*

given in the Fourth Gospel, as is so often maintained, radically different?   Let us take the two essential points —(1) Jesus' relation to men, and (2) His relation to the Father.   1. The peculiarity of the Fourth Gospel is the emphatic and persistent way in which it sets forth the inwardness of His relation to His disciples, the mystical identification of His life with theirs.   This will necessarily seem an incredible claim, if we adopt a very common delusion that the Jesus of the first three Gospels is merely a spiritual prophet of the highest kind; severe, doubtless, towards many forms of false religion, but entrancing us by the beauty of His character and the sweet graciousness of His message; careless about Himself and the ideas men had of His personality, so only He could lead them to think rightly of the merciful Father in heaven.   But the Synoptic account contradicts this at every step.   Let me recapitulate what we have there found.   Christ sums up the past as the full and final revelation of God to men ; He dictates their course, and imposes on them without hesitation the most trying sacrifices ; He judges their hearts now, and will judge them finally hereafter. He possesses an absolutely unique moral consciousness of harmony with God, and stands there, not as a solitary and supreme example to inspire and instruct, but as the sole Mediator of the spirit of sonship which all need.   When we read, therefore, in the Fourth Gospel that Jesus declared, " I am the bread of life," or " I am the vine, ye are the branches," " as the branch cannot bear fruit of itself, except it abide in the vine ; no more can ye, except ye abide in Me,"[1] there is no real change in the idea as compared with the self-disclosures made by Jesus in the

[1] John vi. 48, xv. 5, 4.

Synoptics. There is a certain unfolding of it, a more
direct statement of a personal and inward fellowship, but
no essential advance.   And the proof of this is, that if we
repudiate such words as giving a false view of Christ's
teaching, then we must deny the genuineness, not only
of a few phrases in the Synoptics, but of their entire
presentation ; for the work which Jesus there claims to
do for human souls, and the place which He asserts for
Himself in their allegiance, are only possible to one who
has towards all the divine power of entrance and
possession.

2. Nothing can be more erroneous than to speak of
the view of Christ's Sonship to the Father in the Fourth
Gospel as an abstract and philosophical conception,
having only an external connection with the facts of
Christ's life and experience.   It is not so, even in the
passages where the Evangelist speaks in his own name ;
and in the sayings attributed to Jesus, His Sonship is the
very reverse of an abstract term.   Still more plainly than
in the Synoptics is the consciousness of it definitely
correlated to His mission as Redeemer.   However true
it may be that it involves an eternal background of
Being, yet His expression of it remains ever in inseparable
connection with the fact and purpose of His human life.
He is not merely the Son, but the Son in Humanity,
existing and manifesting Himself as man for the reunion
of souls to the Father.   " My Father worketh even until
now : and I work. . . . For as the Father raiseth the
dead and quickeneth them, even so the Son also
quickeneth whom He will."   " As the Father hath life
in Himself, even so gave He to the Son also to have life
in Himself: and He gave Him authority to execute

judgment, because He is Son of Man." [1]   Wherever His
Sonship is most emphasised by Him, it is always in
relation to the mission entrusted to Him on earth.   He
is *sent* by the Father.   "Yea, and if I judge, My judgment is true; for I am not alone, but I and the Father
that sent Me." [2]   As in the Synoptics He declines the
title Good, because in the fullest sense it is applicable
only to pure Deity, while His own goodness on earth
was human, progressive ; so in the Fourth Gospel He
repudiates the charge of making Himself equal to the
Father.   "The Son can do nothing of Himself, but what
He seeth the Father doing : for what things soever He
doeth, these the Son also doeth in like manner.   For the
Father loveth the Son, and showeth Him all things that
Himself doeth : and greater works than these will He
show Him, that ye may marvel." [3]   No words could
bring out more clearly the three phases of Christ's
person : His inferiority to the Father, as the organ of
His life; His unity with the Father, as being adequate to
receive and communicate that life ; and the expression of
this complete Sonship in marvellous works among men.

   In one particular the Fourth Gospel goes beyond the
Synoptics, namely, the affirmation which Christ makes
of His pre-existence.   "Before Abraham was, I am ";
"Glorify Thou Me with Thine own self with the glory
which I had with Thee before the world was." [4]   Some

---

[1] Chap. v. 17, 21, 26, 27.   In ver. 27, "Son of Man" or "a Son of Man,"
not "the Son of Man," is the true rendering.   The Son hath this prerogative
of judgment committed to Him, because, while being the Son, He is also *Man.*
See Westcott, *Comm. on St. John, in loc.*

[2] Chap. viii. 16.

[3] Chaps. v. 18–21, x. 33–36.

[4] Chaps. viii. 58, xvii. 5 ; cf. also vi. 62, xvi. 28, xvii. 24.

theologians[1] who accept these words as genuine sayings of Christ, maintain that they do not imply a reference to a former life in heaven before His earthly one; that they describe, not a personal existence, but an ideal one, as the object from all eternity of God's loving regard. They maintain that Jesus was following here a prevailing Jewish form of thought. Everything holy or divine that appeared on earth, or was expected, was traced back to a heavenly original. The tabernacle was made according to the pattern in the Mount; the kingdom of God was prepared for the righteous from the foundation of the world; their reward is even now laid up in heaven. So Jesus, recognising that through Him alone God's purpose towards humanity was to be realised, and that all history gathered itself up in Him, portrays His central importance for the race by using this prevalent Jewish idea of a heavenly pre-existence. He was before Abraham and all the prophets in God's thought; *they* were but individual instruments, *He* was the goal of their endeavours. This place which He had in the divine plan was His pre-existence; this high and unshared function of spiritual Messiahship, appointed to Him from the beginning, was the glory which He had with the Father before the world was. As the glory which He prays for stands in necessary relation to His Messianic work on earth, it cannot have really, but only ideally, existed before His appearance among men.[2]

Probably on first reading such an interpretation we are inclined to say of the critic as Voltaire said of the

[1] Wendt, *Teaching of Jesus*, vol. ii. 168–178; Beyschlag, *N. T. Theology*, vol. i. pp. 249–255.

[2] Beyschlag, *ibid*. p. 254. See Orr, *Christian View of God and the World*, pp. 278, 289–291.

prophet Habakkuk, that he is " capable of anything."
It is futile to seek to refute him by pointing out how
unlikely it is that Christ would have used the phrase
" Before Abraham was, I am," if He meant merely to
contrast Abraham's *actual* existence with His own *ideal*
one, or that He would have spoken of returning to a
glory which had never been His, and was only now about
to become so.   An easy escape is found in insisting on
Jewish forms of thought, and the anachronism of import-
ing our Western logic into the fluent expressions of
Oriental mysticism.   If we are to argue the question
of Christ's pre-existence effectively, we must go farther
back.   The consciousness of it rose to expression only
in a few supreme moments of His life.   It was the
culmination of His self-witness.   Therefore it is only
when recognised as involved in, and necessarily growing
out of, those other more obvious forms of self-witness
which preceded it that it becomes credible to us ; and
more than credible, imperative.   To ascribe to Christ
the functions of perfect revealer of the Father, of a unique
Sonship which constitutes Him the one mediator to men
of true spiritual life, of ultimate Judge of human destinies :
to enthrone Him in this solitary supremacy, and then to
demand that men shall not accord to Him the homage
which is due only to an eternal Lord, is to be guilty of a
gross contradiction.   A Christ who, according to Beyschlag, had no personal existence before His birth in
Bethlehem, but somehow lived " in the heart of God," [1]
has no reality for human thought.   In one sense we may
say that the exegesis which refuses to find His pre-
existence in these passages of the Fourth Gospel is no

[1] Beyschlag, *N. T. Theology*, p. 259, *n.*

more forced than that which refuses to see that it forms the indispensable pre-condition of the total demand which He makes in the Synoptics. If we can fairly explain the latter without it, we can explain the former too. It would not appreciably affect the argument though the Johannine verses were discovered to be spurious, any more than the doctrine of the Trinity was affected by the deletion of the " Three heavenly witnesses." [1] For it rests not on isolated phrases, but on the inner necessity of the relation which Christ, with the unbroken sense of carrying out the Father's will, assumes towards all men. The special value of the verses is, that they give expression to a truth without which other truths of which we are already persuaded would be utterly incomprehensible.

The endeavours made to discredit the testimony of the Fourth Gospel by representing it as a theosophical romance, composed by a Greek in the latter half of the second century, have practically been abandoned. It is now perfectly clear that, instead of being a philosophical treatise on the dogma of the Logos, in which the Gnostic antithesis of the principles of light and darkness is worked out in the form of an idealised picture of Christ's life, this Gospel is emphatically a historical document, grounded on a minute knowledge of facts. Not merely does the writer show an intimate acquaintance with the language, traditions, modes of thought, history, and customs of the Jewish people, but he describes events with the incidental touches possible only to an eye-witness.[2] During recent years, Lightfoot [3] and others have produced an enormous

[1] 1 John v. 7.
[2] Chaps. vi. 10, 19, 23 ; x. 22, 23 ; xi. 1, 44, 54 ; xxi. 2.
[3] *Biblical Essays*, pp. 1–198.

accumulation of evidence, both external and internal, which raises to a high degree of probability the ancient unbroken tradition of the Church,[1] that it was written by the Apostle John.[2]

Notwithstanding this, however, it must be acknowledged that a perplexing problem is presented by the discourses. The difficulty does not consist in the substance of their teaching. Wendt has unquestionably succeeded in showing that, with all their divergence in form, they present the same fundamental truths as the Synoptics, though his rejection of the transcendent element in Christ's personality leads him to lower the testimony which both render. The real difficulty is that Jesus should have spoken them as they stand. No one can doubt that the short pictorial sayings and the parables of the Synoptics convey the impression of being nearer to an actual report of His words; while the style of the discourses is somewhat similar to that of the Evangelist himself, as seen in the narrative part of the Gospel and in John's First Epistle. But certain distinctions have to be made.   1. The doctrine of Christ as the incarnate Logos, which is set forth in the Prologue, is undoubtedly the general conception which underlies the whole Gospel,

the word Logos quite answers to the writer's own view of Christ's personality, he never represents it as employed by Christ Himself. It is *his* interpretation, not Christ's declaration.[3] The discussions in which the Jews so eagerly take part as to Jesus' personal claim, do not

---

[1] The one exception, hardly worth mentioning, is that of the obscure sect in the second century, known as the Alogi.

[2] Note 7, p. 392.

[3] See Note 8, p. 392, "Harnack on the Prologue of the Fourth Gospel."

turn on the question whether He is the incarnate Word
of God, but whether He is the Messiah.   They treat of
just such perplexities as would arise in Jewish minds
regarding His relation to their national past, its traditions
and hopes.   It is this historical reference which really
underlies them, though it is sometimes kept in reserve
till, as it were, the close of the discussion,[1] because Jesus
insists on falling back, not on any official title, as vindi-
cating His inherent dignity, but on His own immediate
consciousness of Sonship.   His thought moves in the
sphere of direct practical experience.   One can see how
natural it was that the profound expression of His own
personality should arise precisely as the writer describes,
either when He was alone with " His own," or in converse
with disputants who, conscious of the mysterious authority
which He claimed in God's name, yet, hardened against
His message, sought to force the argument into a controversy about Himself.   Even the expressions of His pre-
existence are not so much formal declarations as intimations of it, springing from the sudden heightening of His
consciousness in moments of intense feeling.   2. While
John's own style abounds in a recurrence of simple
and abstract terms, such as life and light, the discourses
themselves are full of picturesque imagery.   The manna,
the living water, the bread of life, the good shepherd, the
true vine, have all that element of the pictorial and
illustrative which is characteristic of the Synoptic sayings.[2]

---

[1] Chaps. v. 39, 45 ff. ; vii. 26 ff. 40, 43 ; viii. 56 ; x. 24, 25.   The demand of
the Jews, "How long dost Thou hold us in suspense ? If Thou be the Christ,
tell us plainly" (x. 24), shows that they were dissatisfied with His reiterated
allusions to His Sonship, and wanted Him to "place" Himself definitely in
relation to their Historic Hope.   See Lightfoot, *Biblical Essays*, pp. 23, 24.

[2] Wendt, *Teaching of Jesus*, vol. i. pp. 117-119.

6

There are also aphorisms and gnomic phrases closely allied to the Synoptic manner. Though uttered probably at different times, they have been brought together by the writer as if they formed a single address. This grouping accounts for the obvious discontinuity of many passages, and has helped to widen the apparent divergence between the Fourth and the First Three Gospels.

Making all allowance for these considerations, there remains something still to be accounted for. The relation in which the writer stands to his material is very different, for example, from that of Luke. The latter frankly takes up the position of a compiler from documents and narratives which he has collected and verified. One may, indeed, be at a loss to know, in the case of a saying which Luke records differently from Matthew, whether the divergence is to be attributed to him or to the source from which he draws; but he leaves us in no doubt where he means Christ's sayings to begin and end. It is otherwise with the Fourth Evangelist. In the third chapter he so weaves together his own words with those of Christ and of John the Baptist, that it will probably never be certain how we ought to assign the last twenty verses; yet some of them assuredly are the Evangelist's own comment. This fusion runs throughout the Gospel, though it is seldom so easy to detect as here. The author is not a compiler; he is a reproducer of what has come under his own eyes, and been absorbed into his life. Writing some fifty or sixty years after his fellowship with Jesus, a thousand incidents and details of that unforgetable time rise vividly before him, yet he sees the whole as interpreted by the spiritual experience of the

intervening period.[1] The time, the place, the circumstances of any utterance may be written on his memory,
but the utterance itself has another meaning for him now.
It is the actual historical life of Jesus that he is dealing
with, but he looks back at it in the light of what it has
since proved to signify for the Christian Church and for
himself. His Gospel is the expression of that deeper
insight which, according to him, Jesus promised when
the Spirit should bring to their remembrance all that
He had said to them. This remembrance was not
the mere recollection of His sayings, but the spiritual
illumination of them, the opening up of their inner
purport and ultimate significance; and just because that
significance could only reveal itself through personal
experience, they reappear with a certain impress of
John's individuality. Thus, intimate as his knowledge
is of the earlier stages of Christ's ministry, he views them
from a later standpoint. The entire history is for him a
completed unity, and he describes the beginning of it
with the feeling of one who has witnessed the close, and
by much brooding reached the heart of the secret. The
discourse on the Bread of Life in the sixth chapter has
every indication of being a genuine saying of Christ, in
connection with the miracle of the loaves, and turning
upon the story of the Manna which came down from
heaven; but in its present form it seems to be interwoven with thoughts drawn by John from his recollection

[1] " Words which seem strange, if taken to have been uttered by Christ
concerning Himself, are at once seen in another light when they are regarded
as coming from a disciple, and as revealing the after-influence of intercourse
with Him." Weizsäcker, *Apostolic Age*, vol. ii. p. 234. This principle
certainly applies in some measure to the Fourth Gospel, though one may
dissent from Weizsäcker's own application of it.

of the Last Supper.[1]   The Evangelist's comments[2] on
the interview with Nicodemus are plainly such reflections
as could only have been made by one who lived in a
time when the completed Christian faith stood forth to
claim men's homage, and divided them into two opposing camps.   On the one side is the Church, where Christ's
redeeming power is manifest; on the other, the World
which rejects Him, because it loves darkness rather than
light.   This is the outcome and issue, as John now
beholds it and as all the intervening years since Pentecost
had shown it, of the appearance of Jesus among men.
He sees that it could not have been otherwise, that the
message of redemption inevitably awaked antagonism
from those who had no affinity for the Truth.

So deeply is this idea wrought into his soul, that it
dominates his retrospect of the actual ministry.   From
first to last his Gospel dwells on the hatred and captious
opposition of " the Jews "; and then, in contrast to these,
we have Christ's fellowship with " His own."   We naturally ask, How did Christ gain " His own "?   By what
means did He secure their allegiance?   They were not
His at first; how came they to attach themselves so
utterly to Him?   It was not by His simply declaring,
" I am the Son of God," but by the gracious and wonderful human life which the Synoptic account portrays,
and which irresistibly drew them to the confession of His
lordship.   His direct personal claim could not come
first; it required for its basis and interpretation living
words and deeds that appealed to the hearts of men.

---

[1] Chap. vi. 51–56.   See Note 9, p. 393, on the Baptist's designation of
Jesus as " The Lamb of God."

[2] Chap. iii. 19–21.

The tenderness and compassionateness of Jesus as the "Friend of Sinners" is very slightly represented in the Fourth Gospel. But it formed part of the common tradition of the Church; and with that, if not with the First Three Gospels as we possess them, the writer was familiar. His purpose was not to repeat what was already known concerning the process by which Christ gained men to Himself, but to gather together the incidents and sayings that revealed the divine greatness of His personality as the Eternal Saviour. For this reason the general Fatherhood of God is not depicted as it is in the Synoptics; but rather that Fatherhood as it exists only for those who through Christ the Son have received the *spirit* of Sonship. It is this special aspect that John emphasises, not as contradicting the other, but as completing it.[1] In the picture which he gives of the people among whom Jesus moved, both the lights and the shades are fiercer than in the Synoptics, just because the history of Christ's life is written with the deep consciousness of the separation which that life now fully revealed has made between souls, deepening the darkness of those who oppose, and enriching all who welcome it with unspeakable treasures of joy and peace. The conversational character of the Gospel[2] shows that it was composed primarily to meet the needs and questionings of John's own disciples at Ephesus; and so it brings out the present and enduring relation of Christ to believers who had never seen Him in the flesh. Hence it is peculiarly the Gospel beloved by "His own"

---

[1] See Note 10, p. 395, "The Fatherhood of God in the Synoptics and in St. John."

[2] Lightfoot, *Biblical Essays*, p. 197.

in all ages, while it is naturally repudiated as "poor stuff"[1] by those who have not been already won through the Synoptic account to the acknowledgment of His unique lordship.

From all this it is perfectly clear what place it ought to hold in the study of the self-revelation of Jesus. Though giving the general chronology of His life more fully and precisely than the Synoptics, it does not show, as they do in a manner, the actual development of His teaching. Loosely as they sit to the detailed order of events, yet they make clear the means whereby He led up to the turning-point of His ministry,—the confession of His Messiahship, and the first definite intimation of His approaching death.[2] It is to them we must refer if we would ascertain, not only the process by which Christ secured, in the beginning of His intercourse, the disciples' love and loyalty, but also the general views which they had of Him up to the close of His ministry, and even in the earliest days of the Christian Church. We can see from the addresses of Peter in the opening chapters of Acts, that their faith grew out of just such teaching as is contained in the Synoptics. The sayings which John records had in substance been spoken by the Lord, but they had not been assimilated by the apostles. Their profound inwardness needed, not merely the illumination of the Spirit bestowed at Pentecost, but a certain affinity of soul, and the receptivity that only comes from a deepening personal experience of Christian struggle and triumph. John himself could not have reproduced them as they stand in his Gospel till through

---

[1] J. S. Mill, *Essays on Religion*, p. 254.
[2] Matt. xvi. 13–23 ; Mark viii. 27–33 ; Luke ix. 18–22.

long meditation and service he had appropriated and
absorbed them. We have no reason to suppose they
had a place in the earliest traditions of the Church
regarding Jesus, like so much of the Synoptic account.
Some of them may have been known and current, but
the general representation as given by John was certainly
not. He did not gather them from tradition: they
were his own recollections. He had treasured them in
his heart, and he brought them forth at last, interpreted
by his spiritual verification of them, for the instruction
of believers who had already reached their faith in
Christ along other lines.

LECTURE III.

THE GROWTH OF CHRIST'S SELF-CONSCIOUS-NESS, AND THE METHOD OF HIS SELF-MANIFESTATION. JESUS AND THE TWELVE.

SYNOPSIS.

Importance of studying the *method* and *order* of the self-revelation of Jesus.

I. The Growth of His own thought.
    1. As regards His Messiahship.
        Unlikely that His consciousness of it was awaked only at His Baptism.
    2. As regards His Death.
        Improbability of Wendt's view.
        Cannot say *a priori* what Jesus, as the incarnate Son, *must* have known.

II. His Self-manifestation to men.
    A. The Threefold means He employed.
        1. *Teaching.*
            Dealt first with the basal conceptions of God and man as Father and child.
            His purpose not to impart ideas, but to mould character.
            His teaching, therefore, suggestive and germinal, not didactic; but more 'authoritative' on this account.
        2. *Miracles.*
            That Jesus *claimed* to work them, quite certain.
            Not to be judged *in vacuo.*
            Jesus' sinlessness and the argument from the uniformity of nature.
            The miracles as expressions of His character and mission.
            Have a place only in a *disorganised* world.
            The miraculous in Christianity more credible if found in the *physical* as well as the *moral* sphere.
        3. *The Influence of His Personal Presence.*
            Its subtle power in shaping character.
    B. The existence of a Special Circle on whom these three factors continuously operated.
        The Apostolate a necessity.
        The Twelve, a school; but a school *in* the world.
        The Crisis—the acknowledgment by Jesus of His Messiahship: effect on His subsequent intercourse with the disciples.
        The potency of His method lay in its indirectness.

LECTURE III.

The Growth of Christ's Self-consciousness, and the Method of His Self-Manifestation. Jesus and the Twelve.

In passing from the discussion of the manifold and imperious claims made by Jesus to the progressive account of His life as it stands in the Synoptic Gospels, we are conscious of a great contrast. It is the difference between a completed revelation and a revelation in process. The question that supremely concerns us as we look back on the appearance among men of this unique Personality is, What was His real significance? What was the total purport and outcome of His mission? And the answer to that necessarily lies in the later stages of His work, when the truths which it embodies rise to more explicit utterance. The consequence is that the earlier and preparatory period is apt to lose its proper place, in one of two ways. Either we read into it the developed thoughts that belong to the close, and thus fail to do justice to the slow and natural growth of the revelation ; or, on the other hand, recognising that it largely consists of hints and half suggestions, we disparage its value as compared with the fully unfolded message. But to act thus is not only to be untrue to the facts, it is a serious detriment to our own under-

standing of Christ's mission. It obscures from us the
method by which He led men to the recognition of His
indispensableness to their spiritual life. It was not by
overt and unmistakable announcements of His Person
that He won their homage, but by the subtle authori-
tativeness which penetrated His gracious invitations, His
warnings, His works of healing, His daily intercourse.
It is quite as true to say that they discovered Him, as
that He revealed Himself.

Nor is this method in His self-revelation important
merely from a historical point of view. It is an indication of the way in which Christ has always to be
approached, if we are rightly to recognise His supremacy
over us. The record of the time when He went about
doing good, and the people, astonished at His marvellous
sayings and deeds, asked wonderingly whether He were
the Great Prophet or not, is no mere scaffolding which
was of use till the edifice was completed and may now
be discarded. It is a part of the building itself, of the
self-manifestation whereby He was to draw all men unto
Him. And it is because so many form their conception
of Christ simply from the perfected shape which His
claims assumed in the last days of His ministry, or still
more from the dogmatic form in which the Church
presents them, that they repudiate or treat with indifference an authority which seems to them abstract and
dictatorial. Authority is not, in Christ's case, the first
word, but rather the last; it is not so much a right
imposed, as a supremacy finally acknowledged as the
result of a growing and irrepressible conviction.

I. But before considering the gradual development
in Christ's method of self-manifestation, there is a prior

question. Was this development due to His own self-restraint and conscious adaptation of truth to the needs of others, or was it the expression of His own slowly deepening insight into His message? There are certain theories on the subject which are plainly impossible, if any historicity attaches to the Gospel accounts. Dr. Martineau's contention, that Jesus Himself never claimed to be the Messiah, and that the name was subsequently "palmed upon" Him by His followers, has hardly a vestige of plausibility;[1] and one can only marvel at Schenkel's view, that He adopted the title at a late stage as an accommodation to the popular expectation. It was precisely His refusal to accommodate Himself to prevalent ideas which led to His rejection and death. It has become more and more clear that He had from the beginning of His public life the same spiritual conception of the kingdom of God and of His own central relation to it which dominated Him to the end. There is undoubtedly a progress throughout in the unfolding of its content and application, especially in its personal reference, but there is no departure from the essential standpoint of His earlier Galilean Gospel. The inward, ethical, and universal quality in His teaching is present from the first.

1. It seems to me doubtful whether we are warranted even in saying that His Messianic consciousness was born

---

[1] "Some critics have called in question the fact that Jesus called Himself Messiah. But this article of the Evangelic tradition seems to me to stand the test of the most minute investigation." Harnack, *History of Dogma*, vol. i. p. 63, *n.* "Historically considered, the calling which Jesus embraced, and with which was bound up His significance for the world, was and could be no other than to be the Messiah of His people." Weiss, *Life of Christ*, vol. i. p. 295.

only at the moment of His Baptism.[1]   We lack, indeed, the historical data which would enable us absolutely to determine the point ; but psychological probabilities are on the other side.   We have seen that the moral consciousness of Jesus as it manifested itself in His public life, implied that He had maintained from His earliest childhood an unclouded filial relation to God.   But if there never was a time, as Wendt admits, when He did not know Himself as the Son of God, what was the transformation which His idea of Sonship underwent at His Baptism ?   " Whilst hitherto," Wendt says, " Jesus had been conscious of no peculiar excellence which exalted Him above others in respect to His religious views, experiences, and acts, and that just because they appeared to Him so simple, normal, and self-evident, now, all at once, He recognised the import of these qualities.   He saw in them not merely a specific advance beyond the religious standpoint of His countrymen, but also the first and supreme realisation of that ideal relationship between God and men foretold in Scripture as characteristic of the Messianic time."   Such a picture as Wendt here gives of the consciousness of Jesus in His preparatory period has an inherent unlikelihood.   He grew up with the profoundest sense of uninterrupted union with the Father, of joyful and childlike obedience to His will in every detail of inward and outward life ; and yet it never seemed to Him that His experience separated Him from others, it " appeared to Him so simple, normal, and self-evident."   Normal it may have been in a high ideal sense of the word, as the only

---

[1] So Wendt, *Teaching of Jesus*, vol. i. pp. 99-101 ; Beyschlag, *N. T. Theology*, vol. i. p. 58.

experience which accorded with the divine purpose
regarding humanity; but that could not possibly blind
Him to the fact that in this sense all other lives were
*ab*normal. A man's superior goodness does not hinder
him from perceiving in others faults from which he himself is free, it rather quickens his insight into the defects
which by brotherly sympathy he strives to remove. And
the perfect purity of Jesus made Him sensitive, to an
incomparable degree, to the least marks of wilfulness in
the conduct of those around Him. He detected selfishness where it was unfelt by other souls; and it smote
Him with a keener pang from His own intense and
unreserved devotion to the Father. When He worshipped in the synagogue, its prayers were no adequate
utterance of His own aspiration and divine communion.
The piercing cries of abasement in which the psalmists
and prophets gave voice to the deepest consciousness of
men before the Holy One found in Him no echo. " His
soul was like a star, and dwelt apart" in a region un-
entered by the saints of old. At every turn and stage
of His life this isolation was brought home to Him.
Can we imagine that He passed through an experience
like this, continuing unbroken, but growing ever deeper
and fuller, through childhood and youth up to the
maturity of thirty years, without asking Himself what
the meaning of it was, and why He had been chosen
of God for so special a heritage? And when He
turned to those Scriptures which enshrined God's highest
revelations of Himself in the past, He found in His
own consciousness of inward righteousness and harmony
with God the explanation of that salvation which the
purest souls so passionately longed for, but which they

declared could only be attained at the coming of the Messiah.

Thus His own unique experience and the Messianic Hope mutually interpreted one another. His own consciousness taught Him that the redemption which the prophets foretold was not external or national, but personal and spiritual, was, in fact, just the blessing which He already possessed of unimpaired communion with God; and so, conversely, the great Jewish Hope so long and profoundly cherished made clear to Him that the gift granted at present to Him alone was no individual boon, but given that He might mediate it. As Jesus' consciousness of His Messiahship grew out of, and was inwardly determined by, His permanent consciousness of Sonship, His conception of the Messianic kingdom rejected from first to last all the merely outward and earthly elements which mingled with the historic and traditional view of it.

Now what plausible reason is there to suppose that the Baptism was the birth-hour of this Messianic conviction? That the Evangelists are practically silent[1] regarding the previous stages of His life is no proof. The attestation of His unique Sonship, which is represented as given Him at His Baptism, is again given in precisely similar fashion at His Transfigura-

---

[1] In the one scene recorded belonging to this period (Luke ii. 41–51), the words of Jesus' reply, ἐν τοῖς τοῦ πατρός μου, following upon Mary's phrase, "Thy father," as applied to Joseph, appear to involve a certain unique consciousness of Sonship to God, but cannot be said of themselves to imply a consciousness either properly Messianic or properly Divine. (See Gore, *Dissertations*, p. 78, *n.* 1.) They are best described, perhaps, as indicating, to use Godet's expression, "the first revelation of a relation which surpassed all that Judaism had realised."

tion.[1]   It was evidently awaked in Him with exceptional
intensity at certain supreme moments, when, as it were, He
consecrated Himself afresh to His mission.   Just as in the
Transfiguration He received only a renewed confirmation of the assurance, so in all probability the Baptism
merely corroborated the dominant thought in His heart.
The attempt to portray in any other way the conditions
of Christ's mature thought prior to His ministry results in
confusion ; for it attributes what must have been a sense
of unique Sonship to One who could render to Himself
no rational account of His exceptional nature and its
relation to others.   To say with Godet[2] that a knowledge
of Himself and His special function would not have been
compatible with the accomplishment of the task assigned
to the first period of His life, is quite unwarrantable.
Would His consciousness of divine Sonship have rendered
it impossible for Jesus during the silent years to discharge His duty in the home and the carpenter's shop?
Would He have been so possessed by the thought of His
future mission that He would have fretted impatiently
at the meaner tasks prescribed Him?   But the Messiah
was not one who took His office on Himself; He was
chosen for it : and the assurance of God's choice of Jesus
was begotten within Him through the feeling of His
absolute filial surrender to the Father's will.   It was
that Will which determined His steps, which appointed
to Him as surely the preparatory stage, as it fixed the
hour when that stage should close ; and it was under the
guiding of that Will alone that He went forth to be

[1] See Note 11, p. 397, "The Attestation of Jesus' Sonship at the Baptism
and the Transfiguration."
[2] *Comm. on St. John*, vol. i. p. 399,

baptized of John in Jordan.   The consciousness of His Messiahship, instead of impairing His implicit submission to God in the details of a humble and withdrawn life, would have confirmed and deepened it.   As He Himself said in later days, " I do nothing of Myself; as the Father hath said unto Me, so I speak."

I must therefore hold with Weiss that Jesus was sure of His Messianic calling before He reached the Jordan.   The Baptism was remarkable, not as the hour in which His Messianic consciousness was born, but as the hour when under the solemn designation of the last of the prophets He consecrated Himself to the mission which was now to begin ; and received not only a fresh attestation of His call, but the gift of the Spirit needed for its fulfilment.   There is no contradiction in supposing that He was aware of His Messiahship before the special endowment required for realising it was conferred.   The thought of the future would be no burden to One who so utterly knew the Father, and knew also that according to His day His strength should be.   It is this childlike surrender which is the key of the whole.   The Spirit which descended and, in the Baptist's vision, rested [1] upon Him was to be His constant possession, " enabling Him to say and do what was needful for His Messianic calling, and what with ordinary human capacities He could not have attempted." [2] It was precisely this fresh gift of divine power which created the Temptation ; not merely the fact that He was on the eve of His great redemptive work, but the new consciousness of supernatural endowment as regards

---

[1] John i. 32, ἔμεινεν.   See Westcott, *in loc.*
[2] Weiss, *Life of Christ,* vol, i, p. 327.

both the physical and the spiritual sphere, driving Him to self-searching and the resolved consecration of it to purely Messianic ends.

2. Again, it is asserted by many as a certain and almost self-evident fact that Jesus, though conscious, from the beginning of His mission, of its Messianic character, did not anticipate that it would involve the surrender of His own life; that the cruel death which fell to His lot was only borne in upon Him as a necessity through the experience of disappointment and embittered antagonism, and that however clearly He may have seen that trial and renunciation would have to be endured by Himself as well as His followers, yet this coexisted at first with the joyful hope that He would ultimately obtain in His earthly life the gratitude and recognition of men.[1]   Now, while it is plain from all the records we possess that the earliest definite announcement of the death was made at Cæsarea Philippi, on the occasion of Peter's confession, yet that Jesus had previously forecast it in veiled forms is almost a certainty.   The Synoptics tell us that He spoke in the midst of His ministry in Eastern Galilee of a sad time coming for His disciples when the bridegroom should be taken away.[2]   As they do not touch upon the first part of His life spent in Judæa we cannot use them to test the statements of the Fourth Gospel, which represents Him as speaking at His first Passover, only a month or two after the Temptation, of a temple which if destroyed He should raise again in three days,

---

[1] Wendt, *Teaching of Jesus*, vol. ii. pp. 219-221.   Cf. Baldensperger, *Das Selbstbewusstsein Jesu.*

[2] Matt. ix. 15; Mark ii. 20; Luke v. 35.

and of a lifting up of the Son of Man like unto that of
the brazen serpent in the wilderness.[1]   Possibly there is
in the words " in three days " a certain " reading back "
from later experiences, as in other Johannine phrases;
but it is worth noting that these two expressions in
John have precisely the same indirect and half-hidden
reference that belongs to the above Synoptic saying,
which unquestionably could not be the only one uttered
by our Lord on so mysterious a subject in the preparatory months.

But even if the evidence of these dim forecastings
were much weaker than it is, it would not prove that
He was Himself ignorant of the fate in store for Him.
No blunder could be more glaring than to judge of *His*
knowledge of His mission at any point by the degree
in which He communicated it to others.   It is not from
His teaching, so largely determined as it was by the
need of adaptation to the imperfect capacities of His
followers, but from a consideration of what He was in
His unique moral nature, and of what, being what He
was, intercourse with men meant for Him, that we must
form our conception of His thought.   Now the opposition, which as it gathered to a head is supposed to have
convinced Jesus of the inevitableness of His violent
death, was present in some sense as early as we have
any record of His work.   It declared itself in the
synagogue of Nazareth[2] at the very opening of that
Galilean period which seems bathed in such an air of
graciousness and hope; and though it then took merely
the form of local jealousy, Jesus could not fail to see
that this was but one expression of the deep-rooted

[1] Chaps. ii. 19, iii. 14.   [2] Luke iv. 16–30.

selfishness of the human heart which in many forms
would thrust itself across His path.   He was in no
danger of mistaking the enthusiasm of the multitude for
a permanent attachment to His message, knowing that
many of the harder and profounder aspects of His
Truth had yet to be revealed; and just when this
enthusiasm was at its height, the ever-recurring captious-
ness of the Pharisees was a reminder of the sleepless foe
that dogged His steps.   If such was the reception that
He met with even in the Northern province, where the
people breathed a freer and less prejudiced atmosphere,
can anyone imagine that the marks of hostility were
less manifest during His visit to Jerusalem at the first
Passover, or during the period, possibly extending to
eight months, spent by Him in Judæa, of which nothing
but the bare mention survives? [1]   To speak as if Jesus
had to wait till the suspicion and hatred, which were
constantly showing themselves in individual cases, had
assumed bold dimensions before He could be convinced
of the issue, is to attribute to Him an extraordinary
blindness to the moral facts and tendencies of life.   A
great soul does not require this compulsory teaching;
it divines afar off.   It can pierce through the slighter

---

[1] John iii. 22, iv. 1-3.   If any historical value at all belongs to the earlier
chapters of John's Gospel as a record of what took place at the opening of
the ministry, there can be no doubt that when Jesus left Judæa for Galilee,
He had already surrendered all hope of recognition by the representatives of
the nation.   They had not indeed rejected Him formally as the Messiah, for
His Messiahship was not then acknowledged by Him; but they had
repudiated teaching which essentially involved it.   Any success which He
might henceforth attain in Northern Palestine would not conciliate but
strengthen the opposition of the hierarchy in the capital; so that He actually
began His Galilean ministry with the deep consciousness of His ultimate
rejection.   See Weiss, *supra*, vol. i. p. 387 ff.; Ellicott, *Hulsean Lectures*,
p. 203 and *passim*.

incidents of conduct to their essential significance and
the spirit that underlies them : it is surer of its conclusion from one ominous fact than the common mind
is after the most obvious demonstration.   This is the
prophetic gift : it has *fore*sight because it has *in*sight.
It sees the inevitable issue of a certain course of life,
because it knows the laws of the moral universe and
discerns the bias of the personal character.   It was this
which enabled the Old Testament seers to foretell the
destruction of a faithless Jerusalem.   And it was this
quality which Jesus possessed in a supreme degree, and
in virtue of which He knew what was in man.[1]

Further, the fate of so many of the great prophets of
old, and the despite done to them by the Jewish people,
were not thoughts hidden from Him till the close drew
near.   Whatever forewarnings their history conveyed
regarding Himself were surely as clear to Him when He
pronounced the Beatitude on those suffering for righteousness' sake,—" for so persecuted they the prophets which
were before you,"—as when at last He upbraided
Jerusalem with the murder of God's servants.[2]   How
could He expect to escape what the prophets suffered,
when He not only rebuked as they did the vices of the
age, but claimed to be the Messiah in a sense which ran
straight in the teeth of the traditional Hope of the race,
and which by condemning the externalism of the prevailing religion could not but incur the undying enmity
of a powerful officialism ?

The theory that Jesus began His mission in the

---

[1] On the relation of the *prophetic* to the *divine* element in Christ's
knowledge, see Note 13, p. 398.

[2] Matt. xxiii. 37 ; Luke xiii. 33 ; cf. xi. 47–51.

hope of " a peaceful, regular expansion of His teaching and of the establishment of the kingdom of God thereby," seems incompatible with His conception of His Messiah-ship as we know it to have been.   For that conception only grew up through the consciousness of His unique Sonship, and had for its central point the mediation of the filial spirit to others.   But this mediation could not be effected by mere teaching; it involved a personal identification with the sinful in their sufferings.   This was the chief channel whereby, through the manifestation of His sympathy with them, He awoke in them susceptibility and response to the spirit He sought to impart.   The one fact which stood out above all others in the thoughts of the people regarding Him, and which thrilled them with a joyful astonishment, was just that One who so plainly spoke with the authority of a prophet of God, yet took His place by the side of the outcast and distressed as a healer and a brother born for adversity. If, therefore, it was only by entering into the fellow-ship of their sorrow that He could heal the hurt of the soul, then with His profound sense of the alienation of men from God must have arisen an equally profound sense of the depth of the humiliation into which He must descend for their deliverance.   If the Evangelical Prophet long before saw that only through the voluntary self-sacrifice of the Holy One redemption could be wrought out for the guilty,[1] how could He, whose func-tion it was to break the power of sin in humanity and impart a new life of divine sonship, fail to see that He must endure the utmost expression of sin's curse, and taste not only of life's sorrow but of death's bitterness?

[1] Isa. liii.

Nor is it easy to understand how Jesus could possibly conceive, under any circumstances of popular welcome, of the success of His Messianic mission in His own life-time.   The spiritual blessing which He brought was not one that could be even rightly comprehended, far less appropriated, so long as He stood before men under the limiting conditions of earthly life.   This is obvious, even in the case of His most loyal disciples.   Did He picture to Himself a time when the whole Jewish people, including the representative hierarchy, would be as loyal to Him as they?   That would not have sufficed for Him or for them.   And what of future generations?   Had He no thought of the deepest trials of life?   What message of deliverance would He have left to a dying and self-condemned humanity?[1]

I have not at all argued this question from the standpoint of Christ's Divinity and of what as Divine He must have known.   We cannot say beforehand how much or how little of His essential prerogative of perfect power and knowledge the Son of God surrendered in submitting to the conditions of a true human life.   The *a priori* method is utterly illegitimate, and issues in a perverted exegesis.   It led the Fathers almost universally to explain away Jesus' declaration that He knew not the day of the Final Judgment,[2] by affirming that He used the words, not in His own person, but as the representa-

---

[1] See Neander's discussion on Christ's plan as unchanged, *Life of Christ*, pp. 84–88.

[2] Mark xiii. 32 ; Matt. xxiv. 36 (R.V.).   See Gore, *Dissertations*, pp. 117, 136, 160.   The fact of a limitation in Christ's knowledge remains the same, even if the prophetic discourse on the Coming of the Son of Man be held (as by Gould, *Comm. on St. Mark*, p. 241) to refer to the fall of the Jewish State, and not at all to the end of the world.

tive of His mystical Body, the Church.   The appeal
must be purely to the facts; nor is it difficult to see
what their general verdict is.   He had no absolute and
intuitive knowledge of distant or merely external events.
There are indeed one or two instances which seem to
imply it; as when He told Peter how he would find
the piece of money in the fish's mouth, and the disciples
how they would find the colt tied in the village, and the
man bearing a pitcher of water who would take them to
the upper chamber.[1]   These belong to a different category from His prophecy of Judas' betrayal or Peter's
denial, because they are isolated facts not capable of
discovery through their relation to human character.
But whatever difficulty there may be in explaining them,—and they are precisely analogous to the
predictions of special occurrences attributed to the
prophets,—they are not typical but exceptional.   The
distinct impression which the life of Jesus as a whole
leaves upon us is that He gained His knowledge of
outward events through ordinary channels of information.
He frequently expresses unfeigned surprise, asks the
father of the demoniac child, " How long is it since this
hath come unto him? " and inquires where Lazarus is
laid.[2]   He gives no indication of supernatural acquaintance with the facts of physical science or of the history
of the world, Jewish or Gentile.   There is no sign of
omniscience, and no claim to it.   Godet says of Him,
" As a philosopher He would have surpassed Socrates;
as an orator, have eclipsed Demosthenes."[3]   This seems

[1] Matt. xvii. 27 ; Mark xi. 2–6.
[2] Mark ix. 21 ; John xi. 34.
[3] *Defence of the Christian Faith*, p. 218.

to me an excellent example of the way *not* to describe Christ. To compare Him with the great intellectual leaders of mankind, and then to assert that He would have excelled each in his own department, is to seek, as the Jews did, to honour Him with an earthly crown. It is not warranted by the records, and it obscures rather than reveals His true glory. He enters into no such rivalry, but remains enthroned apart, the Lord of the spiritual world.[1] One thing at least is clear, whatever limitations were involved in His secular knowledge, He shows unerring insight into the characters of men, the operation of moral forces, the conditions of spiritual renewal, into all, in short, that entered into His redemptive mission. Now the elimination of His death from Jesus' early view of His Messiahship would carry with it the elimination of a great deal more, and completely transform the nature of that mission itself. It would imply an imperfect conception of sin and of His own permanent indispensableness as the Remover of it, which is contradicted by His initial consciousness of supreme Sonship. We are a thousandfold more likely to err in ascribing to Him in His own sphere too little knowledge than too much.[2]

II. It was, then, with the absolute conviction of the unique relation in which He stood to God as the supreme object of the Father's love and the chosen organ of His people's deliverance, that Jesus entered on His ministry. But it would have been of no avail for Him to say, " I am the Son of God," or " I am the Messiah," so long as these names did not carry for His hearers their true

---

[1] See Note 12, p. 398, " Pascal on the true Glory of Christ's life."
[2] See Note 13, p. 398, " The Limitations of our Lord's knowledge."

spiritual content.   They would then have been mere
titles of courtesy or formal reverence, the use of which
is one of the most perilous things in religion.   Jesus
strenuously set Himself, as in the case of the young
ruler, to challenge all these, and to rescue great moral
or religious terms from such debasement.   He had first
to supply men with the data which alone could give the
names their right place and significance as the expression
and summation of an inward experience.

This preparatory work of deepening and purifying
the primary religious feelings and ideas of men, indispensable as it is for all prophets of God, was specially
necessary for Jesus on account of His affiliation to the
past.   He was not only carrying on, but completing, all
former revelations.   They constituted the basis and presupposition of His mission.   He was compelled to relate
Himself to the great Messianic Hope, which yet He had
to transform.   He could not disregard that Hope with
its entangling misconceptions ; He had both to conserve
and to transmute it.   For Him the essence of Messiahship
was Sonship ; it was through the consciousness of Sonship that He felt Himself called to the office ; and so
the Messianic blessing which He was to realise and
impart to men was just this filial spirit.   He had to
refrain from claiming the title until He had at least in
part made His purpose clear, and led them to feel the
supreme value of this spiritual life which He possessed
and mediated.   He had to draw away their thoughts
from false ideals of national triumph, not by direct
repudiation of these, so much as by arousing susceptibilities and longings which no national triumph could
satisfy.   His initial work was the transformation of the

individual character through fellowship with Himself,
and through the revelation of the divine which that
fellowship brought. Very slowly, indeed, were the external and patriotic hopes surrendered; they lived on
alongside of the new inspirations which He gave to men;
but the latter were the growing factors of their life, and
as His influence deepened, one by one the earthly
dreams lost their power. These no longer formed the
determining element in their principles and impulses,
which were moulded by His spirit and example. Thus
were laid, and thus alone could be laid, the foundations
which made inevitable the ultimate recognition of the
true nature of His Messiahship.

There were three means (*A*) which Jesus adopted for
the creation of this experience : Teaching, Miracles, and
the Influence of His Personal Presence. They did not
operate singly, they blended together and interpreted one
another, as the threefold manifestation of a life-giving
Personality. Each was indispensable as representing one
phase of it, and (*B*) the key to the whole is to be found
in His relation to the twelve disciples, where alone all
three factors existed in their fullest form and told with
complete effect.

A. 1. *His Teaching.* We have seen in the last lecture
the substance of Christ's declarations regarding Himself
and the significance of His imperious claims as viewed
by us in retrospect, or by the apostles when they stood
at the close of the revelation. What we have now to
deal with is, not the complete form, but the order of His
teaching, the method by which He led up to the full
disclosure of His personality, and prepared certain
chosen spirits for receiving its impress. His earlier

ministry, whose characteristics we must gather, not from
John, but from the Synoptics, contains no direct exposition of His place and function comparable to the vividness and certainty of His own self-consciousness, or to
the utterances of the final months.   The conception
which men would have of His mission as Mediator
wholly depended on their prior conceptions of God and
man ; and it was to the rectifying and enriching of these
that He first addressed Himself.

By proclaiming the Kingdom of God as the great
end which He came to realise, He put Himself in touch
with the long-descended traditions and hopes of the Jews ;
but He divested the Kingdom of its limited and external
suggestions by affirming as its determining idea the
Fatherhood of God.   Now, if the relation in which God
stood to men was that of a Father to His children, then
its whole character was not political but ethical; it was
a fellowship of heart with heart.   No service which man
as God's child could render Him had any meaning unless
it sprang from the impulse of a personal devotion.   At
one stroke ceremonial worship and interested philanthropy were branded as a worthless mockery; the
rejection of which but revealed the more clearly the
greatness of the single soul whose least act of genuine
homage brought joy to the heart of God.   Each was of
value to Him, not merely as a member of a society, but
in and for himself, just because he had in him the
capacity of manifesting the filial spirit.   But this spirit
could only be awaked in a man by his perception of the
Father's love as already existing, brooding over him,
encompassing him.   It was under the recognition of
that love as directed to himself personally and going all

lengths of sacrifice to regain him, that the new life was born within him, so that he returned through the gate of self-abasement to self-surrender and the obedience of sonship. The new fellowship into which God had brought him altered his entire relations to those around him. He interpreted others by himself, saw them under the new light which had transfigured his own experience. They, too, were children, each of them as truly as He the object of the Father's care; and however perverted or wilful, had in them the germ of sonship which it was His mission up to the measure of His opportunity to foster and develop. He had to exercise toward them the same free forgiveness which God had shown to Him; to love them, not because they were good, but that He might make them good, and because they were capable of becoming so. Thus the Kingdom which Jesus preached was in its essence implicitly universal, just because it was based on the value before God of the individual soul as such, and had inwardness and freedom for its characteristic marks.

And since the supreme purpose of Christ was not to give men right ideas about the Kingdom, but to bring them within it, He had to cast His teaching into a form which would make it the illumination of their experience. " False opinions," as John Stuart Mill reminds us, " may be exchanged for true ones, without in the least altering the habit of mind of which false opinions are the result."[1] It was this " habit of mind," this disposition and bias of the soul, which Christ laboured to transform. His pictorial and parabolic sayings, by touching the emotions and the imagination, quickened the forces which, far

[1] *Autobiography*, p. 239.

more than the intellect, mould the personal character.
No direct statement could set forth the Fatherliness of
God or the universal brotherhood of man with the incisive
power of the " Prodigal Son " or the " Good Samaritan."
It is not merely that these pictures are more memorable,
but they fasten upon the heart with the power of living
example, and arouse it to new impulses.   Christ's hearers,
in the very endeavour to make out the analogy between
the human and the divine which His parables implied,
were thrown back upon themselves and led to feel the
higher meanings of their commonest life.   The divine
was brought near, and the human was made great.
Even when He enjoined specific duties of patience or
forgiveness, it was not according to the definite method
of the moralist, but in the inspiring manner of the
prophet, who is not afraid of enigmatical utterance, if
only he can stimulate the thought or the conscience.
Nay, it would seem at times as if He deliberately used
expressions which had a certain ambiguity, and which
only unfolded their meaning to the resolute and earnest
soul.   While He came to reveal new truths which
unaided human wisdom could not reach, no one ever
acted more in the spirit of the maxim, that *that* only is
true for men which they discover for themselves.   For
the truth, however it may in the abstract be the same
for all, is in the concrete different for each, comes to him
by a different process, and verifies itself in different forms
of practical experience.   Christ's object was not to
formulate a system of doctrine, but to thrill souls by a
divine impulse.   His supreme interest was in individuals.
He adapted Himself to their special character, speaking
to each the word that he most needed or was most

likely to welcome. A great part of the record is taken up with personal interviews, and many of His deepest sayings come to us coloured by the occasion. Hence the infinite variety and even at times apparent self-contradiction of His teaching. For the purpose He had in view the half of the truth was often more than the whole; it was the surest way in the end of leading the man into possession of the fuller revelation. So He wrought constantly by aphorism and suggestion, because they who could not be aroused to examine and appropriate for themselves would never enter the Kingdom at all. Underlying all that He said was the demand that men should meet Him half-way, should bring the contribution of living minds and hearts to the appreciation of His message. He did not argue, He declared; assured that all who were " His own " would come to Him. " Every one that is of the truth heareth My voice." [1]

By thus throwing upon men the responsibility of intelligent co-operation with Him in the attainment of truth, He was not abnegating His *authority* over them : He was adopting the one certain means of establishing it. This is in some degree hidden from us, because we so readily imagine the final form of authority to be that of a despot or dictator, who wields an unchallenged control over servants whose only function is to carry out his behests, whether they perceive their reasonableness or not. They are but the mechanical instruments of his will; his word is as absolute at the beginning of the relationship as at the close. But such an authority has hardly any place in the moral sphere. The unquestioned obedience which a mother exacts even from

[1] John xviii. 37.

a young child is not simply obedience to a bare command, which the child is conscious can be enforced. He
may be quite unable to understand the necessity or
rightness of the command, but he understands something
of the person from whom it comes. He has learned to
associate her with love and a greater wisdom than his
own, and the injunction she gives carries with it the
sanction of her gracious character. But this initial
obedience, which is rendered rather to the character
than to the special command, develops in course of
time the capacity of the child for recognising the
inherent fitness of the command itself: so that the
relation between mother and child becomes less and
less that of ruler to subject, and more and more that of
the larger to the lesser soul, whom it raises gradually
into closer fellowship.[1]

The authority which Christ exercised as a teacher
was of this moral type. How was it at first acquired?
Not by overbearing men's judgment, but by appealing
to it, by the utterance of truths concerning God and
themselves, to which, even when they could not fully
comprehend them, their hearts bore a surprised witness;
and whose power over them grew, the longer they
pondered and lived with them. It was extended and
deepened by every fresh disclosure on His part, and
every verification on theirs. They became conscious
that this whole world of spiritual strength and joy,
which was but slowly unfolding itself to them, lay
before Him like an open book; nay, that He not only
saw it but possessed it, that He held the keys of that
Kingdom into which they fain would enter. This con-

---

[1] See Gore on the two types of authority, *Bampton Lectures*, p. 177.

8

viction, however, was created in them partly by causes yet
to be explained, and came not from His teaching merely,
but from the interpretation which the teaching gave to,
and received from, the life.   Their increasing assimilation
of the truth He revealed did not tend to the diminution
but to the increase of His authority, as the Way to the
Father, as the sole possessor of the divine secret of peace.

2. *His Miracles.*   In discussing the second factor in
Christ's self-manifestation, we pass into a different atmosphere.   Critics of Christianity are fond of dwelling on
the contrast between the miracles and the teaching,
between marvellous works which are *temporary* and
local, the evidence for which grows feebler with lapse
of time, and truths which once spoken are *eternal* and
increasingly self-verifying in human experience.   This
familiar antithesis, which has attained the dignity of a
supposed commonplace, is not at all, as I hope to show,
a balanced and accurate statement of the relative
character of the two as they exist in the life of Christ.
But it serves to emphasise the fact that the miracles
had a direct significance for those before whose eyes
they were wrought, which they cannot have for others ;
and that even their credibility in later times is dependent
on their correlation to moral forces in teaching or
personal character.   Whatever view men take nowadays of the miracles attributed to Christ, three things
are practically certain : that the people among whom He
lived believed that He wrought them ; that this belief was
a chief element in attracting men to Him as their Master,
and in confirming their faith in His divine mission ; and
that Jesus Himself meant and taught them so to believe.

The Second Gospel, which embodies the earliest

collection of the evangelic facts,[1] and in all probability
is substantially identical with the " Teaching of Peter,"
mentioned by Papias, is largely a narrative of the
wonderful deeds of Jesus ; and thus, as regards mere
testimony, we have more ancient evidence for His
miracles than for many of His sayings.   The incisive
realism of Mark's portraiture is the best proof that he
is recording the reminiscences of an eye-witness.   Take,
for example, the scene in the Synagogue of Capernaum
at the opening of the Galilean ministry, the effect
produced by the healing of the demoniac, the astonished
cry of the people, " What is this?   A new teaching !
With authority He commandeth even the unclean spirits,
and they obey Him." [2]   It is impossible to doubt that
we have here a transcript of the actual impression.
The endeavour, formerly so common, to save the sayings
at the expense of the miracles, inevitably results in the
arbitrary rejection of some of the most characteristic of
the former.   Any plausibility which the mythical theory
might have as an explanation of the cures ascribed
to Jesus, is wholly destroyed by its inability to account
for the pregnant and penetrating words which are indissolubly bound up with them, and which, if internal
evidence has any meaning, bear the indubitable stamp
of the Master.[3]   His recorded unwillingness on certain

---

[1] Mr. F. P. Badham in his recent volume, *S. Mark's Indebtedness to S.
Matthew*, endeavours to rehabilitate Augustine's verdict, so long prevalent,
on Mark as "pedisequus et breviator Matthæi" ; but his argument, however
ingenious in details, is not likely to shake the view now generally accepted of
Mark's originality.

[2] Mark i. 27.

[3] See Godet, *Defence*, pp. 114,115.   "They (the sayings) stand in the same
relation to the miracle as the inscription stamped upon the coin does to the
coin itself."

occasions to work miracles, His strong disapproval of
those who would make them the sole ground of their
belief, His contempt for the generation that was ever
seeking a sign, are not arguments *against* the reality of
His claim to perform them, but *in favour* of it, as being
a protest against the misunderstanding of their character
and aim, and a protest whose presupposition is that He
has already wrought them.   When we take into account
the immense place they fill in the Gospels, the illuminat-
ive details with which they are related, the particularisa-
tion of persons and localities, and the essential consistency
of the Synoptic story amid its threefold diversity, it is
hardly too much to say with Professor Seeley that " the
fact that Christ appeared as a worker of miracles is the
best attested fact in His whole biography." [1]

The scornful incredulity with which they are regarded
arises from the conviction that scarcely any conceivable
amount of testimony would suffice to establish them.
The Agnostic who knows his business is too wise to
entangle himself in an argument as to their abstract
possibility.   He attains his end quite as effectively by
denying their credibility.   " Certainly," he says, " they
may have happened ; but they can never be adequately
proved.   The belief in the uniform operation of nature
is based on such an overwhelming induction from human
experience, that the improbability of a departure from
that uniformity at a single point overbears any probability as to its occurrence drawn from the testimony
of a necessarily limited circle.   Even if that testimony
were corroborated by many witnesses of acknowledged
honesty and intelligence, it would not be possible to

----

[1] *Ecce Homo*, Preface, p. 9.

eliminate the suspicion of inaccuracy or self-deception on their part, in face of the inherent unlikelihood of the event itself." General propositions of this kind are nothing better than a snare. Whatever force they possess, they derive from treating miracles *in vacuo*, as a mere break in the continuity of nature, and taking no account of their quality, the purpose that underlies them, or their relation to surrounding circumstances. To class Professor Huxley's imaginary centaur trotting down Piccadilly,[1] with Christ's healing of the sick or His raising of Lazarus, as if the evidence in the two cases were in the least degree comparable ; to say, as Professor Huxley does, " all miracles are centaurs or they would not be miracles," is to be blind to the first conditions of the problem. Abstract discussions of their credibility or incredibility are unspeakably futile, and only tend to confuse things that differ. The question, if truth be our object, is essentially a particular one. Is this or that miracle, or series of miracles, credible in view of the facts as a whole ?

It so happens that we are able to show, in one outstanding instance, the precariousness of the *a priori* objection. The statement that " all men have sinned " or are conscious of moral failure, is as universally true in the moral sphere as the statement that " all men are mortal " is in the physical. Were we told, apparently on good authority, that some one living hundreds of years ago had achieved spiritual perfection, that he had attained at each stage of life all the goodness possible for him, our first instinct would be to say that the prior improbability, founded on the experience of sin in the

[1] Huxley, *Hume*, p. 134.

race, outweighed any likelihood that might belong to
such an assertion.   Therefore the testimony of the
apostles of Jesus, based upon at least a year's[1] close
companionship with Him, that *He* had reached this
spiritual completeness, would, if it had stood alone, have
been discredited.   But it does not stand alone ; as has
been seen in the first lecture, we have the means of
testing it in the accounts of His life as lived among men.
We have the data in the words which He spoke, and the
attitude which He assumed towards others, on which we
can form our own opinion of what Christ was.   We see
in Him a soul with an extreme sensitiveness of spiritual
perception, and yet conscious of an unbroken loyalty to
the Father's will, which He so constantly and fully
discerned.   Now, the uniform experience of mankind
proclaims the incompatibility of these two characteristics.
Yet nothing is more certain than that they were united
in Him.   Thus the declaration of the apostles concerning the holiness of Jesus, which the so-called general law
of evidence would have repudiated, is ratified by the
judgment which we are able to form on other grounds.
The peculiarity in this case is that the testimony is such
that it not merely asserts the miracle, but puts us in the
position of estimating its truth for ourselves, by bringing
us in a real sense as directly face to face as the first
witnesses were with the manifestations, in His teaching

[1] I am speaking here only of the *continuous fellowship* which the Twelve,
as a whole, had with Jesus.   My own view is that it extended to eighteen
months or two years ; but the point can never be definitely settled.   Of course,
several of the apostles, and these the chief, like John and Peter, knew Jesus,
and had *occasional* relations with Him from His first appearance beside Jordan.
I restrict myself here to a statement which all will admit, whatever views they
may entertain concerning the length of the ministry (see Note 14, p. 401, on
" The Duration of Christ's Intercourse with the Twelve ").

and bearing, of the unique Personality. We know as truly as they what substantially the manifestations were, and are as conscious that these could not have proceeded from a moral nature of the normal type. What, therefore, we are driven to accept in the case of Jesus is not simply certain great *truths* uttered by Him concerning God and human duty, as contrasted with the vanishing marvels of the hour, but the *fact* of a personal character to which there is no antecedent or subsequent parallel, and which was as temporary in its earthly existence as the miracles whose temporariness is supposed to disparage them.

We have, indeed, no such means of verifying Christ's miraculous works as we possess of verifying the miracle of His holiness.[1]   But, in the first place, a single

---

[1] In arguing for miracles as the indispensable proof of a Divine revelation, Dr. Mozley says : " Would not a perfectly sinless character be proof of a revelation ? Undoubtedly that would be as great a miracle as any that could be conceived ; but where is the proof of perfect sinlessness ? No outward life and conduct, however just, benevolent, and irreproachable, could prove this ; because goodness depends upon the inward motive, and the perfection of the inward motive is not proved by the outward act. Exactly the same act may be perfect or imperfect, according to the spirit of the doer. The same language of indignation against the wicked which issues from our Lord's mouth might be uttered by an imperfect good man, who mixed human frailty with the emotion. We accept our Lord's perfect goodness, then, upon the same evidence upon which we admit the rest of His supernatural character ; but not as proved by the outward goodness of His life, by His character, sublime as that was, as it presented itself to the eye " (*Miracles*, pp. 11, 12). According to this view, the proof of our Lord's perfect goodness lies not in His outward life or conduct, but in His miraculous works and in His resurrection. Now this is doubly erroneous. 1. It is the merest commonplace that a single act, taken by itself, however apparently good or self-sacrificing, does not necessarily demonstrate the goodness of a man's heart. But there is no parallel between an isolated action and Christ's intercourse with the Twelve, which, alike from its duration and its essential characteristics, involved a self-revelation on His part that touched the inmost quality of His moral being (Lect. I.). Dr. Mozley would have been among the first to repudiate as irrational the idea that

demonstrated exception to a uniform order of experience should lead us to lower our tone in talking of *a priori* incredibility. And, in the second place, the miracles of Christ's ministry are not isolated marvels, hanging in air, but hold an inseparable relation to One who has already proved Himself an exception to the continuity of nature. They were not only wrought by *Him*, but wrought in fulfilment of the same purpose which explains the existence in our world of His personality. That purpose was, as His claims prove, not simply to reveal the Father, but to mediate His grace, to be the quickening Spirit of a new kingdom of souls. But the disorganisation which it was His mission to cure extended to the physical sphere as well as to the spiritual. The sin which severed man from God's fellowship worked itself out in disease and death. Was the deliverance which He brought to human hearts, in renewing their trust in the Father, powerless to arrest and reverse the *outward* consequences of moral transgression? Was He helpless before those physical laws which demand from the sinner the uttermost farthing of penalty?

Christ's miracles are His answer to that question. (*a*) God's universe is one. He whose will Christ came to do is Lord both of Nature and Spirit, and gave Him power for the redemption of both. But the miracles proved more than the universal dominance of the redeeming power; they showed that nature exists for the sake

---

the impression Jesus left upon the disciples might have been produced by "an imperfect good man, who mixed human frailty" with his excellence. 2. While it is true that the physical miracles form a part of the same whole of revelation with the moral miracle, and have an evidential value of their own, yet it is the latter, not the former, which is the *basal* fact (see below, p. 157, *n*).

of spirit.[1] It has, indeed, its own laws; but their uniformity is modified for the higher revelation of spirit.
Thus the miracles are not pure displays of power: they
are penetrated with a spiritual symbolism. This is so
even in the case of those wrought on external nature,
like the Stilling of the Storm, or the Feeding of the
Five Thousand. It is still more manifest in His works
of healing, which form much the larger portion of the
whole. They are redemptive acts. The bodily cure is
but the analogue in the physical world of the restoration
effected in the spiritual, and is wrought as its typical
representation. "Whether is easier to say, Thy sins
be forgiven thee; or to say, Arise and walk? But that ye
may know that the Son of Man hath power on earth to
forgive sins, then saith He to the sick of the palsy, Arise,
take up thy bed, and go unto thine house."[2] (*b*) This
subordination of the physical to the moral is further
implied in the demand for *faith*, for the right attitude of
receptivity on the part of the recipient of the cure.
Though Jesus, by the simple exercise of authority, controlled outward nature and stayed the tempest, yet when
the natural formed part of the *same organism* with the
spiritual, as in humanity, He related Himself to the
former through the latter as the superior and determining
factor. As no bare word of command suffices for the
soul's regeneration without its own free response, so it
did not suffice for the healing of those bodily evils which

---

[1] As to Spirit being the implicit truth of Nature, and the revelation of Spirit
the end to which Nature points in its progressive stages of evolution, see
Principal Caird, *Introduction to the Philosophy of Religion*, pp. 108–110;
Gore, *Bampton Lectures*, pp. 29–35; Fairbairn, *Studies in the Life of Christ*,
pp. 153–155; Godet, *Defence of the Christian Faith*, pp. 121–126.

[2] Matt. ix. 5, 6.

had their root in the soul's apostasy from God. (*c*) The same respective relation between the two comes out in the restraint of Christ in the exercise of His miraculous gift. It never assumes the aspect of " omnipotence let loose," but is always power controlled from within by love. He does not wield it in His own interest, either by lessening the sufferings which fell to His lot, or by visiting His detractors with vengeance.[1] It is the effluence of a personality which is essentially a renovating moral force. Therefore the miracles are not a proof externally supplied to a message which is independent of them ; they are a part of the message, but they are that part of it which carries with it a peculiar evidential quality. To discard the evidential element in them, no matter from what motive, is to empty them of their special character, and to reduce them to Parables in act. Christ's restoration of sight to Bartimæus was, from one point of view, an illustration in conduct of the same compassion which is taught in the story of the Good Samaritan ; but it was a great deal more. It was at once an interpretation of His spirit of pity, and a guarantee of its supremacy in a form which men could easily test.

If it be said that it is perilous for anyone who maintains an idealistic or spiritual view of the universe to admit that the presence of the divine is proved rather by the breaks in the natural order of things than by that order itself, the reply, after what has been said, is perfectly plain. The acceptance of miracles as evidential does not imply that nature is under the thrall of a blind necessity, and that the only indications of an operative spiritual principle

[1] See Note 15, p. 404.

are given by exceptional interruptions of the natural
course.   When Dr. Edward Caird says, "I should not
expect to find what is above nature anywhere, if there
were not something above nature everywhere,"[1] he is
only repeating what the early Christian writers made the
very foundation of their argument.[2]   In no sense is the
world before, or apart from, Christ, a world without God.
In its different stages of inorganic, organic, and rational,
it presents a progressive unveiling of the divine attributes,
from His power and wisdom up to at least partially His
moral character.   That men fail to perceive these manifestations, or perceive them but dimly, is due to their
moral disorder.   The sin which impairs man's personal
communion with God has, as a necessary result, blinded
him to the signs of God's presence in the universe.   Even
the natural order which he cannot fail to see, he has lost
the power of interpreting.   Nature's uniformity becomes
a blind necessity, not the expression of a quickening Spirit
who in all His workings remains true to Himself.   It is
at this point that miracles enter with a revealing power.
If nature spoke throughout with a divine significance to
man, they would have no place.[3]   But not only is the
spiritual meaning of her order obscured for him, but in
some parts of it that order itself has been perverted.
Deaf ears and paralysed limbs are no part of it according
to God's intent, and the very fact of such suffering leads
many to deny His existence or to impeach His goodness.
Therefore Christ's cures were real signs to men of a spiritual
presence and authority.   For they were both arresting

---

[1] *Evolution of Religion*, vol. i. p. 318.
[2] See Note 16, p. 405.
[3] See Note 17, p. 406, "Miracle as belonging to a *disorganised* world."

indications of the operation of a divine will, and a revelation of its beneficent character.   Thus they were *not* meant to suggest: " there are no proofs of God in nature ; you cannot find Him there : He is shown only in His supersession of natural methods "; but to confirm and correct the evidences of Him which nature supplied; to open men's eyes to the daily working of His power and wisdom in the order of the universe ; and also to show that where the action of His natural laws was injurious, as in physical disease, it was due to the perversion of sin, which it was God's purpose to remove in order to restore the disturbed harmony of the world.

Or, to put it otherwise : Nature is a progressive revelation of God, which culminates in the moral being of man.   But it is at the highest point, for which the previous stages are but a preparation, that the revelation has been perverted.   For God to fail there is to fail altogether. Therefore a new moral centre of life is needed.   For the purpose of restoring the moral order, God manifests Himself in a unique personal life as a renewing power.   But this moral centre is necessarily environed by the operations of natural law.   Will these remain unaffected ? only if in all respects they fulfil their original design.   But that is not the case.   In themselves the natural laws are unchanged by sin ; but they are changed in their effects. Their working is poisoned in many ways, such as disease, by the influence of the moral disorganisation of the world. Therefore the rectification of the *moral* revelation, if it be true, must give some " sign " of the rectification of *disordered nature* : and the " sign " is—Miracle. This is clear in the case of bodily cures.   The miracles wrought directly on nature are not in the same way rectifications of the

disordered operation of natural law, but are wrought for
the rectification of man's thoughts of God as He is revealed
in the universe.   To the man who sees Christ's miracles
in their true setting and significance, as an inherent portion
of a moral unveiling of God, Matthew Arnold's remark [1]
about turning a pen into a penwiper is simply beside the
point.   Nor will he be much affected by Emerson's contemptuous description of miracle as " Monster," because
" it is not one with the blowing clover and the falling
rain"; [2] for he recognises that the clover and the rain
do not represent the highest principles of a universe in
which God manifests Himself,[3] and that a miracle violates
superficial uniformity only " in the interests of deeper
law." [4]

   There is a disposition on the part of many writers
who themselves accept the miracles to minimise their
importance, as if the Gospel were best commended by
saying as little about them as possible.   Even as a policy
it is foredoomed to failure.   The whole Christian revelation is penetrated with the supernatural, and the repudiation or surrender of it in the sphere of nature will not
lessen by an iota the antagonism of unbelief to it in the
spiritual sphere of Christ's person and man's regeneration.
Nay, whatever difficulties exist in regard to it are intensified, not decreased, by confining the miraculous to a
limited or sectional area.   Men are not likely to possess,
or long to retain, a very deep conviction of the unique
divine power which Christ introduced into the world, if
they believe that His capacity to deliver was barred by

---

[1] *Literature and Dogma*, p. 95.
[2] *Address* at Divinity College, Cambridge, U.S.A.
[3] See Note 18, p. 408, "The false view of Miracle."
[4] Gore, *Bampton Lectures*, p. 45.

inexorable law from dealing with physical evils.   Jesus, indeed, always spoke of His miracles as a subordinate part of His self-revelation.   They had two sides, a natural and a spiritual : as natural, they were marvellous displays of power ; as spiritual, they were an unveiling of the moral character and purpose of God.   But while all men could see the former side, only those who already possessed some spiritual appreciation could perceive the latter, which constituted their message.   Hence the miracles had to be preceded or accompanied by Christ's teaching and conduct as their interpretation, as the means whereby their real meaning as a divine work might be borne home.   But when that interpretation made no impression upon men, and the miracles were the only sign to them of a supernatural authority, the faith to which they gave rise was destitute of ethical quality.   It became mere superstition.   It is for this reason Christ says, " If they hear not Moses and the prophets, neither will they be persuaded, if one rise from the dead." [1]   The soul which is destitute of spiritual need and aspiration cannot have these awaked in it by an outward marvel whose meaning it would fail to see, and simply pervert.   But to acknowledge this is very different from saying that miracle is of no account for the formation, and still more for the quickening, of a true faith.   The faith which is necessary to apprehend its significance and appropriateness is in turn confirmed by it.

The common saying, which is supposed to be the note of every intelligent apologist, " We believe in the miracles because we believe in Christ, not in Christ because we believe in the miracles," is true, so far as it

[1] Luke xvi. 31.

means that the miracles derive their credibility and their impressiveness for us from their relation to Christ and the purposes of His life; but it is *not* true, if it means that they constitute a mere burden to belief.   They are, on the contrary, a real alleviation of the burden; they make faith in the moral miracle of Jesus more self-consistent and reasonable by their revelation that the whole universe, outward as well as inward, is under the sway of a restorative and redeeming love.   The more we examine this question, the more will the verdict of Mr. Myers commend itself.   " The common sense of mankind will assuredly refuse to concur with the view, often expressed both in the scientific and the theological camps, according to which the marvels of the New Testament history are after all unimportant, that the spiritual content of the Gospel is everything, and religion and science alike may be glad to be rid of the miracles as soon as possible. . . . According to the cruder view of the Gospel wonders, indeed, this would be reasonable enough.   To wish to convert men by magic, to prove theological dogmas by upsetting the sequences of things, this is neither truly religious nor truly scientific.   But if these Gospel signs and wonders are considered as indications of laws which embrace, and in a sense unite, the seen and the unseen worlds, then surely it is of immense importance to science that they should occur anywhere, and of immense importance to Christianity that they should occur in connection with the foundation of that faith." [1]

3. Interwoven with Teaching and Miracles as the third factor in Christ's self-unveiling was *the Influence of*

[1] F. W. H. Myers, *Essays : Modern*, p. 223.

His Personal Presence. We are apt to depreciate its
potency in comparison with the other two, just because
personal influence is so subtle in its operation, because
it does not, like teaching and miracle, formally challenge
a verdict. Yet everyone knows that the hold which a
moral leader has over his followers is not created simply
by the thrilling utterances or heroisms of great moments.
By these, indeed, he first arrests and inspires them. But
their belief in him only gains depth and completeness,
if those quieter hours which show the real man reveal
the same spirit that shines so brilliantly at special times.
Every part of conduct adds its colour to the impression.
The tone in which he speaks, his bearing under suspicion, his reserve, his silences, are the deep roots out of
which alone springs that sure confidence which, as
Burke says, " is a plant of slow growth." This fact, true
of all men, has a double force in the case of Christ.
For His teaching and miracles all tended to throw the
emphasis on Himself, and thus to compel others to mark
every indication of His inward life. Even if men had
been desirous of drawing a distinction between the
preacher and His message, as is so often done to show
that the imperfection of an individual is no disproof of
the wisdom of his words, He made it impossible for
them. He did not wish them to look away *from* Him
to God, but to see God *in* Him. The more they saw of
Him, the longer they continued with Him, the better.
When Paul had proclaimed his message, and men
received it, they could do without him. It worked out
its own effect, by bringing them under a divine power
which gradually subdued and took possession of them.
Further intercourse with him would, of course, illustrate

and vivify it; but it was not indispensable. It *was* indispensable for the establishment of full faith in Christ's message, for the message itself was a progressive manifestation in life.

B. From the first public appearance of Jesus His characteristic demand from all who showed any capacity of spiritual reception was, " Follow Me." Obedience to this involved in many cases no more than a prolonging of intercourse with Him, and a frequent renewal of it; in others, it implied the total abandonment of earthly occupation.[1] Not a few, like the women who ministered to Him of their substance, accompanied Him in His journeys. Yet an increasing band of miscellaneous adherents, more or less identified with Him, was not sufficient for His purpose. What was requisite was *a special circle of selected spirits with whom He held constant relations and on whom the totality of His self-revelation, His teaching, His miracles, His personal influence, could be brought to bear.*

It is needless to entangle ourselves with the question whether what is called Christ's ministry in Eastern Galilee—closing with the feeding of the five thousand, which marks a turning-point in the attitude of the people towards Him—extended to a year, or to several months, or only to three weeks. The chronology of His life is a problem of which no more than approximate solutions are now possible.[2] It was during that period in Eastern Galilee, and soon after its commencement, that " He appointed Twelve that they might be with Him, and that He might send them forth to preach." [3] Some of them

---

[1] See Bruce, *Training of the Twelve*, pp. 17, 18, 29.
[2] See Note 14, p. 401.
[3] Mark iii. 14.

had attached themselves to Him when He first appeared beside Jordan; others, only after the opening of His Galilean ministry. They were already disciples, when they were called to the privilege of a close and abiding intimacy. Through them Christ was to become a living power for humanity. The Apostolate was no happy accident: it was the necessary condition of a *revelation in personality*.

The education to which He subjected them in preparation for this destiny, was of a dual character. They were a school, yet a school not apart from the world, but in it. On the one hand, He could not train them by confining Himself exclusively to them. No private instruction however full, even aided and illumined by the perpetual witness of His example, could have attained the end. He had to reach them through others. They had to see Him in the daily experience of common life, in contact with human suffering and sin, with captious opponents and deceitful friends. By this means they were drawn to Him at the first; and without the continuance of it, His self-revelation would have been arrested. But, on the other hand, they were no longer, as formerly, part of the general multitude; they were permitted to share His friendship. When His other hearers had departed, He answered their questions, resolved their perplexities, led them into the deeper meanings of His words. Thus the public and the private phases of His life interpreted each other for them. Whether or not this double education was first carried on for a whole year in the vicinity of Capernaum and the Lake, there can be no doubt that it was continued at least for some months during His journeys into

Phœnicia and half-Gentile Decapolis and the uplands of Northern Galilee, where the opportunities for quiet communion with the disciples were much greater than among the populous villages in which His work began. Stroke by stroke He was deepening His imprint upon them. Conceive, for example, the effect produced by the one fact that He who had chosen them to be not servants but friends, to dwell with Him as members of one family, yet never mingled His prayer with theirs. In the heart of the intimacy there remained a great self-withdrawal, an unshared loneliness continually declaring itself, yet in such wise as only to deepen their reverence, not to chill their affection—

> "Like aught that for its grace may be
> Dear, and yet dearer for its mystery." [1]

Towards the close of that period in Northern Galilee Jesus saw the growing conviction of their souls regarding Him, and by a direct question [2] brought it to clear consciousness and utterance. His Messiahship was not a declaration on His part, but a discovery on theirs, an inference to which, under the illumination of the Spirit, they were inevitably driven by what they had experienced in His presence.

It is difficult for us to realise how decisive a moment the acknowledgment of His Messianic claim was to the disciples. It gave definite form to their belief in Him. However sincere might be their convictions hitherto concerning His supreme authority as sent from God,

---

[1] Shelley, "Hymn to Intellectual Beauty."

[2] Matt. xvi. 13. See Note 19, p. 409, "Dr. Martineau on Peter's confession of Jesus' Messiahship."

still they were somewhat vague and variable; henceforth they were gathered up and unified, and stamped by Jesus Himself with the seal of the great Jewish Hope. Yet it is just here that the deepest pathos in His relations to the disciples begins.   He had trained them up to that point where they could recognise for themselves that He was the expected Messiah, and where it was possible for Him to accept the title.   Had He assumed it from the first, they would at once have resented His use of it, while He walked in lowliness before men.   But the preparation which they had since undergone had stirred within them nobler thoughts of God and man. He had so fascinated them by the lofty spirituality of His teaching and life, that they now clung to Him even in spite of His continued frustration of their desires.   It is this belief in Him, notwithstanding His perpetual contradiction of their hopes, that makes the closing six months of their fellowship so touching a tragedy.   He welcomed that belief, because He knew that it was well warranted, and that He was to be to them not less than they thought but more, though this something more meant also something very different.

Thus it was that while He accepted the Messianic name, He was ever labouring to re-interpret and transmute its significance.   He sought to impress upon them the certainty of His suffering and death; but to speak only of these, and not of the resurrection which was to follow, would have been to convey to them the false idea that His work was a failure, and that their personal communion with Him would be at an end.   Yet every reference to the resurrection only undid the impression which His announcement of the death was fitted to

make. Some, indeed, have maintained that the prophecies
of His " rising again " were read back by the disciples
from their after reflection.   But the whole character of
the narrative shows that the intimations of the approaching catastrophe made little impression upon them; that
the manner in which Jesus referred to it always implied
that His outward defeat would be temporary, and His
real victory eternal.   It was not possible for Him to
explain to them at that stage how His communion with
them in the Spirit would be closer than any intercourse
He held with them on earth.   Only through the experience of the pain could they come to its illumination.
They must live through it to understand it.   All He
could do was to supply them now with the facts which a
later and happier hour would interpret.   This was their
trial; it was His also.

So when the final disaster broke, it left them scattered,
helpless.   Yet is it not plain that that single fact would
be the gravest censure upon Jesus, had He only been
and felt Himself to be, as many affirm, a great Teacher
of divine truth?   How easy it would have been for Him
to tell them, " I am about to die; but the message
which I have delivered to you of the Father's love is
imperishable.   It will yet gladden humanity.   Its
triumph does not depend upon Me; I have been but the
chosen voice of God for its proclamation.   And now My
time has come; but be of good cheer, the Father is with
you always."   As a mere prophet, it was His imperative
duty thus to take farewell.   But when they stood at the
close of the apocalypse, and searched their hearts for its
meaning, they had nothing to declare, which had any
power or significance apart from His continued presence.

His message had disappeared with Himself. A clearer proof could not be given that if Jesus was no more than a Teacher, His teaching was a failure.

But if His design was not simply to teach but to bind the disciples to Himself, He could have adopted no more effective method. In its slowness and indirectness lay its incomparable power. It appears a long way round; but it was in truth the shortest and surest way to the goal. The influence which He had on their opinions was the least part of His mastery. They had not reached, and could not reach, while He was with them the recognition of His essential Deity; but He had made attachment to Himself so much a part of their inmost being—their thought, feeling, and conscience— that ultimately it could only find in such recognition its rational explanation and fulfilment. Even when the shattering blow had fallen, which seemed to them utter ruin, they did not stop to compassionate themselves for their pursuit of a delusion, or upbraid His memory for imposing on them unrewarded trials. They loved and longed for Him as deeply as ever; though they would have found it impossible to analyse or unfold to others the causes of their faith, which lay in the accumulated witness of a manifold experience.

LECTURE IV.

THE TRANSITION FROM THE HISTORICAL
TO THE SPIRITUAL CHRIST.

SYNOPSIS.

The Resurrection of Christ : belongs to a different category from the resurrection of Lazarus.

The Appearances of the Risen Christ.
    I. Their Objectivity.
        Failure of the Vision Hypothesis.
        Value of St. Paul's testimony.
        Witness of the first apostles, though referring to an exceptional experience of their own, capable of refutation, if untrue.

    II. Their Unique Character, as uniting the earthly and the spiritual.
        Weizsäcker on the different layers of tradition.
        The two contradictory aspects are of the essence of the problem which the Appearances were meant to solve : the revelation of the spiritual in a world of sense-perception.
        This union of attributes merely temporary, for a specific purpose.
        Why the Appearances were vouchsafed only to believers.
        Not the creation of a new faith, but the reinstatement and transfiguration of the old one.
        The validity of the Resurrection depended on two correlated factors : the outward event and the inward susceptibility.
        Its place in Apologetics.

The Ritschlian disparagement of the Resurrection.
Herrmann's view of the ' inner life ' of Jesus.
Misreads the growth of the Apostolic faith.
The Risen life of Christ not merely an *inference* from His sinlessness, but part of the same *objective* divine manifestation in humanity.
The self-contradictions of Herrmann's theory.

LECTURE IV.

The Transition from the Historical to the Spiritual Christ.

WE have hitherto been considering the life of Jesus as He appears in history. The underlying purpose of all His relations to His disciples was the creation of attachment to Himself, as the bringer of the divine kingdom, as the mediator of the Father's grace. But that attachment had for them one indispensable condition, the continuance of His earthly presence. When the catastrophe of the Crucifixion overtook them, it left nothing but a lingering regret for a bygone blessedness. · How then did they arrive soon after at the indomitable conviction, not only of the persistence of His personal life, but of His assured triumph as Lord of all, leading them to reconstrue the appalling death as an additional demonstration of His Messianic claim ?

Frequently Christ's resurrection is argued both by those who accept and those who deny it, as if it were merely a question of whether a dead man had returned to life. But this is to misconceive it altogether. It does not belong to the same category as the resurrection of Lazarus ; the purpose of it was different, and the tests applicable to it are different. Lazarus was restored out of the tomb to precisely the same human life as before.

He resumed his place under the same conditions of mortality to which he was formerly subject, and which would again assert their thrall over him. But Christ's resurrection was not a temporary reversal of the laws of sin and death, but a permanent supersession of them by a higher law in which mortality was swallowed up of life: it was the revelation of a victorious spiritual life under forms which made it recognisable by those who still dwelt in a world of sense-perception. This dual quality pertains to the essence of the manifestation, and gives it its specific meaning. If Christ's resurrection were amenable to the same tests as any of the three miracles of raising the dead attributed to Him, it would contain no more than they a guarantee of a triumphant immortality. It appeals therefore very largely to another type of evidence. What this is will become clear at a later stage. Meanwhile it is enough to note that there are two inseparable factors in the witness borne by the disciples: first, *the objective reality* of the risen Christ's appearances to them, and secondly, *their peculiar and unparalleled nature.*

I. And first, as to the objectivity. Some of the theories propounded to discredit it have been eliminated from all rational discussion. The only interesting thing about them now is that they should ever have been suggested. The hypothesis of Reimarus, that the disciples stole the body of their Master and then proclaimed that the " Crucified " had risen, contains no single element of a probable solution. Its gratuitous offensiveness is only surpassed by its grotesque inadequacy. Hardly less absurd is the view of Paulus that Jesus did not really die, that on the Cross He only fell into a death-swoon, from which He afterwards recovered, when His body was laid in the cool air of the cavern-tomb, permeated with the restoring fragrance of the spices.   A grain of commonsense, as Strauss has shown in a passage which is almost too familiar for quotation,[1] is sufficient to destroy it.   A half-dead Christ struggling out of the sepulchre could not have given to the disciples their conviction that He was the conqueror of death.   It would rather have weakened the impression which He had made upon them in life, and could by no possibility have transmuted their sorrow into enthusiasm.   And even if He had so returned, the difficulties of the theory are only beginning: it is involved in inextricable entanglements as to what subsequently became of His body.

The Vision hypothesis is the only one which is worth examining to-day.   That it presents some plausibility is shown by the many forms it has assumed.   It gains a certain support from modern feeling in the tribute it pays to a great soul, and to the fascinating power He wields of winning a measureless devotion from His followers.   In Renan's rendering[2] it is seen at its worst.   'Love worked the miracle; it discovered in some sudden noise or tone or atmospheric effect the sign of the risen Lord.   Sorrow was at once lost in ecstasy. Mary of Magdala created the belief.   She first saw the vision; then the others, quickened by her enthusiasm, had their visions too.'   Such an account is its own refutation.   The apostles who afterwards maintained their witness with such sanity and practical judgment,

[1] *New Life of Jesus,* i. 142.
[2] *Les Apôtres,* p. 2 ff.

were not likely to be started on their course by a violent attack of hysterical monomania.[1]

In the rational form of the Vision theory there are two stages. First, it is pointed out that Paul, in his statement of the evidence for the resurrection, ranks Christ's appearance to himself as of precisely the same kind and value as the appearances to the original apostles. But in his case the vision was purely subjective. He was frequently thrown into an ecstatic condition, and beheld visions in which the subjective had all the force and vividness of objectivity.[2] He was in this mood at the great crisis of his conversion. The three-fold narrative in Acts of what then happened is not to be trusted: it is a picturesque development. His own direct testimony in Galatians[3] does not refer to any outward appearance, but to an inward revelation of Christ. In no other sense than the spiritual one, according to Paul, did the first disciples see the risen Lord. Secondly, these optical illusions which they took for objective appearances can easily be accounted for. For some time after the Crucifixion they were prostrate with grief; but gradually the endearing memories of the past re-asserted themselves, and brought Christ near to them. Thrown back by the mysterious collapse of their hopes on a more eager searching of the Scriptures, they found there passages which spoke of death as the very way to a higher life; and in the light of the bitter experience through which they had passed they read these into connection with the redeeming work of the Messiah. " After two days will He revive us: on the third day He

---

[1] See *Essays: Modern,* by F. W. H. Myers, p. 222.
[2] 2 Cor. xii. 1.   [3] Gal. i. 13–17.

will raise us up and we shall live before Him." [1] When they returned to Galilee, where every familiar spot seemed consecrated by Christ's presence, these vague utterances of the prophets stirred their hearts with the expectation of His re-appearance, and out of this passionate longing their visions of Him were born.

Now, whatever view be taken of the appearance of Christ to Paul, the attempt to use it to the disparagement of the earlier appearances to the disciples is wholly illegitimate. It takes all meaning out of Paul's argument. He was keenly aware of his apparent inferiority to the original apostles in that he had no personal acquaintance with Jesus. Confronted as he was at every step by this objection, he was perpetually declaring that the ascended Christ had in boundless condescension "appeared to him in the way," so that he was an apostle, " not from men, neither through man, but through Jesus Christ and God the Father, who raised Him from the dead." [2] His authority had therefore, he maintained, the same direct guarantee as that of Peter or John. This is the idea which underlies the personal reference to himself as the single witness of the final Christophany. The objectivity of the appearances during the forty days is accepted both by Paul and by the Corinthians as beyond dispute. On whatever subjects he might differ from the " pillar " apostles, he was at one with them in holding that Christ was raised on the third day. But an actual rising from the dead on a specific day stands in no harmony with the notion of a subjective illusion: as Ménégoz [3]

---

[1] Hos. vi. 2.   [2] Gal. i. 1.

[3] *Le Péché et la Redemption d'après Saint Paul*, p. 261. See also the admirably succinct discussion of this point by Dr. Marcus Dods in *The Super-*

remarks, "it only accords with an actual reappearance." When he recounts the testimony of Peter and James, and of the five hundred of whom the majority were then alive, he is alluding to well-known facts which had formed part of his teaching at Corinth.[1] The very manner in which he speaks of himself "as one born out of due time,"[2] clearly indicates his belief in the objectivity of *their* vision, and consequently of *his own*, which he parallels to it. He came too late to witness one of the normal appearances of Christ before the ascension; but no one is born too late to be capable of spectral illusions. They may be indefinitely multiplied and repeated. The Corinthians themselves might have had them; but they knew that something very different was intended by Paul's formal catalogue of Christ's appearances. It was a summary of the universal faith of the Church; and it is on the basis of their acceptance of it, that he proceeds to argue against the self-contradiction of believing in the resurrection of the Lord, while denying the final resurrection of the faithful.[3]

Paul's conversion took place almost certainly not more than five years after the Crucifixion.[4] He passed into a Church, the foundation principle of which was faith in the risen Christ. Though absent from Jerusalem at the time of the Crucifixion,[5] he returned soon after, and threw himself immediately into a fierce antagonism

---

natural in Christianity, pp. 103, 104. "Why mention His *burial*, unless it was His bodily resurrection he (Paul) had in view?"

[1] 1 Cor. xv. 3.   [2] 1 Cor. xv. 8.   [3] 1 Cor. xv. 12–19.

[4] So Weizsäcker, *Apostolic Age*, vol. i. p. 20. Caspari argues in minute detail for placing it in the very year of the Crucifixion. See his *Chronological and Geographical Introduction to the Life of Christ*, pp. 45–50.

[5] See Farrar, *Life and Work of St. Paul*, chap. iv.

to the pestilent new heresy. He had the means of knowing what form it had taken from the beginning. In its central testimony it had undergone no development; it sprang full-grown into life.

Even if we admit that the story of his conversion is told in Acts with picturesque additions, nothing is plainer than that what maddened him against the Christians was just the unanimity and persistence with which they proclaimed that the Crucified had been approved by His resurrection to be the true Messiah. Only to one whose soul was preoccupied with this idea, none the less abhorrent to him that he was troubled with apprehensions of its possible truth, was such a vision even conceivable. The Gospel which he afterwards preached in its two great affirmations, the significance of the death, and the reality of the resurrection of Jesus, was one which he in no sense created. He " received " it;[1] first, he repudiated it with detestation, and then embraced it with the fervour of entire conviction. But the first disciples did not receive it. They were themselves the direct witnesses of the revelation. They had no snch predisposing causes towards belief as Paul had in the consistent testimony of others and the manifest spiritual effects of their faith. The discovery of the empty tomb was a bewildering surprise. Yet, according to all the records, in less than two months they had not merely attained the unshakable conviction that they had many times seen the risen Lord, but preached it with an unfaltering calmness, with a steadfast practicality which never yet was born of nervous overstrain.[2] They saw no

---

[1] I Cor. xv. 3.
[2] Keim puts this trenchantly. *Die Geschichte Jesu von Nazara*, vol. iii.

more visions of Him. But ecstasy does not thus speedily grow to a head and then cease. Its manifestations, though in themselves sudden, rise out of a background of prolonged absorption, and tend to increase in number and vividness only when the actualities round which they circle have gained through time the glamour of endearing memories. The ultimate result which they leave behind is invariably freakishness in judgment, and either feverish and spasmodic activity or utter prostration. When we contrast this with the subsequent conduct of the apostles, their clear-minded grasp of the truths they promulgated, and their patient resoluteness in adapting means to ends, we feel that the Vision theory only brings into bolder relief the objectivity of the appearances.

Nor can it be said that their testimony, however true for themselves, was incapable of refutation, because the appearances, from the nature of the case, were an un-paralleled experience vouchsafed to them alone. At a vital point it touched matter of fact, which ordinary evidence could either establish or disprove. They said, He rose and we saw Him ; and thus their witness would have been discredited, if it could have been shown either that the body still lay in the grave, or had been disposed of in any other way. There are those who profess to believe that its disappearance is accounted for by the fact that it was cast with the bodies of others con-demned as malefactors into the common pit, and that as it had lain there for fifty days before the disciples began publicly to preach the resurrection, the plain dis-proof of their account was not then practicable. But though Pentecost was the first proclamation of their faith, yet, unless the Gospels are fundamentally inac-

curate, in less than two full days after the Crucifixion
the disciples had become persuaded of the resurrection.
Does anyone imagine that this belief of theirs, arousing
them from despair, if not to hope, at least to wondering
expectation, was wholly unknown to outsiders, who witnessed the change in their bearing, and that it never
reached the ears of the authorities till it was declared at
Pentecost? The incident related by Matthew,[1] that the
chief priests and elders, being told of the empty tomb,
bribed the soldiers to say, " His disciples came by night
and stole Him away while we slept," though it is not
corroborated in any of the other Gospels, has, I think,
every mark of probability. Even after an interval of
fifty days, the body could not have been either lost or
unrecognisable: it could have been produced. In any
case, if it had simply received the treatment allotted to
criminals, nothing was easier than to bring forward
those who had with their own hands removed it from
the Cross.

But the hypothesis is itself preposterous. For,
according to Roman law, the bodies of criminals were
not so treated; they were given to those who came
to claim them.[2] There was, therefore, nothing unusual
in the request which Joseph made to Pilate for leave to
take down the body and bury it. He was but following
a common usage. Every one of the four Gospels
records the incident.[3] The whole story of the resurrection, as told by the apostles, implied that the grave of
Jesus was perfectly well known. It would have been a

---

[1] Chap. xxviii. 11-15.
[2] Godet, *Defence of the Christian Faith*, pp. 41, 97.
[3] Matt. xxvii. 58 ; Mark xv. 43 ; Luke xxiii. 52 ; John xix. 38.

simple matter for the Jews to have turned their tale to ridicule, if it recounted visits to a tomb which had no existence. On the other hand, the supposition that the body lay for a brief time in Joseph's tomb, and was then stealthily taken away by order of the Jewish authorities, is, if possible, even more inconceivable. For its removal was then a deliberate act, carried out by special agents, who could readily have been called as witnesses to unmask an imposture. The unspeakable futility of every endeavour to explain by natural means the disappearance of the body of Jesus is a strong corroborative proof of the apostles' testimony.[1]

II. Not less important than the objectivity of the appearances, and one of the circumstances that help to establish it, is *their unique character.* It is not necessary for our purpose to discuss the question when the Gospels were composed. Whether or not we adopt the view held by critics[2] who are not biassed in favour of traditional opinions, that the first three Gospels were drawn up between the years 60 and 80 of our era, it cannot be disputed that Matthew and Luke[3] contain, especially in

---

[1] The sudden and permanent transference of the sanctity of the Jewish Sabbath to the Lord's Day is, even if it stood alone, hardly accountable on the Visional hypothesis ; and, when taken in conjunction with the other lines of evidence, it lends a very real, if subsidiary, support to the reality of the resurrection on the first day of the week. Cf. Newman Smyth's *Old Faiths in New Lights,* p. 155; and Mair's *Studies in the Christian Evidences,* p. 248.

[2] Cf. Weiss, *Introd. to N.T.,* vol. ii. See also Harnack's notable pronouncement in his recent book, *Die Chronologie d. altchr. Litt.,* on the substantial accuracy of the traditional dates assigned to the N.T. writings.

[3] Though the last twelve verses of Mark are missing in some ancient MSS., yet the abrupt way in which the 8th verse concludes, shows that it is not the real close of the Gospel, but that the writer meant to add some details as to the meeting of the Lord with the disciples in Galilee, referred to in the 7th verse. See full discussion in Westcott and Hort.

regard to such a matter as the resurrection, the accounts
which existed in the days of the first disciples, and
which had substantially received their sanction. They
simply record what had long been current in the Church
in oral or written form. How do they describe the
risen Christ? When He appeared to the women, they
held Him by the feet and worshipped Him: yet even
among the Eleven there were some that doubted.[1] The
two disciples failed to recognise Him during a two hours'
journey till He was made known to them in the breaking of bread, and then He vanished suddenly from their
eyes.[2] When He stood in the midst of the assembled
disciples,[3] He seemed so strange to them, that they
thought they had seen a spirit; but He proved the
reality of His return by inviting them to touch Him,
and He showed them His hands and His feet.[4] And
as they were still incredulous from joy, He took a
piece of a broiled fish and ate before them.[5] This
double aspect of His appearance is present equally in
John's account.[6] There is the same doubt removed by

---

[1] Matt. xxviii. 9, 17.   [2] Luke xxiv. 30–32.

[3] John adds : "The doors being shut"; xx. 19.

[4] Luke xxiv. 36–43. Some ancient authorities omit ver. 40 : $\kappa\alpha\grave{\iota}\ \tau o\hat{v}\tau o$
$\epsilon\grave{\iota}\pi\grave{\omega}\nu\ \acute{\epsilon}\delta\epsilon\iota\xi\epsilon\nu\ \alpha\grave{v}\tau o\hat{\iota}s\ \tau\grave{\alpha}s\ \chi\epsilon\hat{\iota}\rho\alpha s\ \kappa\alpha\grave{\iota}\ \tau o\grave{v}s\ \pi\acute{o}\delta\alpha s.$ But with a slight modification,
the same statement occurs in John xx. 20, where the words are undisputed.
These passages in the Third and Fourth Gospels probably describe the same
appearance, though there is a discrepancy in the number of disciples present.
See Godet, and Plummer, on *St. Luke, in loc.*

[5] The words "and of a honeycomb" are omitted in the best MSS. See
note in Westcott and Hort.

[6] John xxi. Though this chapter forms an appendix to the Gospel, and
was written later, yet there is no evidence to show that the Gospel was ever
published without it. "Either John himself composed this piece some time
after having finished the Gospel, or we have here the work of that circle of
friends and disciples who surrounded the apostle at Ephesus, who had often
heard him relate the facts contained in it, and who have reproduced them

the same outward proof. The seven disciples knew Him
not when He stood on the beach; but gradually they
were assured it was He, as they sat with Him at the
feast He had prepared, and listened afterwards to the
conversation in which He pronounced Peter's restoration
and commission.

This blending of the spiritual and the earthly is
accompanied also by a total change in His relations to
them. Though He invites them to handle Him and
see,[1] it is only for the purpose of convincing them that
He is no phantasmal apparition, and of creating faith in
Him as their risen Master. But where this faith already
existed as in Mary Magdalene, He forbids her to touch
Him.[2] He is no longer their companion. He speaks
of the time " when I was yet with you." [3] Not only are
His visits occasional, subservient to a special end of

in his own language. It is of small importance which of these suppositions
is chosen. Yet we must say that the first alternative, as it seems to us, is to
be preferred." Godet, *Comm. in loc.* So also Westcott.

[1] It is not said that Thomas put his finger into the print of the nails, or
that the disciples applied the test of touch at the invitation of Jesus (John
xxi. 27, 28; Luke xxiv. 39, 40). But in Matt. xxviii. 9, we read, "They
(the women) took hold of His feet and worshipped Him." If Thomas or the
other disciples did not actually touch Him (which cannot be shown), it was
because they were so convinced, by sight, of His reality, that they abstained
out of reverence from subjecting Him to the further test. That the account
leaves it possible for us to infer that they refrained from doing so, is the
clearest indication of verisimilitude. This is not the way in which legend
works. It would have "made assurance doubly sure," by asserting actual
contact.

[2] John xx. 17. The verb ἄπτεσθαι signifies here more than "to touch."
It describes a taking hold of one, with a view to possession. The prohibition
of Jesus to Mary Magdalene meant that His earthly intercourse with His
disciples, which she desired to have restored, was impossible now, and that
its place would be taken by a new and higher union not attainable as yet,
but only to be realised when He had wholly completed His earthly self-
manifestation. See Westcott, and Godet.

[3] Luke xxiv. 44.

revelation, but His attitude throughout has a strange aloofness. He stands, as it were, apart from them, above them. He calms their troubled hearts; but He does not identify Himself with them. The former intimacy is past for ever.

Weizsäcker,[1] in a very ingenious analysis of the Gospel accounts, argues that these two phases in the appearances of Christ represent different layers of tradition. The Christophanies were, he says, in their earliest form purely ghostly or visional; but, as time went on, the craving for palpable proofs, together with popular realistic ideas as to the return of the dead to life, led to a gradual materialising of the visions. But if this were so, why did the tendency stop at the middle point? Why did it not work to the total exclusion of the impalpable or ghostly element? Surely if this longing for external and indubitable signs endowed a spectral Christ with physical attributes, it would have eliminated every suggestion that seemed to imply His illusoriness. It would not have left untouched those portions of the story which told how affrighted the disciples were when He stood among them, how at first they did not recognise Him, how some doubted His identity. If, as Weizsäcker admits, the narratives shrink to the last from carrying out the physical conceptions to their logical conclusion, it is only because they are the genuine impression made upon the witnesses by the mysterious facts. It is easy to find variations in the details; but all the more remarkable is the essential agreement even in versions of the same incident. The two elements of the spiritual and the physical are interwoven with the

---

[1] *Apostolic Age*, vol. i. pp. 9-11.

texture of the narratives;[1] and even if the former predominates—which is very doubtful—in what Weizsäcker terms the earlier layers of the tradition, it is also emphatically present in the later.[2]

But these contradictory aspects, instead of casting a suspicion on the appearances, are of the essence of the problem which they were intended to solve. Christ hovers, as it were, on the border line of two different worlds, and partakes of the characteristics of both, *just because He is revealing the one to the other.* Had His risen body been but the re-assumption of the earthly, then the indications of its nature would have been self-consistent; but it would have been no revelation of His final triumph over death, or of another mode of existence awaiting humanity in the hereafter. If it were to bear such a witness, it must be in reality a spiritual body, with the qualities of the higher sphere to which it belonged, and yet retaining in part the visible marks which verified the revelation to human experience, and demonstrated the identity of the present with the past.

The visible marks were, as has been seen, of the most decided character. Some have thought to lessen

---

[1] See Note 20, p. 411, "Christ's Resurrection as a ' process.'"

[2] "There is a false impression made by the unusual consistency of the Synoptical Gospels, which weakens unduly their testimony in the parts where they show more independence and variety. Of course Matthew and Mark, on the one hand, and Luke, on the other, give independent and varying accounts of the resurrection. But the variety is caused by the independence; it is no greater than the ordinary variations of independent narratives, and it does not invalidate the main fact of the resurrection. But the Synoptical Gospels, in the main, in their record of the public ministry of Jesus, are interdependent, and so there is an unusual sameness about them. This should not weaken their testimony, when they become independent and so variant." E. P. Gould, *International Critical Comm.*, *St. Mark*, pp. 308, 309. This argument applies quite as strongly to the unique character of the resurrection as to the mere fact.

the difficulty by doubting whether the risen Lord ought to be understood as actually partaking of human food. They point out that this is the least certain, as it is the most paradoxical, element in the objective manifestation : that it is not said either in the case of the two disciples at Emmaus [1] or of the seven beside the Lake [2] that He personally ate of the bread which He distributed to others.   But on at least one occasion [3] His eating is distinctly affirmed ; which makes the argument from the silence of the Evangelists in the other instances rather precarious.   The words of Peter to Cornelius, " We did eat and drink with Him after He rose from the dead," [4] regarded by Weizsäcker as representing the realistic shape which the legend of the resurrection ultimately took, do not necessarily imply that this form of intercourse was usual, or even frequent, but that it simply did take place.   It is useless, however, to discuss this point, as if its elimination would appreciably lighten the mystery.   Human eyes saw Him ; human hands could touch Him.   But a purely spiritual body could not thus have been perceptible to ordinary sense.   That it was thus visible and tangible implied a condition not one whit less miraculous than if it partook of human food. We cannot indeed conceive how this union of opposite attributes was possible.   It was essentially temporary, assumed for the purpose of crowning the revelation already made by Christ to the disciples, and of enabling them to attain the convictions out of which would grow the right interpretation of His earthly life and death. They themselves felt that it had in it no permanency,

[1] Luke xxiv. 30.
[3] Luke xxiv. 43.
[2] John xxi. 13.
[4] Acts x. 41.

and that He did not now belong to them, or to this world. During the forty days His body was in a transition state, and had to undergo a further transformation in entering into the spiritual sphere, its true home.[1] Hence the appearances of the risen One do not give, and are not intended to give, any exact idea of the nature of the glorified body, whether of Christ or of believers. Their aim was wholly different: to prove by adequate signs, to those who had received the ineffaceable impression of the character of Jesus, and had become profoundly convinced that in Him God's Kingdom centred, not only the persistence of His life through death, but its dominance over it, the triumph of His total human personality over every alien influence whether spiritual or material.

Now the conviction of His spiritual supremacy was not a new thought to them. They had in a manner reached it before His ministry closed. But the Crucifixion shattered it, emptied it of all real force, turned it into a memory. What restored it and re-endowed it with greater reality than ever? Just the demonstration that no material forces held lordship over Him, that the law of mortality had for Him been not merely arrested for a time, but finally abolished; that, in a word, He had not been rescued from death, but had passed through it, and put on immortality. The mere belief that Christ still lived, *i.e.* that His spirit had entered the spirit-world, could never have inspired them with their confident assurance of His victory, so long as His death remained to contradict them.

His resurrection is in the New Testament the in-

[1] See Note 21, p. 412, "The Ascension and the Forty Days."

disputable mark of the divine *power*, the ultimate warrant
for faith in God's promise to establish His Kingdom ;
" declared to be the Son of God with power . . . by the
resurrection of the dead." [1]   Through it the apostles had
their former faith in His spiritual authority requickened,
deepened, illuminated.   In what other way could this
have been done than by the manifestation of a risen
Christ, who, though spiritual, still retained the outward
form by which they could recognise His identity, and
whose presence spoke of an unseen life in the language
of earth and time?   The temporary union in Him of
two diverse modes of being will not seem strange to us
if we realise that only by this means could God assure
us that the redemption of Christ was no less the rectification of the material than of the spiritual universe.   Yet
it is precisely such an assurance that is needed to give
religious faith a final basis and guarantee by showing
that it cannot be explained as a psychological hallucina-
tion.   Had the recorded appearances been the result of
a growing legend, it is incredible that they would have
exhibited throughout a variety of minutely detailed
circumstances, just this combination of transcendence
and objective reality.   The one side would have pre-
dominated to the absorption or obliteration of the other.

Closely connected with this unique quality in the
appearances is the fact, attested by all the evangelic
accounts, and proclaimed by the apostles,[2] that they were

---

[1] Rom. i. 4 ; cf. 2 Cor. xiii. 4 ; Rom. vi. 4.

[2] Acts x. 40, 41 (R.V.), "Him God raised up from the dead and gave
Him to be made manifest not to all the people, but unto witnesses that were
chosen before of God, even unto us who did eat and drink with Him after He
rose from the dead."   Even those who are most sceptical of the historicity of
the first half of Acts, will admit that such a statement of the restriction of the

vouchsafed only to believers. They were not the beginning of the Gospel, but its seal and crown. They were
the interpretation of the past, and could convey no
proper meaning to any but those who had in some
measure received the revelation given in the ministry of
Jesus. The disciples, from their previous intercourse
with Him, had reached the belief of His Messiahship.
He already possessed a supreme greatness for their hearts.
He had claimed an immediate and absolute homage
from them: He had searched and judged them: He
had declared that He would yet judge all men. These
assumptions of an unshared authority were vindicated in
their eyes by His self-verifying teaching, above all by
the whole impression created by His person and miracles,
that He was the chosen possessor of a divine holiness and
power. " They trusted that it was He who should
redeem Israel." [1]

But the Crucifixion came and severed the tie that
bound them to Him who was their true life. It made
their hope a mockery. Their love for Him remained,
but it was turned into a poignant regret. God had
forsaken Him; that holy soul who bore so many marks
of the deliverer. The reappearance of Christ was the
restoration of this lost hope: it was not the creation of a
new faith, but at once the re-instatement and the transfiguration of the old one. It was credible to them, just
because it took up and continued the broken threads of
a fellowship which contained in it elements that spoke
of immortality, though it was for the moment apparently

area of testimony, antagonistic as it is to the craving for external proofs, is
literally historical, and represents the consistent teaching of the Early
Church.

[1] Luke xxiv. 21.

destroyed by one terrible fact. While the resurrection was wholly unlooked for by them, yet, when it had taken place, there was that within them which proclaimed it not merely probable, but necessary. Without it, their divinest experiences in the past would have been incomprehensible. The one thought which underlay all their other thoughts regarding Jesus had been that He was personally indispensable to them. In every possible manner He had fostered this conviction, and it leapt out to recognise its fulfilment when He reappeared under conditions which assured an abiding communion.[1] Apart from such an actual manifestation, attesting both the reality of His return and its transcendent and permanent character, their previous sense of His indispensableness would either have been finally destroyed by His death, or would have expressed itself in fitful dreams. It would never have become the central force of their being, nor given birth to their clear apostolic message and confident service.

On the other hand, it is true, as Harnack says, that " no appearances of the Lord could permanently have convinced them of His life, if they had not possessed in their hearts the impression of His Person." [2] Here is the paradox of the resurrection. It came as a surprise, yet it was felt to be a divine necessity. Its validity depended on two correlated factors : the outward event and the inward susceptibility. The absence of either

---

[1] The strangeness of His risen manifestations, so different from all the current conceptions of human resurrection, did not alienate the disciples, for they had already learned to trust Him even when He most contradicted or surprised their ideas ; and they soon saw in that very strangeness the witness of a higher and endless intercourse.

[2] *History of Dogma*, vol. i. p. 86, *n.*

would have nullified it.   Therefore he never appeared either to His opponents or to the Jews generally, in whom the latter factor was absent.   His resurrection was not a sign, in the sense in which the miracles of the ministry were signs, of supernatural power.   When He stayed the raging fever, He simply accomplished by a word the cure which might have been slowly wrought out by ordinary processes.   When He gave sight to the blind or raised the dead, He merely restored the powers of the natural life.   Consequently, He performed these miracles in presence of the multitude.   Their reality could be easily verified.   Common observation and knowledge could judge of them.   Physical science can tell whether a man who is dead at one moment has returned the next to a normal human life.   But the resurrection of Christ was not such a return.   The revelation which His risen body gave of the spiritual was itself necessarily half spiritual.   There is indeed no reason for supposing that it was impossible for Jesus to be as visible to the Pharisees as He was to the disciples when He showed them the print of the nails, and ate before them of the broiled fish.[1]   But His appearance to unbelievers would have served no real purpose.   They would probably

---

[1] The literal character of the proof which Jesus offers to Thomas points distinctly in this direction.   Westcott, *Revelation of the Risen Lord*, p. 11, says : " If it (the resurrection) was a foreshadowing of new powers of human action, of a new mode of human being, then without a corresponding power of spiritual discernment there could be no testimony to its truth.   The world could not see Christ, and Christ could not—there is a Divine impossibility— show Himself to the world."   Perhaps it would be more accurate to say that even if the world could have visibly recognised the identity of the risen with the earthly Jesus, yet it could have had *no perception of what His risen life meant*, seeing that the transformation in Him, which was quite as real and essential as the identity, required spiritual receptivity for the discernment of its significance.

have declared it phantasmal; and even if they had admitted it was He, it would have revealed nothing to them, because they had no spiritual perception, no background of experience to interpret it, no adequate sense of what He had proved Himself to be as the anointed of the Father, and the Lord and helper of souls.

This shows us the true place which the resurrection occupies in Christian evidences. The apologist who seeks to refute scepticism by setting it in the front rank, by demonstrating it as " the most certain of all historical events," and arguing back from it to the divinity of the mission and character of Jesus, inverts the method in which the revelation was historically given. He tends inevitably to alter the true character of the resurrection by treating it as on a level with the miracles of the ministry, and then He violates the example of the Lord Himself by using it as a miracle to create faith. On every ground the attempt must fail. The sceptic can readily show, by pointing to the Christian records themselves, that it was no miracle in the usual sense, and was not open to the ordinary external or historical tests. Though a fact, it was different from all other facts, in that its real significance lay in its spiritual content; and apart from that content, the fact remains no Christian fact at all.   It is a mere incident in ancient history.   A man will not be able to accept this most mysterious of all supernatural manifestations, if he has not first been led up, as the disciples were, to find the supernatural in the life and person of Jesus; to find it, that is, in a form in which it can be verified by human experience.[1]

[1] The miracle of Christ's holiness is directly verifiable by us, because the various forms of His self-manifestation recorded in the Gospels irresistibly

Until we have received the impression from the
Gospels of Christ's moral supremacy, of the unshared
relation to the Father to which His inmost consciousness testified, and of the correspondence between His
unique personal experience and His unique claim to be
the mediator of a new life of sonship to others, the
resurrection will seem but an idle tale. Now such an
impression is not simply a stamp made upon us from
without ; it is a growing recognition on our part of what
He truly was, and of what *we* are before God.   Contact
with Jesus as we see Him in the records creates for us
a new moral atmosphere, and increasing capacity of
spiritual discernment, which reveals Him to us, because
it reveals in us the needs which He alone can supply.
It forces us to face the dark problem of human sin,
hitherto unrealised but now felt in its pressure, and thus
to discover that just such a One as He provides the
solution.   Only to those who have passed through this
experience and been inwardly impelled to assume this
attitude towards Him is the resurrection truly credible.
It fits in, like the half of the Roman *tessera*, to what they
are already assured of.   It makes complete what would
otherwise be a revelation inexplicably arrested.

The resurrection thus constitutes the great point of
transition in the Christian faith, at which He who
appeared as a single figure in history is recognised as
in reality above historical limitations, the abiding Lord
and life of souls.   As it leads inevitably to the doctrine

imply it (see Lecture I.).   It is not an inference from His other miracles ; it
is the basis on which faith in them rests ; and it alone gives reality and intelligibility to the exceptional miracle of the resurrection, with its dual character.
If it is denied, the rest become meaningless.   It then matters little what we
believe about them.

of Christ's transcendent Sonship, the Ritschlian school,
to whom all religious conceptions are but "judgments of
value," naturally deny or disregard it.   For them the
revelation of God in Christ closes with the Cross.   How
then are we to think of Jesus and of the salvation He
brings, when the resurrection is eliminated?   In some
respects the best representative of this view is Professor
Herrmann, who, by his religious insight and his intensity
of conviction, has perhaps done more than any other to
commend it as practically helpful.   God, he says,[1]
makes Himself known to us through a fact.   Our
certainty of Him has its root in this, that in the realm
of human history we encounter the man Jesus as an
undoubted reality.   His incomparable moral strength
and adequacy to His loftiest ideal, His confidence that
He could uplift men to enjoy the highest good in a life
of utter submission to God, are borne home to us with
irresistible force.   The irremovable persuasion of His
historical reality does not imply the acceptance of the
Gospel story as literally accurate.   We start from the
records, but the power of His personality over us is quite
independent of the correctness of the details.   Help lies
for us, not in what we make of the story, but in what
the contents of the story make of us.   We receive the
impress of His "inner life," as it is portrayed by those
who were lifted by it into communion with God, and
interpreted for us by the living Church around us.
When we have found this inner life through the mediation of others, we become free even of their mediation
by the significance which that life has for our own experience, and we ask no more questions regarding the

[1] Herrmann, *Communion of the Christian with God.*.

trustworthiness of the Evangelists.[1]   In Jesus we cannot
but see a Power greater than all things, and we are
assured that He must succeed though all the world be
against Him.   The more keenly we feel our own shortcoming, the more do we become alive to the strength of
His character, and recognise that nothing but the presence of God can account for it.   The personal attitude
of friendship which Jesus takes to sinful men certifies to
us that His God is our God, and that God enters into such
communion with us, that He thereby forgives our sins.
Hence, while Jesus compels us to realise as never before
the self-contradiction of our being, He is at the same
time the "sure sign" that good is not essentially foreign
to our nature.[2]   By our conviction that in Him God
communes with us we are placed inwardly in a position
to overcome the antagonism between our natural life
and the law of duty, and are conscious that we stand in
and belong to a historical movement in which the good
wields ever greater sway.   This communion with God
includes the experience of moral deliverance; and it
gives such satisfaction to our spiritual need that it
becomes to us the clearest of certainties.   But though
our only real knowledge of Christ is as He is seen in
His historical appearance, yet "we cannot think of His
personal life as something that could ever be given over
to annihilation."[3]   The same faith that sees that God is
present to us in Him must also grasp the thought that
Jesus lives now.   It is convinced that the exalted Lord
knows how near we have come to Him, or how far we
are from Him, and that He is taking part in our battles

[1] Herrmann, *Communion of the Christian with God*, pp. 61, 62.
[2] *Ibid.* p. 81.   [3] *Ibid.* p. 222.

with all His human sympathy and power. But this is only an affirmation of the religious experience. We hold no communion with the exalted Christ. We are simply compelled to think of Him as living and ruling, because such a thought is the necessary outcome and completion of our faith in God, who touches and redeems us in the historical Jesus.

This is not the place to discuss whether Professor Herrmann gives an adequate account of the work of Christ as our Redeemer. Unquestionably, on his theory, sin is not that desperate and dissolvent reality in God's world, requiring a supreme mysterious sacrifice for its removal, which it consistently is with the writers of the New Testament. Nor does he connect our deliverance from it, as they do, with the death more than with the life of Jesus. Leaving this aside as a subject which belongs to a subsequent lecture,[1] Herrmann is certainly right in maintaining that the idea which we have of Christ's person depends on the spiritual impression which He makes upon us. But though his analysis of that impression has much beauty and truth about it, the first thing that occurs to one is its complete divergence from the apostolic view.

The inner life of Jesus through which we feel ourselves in contact with God is, says Herrmann, His personality as manifested in His earthly ministry. It is there, and there alone, that we gain the conviction of His supremacy, and the guarantee that God is giving us the victory over all forces, without or within, that are alien to our spiritual good. But this is not the way in which Christ's Church came into existence. If anything

[1] See Lecture VI.

11

is clear, it is that the first disciples did *not* attain their sense of Christ's dominance, as the Head of a divine kingdom, merely from the witness of His earthly presence and work. Deeply as He had stamped Himself upon them, the disastrous close of His career would have paralysed whatever confidence they had in His triumph, had it not been for the indisputable proof of His risen appearances. Whatever judgment be passed on the genuineness of the words ascribed to Peter on the day of Pentecost, " Being therefore by the right hand of God exalted, *He* hath poured forth this which ye see and hear," [1] they represent the abiding consciousness of the apostolic Church. So far as the apostles saw in His earthly person the sure sign of His mastery over all that impaired the soul's life, it was because in the light of His resurrection they discovered a significance in the past which of itself it could never have yielded. It is quite true that this conception of the risen Christ drew its content from their knowledge of what He had been as a man; yet even the content had undergone a transformation. The supremacy which had been restricted by earthly conditions was liberated; and it was through the liberated and dominant Lord that God held real communion with them.

This applies to us to-day not less than to the first disciples. Herrmann insists, with almost needless reiteration, that what makes us Christians, what emancipates us from the pressure of sin and raises us into an assured fellowship with God, is the inner life of Jesus, which, breaking through the veils of the record, attests its reality to us as an actual power in our world. But what is our

[1] Acts ii. 33.

conception of this inner life? It certainly is not only that Jesus remained ever in that state of soul which we count blessed, and that He retained this divine peace in presence of the awful death which befell Him; but that, as His life stood apart from ours, so death also had not the same meaning for Him as for us, and that His victory over it was not, as in our case, a deferred hope, but an immediate reality. It is nothing to the purpose to say that His risen appearances belong to a bygone time, and therefore cannot be directly verified by us. This is no more true of them than of the incidents of His ministry. His whole earthly manifestation lies in that sense in the past. For the knowledge of it we are wholly indebted, in the first place, to those who witnessed it, and who had the spiritual perception to recognise it.[1] But if, as Herrmann says, *their* representation is but the means of leading us into direct contact with the reality of His personality, then that personality verifies itself to us as truly in the picture they give of His triumph over death as of His triumph over the evils of life. The former triumph is not a mere inference which we draw from the latter. Both come to us, in their representation, as facts to which they bear testimony. Neither in the one case nor in the other does the truthfulness of the fact depend on the accuracy of the details. Just as, despite all the particular divergences in the accounts of the ministry, we feel ourselves in the presence of One who actually overcame the world, so despite the divergences or contradictions[2] in the story of the resurrection, we are compelled to

[1] *Communion of the Christian with God*, p. 90. "We find the Person of Jesus only in the preaching of disciples who believed in Him."

[2] See *International Critical Commentary on St. Mark*, by E. P. Gould, p. 308, and on *St. Luke*, by Plummer, p. 546.

acknowledge the reality of His risen power. The impression of it is irresistibly borne in upon us from the recorded effects in the experience of the disciples. And all the more is this so, that the Christophanies, as has been shown, contain just those contrasts which inherently belong to a revelation in humanity of a higher mode of existence.[1]

If, on the abstract ground of the incredibility of physical miracle, Herrmann is entitled to set aside the resurrection, with all that it involves of an actually revealed immortality and an assured hope, then what answer can he offer to the agnostics who say that *their* intellectual presuppositions make the miracle of Christ's unique character incredible to them, and that the possibility of His spiritual victory is rigorously ruled out by the essential laws of human development? What Herrmann calls the self-attesting power of the inner life of Jesus is to them the product of mingled emotion and imagination. When he replies that not every one can see the personal life of Jesus, and that we see it only when it pleases God to reveal His Son in us,[2] this very answer is fatal to his own position. For if the witness of Jesus to the receptive soul warrants it in disregarding abstract probability, and affirming His *moral* nature as a reality in history transcending the human limitations that prevail everywhere else, then abstract probability cannot be interposed as an objection to the truth of that witness in any sphere.

It is strange that Herrmann, who perpetually contends

---

[1] See Note 22, p. 414, "Harnack and Martineau on the Significance of the Christophanies for subsequent ages."
Communion of the Christian with God, p. 68.

that we cannot know God as our God through any teaching, but only through a fact, should yet hold that belief in a living Lord who makes our affairs His own, and to whom we belong as members of the body to the Head, is not based on any verifiable fact, but is only an inference from a fact.   Surely if this belief alone opens up in us, as he says, "a channel for all the true power of redemption," it ought to be guaranteed in the same sphere of actuality as the moral victory of Jesus.   Is it not a gross inconsistency to say that God could not be truly known by us unless through the reality of Christ's perfect Sonship, and yet that we are left to a mere inference of our own, with no real occurrence in history to establish it, regarding both Christ's triumph over death and our immortality in Him?   The Church from the first has felt by a sure instinct that, if His sinlessness is a fact, His risen life is no less a fact, recognised indeed to be so only from its relation to the other, yet not merely ideally inferred from it, but forming with it an integral part of the same *objective* divine manifestation in humanity; that the impression upon us of Christ's personality which declares the sinlessness includes the resurrection, and that the disbelief of the latter leads by no uncertain path to the denial of the former.

According to Herrmann, the personal life of Jesus can be grasped as a real fact in history by a man who has no faith, and the invisible God so uses this fact to make such men certain of Himself that we can say He communes with us.   Thus by an act of self-revelation God reaches down into the realm of our earthly experience.[1]   But, he adds, we cannot say this of the

[1] P. 224.

exalted Christ.   He is still hidden from us; and when
we declare that Christ lives in us, we are only expressing
our faith in our redemption through Him.   Now, undoubtedly, it is through the historical Jesus that faith
is created; but though the records of the Gospels lie
open to all, yet, as Herrmann admits,[1] to realise the inner
life of Jesus as a veritable attestation of the presence of
a redeeming God involves a special experience wrought
by the Spirit.   But where anyone has attained this
insight, he perceives that the victory of the risen Christ
belongs to the same spiritual order as a real fact in
history, and it is through that fact of the living Christ
that his whole thought of God is henceforth determined.
All that Herrmann says against the false mysticism
that regards Christ as simply the indispensable means of
reaching God, and when it reaches Him leaves Christ
behind, is thoroughly true to the Christian consciousness; but there is a sense in which the Christian *does*
leave the Christ of the earthly life behind, and grasps
Him as a present reality, dominant now as He never was
then, and through whom the love of the Father descends
into his heart and possesses it.   By no analysis is he
able to distinguish his communion with the Father from
his communion with Christ.   They are blended as consciously real in one indivisible experience.   It is quite
certain that this experience does not spring from the
negative conviction that God " would not suffer the Jesus
of the Gospels to be annihilated."

What self-consistency can be found in a theory
which assures us that we must think of the exalted
Christ as taking part in our battles with all His human

[1] P. 68.

sympathy and power, and yet tells us that in no single point can we verify His co-operation? The truth is, the co-operation has no reality; it exists only in our conception of Him, and it is no marvel if a non-existent co-operation is not verifiable. We must indeed believe, we are told, that Jesus is now alive, and because He is Jesus He must sympathise with us. But how this thought, which is a subjective affirmation, gives the personal life of Jesus "free course in us," except as *Aberglaube*, may remain a question. It is but the ideal projection into a higher world of the capacities of His human life. Herrmann continually employs phrases regarding Jesus which cannot but create an illegitimate impression. When he speaks of the inner life of Jesus "as a present fact in our own life,"[1] of the "essence of God as nothing but this inner life of Jesus,"[2] of "God and Christ as one in the Christian's own experience,"[3] and of the recognition of the One as including the Other, he conveys suggestions of the transcendence of Christ's person which his entire theory repudiates. He talks of touching Him as "the living One,"[4] yet it is only in the sense in which any personality must be a "living" power to us before we can be said to know it.

It is time to protest against this abuse of language, which ascribes to a theory fatal to the historic faith the intimate and continuous fellowship with Christ which that faith alone makes possible. Sometimes the contradictions are such that one is puzzled to say whether they spring from an eclecticism which has no rational coherence, or from mere confusion of thought.[5] He

---

[1] P. 78.   [2] P. 133.   [3] P. 139.   [4] P. 62.
[5] See Note 23, p. 415, on "Herrmann's Conception of the Exalted Christ."

rightly emphasises the fact that we need the communion of Christians in order that, from the picture of Jesus which His Brotherhood has preserved, there may shine forth that inner life which is the heart of it. It is within the Christian Church that Herrmann has himself received his inspiration; but had the "inner life" of Jesus contained no other elements than he ascribes to it, there had been no Church to perpetuate and expound it. The enthusiasm with which he unfolds his conception, and the attaching power which it has had for many of his readers, are the survival of a faith which strikes its roots into ultimate realities that he ignores. The result is a half-way house, which, like ancient Arianism, affords no abiding resting-place to spiritual intelligence. What has been said in another connection may be applied to his view of Christ, as compared with that of the historic Church: "It is a weary way to God, but a wearier far to any demi-god."[1]

[1] R. H. Hutton, *Essays, Literary*, 2nd ed., p. 79.

LECTURE V.

THE PERSON OF CHRIST AND HIS REVELATION
OF THE GODHEAD.

SYNOPSIS.

The problem of Christ's Person as it presented itself to the Apostles.

Their *first* conception of Him, as the adequate organ of God's working in the *redemptive* sphere.

Their *later* view simply a realisation of what this involved.

The Pauline doctrine in Colossians : anticipated in Corinthians.

The Prologue to St. John's Gospel : his use of the term *Logos*.

The Christology of St. Paul and St. John makes the universe intelligible by revealing its unifying principle.

Man, as a centre of free spiritual activity, expresses and reproduces the Son.

Therefore the Logos can become personally Incarnate in humanity.

Was the Incarnation a necessity apart from Sin?

Examination of the arguments for the affirmative view.

In what light the Christological decisions of the Church Councils are to be understood.

Defect of the Chalcedon Formula.

Kenotic Christology.

The doctrine of the Holy Spirit : how it arose.

In the Pauline Epistles and the Fourth Gospel the Spirit is the *alter ego* of Christ : yet only within limits.

Knowledge of His personality only reached through the personality of the Son.

The Trinity a Christian, not a Jewish, conception.

The adumbrations of it in the Old Testament.

Speculative renderings of it.

The Trinity essentially a *historical* revelation.

LECTURE V.

The Person of Christ and His Revelation of the Godhead.

As we have seen, the plausibility with which Herrmann seeks to arrest any inquiry concerning the person of Christ arises from the truncated view he gives of the impression produced upon us by Christ, by limiting our knowledge of Him to what pertained only to His human life, closing with the Crucifixion. Even on this basis, the plausibility is purely deceptive. He who attributes to Jesus the unique pre-eminence which the Ritschlians assign to Him, cannot at the same time treat Him as requiring no more explanation than any other historical figure, and must either rise to such a conception as will vindicate the impression, or sooner or later discard the impression itself as subjective and illusory.

But the problem that actually presents itself is quite different. For the self-attesting impression of Christ's life to the Christian soul is that of a personality which is unique not only in its spiritual quality, but also in its persistence through death and over it; which verified under temporal forms its entrance into the spiritual world as the living Lord of humanity. If it were possible, which in reality it is not, to abstain from all question as to the nature of One in whose earthly

appearance God gives us the incontestable assurance
of His redeeming purpose and power, it is totally impossible in the case of One whom we cannot but conceive
as still the sole mediator of the divine life to men, and
mediator now in a full and supreme sense as He was
not upon earth.   Yet this was precisely the conviction
which was wrought into the being of the apostles.   The
new spiritual life which streamed down upon them
shortly after His ascension was indeed a gift from the
Father, but none the less was it for them mediated by
Christ as the exalted Son of Man.   Their thoughts
centred in Him as the one channel of the Father's love.
All the riches of God were summed up in Him for
humanity.[1]

   But it would be absurd to expect that they were
able at once to realise all that was involved in this new
attitude towards Christ which they felt constrained to
take.   They kept close to the historic facts out of which
their faith in Him grew.   He was the Servant of God,
the holy and righteous One, whom God for His fidelity
to His mission as Messiah had raised to His own right
hand and made to be a Prince and a Saviour.[2]   The
addresses of Peter in Acts bear the stamp of verisimilitude, just because they set forth the unequalled supremacy
of Christ in terms of direct and realistic simplicity.
They are an attempt to express a new and overwhelming
fact of experience, when reflection upon it has only

---

[1] See Note 24, p. 416, " The Universalism of Christ."

[2] Acts iii. 13, 14, 26; v. 30, 31; x. 38.   Cf. iv. 27, 30.   The word παῖς so
frequently applied to Jesus in these passages does not signify " child," with
any transcendent reference ; but simply "servant," or, in this connection,
" the supreme Servant " of God, *i.e.* The Messiah.   See Grimm's *Lexicon*,
edited by Thayer.

begun to work. Two influences entered to determine
the earliest form of the apostles' thought. The first was,
that this Jesus, who was now the Lord of all, had
recently lived with them in all the intimacy of human
companionship. To them He was emphatically a man
approved of God, who went about doing good. That
earthly life, which formed the basis of all they knew
or believed of Him, effectually restrained them from any
abstract or speculative statements. And, secondly, they
construed His work of redemption under the forms of
Messiahship. But however varied were the qualities
belonging to the Messiah of the Jewish hope, he himself
was not divine, but the delegate of God.[1] The prophetic
picture of him dealt not with his person, but with the
functions appointed to him. Attention was wholly
concentrated on his earthly appearance, and on all
that he continued to be to his people in consequence
of that.

In declaring, therefore, that Jesus was the Fulfiller
of the promises made to the fathers, the apostles felt
at first no necessity either for themselves or for their
hearers to form any conception regarding Christ previous
to His manifestation. They were not primarily concerned with a theory of the universe, but with the
problem of human sin and the revelation of God's
pardoning and quickening grace. It was the consciousness of God, not as Creator but as Saviour, that had
been awaked in them by the Coming of Christ. That
God was the Maker and Upholder of all things, that
every good gift was from Him, that their bodies and
spirits were His and to be used for His glory, were

---

[1] See *ante*, pp. 69–73.

already deep convictions of their Jewish faith. The
specifically Christian message was the good news of
spiritual deliverance and of the new fellowship with
God which Christ mediated. They did not set themselves to unfold the whole doctrine of God. They
presupposed much that was contained in the earlier
revelation, though incidentally from the standpoint of
their fuller knowledge of Him it was enlarged and
deepened. But essentially it was the redemptive aspect
under which they regarded Him. All the attributes
of God were viewed in this light; and the risen Christ
was to them the adequate organ for the expression of
all God's attributes in the redemptive sphere.[1]

But this position could not be final. It might suffice
for minds purely practical and unspeculative; but the
more the Church realised through its own deepening
experience the supreme place and function of the exalted

---

[1] The Christology of the First Epistle of Peter, which was written
probably about the year 64 A.D., has much of the same simple and realistic
character that marks the Petrine discourses in Acts. Many have questioned
(*vid.* Beyschlag, *N.T. Theology*, vol. i. p. 391 ff.) whether the Epistle teaches
the pre-existence of Christ. When we remember that Peter had now lived
through more than thirty years of Christian experience, and that he had in
the interval been largely influenced by the teaching of Paul, of which this
First Epistle gives evidence (cf. Salmon, *Introd. to the N.T.*, chap. xxii.), it
is hardly doubtful that he had himself reached by this time the conviction of
Christ's true and essential Deity. But it is characteristic of his cast of
thought, that in the Epistle his treatment of Christ's person remains properly
soteriological. He speaks of Him as "foreordained before the foundation
of the world, but manifest in these last times," and declares that His Spirit
testified in the prophets. He proclaims Him to be Lord not only of the
spiritual world, but of the material as related to the spiritual and subserving
it, "angels and authorities and powers being made subject unto Him." In
Peter's view, the miracles of the ministry and the triumph over death were
the symbols in Christ's earthly existence of a mastery now complete over all
created things for the purposes of human salvation. But he never *directly*
raises the question whether Christ holds any other relation to the world than
that of Saviour.

Christ, the more needful it became for some at least to address themselves to the problem which this conception of Him forced upon them. The work which He carried on of moral deliverance and renewal was seen to be interwoven with the whole texture of human life. It implied a perfect knowledge of the variety and complexity of individual characters, and the capacity to meet their needs. But the redemptive power which had this penetrating and universal bearing could not be merely superimposed on an organic world which was independent of it: if it were to become an inherent part of it, and blend with its inner development, it must be in a real sense there already. It could not be external to the formation of a system to whose consummation it was indispensable. He who was central for the redemption of man must be as central for his creation. If He were to satisfy the deepest longings of the soul, He must have been their Inspirer. Had they arisen without Him, He had never been able to comprehend and fulfil them.

Not only so. Man's life is itself an integral portion of God's world, not an isolated and self-contained unity, but correlated to a material environment which influences his whole spiritual being. Since, in one aspect, he is the highest stage of a long process of evolution, the same personal Power whom he recognises as supreme in his own life he cannot but regard as operative, however implicitly, in every prior stage. The more we feel God's universe to be a single whole, the more we perceive the impossibility that the supremacy of Christ in the loftiest sphere of human experience can be arbitrary or sectional. It must, however at times hidden, have a universal reference.   It must have its root in the necessity of things.

It is this idea to which Paul gives formal expression in Colossians.[1]   " The Son of the Father's love, in whom we have our redemption, is," he says, " the image of the invisible God, the first-begotten of all creation.   For in Him were all things created, in the heavens and upon the earth, things visible and things invisible ; all things have been created through Him and unto Him; and He is before all things, and in Him all things consist.   This is He who is the Head of the Body, the Church.   In both spheres, the natural and the spiritual, He has the pre-eminence."   Nothing could be more emphatic.   Nor was this a conception of Christ which came to Paul only towards the close of his life, and quite at variance with the teaching of the Epistles of the Judaistic controversy.[2]   In these he discusses the conditions and method of salvation ; shows that if Christ is anything for forgiveness and sanctification, He is everything ; that the law of the spirit of life in Him wholly supplants the old law of ordinances; that He is central for the race as for the individual soul.   The apostle almost wholly confines himself here to the historical point of view, but he assigns to Christ in history divine functions. He was too keen a thinker to imagine that any single function of the divine could be discharged by one who was unable to fulfil all.   His type of mind was dominantly systematic : he was inevitably driven to seek the issues of his thought, to find some unifying principle which would make the truth he held luminous.   The theology which speaks of Christ having merely " the value

---

[1] Col. i. 13–18,   [2] 1 and 2 Cor., Gal., and Rom,

of God " he would have stamped as a piece of hero-worship, intolerable alike for its intellectual inadequacy and its emotional idolatry.   There were, perhaps un-fortunately, no Ritschlians in Corinth ; but in the letters addressed to that Church there are not wanting indica-tions how he would have dealt with the subjective impressionism to which they would reduce his historical Christology.   He bases his appeal for liberality on the transcendence of Christ and His immeasurable self-impoverishment for our sakes, " that we through His poverty might be rich." [1]   It is not Christ's sufferings, or even His death, but His very existence in humanity, which constitutes for Paul the final proof of His self-renunciation.

In another passage he anticipates almost the exact phraseology of Colossians.   When referring to idol-worship, he says, " Though there be that are called gods . . . yet to us there is one God, the Father, of whom are all things, and we unto Him ; and one Lord Jesus Christ, through whom are all things, and we through Him." [2]   The idea is not elaborated as in the late Epistle, but the very indirectness with which it is in-troduced as a truth acknowledged and beyond challenge is the strongest proof of the permanent and ruling place it had in his thought.[3]   These allusions rise incidentally, but with perfect naturalness and clearness, when he is dealing with some subsidiary question or duty.   He had no cause to develop them at length in the Judaistic controversy.   The doctrine they expressed was not

---

[1] 2 Cor. viii. 9.   [2] 1 Cor. viii. 5, 6.

[3] The Epistle to the Hebrews presents a curious parallel in this respect. The author introduces (i. 2-3) in the same brief and almost incidental way, as an indubitable truth, the cosmic function of the Son.

directly in dispute.   But it *was* in dispute among the
Colossians, who, with their Gnostic speculations and
their exaggerated asceticism, were perverting the character
of Christ's redemption by postulating various mediatorial
agents between God and the world.   Paul declares that
there are no such agents, that Christ is the sole mediator
of the Father's purpose, that He is pre-eminent in the
sphere of grace because He is pre-eminent in the sphere
of nature, and that the denial of His supremacy in the
latter necessarily denudes His supremacy in the former
of its real significance.   But while he is compelled by
circumstances to develop in Colossians the truth of
Christ's cosmic relation, his treatment of it is as far
as possible from a mere abstract argument.   There, as
in Corinthians, the whole emphasis is laid on the renewing and emancipating power of the Gospel.   His
eye is ever on the soteriological aspect of Christ's person
and work ; and it is only as the necessary vindication
of that, and of the presuppositions that it involves, that
he dwells at all on the transcendent side.

There has been a great deal of questionable theorising
as to the slow development of Paul's view of Christianity.
Because the earliest group of his letters is simple and
uncontroversial, it has been maintained [1] that what he
specifically terms " my Gospel," [2] as expounded in
Romans, was only apprehended by him after the Epistles
to the Thessalonians were written.   But the council
of Jerusalem, where Paul appeared as the champion of
Gentile liberty against the Judaising section, was held
before he wrote to the Thessalonians, or even had visited

[1] Very elaborately by A. Sabatier in *The Apostle Paul.*
[2] Rom. ii. 16.

them.[1]   It is against all probability that one of his logical acumen and insight could pass through such a crisis of conflict without perceiving the vital principle involved.   But we are not left to mere inferences.   His dispute with Peter at Antioch,[2] in which he distinctly enunciated his " Gospel," occurred either before the Jerusalem congress, or at latest immediately after it.[3] The omission from his first two letters of the doctrine of justification by faith was due, not to its absence from Paul's own thought, but to the fact that the controversial exposition of it was not called for by the state of the Thessalonian Christians.   So, also, the contrast that is visible between the second and third group of his Epistles does not imply that the intervening three or four years had unfolded to him a cosmological conception of Christ previously undreamt of.   They only brought to him a firmer grasp of the truth he already held, and a deeper perception of its ultimate meanings. The vagrant heresies of Colosse were the occasion, not of revealing to him the transcendent side of Christ's nature, but of leading him to express and develop it.

The same idea of Christ's essential relation to the universe is set forth by John in his Prologue,[4] but is there worked out progressively, and with greater elaboration. The Word is described, not merely as the Agent through whom the worlds were made, but as the Illuminator of

[1] Cf. Bruce, *St. Paul's Conception of Christianity*, pp. 10, 11.
[2] Gal. ii. 11–14.
[3] The generally accepted view, advocated by Lightfoot (*Comm. on Galatians, in loc.*), regards the controversy at Antioch as slightly subsequent to the Apostolic Council of Acts xv.   Professor W. M. Ramsay contends very strongly for an earlier date.   See his *St. Paul the Traveller*, chap. vii.
[4] John i. 1–18.

reason and conscience, the Light that lighteth every man. The peculiarity of the Fourth Gospel as being not only a record of the facts of Christ's life, but the interpretation of them to which the apostle had been led after prolonged experience and reflection, made it necessary for me to deal with the Johannine doctrine in connection with the problem of the historicity of the Gospel.[1] It is only needful now to repeat that the Logos of the Prologue is no abstract conception, but filled with the definite content of the historical personality of Jesus which John afterwards proceeds to depict. The term was no doubt derived originally from the Judæo-Alexandrine school,[2] but the significance of it for the apostle is not to be determined by its traditional use, but by the connection in which he sets it. His long residence in Ephesus naturally familiarised him with the Gnostic theosophies that were rife in Asia Minor, but his employment of a Hellenistic phrase is no proof that he used it in a Hellenistic sense. He " took his own wherever he found it," and seized on the current word *Logos* as best expressing for that age in succinct shape Christ's real place in the universe as demanded by the facts of His self-revelation. He turned it to his own purpose, just as Jesus Himself accepted and transformed the Jewish title of Messiah. In itself, indeed, it is intellectual rather than moral, and does not convey the thought of a distinct per-

---

[1] *Vid.* Lecture II.

[2] " There are reasons apart from the identity of the name for supposing that the apostle had met with the Alexandrine doctrine, and had been influenced by it. And there is a great difficulty about the opposite view, viz. that the Logos-doctrine in S. John belongs to an independent development in the Palestinian schools, and not at all to Alexandrine Judaism."—T. B. Strong, *Manual of Theology*, p. 101, *n.*

sonality ; nor does it bear any direct association with that
humanity of Christ which is yet its fullest manifestation.
But this is to treat the word *in abstracto*. As it stands
in the Prologue, which is both the summation and the
key of the historical portion that follows, it has for its
determining element the idea of sonship, through which
it imparts a moral meaning to the essential nature of God
as revealed in every sphere of creation.[1]

The doctrine of Christ's transcendence is sometimes
dismissed as simply a theologoumenon of Paul or John,
natural in their circumstances and under the forms of
thought with which they worked, but not at all binding
on us, and with no abiding force for humanity. If by
this is meant that the *ipse dixit* even of an apostle is not
obligatory, it may be readily admitted. The only binding thing is truth itself; and the compulsion with which
it arrests us comes from its self-verifying power. Where
this inward witness is wanting, there can be no genuine
belief or acceptance of any doctrine. No teaching of the
apostles, any more than any utterance of the prophets,
is "of private interpretation." The one interpreter of
the divine is the Spirit of God Himself, and it is only
in so far as Paul's thought finds an inevitable response
in the mind and heart that it possesses a permanent
authority. If his message be true, it is not his; it is

---

[1] The Logos or Reason of God is a favourite word with many of the Fathers
(cf. Newman, *Arians of the Fourth Century*, p. 170), who argue that to deny
the eternity of Christ is the same as to say that Almighty God was once without
intelligence (ἄλογος). But the same argument is equally valid for the eternal
Sonship, inasmuch as the denial of the eternity of the Son is the denial of
Fatherhood as God's essential character. Fatherhood and Sonship are correlative facts ; "the one is only as the other is." (Fairbairn. See his admirable statement, *Christ in Modern Theology*, p. 393.) The "eternal generation
of the Son" is involved in the Christian conception of God.

given him by the same illuminating Power that gives me the capacity to receive it. The whole force of it for teacher and recipient alike lies in the Spirit, who is the possession of both. Christ's cosmic function appears naturally but a fantastic speculation to those who see in Jesus only one, though the highest, of many similar revelations of the divine. On that basis it *is* fantastic, and would never have existed. But a faith such as we have seen to be common to the first disciples, and to be warranted by the facts of Christ's unique moral nature, His claims, and His manifestation as the risen and dominant Lord, not simply accepts but demands it as its rational ground and presupposition. There was a stage in the history of the early Church, as the Book of Acts shows, when many held this faith, while unconscious of its implications. The question of the transcendence was not negated ; for them it did not exist. But with the advance of analytic thought it was bound to arise ; and, when once raised, the believer recognises in the cosmic Christology of Paul and John the imperativeness of a true revelation.

For it renders the universe intelligible, by revealing its unifying principle. The redeeming work of Christ not merely presents to us the aspect under which *we* must think of God as related to us ; it is the veritable unbaring of the inner heart and life of God, of what He is in Himself and in every phase of His activity. The operative power in all worlds is the eternal Son, who is the object of the Father's love and the organ of His love's expression. Creation and redemption come into line. Redemption, being in essence a recovery, is the luminous centre which interprets for us the meaning of creation which sin has obscured. All things have their being from the outflow of God's heart through the Son of His love. Sonship is the ultimate principle that underlies creation, physical as well as moral. The material world would not exist if it had not its final cause and explanation in the spiritual.[1] Sonship is the secret of its being,[2] just as the fruit is the secret hidden in the seed; it is the issue to which it is blindly working, and the vindication of its existence. Therefore the divine love cannot rest in its creative activity through the successive stages of the inorganic and animal spheres till it has embodied in its works the likeness of its inner character. God is essentially and of Himself perfect love; but love implies both a giving and a receiving—a double personality; and this double personality God includes in Himself as Father and Son, the originative and the dependent love.[3] And as all creation is in its final purpose but the self-projection of the divine, or the realisation *without* the Godhead of that sonship which eternally exists *within*, it can only find its goal in a rational and spiritual being, who not merely receives but returns love in a conscious fellowship. The filial will in us is not simply *our* human response to the divine; it has its root in the divine nature.[4] Man is made in the image of God, because he is the analogue in creation of the uncreated Son, whose working is in him consummated.[5] His sonship is

---

[1] See *ante*, p. 121, *n.*

[2] See Note 25, p. 422, on " The apparent Antagonism between Nature and the Moral Life—Sin and Death."

[3] See Note 29, p. 436.

[4] See Note 26, p. 432.

[5] In speaking of Man as the crown of creation, I am not to be understood as forgetful of, or denying, the New Testament doctrine of the existence of angels. But angels and men belong to the same order of spiritual intelligence,

grounded in the Filial and Recipient Love which is eternally in God.

It is this fact that makes the Incarnation possible. Though all created things have their ground in the Son, yet in inanimate nature or the purely animal world they do not express His character. Man *does*; because he can represent and reproduce the Son as a centre of free spiritual obedience and activity. Therefore the Logos can personally identify Himself with, and reveal Himself through, humanity. But are we entitled to say that His Incarnation is not only possible, but necessary—an indispensable stage in the self-revelation of God? It is well to remember that in the New Testament no such question is ever raised. All its interpretations of the world and human experience, all its forecastings of the future, are focussed on the actual life and death of Christ. *There* they take their rise, and never, even in their furthest movement, lose the consciousness of the Cross. This, however, does not of itself prove that an Incarnation, apart from the problem of sin, is not implied in the truths that Scripture declares, or may not be fairly deduced from them.

What, then, is the motive of the Incarnation as the New Testament views it? It was God's rectification of His moral world. All creation, which was but the

as self-conscious beings possessing freedom and immortality, and of that order man is the typical representative, because he has race-existence, which the angels have not (see Edwards, *The God-Man*, pp. 12, 13). He is thereby correlated to the evolution of creation, as we know it. The race, not the individual man, is the true unit of humanity. The Son, in assuming manhood, became not only *a* Man, but *Man*; and thus the Incarnation has a universal significance. I confine myself in this discussion to what comes definitely within the sphere of our experience; and whatever our faith may affirm as reasonable, it cannot be said that the existence of angels is verified by actual knowledge.

working of His love, led up to man; and he who was
its crown had ceased to reflect that love. The meaning
of the whole created process was lost. The only means
whereby its significance could be restored, and man
lifted up to that filial relation to God which was the
highest work of the Logos, was by the personal indwelling of the same Logos in a human life. And in
restoring man to his sonship He re-quickened in him the
lost vision of the world as the sphere where the same
love was at work which revealed its highest glory in the
humiliation of the Cross. The Incarnation of the Son
was not His one revelation of God, but the interpretation
to sinful humanity of all His other revelations of Him in
nature and history and moral experience, which have
been darkened by sin. This act of unspeakable condescension, outreaching every other expression of His
nature, this locating of Himself within the limits of the
humanity He had created, was worthy of Him, and with
all its mystery is credible by us, because it was love by
an unmeasured sacrifice regaining love's own lost work.

There are two chief considerations which have led
many to maintain that the Incarnation has a deeper
significance than this : that it has its root, not in redemption, but in creation, and that the conditions of pain and
death associated with it as a historic fact are only modi-
fications in its essential form, caused by redemptive needs.

1. The first of these is, that Christ as redeeming
Lord is represented in Scripture as the final cause of
creation, in whom all things, " the things in the heavens
and the things upon the earth," find their unification.
He is not merely the creative agent, He is the goal and
crown, of the universe. And it is argued that it is in-

conceivable that He could be so, unless this function belonged to Him, as incarnate, in the essential plan of the world.   If in Him alone God's purpose in creation is summed up, He could not be an intercalated or super-induced factor.   But the Incarnation, even if conditioned by sin, does not constitute a departure from God's plan of the world :   it is emphatically the realisation of it in a particular form, due to a tremendous and unparalleled necessity created by the action of free spirits.   The Logos, whether Incarnate or not, is the τέλος as well as the ἀρχή of creation.   The κένωσις did not alter his rela-tion to the universe.   Even if we adopt the extreme view [1] that it implied the absolute abandonment by the Son of His cosmic prerogative, it was a temporary sur-render, followed by a complete resumption.   Conse-quently, in this aspect of the matter, which is funda-mental, the only difference introduced by the Incarnation was at most that between the continuous exercise, and the momentary or partial suspension, of an inherent sovereignty.

In another aspect, indeed, a new element is added,— the human nature which He assumed, and which remains indissolubly bound up with the divine in the unity of His person.   This, it may be said, inevitably changes the proportion of things by raising humanity to a supre-macy which it did not formerly possess, and making it the medium of His relation to all other parts of crea-tion.   But, as has been shown, man holds already by the constitution of his being the primacy in nature.   He is its point of conscious contact with God, the eye with which it sees Him, the head to which it grows up and in

---

[1] See below, pp. 200–3.

which it reaches its fulfilment. He, as the sole true type of sonship, is creation's one image and analogue of the eternal Son. A disorganised humanity means a disrupted universe, and a disrupted universe is the failure of God's original plan. Therefore the Incarnation is not in itself the conferring upon man of a priority which is not his; it is the restoration to man of a priority he has forfeited, and a priority without which the world would cease to be the expression of God's will. It is not the altering of the relation in which the Son originally stands to all things, but the re-establishment of it. Hence the apostle declares that the whole creation will only attain its deliverance and realisation at the *revealing* of the sons of God.[1]

Thus, even if we regard the Incarnation as conditioned by sin, it is in no sense a subversion or essential reconstruction of God's plan of the world. It is indeed a modification of it, only because that plan is to the eye of Him " in whom is no before " disastrously modified already.[2] Nor do we get rid of the fact of modification by saying that redemption was no afterthought in God, that His plan of the universe was one, and that " the foresight and permission of sin was from the first included in it." [3] For we speak of God's " foresight and permission of sin," but we do not speak of His foresight and permission of man's sonship. The sonship is His clear purpose, the end towards which He works and subordinates all. It is of His calling and operation, which sin is not. Sin is there, not according to His

---

[1] Rom. viii. 19–23.
[2] On the expression "God's Plan of the World," see Note 27, p. 433.
[3] Orr, *Christian View of God and the World*, p. 323.

will, but against it; and the Christian conscience is
violated when, through any metaphysical theory of the
necessary unity of the world, it is treated as an indispensable factor in the moral evolution of man.[1]
Ideally, therefore, *i.e.* from the standpoint of God's intention, it is an intruder; and it is surely natural to
suppose that the means adapted to its expulsion and a
reversal of its effects should contain elements or conditions not required in the normal development of the
world as it lay in the heart of God. You cannot get
your aboriginal unity of plan, unless you make the
disease inherent as well as the cure.

2. The second reason adduced in support of this
view is that, as the Incarnation contains the fullest
manifestation of God, it is irrational to think that the
highest blessing to mankind could be contingent on
human sin; it must depend, not on what lies outside of
God, but on His own nature.[2] The apparent force of
this argument comes from an inadequate realisation of
what the absence of sin would mean for humanity. The
ideal sinless state which we figure to ourselves, apart
from the glory of the Incarnation, retains too much the
characteristics of our dim and struggling experience.
But every obedience leads to a further revelation of the
divine will; and the continuous obediences of a lifetime,
unmarred by revolt or pause, would issue in an incomparable knowledge of Him whom the pure in heart see.
And if the whole race from its first beginnings had

---

[1] See Note 33, p. 450.

[2] Cf. Martensen, *Christian Dogmatics*, pp. 260–263; Westcott, *Epistles
of St. John*, p. 315. Westcott's Essay on "The Gospel of Creation" is
specially valuable for its full account of the history of the question. See also
Dorner, *Person of Christ*, div. ii. vol. i. pp. 361–369.

remained true to itself and to God, each generation bequeathing to its successor the heritage of its acquired moral strength and insight, it is impossible for us to conceive the height of spiritual vision to which humanity could rise. The same spirit that descended on the sinless Jesus, and dwelt in Him, would rest upon the sinless race continually, and through His constant illumination it might attain even to such knowledge of its sonship as would reveal to it the eternal Son as the source of sonship. "The revelation of God," as Principal Edwards puts it, "might still be mediated without the Incarnation."[1]

But we are here in the region of pure speculation. We have no calculus that would enable us to compare the knowledge of divine things possible to the redeemed soul with that attainable by the sinless through an unbroken obedience. We cannot say that the latter knowledge would be lesser or lower, though it would be of a different character. And the difference remains, whether we eliminate a personal Incarnation altogether, or only the redemptive aspect of it. For the Incarnation *without the Cross* would lack precisely that revelation of God's love which is to us the most immediately impressive and soul-subduing—His yearning compassion for the unworthy. "God commendeth His love toward us, in that while we were yet sinners Christ died for us."[2] If we cannot in thought get beyond the "O felix culpa,"[3]

---

[1] *The God-Man*, p. 82.   [2] Rom. v. 8.

[3] "O felix culpa quæ talem ac tantum meruit habere redemptorem,"—part of a hymn used in some mediæval Churches. Cf. the words of the sequence :

> "O culpa nimium beata
> Quâ redempta est natura."

See the references in Westcott, *ibid.* pp. 280, 284.

and yet believe that the loss entailed by the absence
of the redemptive aspect of love's manifestation would
be in some way compensated, nay, swallowed up in
glory, then there is no difficulty in believing that
the further apparent loss involved in the absence of
the incarnate Christ would be equally compensated out
of the depths of the divine riches. We may be
able to compute the loss; we cannot measure the
gain,

And if the view which associates the Incarnation with
sin be not open to these objections, it has this to say for
itself, that it helps to make the Incarnation morally
more credible. There is a correspondence between
means and end. There is an appreciation of its mystery
as an unparalleled stage in the self-revelation of God.
That the Son in His creative agency should work
towards the realisation in creation of a humanity bearing the stamp and character of His sonship is one thing;
it is a normal process of evolution through the power of
the Logos from inanimate matter up to human sonship.
That He should become *personally* incarnate is quite
another: it is a unique act. For what does it involve?
Even when we eliminate all the disastrous conditions
that sin has produced,—ignorance and pain and death,[1]
—man still remains subject to the limitations of his
finitude. He is present here, and not there; he appears
and disappears with his generation. However far his
knowledge develops, it is not omniscience. Therefore
the Incarnation, in a sinless as really as in a sinful world,
implies a κένωσις, a self-emptying of the Son in order to
His identification with man under the limits of time and

---

[1] See latter part of Note 25, p. 422.

space.[1]   That this unimaginable surrender of divine prerogatives was a part of the essential plan of God's revelation of Himself, appears to me wholly improbable, and only to *become* probable through the arising of a dire and exceptional problem, which love for its own sake had to solve.

Moreover, when we ascribe it to the creative rather than the redemptive work of the Son, we take from the latter some of its incomparable significance.   It is true that, from the peculiar appeal which suffering, voluntarily embraced for a high cause, makes to the human heart, it is the Agony and the Cross that most directly arrest the sinner, and give him his penetrating sense of the pitying Fatherhood of God.   But it matters a great deal to the depth of his spiritual life whether he ultimately measures the darkness of his guilt only by the suffering that accompanied the Incarnation, or also by the Incarnation itself; whether sin, as he thinks of it, only brought the Son of God—who in any case would have become incarnate—to a ministry of sorrow and the bitterness of death, or whether it actually drew Him to the κένωσις of a human existence, with all that that

---

[1] If it be said that in that case His humiliation must continue for ever, seeing that He has permanently "taken the Manhood into God," the reply is obvious.   Though we do not possess the data which would enable us to realise the nature of our Lord's risen and glorified Humanity, yet, *ex hypothesi*, it is such as does not limit His divine power and knowledge.   His earthly Humanity did so, as we see ; and, under any conceivable conditions of sensuous existence, must have limited them.   To argue back from the former state to the latter, and maintain that, because a non-sensuous and spiritual manhood, which exists only for faith, involves for the Son no humiliation, therefore a manhood in flesh and blood, as we know it, might involve none, is simply to denude the latter state of all that gives it meaning in our experience, and to ascribe to it the mysterious attributes of the spiritual body and the risen Humanity.

involved. Let anyone read Paul's great passage [1] on the progressive self-sacrifice of Christ from " being on an equality with God " to the shame of the Cross, and let him say, " Up to the self-emptying, or assumption of humanity, it was a necessary creative act, and only the subsequent stages of it had a redemptive meaning," and then let him ask himself whether the conception of sin, and of the revelation of love it has called forth, has not lost something of the overwhelming intensity that it bore for Paul himself. A philosophical theory of Christianity, however attractive, which lessens the horror of guilt or the greatness of love's mystery in redemption, is purchased at too dear a cost.

Can we, then, form to ourselves any conception of the kind of personality implied in the Incarnation ? The early Church was compelled to face the question, because it found that under the categories derived from Greek philosophy, which supplied a new and permanent organon to thought, interpretations were given of Christ's personality which emptied it of its essential significance. It had to formulate its faith in order to prevent the spiritual content, of which it was well assured, from being explained away.

---

[1] Phil. ii. 5-11. Considering the long-continued conflict of eminent exegetes on the significance of the different clauses in Phil. ii. 5-11, it would be rash to say that Dr. E. H. Gifford, in his recent volume (*The Incarnation*), has settled the question ; but he certainly gives some good reasons for holding that " the form of God " in which the Son originally existed He retained in His Incarnation, and that it is therefore to be distinguished from " the being on an equality with God " which He then surrendered. But this interpretation leaves the Kenotic problem (see below, pp. 195 ff.) precisely where it was. Everyone is agreed that Paul did not mean to represent the Son of God in His great act of self-renunciation as ceasing to be divine. What, then, did He give up? *i.e.* what is included in the phrase, τὸ εἶναι ἴσα θεῷ? So far as any answer is possible, it must be found in the recorded facts of Christ's life. See, however, Dr. Bruce's exegesis of the passage, *Humiliation of Christ*, 4th ed., pp. 15-22.

It is in this light that the findings of the four great Councils are to be understood. When the Creed of Chalcedon, after repeating the declarations of Nicæa and Constantinople as to Christ's true Deity and true Humanity, went on to affirm that the Incarnation was not the union of two personalities, a divine and a human, but the assumption by the Son of human nature in such wise that the two natures remained the same, without confusion yet without separation, in the unity of a single personal life, it was not attempting to explicate the *method* of the Incarnation, but to assert its reality. Had it been intended to make it more comprehensible, it would have been a pitiful failure. Almost any of the antagonistic views had more logical self-consistency than the Church doctrine. The Deity of Christ was more formally credible on the supposition of a doketic than of a real humanity; the inseparableness of the divine and human natures, as asserted against Nestorius, more apparently credible on the Eutychian hypothesis of a blending of the two, or a transubstantiation of the latter into the former, than on the retention by each nature of its permanent characteristics. But the Church cared nothing about logical contradictions; what it *did* care for was to see that it was not robbed of any side of the truth implied in the revelation of God in Christ, under the pretext of a more exact and systematic theory.[1] It was led from one definition to another, because the same metaphysical interest, which had failed in a direct attack on the reality of Christ's Deity and Humanity, proceeded

[1] Canon Gore well remarks that there is no more signal evidence of a divine providence watching over the fortunes of the Church than the Church's persistent loyalty, *in its authoritative decisions*, to the true humanity of Christ, in spite of strong individual prepossessions. *Dissertations*, pp. 138, 139.

13

to such a rendering of their relations as *involved* a denial
of that reality.   It affirmed the diverse elements in the
complex impression which Christ made irresistibly upon
its experience.   In embarking on its career of definition, the Church was essentially not speculative, but
declaratory.   Its formulæ were negative rather than
positive.   Their purpose was to conserve, not to vindicate philosophically, the content of the Faith.[1]

The Chalcedon symbol owes to this characteristic at
once its merit and its defect; its merit as emphatically
safeguarding a real Incarnation of the Son of God, its
defect as containing an exaggeratedly antithetic presentation of the two factors in the double truth.   It
conveys too abstract a conception of Christ's Deity *as it
existed in the Incarnation*, by bringing together the two
natures in their totality, as if the divine attributes
remained in all respects unchanged.   But this is to be
untrue to the actual revelation which it professes to interpret.   It takes no account of the sacrifice which Christ
made in exchanging, to use Paul's expression, " the form of
God "—or, if a different exegesis be adopted, " the being
on an equality with God "—for the " form of a servant "
and " the likeness of men."   The Gospels reveal something at least of what that sacrifice meant.   They show
that, however wide and deep his knowledge, especially in
the sphere of human character and the Father's purpose,
—so deep and unique, indeed, as to suggest, if not to
imply, a transcendent quality in His nature,—yet it was
not omniscience.[2]   Still more plainly He was not omni-
present, for the " illocal ubiquity " which the Lutherans

[1] See Note 28, p. 435.
[2] *Vid. ante*, Lecture III., and Note 13, p. 398.

attribute to His humanity is as fantastic as it is incomprehensible.[1]   Nor did He retain His omnipotence; He
wrought His miracles by virtue of the power committed
to Him by the Father, received in answer to prayer, and
conditioned in its exercise by the Higher Will to which
He submitted His own.[2]   So long as these facts were
not perceived or faced, it was natural that the Church,
notwithstanding the Creed of Chalcedon, should remain,
as it did for centuries, practically monophysite.   The
human consciousness of Christ was phantasmal.[3]

There can be no doubt that what is known as Kenotic
Christology is in this respect immensely nearer to historical truth than the old abstract idea of Christ's Deity,
and that it avoids some of the antinomies into which the
latter is driven.   But it has difficulties of its own which
it cannot overcome.

Perhaps no better statement can be given of it in its
more thoroughgoing form than that of Godet.   " He
knew Himself as Son with that knowledge with which
the Father Himself knew Him eternally, and—here is that
putting off [4] upon which all the rest depends—that consciousness of sonship which was His light, He allowed to be

---

[1] Bruce, *Humiliation of Christ*, 4th ed., pp. 90, 91, 108.

[2] Cf. Godet, *Defence of the Christian Faith*, p. 255.

[3] Cyril, the famous Bishop of Alexandria, who died (A.D. 444) shortly
before the Chalcedon Council, and whose views as against the Antiochenes
became dominant throughout the Church, uses language with regard to the
retention of the divine " properties " in the Incarnate life, which inevitably
denuded Christ's human nature of its reality.   " When the disciples," he says,
" wished to learn things above them, He (Christ) *usefully pretended not to
know*, that they might not be grieved because they were not admitted to the
knowledge of the mystery."   See the catena of passages from Cyril's works,
quoted by Professor Bruce, *op. cit.* p. 366 ff.   Cf. also Gore, *Dissertations*,
passim, and R. L. Ottley, *Doctrine of the Incarnation*, vol. ii. pp. 80–86.

[4] *Dépouillement*.

extinguished within Him (*il l'a laissée s'éteindre au-dedans de lui*), to retain only His inalienable personality, His ' ego,' endowed with liberty and intelligence as every human ' ego '; for our personality is formed in the image of His.   In virtue of this self-abasement, He was able to enter into a human development completely similar to ours." [1]   In Godet's view, up to the age of thirty Jesus underwent a purely human growth from innocence to holiness.   He did not yet know Himself.   The distinct consciousness of His dignity as Logos only awoke in Him at His baptism, when His special mission as Revealer and Redeemer began.   But while the baptism restored to Him His consciousness of Sonship, it did not restore Him to His filial *state*, the divine " form of God," belonging to Him.   There was an immense disproportion between what He knew Himself to be and what He really was.   Therein lay for Him the possibility of temptation, therein for Him the work of patience.   It was by His ascension that His return to the divine *state* was accomplished.   He was then clothed with all the attributes which He possessed before His Incarnation, but clothed with them as the Son of Man.   " For the very reason that we hold the divine existence of the Son to be a matter of love (*the bosom of the Father*), and not of necessity, as with Philo, we think that when the Word descends into the world, there to become one of the beings of the universe, the Father can enter into direct relation to the world, and Himself exercise the functions of Creator and Preserver, which He commonly exercises through the mediation of the Word." [2]

[1] *Études Bibliques* (*Nouveau Test.*), p. 135.
[2] *Comm. on St. John*, vol. i. pp. 396–404.

Now, there are two aspects in this theory which may
be considered apart, though really inseparable : (1) Its
construction of the personality of Christ, *i.e.* of the Incarnate life itself.   (2) What this construction implies regarding the revelation of the Godhead given in Him.

(1) It may at first sound startling to speak of the
temporary loss by Christ of His divine consciousness, yet,
as that consciousness plainly operated during His ministry
under the forms of human thought, and as a child immediately after birth has no self-consciousness at all, how is
this conclusion to be avoided?   To ascribe to the child
Jesus a divine consciousness before His human consciousness awoke, is not merely to declare the matter hopelessly
unintelligible, it is to contradict the whole analogy of His
later life.   Nor is there, as Godet remarks, a saying or a
deed in the Gospel history which necessitates or supports
such a conception.   Principal Edwards holds that during
the infancy the divine consciousness was not lost, " but
only quiescent " ;[1] but is anything gained for thought by
the change of expression ?   If the Logos " emptied Himself" so as to become truly incarnate in humanity, was it
not essential that He should pass through all the stages,
unconscious as well as conscious, of a human life ?
Christ's knowledge of His unique sonship ought most
probably to be assigned to a period earlier than the
baptism ;[2] but, at whatever point attained, it was reached
through His deepening human experience.

Undoubtedly, Godet's view of Christ's person as disclosed during the ministry is not in formal accordance
with the Chalcedon doctrine.   But the very meaning of

---

[1] T. C. Edwards, *The God-Man*, p. 131.
[2] See Lecture III. pp. 93–99.

a Kenotic theory is that it is an attempt to surmount the
abstract opposition in which that doctrine placed the two
natures. Even the Chalcedon formula, at least in its
necessary development,[1] strove to mediate the opposition
by its assertion of the impersonality of the human nature
in Christ. Obviously, however, there is little illumination
in the conception of a complete human soul, which yet
is not personal, and only becomes so by the indwelling
of a divine ego, so long as that " ego " is supposed practically to retain all the attributes that properly belong to
Deity.

How far, then, does Godet's representation help us to
realise to ourselves the nature or the extent of the " self-
emptying" of the Son ? Any rendering which we give
to the personality of Christ must include the relation of
supremacy in which He consciously stood to the race.
How do we correlate this with human experience?
Godet's explanation is: " The limits of our individuality
impress a *relative* character on the receptivity for the
divine belonging to each of us. But, in consequence of
His miraculous birth, the Logos, while entering into
humanity, reproduces not the type of a determinate
hereditary individuality, but that of the race itself in its
essence and generality." That is to say, Christ's consciousness possessed this " collective receptivity " for the

---

[1] I have said, "in its necessary development," for it is hardly accurate to
represent the Chalcedon Creed, as Schaff seems to do (*Creeds of Christendom*,
p. 32), as formally teaching the "impersonality" of Christ's human nature ;
but it unquestionably involves it. The orthodox view, expressed both by
Athanasius and Cyril, was that the manhood of Christ had no independent
personality. But the doctrine of the *anhypostasia*, or rather of the *enhypostasia*,
is specially associated with its subsequent exposition by Leontius and John of
Damascus. See Dorner, *Person of Christ*, div. ii. vol. i. *passim* ; and R. L.
Ottley, *Doctrine of the Incarnation*, vol. ii. pp. 123–125, 139.

divine, not in virtue merely of that which made His humanity one with ours, but also of that which was its peculiar characteristic. In one sense, indeed, personality is the most inclusive as well as the most exclusive of realities, the most universal as well as the most individual. The true definition of it may perhaps be its capacity for love, "not for self-consciousness but for self-sacrifice, for life in others." But even if we imagine a sinless human soul, utterly filled and dominated by the passion of service for men, though it would possess a kind of universal life, yet its universality would not be in the least comparable to the universality of Christ. For the last thing possible to it would be to assume that air of sovereign authority which He invariably maintained. That is a characteristic which can only belong to One who has not merely a universal, but, as Godet expresses it, a "collective" consciousness. That there may be such a consciousness is distinctly suggested to us by the fact that the race, not the individual man, is the true unit of humanity.[1] But can we form any idea of what it is, or of a human individuality when the "limits" that make it "relative" are removed? The Logos, however self-emptied, still retained of His essential nature what was necessary to give to the humanity of Christ this transcendent element.

It is only the other side of the same fact which is presented in what we call His divine consciousness. We may say, if we choose, that there was but one consciousness in Him, as there was but one personality—that of the *Word made flesh*. But it was a consciousness which had in it a double quality, or at least a double

[1] *Vid. ante*, p. 183, *n.*

reference. The " inalienable ego " who lived and thought
under true human conditions knew Himself to be the
Son who dwelt in the glory of the Father before the
world was; knew therefore that the very essence and
principle of all sonship was itself incarnate in Him.
And it was because He was conscious of this that His
self-disclosure necessarily took the form of a self-assertion
which could not belong to a normal sinless humanity.

If, then, the Incarnation signifies " the coming to be
of a manhood," [1] it is yet a manhood, a human personality, capable of a content impossible to human individuality as we know it—a unique and incommunicable
relation to God, and a " collective " and equally incommunicable relation to the race.   Are we not still face to
face, in our construction of the incarnate Deity, though
not with the same antinomy as before, yet with a union
of characteristics which eludes definite conception?   The
forms and conditions under which Christ develops are
truly human, yet the personality developed, though
human also, is of a type of which other men do not
possess the possibility, and which they cannot even
imaginatively realise.

(2) When we pass to the second aspect of this theory,
and consider what it implies as regards the Godhead
revealed in Christ, we are confronted by something very
like a self-contradiction.   If we confine our thought to
the Incarnate life itself, probably we cannot interpret it
better than by saying that it meant the renunciation by
the Son of the metaphysical attributes of God—omnipotence, omniscience, omnipresence—for the fuller realisation of that love which is the inmost nature of the

———
[1] See Fairbairn, *Christ in Modern Theology*, p. 354.

divine.[1] But how can we reconcile the cessation of the
Son's cosmic function during the period of His humiliation with what Christ reveals of Fatherhood and Sonship in the Godhead? " It is a Father's perfection to
originate, a Son's to receive." But our life is in its
very nature a receptive life, and is rooted, not in the
Father, but in the Filial Will that is eternally in God.
Hence it was not, and we may even say could not be,
the Father who became incarnate, but the Son, who is
" the symbol of the created within the uncreated," " the
basis of objectivity within the Godhead."[2] Can it be
supposed that the Father could assume the Son's prerogative in creation more than in incarnation and redemption? Does not such an assumption, though only for a
time, suggest that the Son is not really as essential to
the Godhead as the Father is? If the Latter can discharge temporarily, no matter for what high redemptive
purposes, the cosmic function of the Former, and become
the ground of the sonship which our moral life denotes,
what satisfactory reply can be made to those who ask,
Why not always look to the Father *directly* for the
creation of the filial will in us?[3]

Godet holds that this surrender was possible, because
the divine existence of the Son is a matter of love, and
not of necessity. There is certainly no necessity *external*
to the Father which accounts for the being of the Son;
but His existence is an eternal moral necessity in the
Godhead, just because God is in Himself love. To say
that the Father's originative love as operative throughout

[1] Fairbairn, *Christ in Modern Theology*, pp. 475–477.
[2] *Ibid. l.c.*
[3] Cf. R. H. Hutton, *Essays, Theological*, 2nd ed., pp. 238–239. See
Note 26, p. 432.

creation could for a period dispense with the dependent and responsive love of the Son within the same sphere, is surely to introduce confusion into the Christian conception of God.   It is to ascribe to the Father the filial nature; for in the absolute divine life the function is as the nature is.   Nor is it a small thing that the idea of the abandonment by the Son of His cosmic prerogative, and therefore of His relation of full equality with God, has against it the overwhelming preponderance of Church judgment in the past.[1]   That judgment may have been partly determined by too abstract a view of the two natures in Christ.   But we may recognise to the full the absence, in the life of Jesus, of the metaphysical attributes of God, and yet feel it impossible to rest in an explanation of that absence which perplexes our whole thought of the interior life of the Godhead.

It is to be acknowledged that Scripture does not explicitly declare the permanence and continuity of the Son's cosmic relation as it explicitly reveals His self-limitation in the Incarnation.   The reality of His self-impoverishment is for us the primary fact in the manifestation of God in flesh.   But it is the same manifestation which also discloses to us such essential distinctions in the Godhead as seem to preclude the possibility of any suspension of function.   If, therefore, our theory is to cover the complete truth revealed to us in the person of Christ, it would appear necessary to suppose that the Son, in becoming incarnate, lived a double life;[2] that, while still exercising His inalienable prerogative as Mediator

---

[1] See Gore, *Dissertations*, pp. 91–93, 98 ff., 189.

[2] See Martensen, *Christian Dogmatics*, pp. 265–268.   Substantially the same view is taken by Canon Gore, *Dissertations*, p. 215 ff., and Principal Edwards, *The God-Man*, pp. 108, 109.

in the universe, He began to live from a new centre of
personality under the conditions of manhood, for the
gracious purpose of redeeming and restoring the created
sonship which had ceased to reflect His image. But
though such a supposition may represent the facts,
the attempt to think it out ends in bewilderment. It
has been suggested that a faint illustration of this
double life of the Logos is found in the capacity which
intense sympathy gives a man to go out of himself and
live under the conditions of another's more limited
thought. " He must not abandon his own higher
standing-ground if he is to benefit the object of his
compassion. But remaining what he was, he must also
find himself in the place of the lower; he must come to
look at things as he looks at them; he must learn things
over again from his point of view." [1] Is it not, however,
rather extravagant to regard this as an instance of a
personality living from two different centres? In any
case, the centres are necessarily inter-related, which
implies some bond or principle of unification. How,
then, do they illustrate the two *non-communicating* con-
sciousnesses of the Logos?

   The service which Kenotic Christology renders is
twofold: (1) It represents an advance on the Chalcedon
symbol, in that it gives a truer impression of the New
Testament facts and teaching as to the divine *sacrifice*
involved in the Incarnation, and thus emphasises the
very quality that endues the Incarnation with its power
of moral appeal. (2) By insisting that the elements in
Christ's character which verify His Deity are not metaphysical, but ethical and spiritual, it reminds us that

[1] Gore, *op. cit.* p. 218.

the deepest qualities in God and man are akin,[1] and that humanity is grounded in and reproduces the eternal sonship in God.   But man, as the created image and reproduction of the Logos, is still only His work: the personality of the Logos remains unaffected.   In the Incarnation, it is this central personality itself which assumes human nature and becomes a human person. It can hardly be said that any of the Kenotic theories make the type of personality thus resulting really comprehensible to us, though they may indicate the lines along which the solution lies.   Above all, with regard to the Son's function in relation to the universe, they present us with the alternative of contradicting what seems involved in the revelation, or of stating the revelation in terms which bring no real aid to intelligence.

But, perplexing as the union of the divine with the human in Christ is, it is not to be reduced to greater intelligibility by declaring that "it must be a union of which humanity is capable," if by this is meant that we have a definite idea, drawn from the experience of the race, of what the capacities of humanity are, and that this supplies the standard by which each individual life must be tried.   Thus the sinlessness of Christ is rejected by many as an incredible violation of the law of development.   They have gathered a certain conception of what a human character must be, and then imposed it upon Him, ignoring the realities of His earthly life, or explaining them away.   But this is a reversal of all intelligent investigation.   If we would understand Nature, we have to accept her surprises, however they

[1] Cf. Orr, *Christian View of God and the World*, pp. 284, 285.

contradict our preconceptions. And if we would know
God, we must be content to keep our eyes open to His
revelations, whether they seem to us unique or not.
Now, the uniquenesses of Christ are manifold and indubitable; and they have forced the Church to recognise that
He was not only divinely possessed beyond other men,
but the Very Incarnate Son of God. He is not to be
judged by a standard outside of Him, but by what He
is in Himself. The Church holds to the Incarnation,
not because it can speculatively resolve its contradictions, but because it faces the facts, and finds in this
faith the one explanation of the correspondence between
these facts and the abiding needs of the soul. To set
up an *a priori* test, and rule out whatever seems exceptional, is the surest way, whether in the natural or the
spiritual sphere, to miss the truth we seek.

We have seen that it was through the self-revelation
of Christ that a new conception was attained of God as,
in His essential being, both Father and Son. How came
this conception to be further enlarged by the doctrine of
the Holy Spirit as equally with the Father and the Son
to be worshipped in the unity of the Godhead? It arose
historically. Believers in Christ as the risen Lord were
conscious from Pentecost onwards of a new gift of
divine life and power, and they could only express it in
the words of Joel, that God was pouring out His Spirit.[1]
Yet the Spirit so poured out had a different significance
for them from that borne in the Old Testament. He
was no longer simply the gift of God, but the gift of the
Father through Him whom He had raised up and
exalted. And this experience of the apostles agreed

[1] Acts ii. 16–18.

with what, according to the Fourth Gospel, Jesus had led them to expect, when He spoke, before His departure, of the Paraclete who should abide with them for ever, and whose function it should be to take of His and show it unto them.[1] The loving fellowship which He had vouchsafed to them was not to cease with His death; it was to be realised in a character and degree hitherto impossible. It was expedient that He should go away:[2] the best was "yet to be." But that could hardly be said, unless they were to be under the continual influence of a *personal* Spirit, who knew them, sympathised with them, rebuked, consoled, and in whom the life of the redeeming and reigning Christ was made theirs.

Hence the New Testament writers instinctively think of the Spirit as a person, and ascribe to Him actions that are the expression of personality.[3] His activity is so absolutely bound up with the person and the work of Christ, that Paul employs the terms Christ and the Spirit of Christ as convertible, just as he uses the terms God and the Spirit of God. When he speaks of " Christ in you," he means substantially the same thing as the assertion of the indwelling Spirit, and in one remarkable passage he identifies them, " The Lord is the Spirit."[4] Both in the Pauline Epistles and in the Fourth Gospel the Spirit is the *alter ego* of Christ.[5] He is Christ in an inward and abiding form. But with this identity there

---

[1] John xiv. 26, xvi. 13, 14.   [2] John xvi. 7.

[3] See *International Crit. Comm. on Romans*, by Sanday and Headlam, pp. 199, 200.

[4] 2 Cor. iii. 17.

[5] See Bruce, *Apologetics*, p. 481, note 1 ; *St. Paul's Conception of Christianity*, p. 254.

is also a difference.   Just as for John the promised Spirit is "another" Paraclete,[1] not the Master, who was soon to depart, so Paul never speaks of the Christ who died and rose as the Spirit.   Hence, though it is true that the phrases, " He will come unto you," " I will come unto you," " We will come unto you," are interchangeable, that is not because there is any confusion of persons or functions between the Father, Son, and Spirit, but because the action of the One essentially involves that of the other Two.   All things proceed *from* the Father as the fount of life, *through* the Son, *by* the Spirit.   The Three are one inseparable God ; and the presence of the Spirit is not a substitute for the presence of the Father and the Son, but the assurance and realisation of it.[2]

Thus the doctrine of the Spirit's personality was first attained through the revelation of God in redemption. He who was the Bringer and Interpreter of the personal Christ, and the one organ of carrying on His perpetual work of spiritual renewal, could not be other than a person.   But when Christ was recognised as the eternal Son, by whom the worlds were made, it carried with it the recognition of the Spirit as eternally operating through Him.   Like the Son, He is a universal presence, and, like Him, He attains His full and proper manifestation only in the moral sphere, as specifically the Holy Spirit, the Inspirer of all good in the hearts and consciences of men.   But the knowledge of His personality is only to be reached through the personality of the Son ; and the Son is only known as personal through

---

[1] John xiv. 16.
[2] *Vid.* Gore, *Bampton Lectures*, pp. 132, 133.

His Incarnation.[1] In the case of those who are ignorant of the redemption of Christ, the Spirit cannot be
the medium whereby the Son is revealed, for it is only
by and with the knowledge of the Incarnate life that
the full consciousness of sonship is communicated. None
the less He is the light of their seeing, dim though it
be, just as He cleansed the vision of saints long before
the Son's earthly manifestation. But since that manifestation has taken place, He has now a special and
incomparable gift to confer from Him who is the Lord
and Head of humanity. They who have received this
gift of sonship through the eternal Son interpret by its
light all other revelations of God in the natural and
moral world.

The Trinity is essentially a Christian, not a Jewish,
conception. But it does not follow that no adumbrations of it are to be found in the Old Testament. It
would indeed be an extravagant literalism which interpreted the terms God, Word, and Spirit in the narrative of
the Creation,[2] or the appearances of the mysterious Angel
of the Lord, as signifying in the Christian sense a
distinction of persons in the Godhead. But, figurative

---

[1] This is true of humanity as it is, but not necessarily true on the hypothesis of humanity as unfallen. See *ante*, pp. 188–9.

[2] " God's vital force," says Schultz, in reference to the Creation-narrative,
"which is represented in a concrete way as His breath, proceeds from Him
and becomes the source of created life in whatever it breathes upon. Over
the lifeless and formless mass of the world-matter this spirit broods like a
bird on its nest, and thus transmits to it the seeds of life, so that afterwards,
at the word of God, it can produce whatever God wills. And His word
creates the world—that is, God's inner world of thought becomes, through
His will, the source of life outside of Himself. The Spirit and the Word of
God are represented as forces locked up in God. The Spirit appears as
very independent, just like a hypostasis or person." *O. T. Theology*, vol. ii.
p. 184. On the Jewish conception of God, see *ibid.* pp. 116–179, and
Oehler, *Theology of the Old Testament*, vol. i. pp. 187–196.

as these expressions may be, they at least show that
Hebrew monotheism did not conceive of God as a mere
unit.   The very multiplicity of names and attributes
which it ascribed to Him, while rigidly conserving the
monotheistic idea, implied that His nature could only
be apprehended as that which involved diversity as well
as unity.[1]   The hypostatised form in which the Spirit
is spoken of in Second Isaiah, and the personifications
of Wisdom in Job and Proverbs, point in the same
direction.   These personifications, says Prof. A. B.
Davidson, " mark the highest point to which Hebrew
thought on the world rose." [2]   There is, doubtless, a
danger of our imaginatively reading back Christian truth
into the earlier forms of God's self-revelation ; but, on
the other hand, if God be indeed a Tri-une personality,
surely some suggestion of that fact would not be wholly
absent even from the preparatory stages of His manifestation.   It could not be more than a suggestion, or
faint adumbration ; otherwise, the Trinity would be not
a Christian but a Jewish doctrine.   But just as the
Jewish idea of the Messiah, though it did not regard the
coming deliverer as divine, yet unconsciously attributed
to him functions which only a divine person could
discharge, so the pictorial representations in the Old
Testament of the self-revealing activity of God were
the expression of half-realised needs, only to be fully
met in the historic revelation of the Father in the Son
by the Spirit.

The attempts to vindicate speculatively a triple distinction inherent in the Godhead do not seem to me

[1] *Introduction to the Philosophy of Religion*, by Principal Caird, p. 312.
[2] *Job* (*Cambridge Bible for Schools*), Introduction, p. 62.

14

to have attained much success, suggestive in many ways
as they are.   One can appreciate the argument that,
as all self-consciousness implies a subject and an object,
so God as the eternal Self-consciousness must contain
both factors within Himself, if the object is to be
adequate to the subject.   One can still better appreciate
the argument that, as love implies a giver and receiver,
so God as the eternal Love is both in one—the Father
who is the source of love, and the Son who receives and
returns it.   That God is in Himself a fellowship, that
Sonship in Him is as essential as Fatherhood,—this
commends itself as the one rational interpretation of
the spiritual world.   Speculatively we get a Duality in
the Godhead ; we do not so easily get a Trinity.   The
difficulty lies in the third movement of thought, in which
the Spirit is construed as the unity of subject and object,
of Father and Son, the bond of Love between Them, as
Augustine first expressed it ; and Mr. Illingworth puts
the case very mildly when he says that " a personal
object is easier to imagine than a personal relation." [1]
Probably, however, this is the nearest approach that can
be made to an intellectual rendering of the interior life
of God.   There will always be some who find it helpful
and impressive, though it may be questioned whether it
does not tend to reduce the idea of the Spirit to that
of an impersonal influence.

    Whether such a rendering of the inner life of God
be possible in regard to the Spirit, as it assuredly is in

---

[1] Illingworth, *Personality, Human and Divine*, p. 73.   For Hegel's conception of Trinity as involved essentially in Thought itself—a conception
which has profoundly influenced all subsequent speculation—see his *Philosophy
of Religion* (E.T. by Speirs and Sanderson) : Part III.—The Absolute
Religion.

regard to the Son, is extremely doubtful.   Dr. Fairbairn
states the truth admirably : " While the Son enables us
to understand the being and action of personality *within*
the Godhead, the Spirit enables us to conceive its being
and action *without*." [1]   The Spirit, that is, is to be known
in His working rather than in what He is in Himself.
This is true to the whole Scripture presentation.   Yet
even in His working it is hard, in the *creative and
cosmical* spheres, to distinguish His operation from that
of the Son ; nor is it easy in the *moral* world to
differentiate the illuminating Spirit from the Logos
" that lighteth every man."   It is only when we realise
His function in the order of God's redemptive revelation
of Himself in history that the personality of the Spirit
becomes to us a clear conviction.[2]

[1] *Christ in Modern Theology*, p. 491.
[2] See Note 29, p. 436, " The Personality of God."

LECTURE VI.

THE OBJECTIVE ELEMENT IN THE REDEMPTIVE WORK OF CHRIST.

SYNOPSIS.

I. The two aspects, Objective and Subjective, of the Work of Christ : danger of isolating them.

Their correspondence to the two inseparable Needs of the soul.

Does God's condemnation of sin imply an actual alienation on His part, or only a severance on ours?

Misleading analogies drawn from human propitiation.

II. The Apostles regarded the *Death* of Christ as the Ground of Forgiveness.

Was this due to an Illusion caused by their Jewish training and their specific experience?

The attitude of Christ towards His Death : the effect which its anticipation had upon Him.

The significance of the Last Supper.

Christ's consciousness both individual and representative.

III. His Death the Ground of Forgiveness only as related to—

      (1) His earthly life.

      (2) His risen life.

The order of St. Paul's exposition in *Romans* : Justification and the New Life.

The need of appropriation on our part shows that the Sacrifice of Christ is not a 'quantitative equivalent.'

Dr. Dale's view that there may be saving faith in Christ without conscious recognition of His Death as a propitiation for sins.

LECTURE VI.

The Objective Element in the Redemptive Work of Christ.

When we come to the question of the work of Christ in relation to sin, it is of the first importance that we should not isolate its aspects, as if they had a separate and independent significance. It is because this has been done so frequently that the objective element has awaked such opposition on moral grounds.

I. The purpose of Christ's life and death was to " redeem us from all iniquity, and purify unto Himself a people for His own possession, zealous of good works."[1] It was to regenerate the hearts of men so that they might be in truth what they were ideally meant to be— the children of God; to create in them the filial spirit. Now, it was just this filial spirit He Himself possessed— He alone, as we have seen; and no achievement *for* them would be of any avail unless it were a means to the end, an achievement *in them*, a realisation in their personal nature of the spiritual quality of sonship which belonged to Him. Therefore the problem is, In what sense can it be said that what He did for them, or in their stead, was indispensable to secure for Him the power to be a new life in them?

[1] Tit. ii. 14.

215

First, it is essential to remember that Christ's relation to men is not that of one individual to others, that He is not simply a man, but Man. He bears a universal relationship as the eternal Son, the light that lighteth every man. He is more than a member of the race; He is the one man in its history who chose to be born into it. In His earthly life He spoke of Himself as " the Sent of the Father." That was the natural language of the position in which He then stood. But in His absolute nature His will as Son was one with the will of the Father. He was sent; He also came. And He came into a race, descended into it from above for a purpose which affected the whole of it and every member of it. It was humanity in its solidarity that He entered, and the fact of His tabernacling in flesh did not concern those whom He met in the streets of Jerusalem, or on the hillsides of Galilee, more than the countless multitudes who died before He appeared, or to whom His story is a tradition out of the long past, or who have never heard His name. In the days of His mortal humiliation this was hid from the eyes of others, who saw Him as a single figure among many in His own generation; but it was not hidden from Himself. This universal function lay at the heart of His self-consciousness, and even occasionally found expression in words which could not be fully understood at the time.[1] Just because in His essential being as the Son He bore this transcendent relation to humanity as a whole, He could, as the incarnate Son, take up a position relatively to men, and accomplish a work for them, which none other could do.

[1] See Note 24, p. 416.

Secondly, into this humanity He voluntarily entered in His own proper person, and identified Himself as the Sinless One with the sinful. It was not simply that He appeared in it, He became one with it in order to raise it into its true life of communion with God. That implied more than the fact that being perfectly holy He had to suffer through association with the selfish and unworthy. Suffering indeed is the inevitable experience of all human goodness, environed by evil. It has been, and must be, both as inflicted and as voluntarily undergone, the lot of all prophets and reformers, of every soul that lives for higher ends than its neighbours comprehend. And as Christ's goodness was unspeakably higher than that of the best of men, differing from it not so much in degree as in kind, so His suffering, through intercourse with human wilfulness, misunderstanding, and treachery, infinitely surpassed theirs. But beyond this, and underlying it, was a sorrow in which others could have no share, and which came through His union with humanity as such, and with all who belonged to it. His divine nature enabled Him to identify Himself with them in their sinful state, so that in a very real sense He could act for them, suffer for them, win for them the right to become sons of God. We are apt to speak as if Christ's work were only to *impart* a divine life, but that is to miss the central point, which is that He came *to impart it to those who had a blighted record behind them, and an old and lower life within them.* Before Christ could acquire the power to convey to them the new life, He had to relate Himself to their old and sinful one, to take upon Himself its burden and bear it away. Until He had done this, the blessed spirit of sonship could not be inspired into them: there would still remain the remorse of bitter memories, the consciousness of a gulf separating them from God.   Not only could *they* not have received the new spirit, *He* would not have acquired the right to impart it.   He might as a man have had it Himself, just because personally He was holy; but He could not have made it theirs.   If He were, in a word, to be the head of humanity in its renewed and regenerate state, He must first be its representative in its sinful and alienated condition, so that the same humanity might pass from condemnation and subjection into spiritual peace and power.

It is this objective side of the work of Christ which has roused such antagonism and repudiation.   The fierce denial of it, with which we are familiar, has been caused in part by the arbitrary and one-sided presentation of the atonement, for which many theologians are responsible.   They have spoken at times as if on the mere basis of Christ's sacrifice of Himself our sins are done away, and the guilty are treated as possessing an imputed righteousness, which does not in any actual sense belong to them.   No doubt, when they have proceeded to discuss the proclamation of salvation, and the means whereby the soul is made to be a partaker of Christ's deliverance, they have to some degree supplied the defect; but in expounding the atonement itself they have so isolated it from its inherent and abiding relation to the new life which Christ brings, that they have quite naturally stirred vehement protests against a doctrine which fails to meet the moral needs of men, and which seems even to contravene the dictates of conscience.

When, however, it is viewed in its essential connection with the other and subjective aspect of Christ's work in the soul, instead of being either a superfluity or a contradiction of ethical law, it is seen to be a profound necessity for man's spiritual experience.

What essentially is it that draws a man to Christ, and what is it he finds in Him? He is oppressed by the fact of his own helplessness to rise into a true fellowship with God—oppressed in two ways: both by the thought of an unworthy past which he cannot undo, and by the consciousness of an evil nature within him which he cannot transform, out of which that past has sprung, and which will inevitably work the same woe in the future. There are, therefore, two supreme deliverances which he longs for—pardon and renewal: pardon first, because, till the burden of sin is removed, the spirit cannot attain to perfect peace, nor rise to a hope for nobler life in store; but pardon only as allied to and involved in the reception of the divine power, which can alone guarantee his communion henceforth with God. "According to the multitude of Thy tender mercies blot out my transgressions,"—that is merely the prelude, but the indispensable prelude, to the further appeal: "Create in me a clean heart, O God; and renew a right spirit within me."[1] The former prayer has in reality no meaning apart from the latter. It could not be answered, nor even offered, without it. He whose heart has learned the need of forgiveness has in the very act learned also the need of cleansing. Nothing could be more preposterous than to suppose that God could forgive the misdeeds of any man who

[1] Ps. li. 1, 10.

yet remained of the same temper and attitude toward Himself out of which the misdeeds grew. If there be forgiveness, it must be bound up with a radical change of soul in him to whom it is accorded.   And both these ethical demands are fulfilled in the gift which Christ has secured by His work and conveys by His Spirit. What does the believer find in Christ?   He sees in Him One who, being the Son of God, has identified Himself with humanity and presented to God in its name the offering of a perfect human will, and who, being raised from the dead by the glory of the Father, has all power to confer upon and realise in man His own triumphant life of sonship.   But he sees also that this power was obtained by Christ, not merely by His becoming man, but by His submission to the sorrowful conditions of His intercourse with sinners.   He sees in the suffering of Christ as the incarnate Son something unique and apart from all other suffering of man, because Christ was as man fulfilling a function which none other could discharge, in obtaining for humanity the gift of a new life.   And just as he finds in Christ alone, on the ground of what He was on earth and is now, this new life, this right spirit for which the psalmist prayed, so in Christ alone, on the ground of what He was and suffered, he finds pardon.   The blotting out of his transgressions is as really conditioned by Christ's sacrifice of Himself, as is the communication of the spirit of sonship and his re-established fellowship with the Father.   The guilt which previously oppressed him is not charmed away as an evil dream that Christ has dispelled,—it remains the most awful of realities, and made more real to him by his vision of Christ; but it is no longer his, because he is in Christ, who had to bear the sin of the old nature ere He could mediate the new to mankind.

This sense of guilt as a real thing, and as creating a gulf between the soul and God, sets forth on the subjective side precisely the same fact as the Scriptures portray on the objective or divine side, when they speak of the wrath or condemnation of God directed against sin. " He that believeth not the Son shall not see life, but the wrath of God abideth on him." " There is therefore now no condemnation to them that are in Christ Jesus." [1] These two terms, wrath and condemnation, are practically synonymous; they express the intense antagonism of God to all unrighteousness of men, and the penalty which that antagonism and displeasure will inflict on the impenitent. " God commendeth His love toward us, in that, while we were yet sinners, Christ died for us. Much more then, being now justified by His blood, shall we be saved from wrath through Him," [2] *i.e.* saved from God's final judgment, when His condemnation now resting on sin shall express itself in punishment. What, then, is implied, as regards God Himself, in this condemnation which He passes on sinners? Does it represent an actual alienation on His part, or only a severance on ours? Bishop Westcott says: " Such phrases as ' propitiating God ' and ' God being reconciled ' are foreign to the language of the New Testament. Man is reconciled (2 Cor. v. 18 ff.; Rom. v. 10 f.). There is a propitiation in the matter of the sin or of the sinner. The love of God is the same throughout; but He ' cannot,' in virtue of His very nature, welcome the impenitent and sinful: and more than this, He

---

[1] John iii. 36 ; Rom. viii. 1.   [2] Rom. v. 8, 9.

'cannot' treat sin as if it were not sin. This being so, the ἰλασμός, when it is applied to the sinner, so to speak, neutralises the sin."[1] Now, it is quite true that the New Testament does not speak of the reconciliation of God to man as it speaks of the reconciliation of man to God; but it makes it perfectly plain that there is a barrier on God's side, which prevents the forthgoing of the divine forgiveness towards the sinner, and that that barrier is only removed through the sinner's identification of himself with Him, whom God hath set forth to be a propitiation through faith in His blood.[2] Sin, Paul argues, cannot simply be passed over; it needs a propitiation, in order to show forth and to vindicate the absolute righteousness of God. That righteousness is no abstract law; it is His own character. He had, indeed, passed by sins of former times; but that long forbearance on the part of God had in view this signal exhibition of His righteousness in the gift and death of His Son, whereby He could be at once righteous Himself, and accept as righteous him that hath faith in Jesus. This redemptive process is God's own act. The propitiation which His character demands, it also provides. Nor do the demand and its satisfaction spring from two opposite principles within Him—His justice and His mercy. His love is not something apart from His righteousness, which prevails

---

[1] *Epistles of St. John*, p. 85.

[2] Rom. iii. 24–26. Whether we take ἰλαστήριον as a noun ("a propitiatory victim") or as a neuter adjective, signifying a means of propitiation, the sense remains the same. The old interpretation, which regarded it not as the sin-offering, but (following the Septuagint usage) as the mercy-seat, is now generally given up as alien to Paul's method of thought; *vid.* Bruce, *St. Paul's Conception of Christianity*, p. 168. But, even on this rendering, the fundamental idea which underlies the word must be that of propitiation. *International Crit. Comm. on Romans*, p. 91.

upon it to assume a new attitude towards men : it is but
one manifestation of it—the form which it takes in order
to fulfil itself in God's relation to a sinful humanity.   As
Dr. Sanday well expresses it : " That which seems to us,
and which really is an act of mercy, is the direct outcome
of the ' righteousness,' which is a wider and more
adequate name than justice.   It is the essential righteousness of God which impels Him to set in motion that
sequence of events in the sphere above and in the sphere
below which leads to the free forgiveness of the believer,
and starts him on his way with a clean page to his
record." [1]   Yet this propitiation only avails for the
sinner through his faith, which makes it his own before
God.   It is obvious, then, how profoundly spiritual is
the entire idea of reconciliation which the apostle here
expounds.

The same idea is contained in 2 Cor. v. 14 ff.: " The
love of Christ constraineth us ; because we have formed
this judgment, One died for all, therefore all died ; and
He died for all, that they which live should no longer
live unto themselves, but unto Him who died for them
and rose again."   Much has been made of the fact that
the word translated " for " is ὑπέρ, on behalf of, not
ἀντί, instead of.   And certainly these words express no
mere substitution of Christ for us ; for the real value of
that death depends on the way in which men relate
themselves to it, by reckoning it as their own, and living
no longer unto themselves, but unto Him that died for
them and rose again.   But the entire argument of the
passage implies that the death of Christ has in itself an
objective power as regards man's redemption : " God was

[1] *International Crit. Comm. on Romans*, p. 91.

in Christ reconciling the world unto Himself." That
reconciliation is in a deep sense an accomplished fact ;
not on the human side, however, for the apostle proceeds :
" We beseech you on behalf of Christ, be ye reconciled
to God." [1]   Notwithstanding the death of Christ for us,
the antagonism of man towards God remains, until he
personally surrenders himself to the Risen One, in whose
death he is dead to sin, in whose life he lives to righteousness.   Hence the reconciliation of the world to
Himself, which God has already wrought out in Christ,
can refer to nothing but God's own attitude towards
the world—an attitude rendered possible only by the
taking away of that which prevented His full fatherly
relation to mankind ; [2] and it is on the ground of this
divine reconciliation that Paul pleads for the responsive
change in men.   But to speak thus is wholly to mis-
represent Paul's thought, if we do not remember that it
is God Himself who is the author of the reconciliation.
This is doubtless the reason why the New Testament
always speaks of a propitiation for sins, never of a propitiation offered to God, because that would convey the
false and debasing idea that He had been reluctantly
won to mercy.   It is the mercy that is the source of the
propitiation, not the propitiation of the mercy.   When
we realise this we see at once how inadequate the term
propitiation is, with its suggestion of external relations.
It may easily be abused.   It does *not* mean that God
is persuaded to gracious thoughts towards sinners by
the sacrifice which Another offers to Him.   It does *not*

---

[1] Vers. 18, 20.

[2] On the relation of Fatherhood to Atonement, see Dr. T. J. Crawford's
Fatherhood of God, pp. 66–75.

mean that His condemnation of them is removed by simple virtue of that sacrifice, and apart from their appropriation of it.   It *does* mean that God's condemnation of a sinful race is expressed in the death of Christ, who died and rose again as its representative, so that the riches of God's fatherly heart might through Him descend upon it in forgiveness and renewal.

Our whole conception of this reconciliation becomes vitiated if we lose sight of the fact that this propitiation has its motive and origin in God Himself.   But this is just what is too apt to happen when we strive to interpret it by detailed analogies drawn from human experience.   Few who have written on the atonement have been more keenly aware than Dr. Mozley of the transcendent and mysterious element in it, or have shown more forcibly the necessity of viewing the doctrine in its proper setting, as one factor in God's redemption of men.[1]   Yet, in endeavouring to bring out the rational, moral value before God of Christ's sacrifice on our behalf, he writes thus: "Its effect proceeds, not from the substitution of one person for another in punishment, but from the influence of one person upon another for mercy—a mediator upon one who is mediated with.   Let us see what it is which a man really means when he offers to substitute himself for another in undergoing punishment. He cannot possibly mean to fulfil the element of justice literally.   What he wants to do is to stimulate the element of mercy in the judge. . . . How is this mercy to be

---

[1] Nothing, *e.g.*, could be finer or truer than this: "Justice is a fragment, mercy is a fragment, mediation is a fragment; justice, mercy, mediation as a reason of mercy—all three ; what, indeed, are they but great vistas and openings into an invisible world in which is the point of view which brings them all together ?"—*University Sermons*, p. 177.

15

gained, enlisted on the side you want? By suffering
yourself. You thereby soften the heart of the judge.
The judge only accepts the act as a stimulant to mercy.
. . . Let anyone have exposed himself to the appetite
for punishment in our nature," *i.e.* the appetite which is
the characteristic of justice in relation to evil, " and it is
undoubtedly the case, however we may account for it,
that the real suffering of another for him, of a good
person for a guilty one, will mollify the appetite for
punishment which was possibly up to that time in full
possession of our minds; and this kind of satisfaction to
justice and appeasing of it is involved in the Scriptural
doctrine of the Atonement." [1]

It seems to me extremely doubtful whether this *is*
involved in the atonement, and assuredly whatever element of truth it contains is more than nullified by the
false suggestions which Dr. Mozley's illustration inevitably conveys. Nothing could be more misleading than
to talk of Christ's sacrifice producing any such effect
upon God as is implied in the terms, " stimulating the
element of mercy " or " softening the heart of the judge."
That sacrifice is the *product* of God's love, not its *creator* ;
it is love's expression, the means by which the divine
love secures a place for itself within a sinful humanity,
and the power of reconciling and renewing it. True,
Christ is a mediator between God and us, but not in the
sense of prevailing upon the Father to treat us otherwise
than He desires to do. He is mediator, because the work
of redemption could only be carried through *in humanity* ;
that is, by One who shared the nature of those whom it
was the Father's purpose to save. All that He endured

[1] Mozley, *University Sermons*, pp. 168, 169, 175.

for us He endured according to the Father's will, who
" so loved the world that He gave His only begotten
Son." Nay, though Christ is mediator, His work as
such is not that of a third person interceding with an
unwilling or unconcerned judge for a guilty mankind; it
is the work, achieved in the sphere of humanity, of the
Son who is eternally one with the Father in the unity of
the Godhead, and who, " in submitting to Another, sub-
mits also to Himself." Therefore the divine love not
only provides the sacrifice, but actually offers it. From
first to last it is the act of God's free grace. And, finally,
the relation in which Christ stands to men is no such
incidental one as that between the voluntary sufferer and
the criminal. All such examples fail, because the essential point is left out—the identification of Christ with the
whole race. He who died for men is He through whom
they and all created things have had their being, and
who, as incarnate, can, because of His connection with
organic humanity, rightly act as its representative. Only
One who as divine has the power to impart to human
souls a renewed life, could suffer in their name God's
condemnation of their sin. It is Christ's oneness with
the race, the universality of His humanity, which makes
possible both the tasting of death for them and the
mediating of life to them. To this oneness with those
for whom He suffers, there is and can be in the moral
relations of men to each other no parallel. He can be
to all of them what none of them can be to another.
There are many aspects of the sacrifice of Christ, and
these of essential moment, which find their interpretation
in human self-sacrifice. To show how it is correlated to
the deepest facts of our daily life and our spiritual expe-

rience is an immense service.   But on the objective side
that sacrifice is unique, because He is unique; and human
illustrations of it import an externality into a relation
which is supremely spiritual, and too often but darken
and perplex the truth they are intended to illuminate.

II. The unanimous testimony of the apostles is, that
the sacrifice of Christ as the ground of our forgiveness
centres itself in His death.   It is needless to quote passages.   This idea is fundamental and pervasive.   We
have not only the direct witness of the apostles Peter
and John, and of the author of " Hebrews," who, though
not an apostle, was an apostolic man and reflected the
view of the apostolic circle;[1] but we have, above all, the
distinct declaration of Paul, who has so emphasised and
elaborated this thought that it is supposed by many
to be his peculiar creation, that on this point he was but
repeating and unfolding the faith of the first disciples
and of the whole Church.[2]

---

[1] 1 Pet. ii. 20-24, iii. 18; cf. i. 18, 19: 1 John i. 7; cf. ii. 2, iv. 10:
Heb. ix. 12, 26.   The importance of this conception for the writers of the
Epistles is not to be measured by the number of times in which it is directly
stated, but by the fact that it forms the presupposition on which they argue and
appeal, and that its displacement would destroy the unity and coherence of
their teaching.   An Epistle was addressed to those who already accepted the
central verities of the faith, and who in their Christian assemblies were perpetually hearing them rehearsed and expounded.   Consequently, it often
dwells far more on the implications of Christian doctrine for belief or practice than on the doctrine itself.   Some have contended that, because Peter
and John (1 Pet. ii. 20–24, iii. 17, 18; 1 John iii. 16) introduce references
to Christ's death in connection with the duty incumbent upon all of patient
endurance and self-sacrifice, they mean to represent it only as the supreme
example of the same spirit.   But the whole context, and sometimes the very
words employed to describe Christ's death, show that they do not appeal to
it simply as an example, but as a *unique motive*, as an act which is fitted to
inspire human self-sacrifice, just because it so utterly transcends it and supplies it with a pledge of victory.   See Dale, *Atonement*, chaps. iv. and v.

[2] 1 Cor. xv. 3, 11.

There are not a few who regard the association of
Christ's atonement specially with His death as due to a
certain illusion or blurring of perspective, natural to
the apostles on account of their individual experience
and their Jewish traditions.   The illusion, it is said, is
easily explained.   The disciples were possessed from the
first by the prevalent conception of a kingly and triumphant Messiah.   The obstinacy with which they clung
to this, and the persistence with which Jesus strove to
undermine it, form one of the tragic and pathetic
elements in the Gospel story.   They lived in a constant
state of mingled expectation and perplexity.   Disap-
pointed in their hopes at every turn, they yet became
more deeply persuaded, as the months wore on, that He
whose conduct so tried their faith was indeed the promised Messiah.   But they could attach no meaning
to His most solemn allusions to His coming death.
Till the end, even when all seemed lost, they appear to
have been buoyed up by a half-conscious feeling that,
somehow, the problem would yet be solved in their way.
Then came the final disaster, obvious to all—shameful,
irreversible.   They were broken men; the past lay in
ruins.   The " longing, lingering look behind," to which
the two disciples on the way to Emmaus gave expression, was all that remained to them of that unforgetable
time : " We trusted it had been He."   Then suddenly
the great transformation.   He stood before them—Himself, not another—with the marks of that awful Cross
upon Him still, but changed, victorious.   God had vindicated Him.   His resurrection, His ascension, proved
that He *was* God's Messiah, after all.   But their old idea
of the Messiah was gone.   It might have survived His

lowly life, His poverty, His homelessness, even the despite
with which men treated Him: He might have passed
through all these, and yet triumphed.   But one thing
they could not get over—*the Cross.*   Their old hope
was buried in His grave.   It rose purified, spiritualised.
But what could they say of that death by crucifixion, so
degrading in the eyes of men, so peculiarly hateful to
Jews, and only inflicted even by Gentiles on slaves and
the lowest criminals?   There it stood, barring the way
to the acceptance of Jesus' Messiahship, the one great
σκάνδαλον [1] to Jewish hearts.   But God's verdict was
just the opposite of man's.   "This Jesus, whom *ye*
crucified, whom *God* raised." [2]   The resurrection did not
come in spite of the crucifixion, but because of it.   In
the very awfulness and shamefulness of the death consisted its eternal power and value.   Nay, had not Jesus,
when He appeared to the disciples, showed them His
pierced hands and feet, glorying in the στίγματα which
man thought of with contempt?   They felt that here
lay the key of the Messianic deliverance.   The great
"scandal" became the great "mystery," the great secret
of rejoicing.

   But this concentration of their thought on the dying
Christ was, it is argued, very much the result of a
reaction from their previous condition of mind.   Just
because they could not bear to think of death as associated with the Messiah, they came to make too much of
it when it *had* to be taken into account, with all the
attendant horrors of a criminal execution upon a cross.
It lost its proper place in relation to Christ's life, and
stood out very much as a sheer, isolated fact, which they

---

[1] 1 Cor. i. 23.   [2] Acts iv. 10.

interpreted too exclusively by ideas drawn from the
sacrificial usages of the Jewish ritual.   But Christ's
whole work as Redeemer was of a piece.   As we cannot
separate His divine from His human nature, and say,
" This He did as man, this as the Son of God," so we
cannot separate His death from His life, and say that
His life was a revelation of the love and pity of the
Father, and His death alone the ground of forgiveness
and remission of sin.   Both have to be taken together,
and every blessing of His salvation is related to both.
His work from first to last has an objective meaning for
our pardon and renewal.   In Him alone we have life
eternal; but that life could not have been His to
impart had He not passed through a complete human
life, and identified Himself with humanity, enduring as
the Sinless One the condemnation of its sinfulness, alike
in His daily fellowship with sinners as in the bitterness
of death inflicted by their hands.   It was through His
whole humiliation that He redeemed us, not by His
Incarnation merely, but by His Incarnation into a sinful
race as born of a woman, made under the law, in the
likeness of sinful flesh, and subject in His earthly experience to all that " is unblessed in man's unredeemed
state."   Neither His life nor His death was like that of
other men.   The fact that the New Testament does not
connect Christ's endurance of hunger, thirst, weariness,
or poverty, or any of the sufferings of His ministry, with
the remission of sins,[1] as it connects His actual death, is,
we are told, partly to be accounted for by the natural
one-sidedness of view into which the apostles fell; but
it is also the safeguarding of the great truth that the

[1] See Dale, *Atonement*, p. 69.

work of Christ in redemption had no validity till it was
finished, that only in death was that life of sacrifice
completed, and only through death could it triumph and
communicate its pardoning and renewing power.   Still
further, it was in His death that the pressure of sin bore
upon Him with its full weight.   That burden was borne
by Him through all His intercourse with men ; in His
intense sympathy with the suffering and diseased, so
that, in every cure He wrought, virtue went out of Him ;
in the pain that He felt at the malice and antagonism
which His goodness awaked, and the utter shame of
which in humanity only He, the Son of Man, could feel.
But every element of sorrow was gathered up and intensified in the Cross—hate, treachery, desertion ; and in
that unspeakable loneliness the Sinless made Himself
one with the sinful in the utmost agony of death, as He
had already made their suffering life His own.   So,
having become one with them in their condemnation,
He acquired the right to make them one with Him in
His triumph, to deliver them from the curse and the
bondage of sin, and impart to them the glorious liberty
of the children of God.

That there is much truth in this insistence, as
regards the atonement, on the connection between the
life and the death of Jesus, we shall see later.   But the
great objection to this interpretation is, that it does not
do justice to the words and attitude of Christ Himself.
If one carefully examines the chronology of the Gospels,
he will probably be surprised to find how frequently
during the last six months Christ refers to His death.
It is no sufficient explanation to say that He was
endeavouring to correct the misapprehensions of the

disciples, and to dispel their hopes of an earthly Messianic kingdom.   His language had no such effect, and,
we may say, could not have it.   Not merely did it
appear to them the flattest contradiction of what they
already believed regarding Him, but it did not correspond with other facts which He was always insisting
on.   For, as we have seen in a previous Lecture,[1] He
did not speak of His death in the tone of one who
viewed it as a mere disaster and separation.   At every
step He seemed to bind them faster to Himself, and to
impress upon them that their union with Him would be
continuous and abiding.   This was not only involved in
His declaration that the death would be followed by a
resurrection; it was the underlying spirit of all His
teaching as to His personal indispensableness for the
realisation of the new kingdom.   His words neither
helped to prepare them for the catastrophe, nor saved
them from panic when the blow fell.   Why, then, did
He persist in His prophecy?   Not for any purpose
which could be fulfilled before the resurrection, but to
lead their minds back, when His triumph over death was
accomplished, to the paramount significance of that
death, to the emphasis *which He Himself placed upon it*
in the achievement of redemption.

   And this view is corroborated by the *effect* which the
anticipation of the death had upon Himself.   There are
no passages in the Gospels which bear a stronger stamp
of genuineness than those which relate His prophecies
of the end.   Had the disciples been fancifully reading
back from the lessons of subsequent events, they might
have attributed to Christ some sayings about His death,

[1] Lect. III. pp. 132-4.

but they would not have dwelt on their own blindness to
His meaning at the time.   Yet that is the contrast that
pervades the entire record, and it has verisimilitude on
the face of it—the contrast between Christ's view and
theirs, *their* sheer inability to attach any real thought to
what not only absorbed but oppressed *Him*.   It hung
over His spirit like a great cloud of sorrow.   He had
foreseen it from the beginning;[1] but it is notable that
the first plain intimation of it to the Twelve followed
immediately upon the confession of His Messiahship,[2] as
if He must make the announcement at the earliest
possible moment, in order that they might realise afterwards that His coming greatness and glory were never
dissociated in His mind from the mysterious efficacy of
His death, and that His acknowledgment of the former
involved the latter.   And the stern impatience with
which He rebuked Peter showed how intolerable it was
to Him that anyone should even unwittingly disparage
the dread necessity.   At times the thought so burdened
Him that, as He journeyed, it quickened His steps, and
withdrew Him from the disciples in a depressed self-
communing.   " He went before them, and they that
followed were afraid."[3]   They were overawed by His
ominous self-absorption.   At last He turned to speak:
it was of the one great ordeal through which He must
pass.   When on the Tuesday before the crucifixion He
cried, " Now is My soul troubled, and what shall I
say?   Father, save Me from this hour.   But for this
cause came I unto this hour,"[4] He was but repeating

---

[1] See *ante*, pp. 99-106.
[2] Matt. xvi. 13-28 ; Mark viii. 27-38 ; Luke ix. 18-27.
[3] Mark x. 32 (R.V.).   [4] John xii. 27.

what He had said months before: "I have a baptism to be baptized with, and how am I straitened till it be accomplished!"[1] In both cases there is visible the same strange dread of a fate which yet He welcomed as necessary—the same longing, so natural and human, that the dark and inevitable hour were over. It was His foretaste of the Agony.

Nothing could be more hopelessly blind and banal than the notion that the horror which smote Christ's spirit in Gethsemane sprang from the thought of the physical torture of the Cross. Picture that torture in its extremest form,—the thirst, the fever of the blood, the throbbing pain: does that in the remotest degree help us to understand the scene in the Garden? He was astounded, struck with terror:[2] "My soul is exceeding sorrowful, even unto death." Then the reiterated pleading, the wrestling, the half-despair. They who suppose that Christ's being was thus terror-stricken, shaken to its centre, by the anticipation of any physical suffering, attribute to Him a fatal unmanliness. He could not be the Lord of martyr souls if His own heart quailed under a trial not heavier than theirs. The whole

---

[1] Luke xii. 50.

[2] Mark xiv. 33. The word ἐκθαμβεῖσθαι (especially here, where it is conjoined with ἀδημονεῖν) conveys the idea of amazement culminating in consternation (see Morison, *Comm. on St. Mark*, p. 399). The same thought is contained in the word ἀγωνία (γενόμενος ἐν ἀγωνίᾳ ἐκτενέστερον προσηύχετο, Luke xxii. 44). The meaning is not, "intense or vehement prayer," but "deadly horror," *i.e.* being in a deadly fear, He prayed the more earnestly. It is to be noted, however, that the genuineness of this passage in Luke is doubted. Westcott and Hort regard it as a "precious fragment"—inserted by a scribe of the second century—of the evangelic tradition locally current beside the canonical Gospels. In that case, its historical value is quite as high as if it formed part of the original text. Cf. Godet, *St. Luke, in loc.*

story of the Passion, even if it stood alone, is a protest
against such a view. But it does not stand alone: the
Agony is but the climax of the oppression which had
again and again descended upon Him. Will anyone
say that He was brooding during all these months
on the bodily tortures before Him? It was the
same vision throughout that darkened His spirit—
that death which held in Christ's thought, as in
that of the apostles, a unique place in the work of
redemption.

Nor can there be any doubt that the institution of
the Holy Supper, and the words used by Jesus when He
gave the Sacramental cup, teach the saving efficacy of
His death. Clouds of controversy have failed to obscure
the salient facts. The omission of the clause " unto
the remission of sins " from all the accounts except
Matthew's,[1] even from that of Paul, who certainly might
be supposed to have every reason for inserting it, unquestionably throws a suspicion on its historic accuracy.
But the idea it conveys is really covered by the well-
attested phrase in which Christ speaks of His blood as
shed for others, and shed for them as the source and
ground of a covenant. This covenant can be none
other than the new one referred to by Jeremiah,[2] which
contained the blessings of inward cleansing and full
forgiveness; and the blood in which it is founded is of
necessity sacrificial blood.[3] The two thoughts suggested
by the Covenant and the Paschal Lamb together imply
the truth which Matthew's account formally expresses.[4]

[1] Matt. xxvi. 28.   [2] Jer. xxxi. 31.
[3] Cf. Meyer, *St. Matthew, in loc.*
[4] *Vid.* Bruce, *Kingdom of God*, pp. 246–248.

No other interpretation than this could be rationally assigned to the Holy Supper by the apostles. Christ had taught them that He had come, not to destroy but to fulfil the Jewish law, that every detail of it had a spiritual truth which would abide. How could they help believing that the ritual of sacrifice would find a fulfilment, and that that fulfilment took place in the shedding of His own blood? If He did not mean them to draw this inference, then it must be said that He Himself was largely responsible for the misconception.

I am not inclined to place much emphasis on the possibility of instructions given by Him during the forty days after His resurrection.[1] If, as the risen One, He expounded to the apostles the full significance of His death, it is strange that they did not afterwards record His words as the final authority for their special interpretation. And it is at least worthy of note that there were great questions, such as the bearing of His redemption on the Gentile nations, and the anticipation of the end of the world as near at hand, on which we might have expected Him to pronounce beyond the possibility of mistake, yet for the solution of which He largely left them to the teaching of experience under the guidance of the Spirit.[2] It is not by resorting to these precarious suppositions, but by making clear to ourselves the indubitable facts, in Christ's own attitude towards His death, and the horror with which its anticipation filled Him, and in the observance of a service[3] which inevitably gave to it a supreme and sacrificial worth, that

---

[1] See Note 21, p. 412.   [2] See Note 24, p. 416.

[3] On the perpetuity of the Supper as an institution, *vid. ante*, p. 58, *n.*

we shall find the adequate vindication of the apostolic testimony.

God's condemnation of sin, which fell upon Christ on the Cross, consisted in this, that He died a death which was not His own, and which yet in a sense He made His own by His voluntary identification of Himself with sinners ; so that, though conscious of His own sinlessness, He suffered as their representative the penalty of God's displeasure at human sin, and acknowledged it to be just. Some object to this view, on the ground that it attributes to Christ a double consciousness : that which He had in His own proper personality as the Son of God in flesh, and that which He had as the representative of mankind. But it is precisely this double consciousness which is the essence of the sacrifice. It was the offering of One who, though sinless, suffered in the place of the sinful. Just because there lay deep in the heart of Christ through all the dreadful ordeal of the Cross the sense of His personal sinlessness, we are able to say, in the full sense of the words, that He " through the eternal Spirit *offered Himself without spot* to God." [1]   The obliteration of His individual self-consciousness, the idea that He regarded Himself as the object of the Father's anger on the ground of sins which yet He had never committed, and whose punishment He was only enduring that He might bear it away, is not merely in itself inconceivable and monstrous, but it impairs the whole character of the atonement which He made. On the other hand, His consciousness of identification with a sinful humanity, and of the condemnation of God resting upon Him as its representative, was just as real. It has been argued that,

[1] Heb. ix. 14.

so long as we maintain Christ's personal consciousness of perfect obedience to God, this condemnation was only the vivid mental realisation of God's wrath against sin to which Christ inwardly responded, not the actual experience of it. It *was* the experience of the divine displeasure towards a race of which He had freely chosen to become one. We have need to take heed when we talk of the pain arising from the sympathy that makes another's woe its own, as if it were but a sentimental feeling.[1] It is a real anguish; and, in Christ's case, not only is this sympathy carried out to its last intensity, but there is more than sympathy,—there is a oneness of life with men, in virtue of His Incarnation, which has no parallel in human experience. What awful agony this implied when He submitted to a death which was not His own, but the death of sinners with the sting of sin in it, it is not possible for us to imagine. To say that He died our death is a permissible expression, but it is not Scriptural; and it may fatally mislead. The death which is due to the sinner is abiding separation from God. That death He did not die, but averted from us. To attempt to find in His death for us some exact equivalent to the condemnation from which He redeems the sinner, is to de-spiritualise His sacrifice. It is doubtful whether this tendency has not led to a forced interpretation of the cry of desolation: "My God, My God, why hast Thou forsaken Me?"[2] No explanation of it, indeed, will ever suffice which attributes it merely to the obscuring of His spiritual vision through the

[1] Cf. Prof. Orr's criticism of Dr. Macleod Campbell, *Christian View of God and the World*, p. 360.

[2] Matt. xxvii. 46; Mark xv. 34.

extreme tension of His physical and mental suffering, and which does not connect it with His identification of Himself with sinners in their condemnation.[1]   It is *there* that the secret lay of this, as of the whole tragedy of the Cross.   But, whatever else that cry meant for Him, it certainly had for one of its elements, as Canon Gore has said, " the trial of the *righteous* man forsaken.[2]   The desolation, the loss of the sense of God's gracious presence, though He bowed to it as a just judgment on human sin, was to Him unspeakably awful, just because He retained His own integrity, His yearning for God's fellowship.   And this yearning for God, " *My* God," is exactly what could not exist in the case of the sinner suffering death as the wages of sin.   So impossible is it for us to find any human equation for the experience through which Christ passed when He " tasted death for every man." [3]

III. But while Christ's death possesses this central significance as the ground of our forgiveness, yet it possesses it only because of its relation to His life. Nothing can be more fatal, or more contrary to the spirit of the New Testament, than to ascribe this virtue to it as an isolated event, and to assign to His ministry a merely preparatory and subordinate place.   It is no more true to say that He came into the world to *die*, than that He came into the world to *live*.   The former statement is destitute of spiritual meaning, unless read in the full light of what is involved in the latter. The purpose of His Incarnation was to introduce into

[1] Cf. Dale, *Atonement*, pp. 60–62, 470–474, and Preface to 7th ed., pp. 40–44.

[2] *Bampton Lectures*, pp. 148, 149.

[3] See Note 30, p. 439.

the race a new life of sonship to the Father; and this
voluntary spirit He had first to realise in His own person,
through all the stages of a complete human experience
from birth to death.   His absolute submission to the
will of God in the lot appointed to Him, in His childhood, in the daily toil of His silent years in Nazareth, in
the trials of His public ministry, was the indispensable
foundation of His final sacrifice: it was, so to speak, the
acquiring of that life which for our sakes He laid down.
His death came to Him, as Ritschl puts it, in the fulfilment of His vocation; it befell Him in His conflict with
the world's evil.   In the New Testament it is never
spoken of as God's act.   It is man's: "Whom ye crucified, whom God raised up."[1]   The Father's love is
shown in delivering up His Son for our salvation; and
the working out of that salvation involved Christ's death,
not as the direct visitation of God, but as the inevitable
result of the human sin that surrounded Him.   Yet it
was not simply inflicted; it was voluntarily undergone
and accepted as an inherent part of the unique vocation
to which God called Him, and which He had Himself
chosen.   He lived out His stainless life of humanity as
our representative before the Father, and though as a
consequence He was "by lawless hands crucified and
slain," yet none the less no man took His life from Him:
He laid it down of Himself.   For the work which He
had freely undertaken included this as a condition of its
fulfilment.

   And just as necessary as the relation in which
Christ's death stands to His life is its connection with

---

[1] Acts ii. 22–24.   Cf. Gore, *Bampton Lectures*, p. 127, and p. 261,
Note 37.

His resurrection: 'I have power to lay down My life, and I have power to take it again." [1]   The surrender and the resumption are inseparable parts of the one act of redemption, of the one "commandment which He received" from His Father.   It was by His identification of Himself with us in the sacrifice of the Cross that He acquired the right to take His life again, not simply as His own, but as the mediator of it to the sinful, as the first-born among many brethren.   Therefore, while His death is the ground of the remission of sins, it is so not in itself merely, but as the death of Him who is now the living One, "who was dead and is alive for evermore."   If Paul determined to know nothing among the Corinthian disciples "save Jesus Christ and Him crucified," [2] that was not because the Cross constituted the whole Gospel, but because it was the central mystery and glory of the Gospel; and because only One, who by His humiliation and death had taken upon Himself man's burden, could be God's Messiah to deliver and renew him.   A dead Christ would have been no Christ at all.   He redeems us not simply by the act of His death, but by His person, by His total work. [3]   Hence Paul, in speaking of the justifying faith of Abraham, declares, "It was reckoned unto him for righteousness. Now it was not written for his sake alone that it was reckoned unto him, but for our sake also, unto whom it shall be reckoned, who believe on Him that raised Jesus our Lord from the dead, who was delivered up for our trespasses, and was raised for our justification." [4]   The

---

[1] John x. 18.   [2] 1 Cor. ii. 2.
[3] See Sanday and Headlam, *Internat. Crit. Comm. on Romans*, p. 117.
[4] Rom. iv. 22–25.

emphasis here laid on the resurrection of Christ implies
far more than that it is the ground of our faith in the
atoning character of His death.   In that case it would
have a significance merely for *us*, as the proof that the
death had an availing power to justify us.   It has a
meaning relatively to Christ Himself and the efficacy of
His sacrifice on the Cross.   Without the resurrection He
would not have taken the complete manhood into God,
and therefore would have been unable to be the " quickening spirit" and head of the new humanity.   But if
He had no new life to impart, He could have no pardon
to bestow.   Hence there are passages, like that which has
been quoted, in which Paul puts the resurrection even
before the death of Christ as the cause of justification.[1]
This variety in the apostle's expression is a proof how
little he is bound even to what may be regarded as his
own formulæ, how inevitably he keeps himself true to
the facts of redemption as a whole.   Christ's death is, in
truth, but one stage in a process.   It is embedded in
the life, the earthly life before it, the risen and ascended
life after it ; and he who forgets this, and divides up the
essential unity,[2] assigning to each part its separate virtue,
will only fall into a pedantic scholasticism.

When Dr. Dale says, " That the remission of sins, if

---

[1] Rom. vi. 9, 10, viii. 34.   This point is emphasised by Schäder, *Die
Bedeutung des lebendigen Christus für die Rechtfertigung nach Paulus*.   See
the reference in Sanday and Headlam, *l.c.*

[2] This unity is expressed by Dr. Hort's pregnant aphorism, 'at which
many will start': " Reconciliation or atonement is one aspect of redemption,
and redemption one aspect of resurrection, and resurrection one aspect of
life" (*Hulsean Lectures*, p. 210).   Dr. Sanday's comment may be added
(*Romans*, p. 118): " All definitions of great doctrines have a relative rather
than an absolute value.   They are partial symbols of ideas which the human
mind cannot grasp in their entirety.   If we could see as God sees, we should
doubtless find them running up into large and broad laws of His working."

it stood alone, would leave us unsaved, is one of the commonplaces of Christian theology; but it does not follow that the remission of sins includes the blessings which are necessary to complete our salvation,"[1] he is putting a purely abstract hypothesis. He himself admits that forgiveness and the new life always go together, but he insists that they are two things, and not one. They are two only as the sides of a shield are two, but you cannot have the one without the other; and the mere suggestion of what would result if pardon stood alone, indisputably leads to misconception. It conveys the impression that a sinner is first forgiven because of the attitude he takes to Christ's death, and only after that becomes related to Christ's quickening life. Some maintain, indeed, that this is exactly Paul's argument in Romans,[2] where he does not take up the function of faith in establishing a vital union with Christ in sanctification till he has completed his exposition of justification as based wholly on the objective merits of Christ, and apart from human merit. They say that the supposed objection to his own teaching, which he starts, " Shall we continue in sin that grace may abound ? " shows that he represents God as justifying us solely through our faith in the atoning work of Christ, without reference to our future renewal. But if this bare formal acceptance of Christ's work for us were all that Paul intended, it would have been impossible for him to reply as he does to the objector : " We who died to sin," he exclaims in horror, " how shall we any longer live therein ? " By the very act that led to our justification we were baptized into Christ's death, that as He

[1] *Atonement*, p. 336.   [2] Chap. vi.

was raised from the dead by the glory of the Father, so
we also might walk in newness of life.[1]   But if this
moral identification of our life with Christ's is involved
in our act of justifying faith, then the latter becomes not
formal acquiescence, but real surrender.   Were it not so,
the two sides of our spiritual relation to Christ, our
justification and sanctification, would fall apart.   The
personal acceptance of Him would be a totally different
thing in the two cases.   But Paul's system is not a confused dualism.

It is not difficult to see why, in building up his philosophy of redemption, he deals first and almost exclusively
with justification.   He is striving, above all, to make clear
the *objective* ground of salvation, to show that in no sense
is the work or conduct of the Christian an element in
what constitutes his reconciliation to God.   Until this is
acknowledged, all the falsities of legalism will but repeat
themselves.   If we were only justified so far as we were
sanctified, no man could be at peace.   The whole effort
of the Christian soul would be a struggle after an endless
and impossible ideal.   But " being justified by faith,"
says the apostle, " let us enter into full possession of that
state of peace with God which we owe to our Lord Jesus
Christ."   This consciousness of present reconciliation is
fundamental.   It is the condition, as it is the inspiration,
of the " new walk " in righteousness.[2]   Had Paul gone

---

[1] Rom. vi. 2-4.   The root-idea of these verses is that baptism into
Christ is *incorporation* into Him, into a Personality who passed through both
death and resurrection, and that therefore we cannot be identified with the
one without the other.   " The idea of sacrifice which was applied to the
death of Christ was not completed in the idea of death, but held within it in
the notion of life liberated and availing."—T. B. Strong, *Manual of Theology*,
p. 304.

[2] Cf. T. H. Green, *Miscellaneous Works*, vol. iii. p. 200.

on, before he had fully established this fact, to speak of
what is implied in it as regards our relation to God in
consecrated living, he would have run the risk of obscuring the objective ground of our acceptance.   For though
Christ is made unto us sanctification as well as justifying
righteousness, and therefore in reality our good works,
being the fruit of His grace within us, constitute no claim
of merit before God, yet in the realisation of personal
holiness there is a blending of the human activity with
the divine; and it might have been falsely inferred that
the human contributed something towards creating the
ground of pardon.   The apostle renders such a supposition impossible by completing his argument regarding
the justification of the soul, before he proceeds to unfold
what is involved in the relation to Christ, which the soul
has taken up through faith.   But the order of his exposition does not alter the fact that the new life, whose
nature he explains in chaps. vi.–viii., is not an external
addition to the faith that justifies; it is inherently bound
up with it.[1]   We are justified solely on account of what
Christ is and has done; but the faith that accepts Him,
that sees in His death the atonement for human sin, and
identifies itself with that death, is in its essence an act
of self-committal to the living Christ, and a reception of
His Spirit.   If it be not this, it brings neither life nor
forgiveness; if it brings either, it brings both: and the
ground of both is objective, the work and the person of
Christ.

The fact that appropriation on our part is necessary,
proves that the death of Christ for us is no mere substi-
tutionary *quid pro quo*; otherwise, it would be in itself

---

[1] See Note 31, 440, "*Justitia imputata* and *Justitia infusa.*"

objectively valid, and secure a universal pardon. If
Christ has paid your debt and mine, apart from our individual relation to Him, then, so far as guilt is concerned,
we should already have our discharge, and only the
spiritual quickening which He alone can communicate
would depend on the response of faith. But as this
response is the condition of the pardon as well as the
quickening, Christ's whole redemption is an ideal one,
which faith transmutes into an actuality. If He were
the propitiation for the sins of the whole world in the
sense of enduring the quantitative equivalent of the
penalty of every man's transgressions, then, in the case
of every unbeliever whose sin remaineth on him, Christ's
endurance of the penalty was an overpayment of the
debt. Christ did not, in His death for us, suffer so much
for each man born into the world, so that had there been
fewer men He would have suffered less. He atoned for
the *sin of the race*, because, by identifying Himself with
humanity, He had to bear God's condemnation of its sin
ere He could impart to it the spirit of sonship. In Him
alone resides the power to confer both blessings on men,—
they are already present in Him for all mankind; but
as regards the individual, they only become an actual
possession through his receptivity.[1]

[1] The question, therefore, of a "limited Atonement," once so eagerly
debated, which necessarily arises on the quantitative view of its character, has
in reality no point. Just because it was an atonement for the race, what it
accomplished objectively, or *per se*, for one, it equally accomplished for all,
in securing the possibility of pardon. It is no more strange that Christ possesses through His death the power to *pardon* some who yet possibly remain
unforgiven, than that He possesses through His risen life the power to *renew*
some who possibly remain unquickened. Both facts are but illustrations of
the universal principle, that all spiritual service, human or divine, is conditioned in its effect by the receptivity of the person to whom it is rendered, and
thus so far may be spent in vain.

No merely external category can express the redemption of moral beings by another.   To override their individuality is not their deliverance, but their destruction. When Paul argues most strongly that the death of Christ is alone the ground of justification, he is just as emphatic in declaring that it is so for us, because we perform the personal act of accepting that death as God's righteous condemnation of our sin.   In other words, we endorse and embrace the spirit of His sacrifice, and so of necessity we rise with Him into newness of life.   The entire course of our Christian experience is but an affirmation in an ever-deepening sense of the will and work of Christ; and the word which in some respects best describes the whole scope of His redeeming work as both objective and subjective, is not substitution, but representation.[1]   No doubt even representation fails to bring out the real unity of Christ with us, whereby it is He who fulfils Himself in us, and not simply we who, standing apart, "think His thoughts after Him."   But it at least sets forth the fact that the simplest faith that saves has in the heart of it a genuine surrender to Christ, without which He would not be in any true sense our personal representative before the Father.

There is a preaching of the death of Christ for us, which tends to empty faith of its moral content, and to reduce the soul's relation to Christ to a simple acquiescence in a past deliverance.   No one need be astonished that the converts whom it makes are too often awakened, not so much to a sense of guilt as to a terror of judgment; and the relief they obtain is far more a shelter from wrath than the peace of forgive-

---

[1] *Vid.* Bruce, *St. Paul's Conception of Christianity*, pp. 177, 178.

ness.   The more violent and one-sided the presentation
of the atonement, the more effect it will produce on
many simple and untutored minds.   But such agonised
emotion is not necessarily a spiritual experience at all,
and very little knowledge of character is required to
forecast the inevitable reaction and prostration.   Even
when the salvation of Christ is associated in their minds
rather with sin than with its punishment, yet so wholly
is it an accomplished fact, that the need of a personal
struggle against evil, as the imperious call of their
new relation to Christ, is regarded as a disparagement
of the all-sufficiency of His redemption.   No other
result can possibly follow, if the death which He died
once for all is severed from the life which He liveth
for evermore.   The latter is the only guarantee against
that misinterpretation of the former, which degrades
faith into the formal acceptance of a divine arrangement.   When the life is thrown into the background
and the whole emphasis laid upon the sacrificial death,
the evil is twofold : not only are the converts likely
to have false or distorted views of the Christian redemption, but many who might otherwise be won to
Christ are alienated by a doctrine which has for them
no force of spiritual appeal.

Dr. Dale well observes that " the faith which is the
condition on our side of receiving ' redemption through
His blood ' is trust in Christ Himself as the Son of
God and Saviour of men. . . . For this trust it is not
necessary that men should even acknowledge the *Fact*
that the death of Christ is the propitiation for the sin
of the world ; much less is it necessary that they should
receive from others or elaborate for themselves a *Theory*

of propitiation. It is enough that the authority and love of Christ have been so revealed to them that they rely on Him for eternal salvation."[1]   For multitudes, this is the path by which they come. They are driven to seek God by an inward restlessness ; the longing for His fellowship and His service grows into a passion ; but as they press on they become weary of the futility of good resolves, and sick at heart of their moral feebleness.   The vision of Christ rises before them, not of this or that aspect of His character or work, but of His total triumph in life, death, and resurrection. They see in Him the revelation of God's redeeming love, the pledge of man's victory, and yield themselves to Him to be lifted up into the divine communion and peace. Their one desire is to escape from themselves, to be taken into the shelter of His goodness, and filled with His grace. Being in Him, they know that condemnation no longer rests upon them ; but that is not because they feel it has been borne by Him in their stead, but because it has no longer any meaning for that redeemed life of which He has made them partakers. Nor do they associate their pardon specifically with His death more than with His life. That such a view is inadequate to the facts, I have already sought to show. But, however inadequate, it has the reality of saving faith in it. The truth is that the sacrificial character of Christ's death, instead of being necessarily a conscious element in conversion, is often borne in upon the believer only in the later stages of his experience.   It is through his " following on to know the Lord," through the deepening insight that springs from a constant abiding

---

[1] Dale, *Atonement*, p. 314 ; cf. pp. 111, 112.

in Him, that he comes to realise the strength and enormity of sin as a poison in the race, as a dissolvent in the moral organism of humanity, and thus demanding for its removal just such a vindication of the divine righteousness towards humanity as is involved in the atoning death. Some, indeed, never reach this at all, and yet are truly surrendered souls whose hope is only in the mercy of God in Christ. But if it be so,—if, as Dr. Dale says, there may be Christian faith without any distinct perception on our part of the atoning value of the death,—then the one essential thing for faith is the recognition of the objectivity of Christ's redeeming work, of that life which He has gained for men, and in the receiving of which they obtain reconciliation and renewal.

LECTURE VII.

THE NEW LIFE IN CHRIST
AND THE CONDITIONS OF ITS REALISATION.

SYNOPSIS.

I. The righteousness of the Law and the righteousness of God.
The relation of the Law of God to His Life.
St. Paul's philosophy of history : its Three stages.
Faith the one condition of spiritual life for man, whether fallen or unfallen.
Relation of the New Life to man's *natural* character.
Did St. Paul hold that it ought to be complete from the first?
The truth of the Pauline doctrine not dependent on its historical setting.
Its essential harmony with the teaching of Christ.

II. The Church as the *Home* of the New Life :—
    (1) As the Bearer of the historic Message.
    (2) As its Interpreter to the individual.
The communion of the Church regarded by the Apostles as indispensable for Christians : their view of Baptism.
The New Testament conception of the Church :—
    (1) Absence of Sacerdotalism.
    (2) No form of ecclesiastical Polity prescribed as necessary.

III. Humanity as the *Sphere* of its realisation.   The New Life not meant to suppress the natural qualities of man : depends on them for its Content.
The error of the Monastic and Puritan ideals.
Due in part to a false conception of Christ's example.
Adaptive and absorptive power of Christianity ; only slowly realised by the Church.

LECTURE VII

The New Life in Christ and the Conditions of its Realisation.

THERE is no point on which Paul insists more strenuously than that the righteousness of God is directly opposed to the righteousness which is of the law. But it is impossible to leave the contrast simply in this bare antithesis. For the moral law is no accidental thing, it is the norm and principle of our rational being; it is itself "spiritual," "holy and righteous and good";[1] and therefore the new life of sonship which Christ mediates to us by the Spirit must be brought into some intelligible and necessary relation to it. From the form in which the apostle at times expresses himself, we might be led to imagine that, ideally speaking, there are two ways in which man may be accepted of God : on the one hand, through the perfect keeping of the law, in which case he would *ipso facto* have a title to the divine favour; on the other hand, being unable to keep it, he may be justified through faith in Christ, who is the righteousness of God, and who fulfils in him the require-ment of the law.[2] On this view, the latter method would be one devised by God in default of the practic-ability of the former.

[1] Rom. vii. 14, 12.   [2] Rom. viii. 4.

But nothing could be further from Paul's conception. Whatever stainless spirits there be before the Throne keep their estate through their free submission to God as the instruments of His will and power. They have no righteousness of their own as distinguished from that which He confers. It is theirs only because it is *given* them, and they cannot glory as if they had not received it. So, if the final cause of man's existence be to realise his sonship to God, then, however much that may imply a homage rendered, it is based on a grace bestowed and appropriated. He who is the Father of souls is not only their origin and their guide, but the abiding inward Spirit of their sonship, without whose indwelling the sonship could not be. Any theory which assigns to men, fallen or unfallen, a primary and uncommunicated virtue mutilates the moral universe. Instead of One " from whom all good counsels and all just works do proceed," you have innumerable independent centres of goodness among whom God is, though it may be in a supreme and inconceivable degree, only the first and most dominant. This is to deny God altogether, in any valid sense of the name. If He exists at all, He is the life and harmony of the entire creation, and in a moral world the only possibility of real communion with Him is the acknowledgment by the souls whom He has made that of Him and to Him are all things. Had man, therefore, fulfilled the purpose of God regarding him, he would, up to the measure of his capacity, have perfectly kept the law; but this undeviating loyalty would have endowed him with no merit which he could claim as his own, for it was rendered possible simply through his faith, his constant receptivity to the inflow of the one Spirit of good. He would have no standing outside of God, but only *in* Him.

This, then, is the one final conception of the law of God ; it is the presence of God's own life ruling in the soul as a guiding, sustaining, quickening power. The same divine Spirit that appoints the duty fulfils it in us, and " boasting " is excluded.[1] How, then, comes it that boasting, or the sense of merit as over against God, is precisely what we associate with the observance of the divine law ? Because of the entrance of sin creating a gulf between God and us, which we feel must be bridged over before we regain our essential fellowship with Him. As our conscience tells us that it is *we*, not God, who have created the gulf, so we easily pass into the delusion that it is *we* who have to build the bridge of reconciliation. The law which we have broken becomes separated in our thought from Him and His life. It becomes a mere command, a *tertium quid* intervening between us. He ceases to be for us ; He is against us ; not a Father but a taskmaster, whose rigid behests overwhelm us with despair, both because of their confessed justice, and of our inability to keep them. He is not to be reached apart from them, but only through them, through our strictest observance of them. Consequently we are thrown back upon ourselves, and upon what we regard as our own moral resources ; or if, in the stress of agony, we still cry to Him for help, it is in reality rather for the aids of His grace to reinforce the natural strength which of itself does not suffice, than for the cleansing of hearts dis-

[1] Rom. iii. 27.

17

ordered at the core. And when we *do* obey His
command in any particular, we instinctively congratulate
ourselves on our fidelity, and look upwards for our
deserved reward. " What shall we have, therefore? "
But as it is the loss of God's life which has brought woe
and condemnation to the sinner, it is futile to fancy
that anything but the regaining of it can satisfy him,
or that it can be regained in any other way than by
the surrender which conditioned its first possession.
The good works which he performs or believes himself
to perform *as a mere individual* can never be a substitute for it, or even a means of attaining it; for
the principle which animates these breaks his connection with the unity of the moral world. The
first and fundamental thing is to re-establish this
connection, and it can only be re-established through
his resuming the attitude of self-committal, of receptivity
towards God, which he has wilfully forsworn.

Paul's whole philosophy of redemption is simply
an elaboration of this thought, an exposition of the
method by which God restores a sinful race to the
glorious liberty of His children. The argument in its
historical form is twice repeated, in Galatians and
Romans.[1] He marks three stages in God's self-revelation: the Promise, the Law, and the Gospel, or fulfilment of the Promise. Whether this triple division
has the same significance for us as for Paul and his
age, will be considered later. We have at present to
deal with the development of the apostle's own thought.

Very early, he says, in the history of mankind it
pleased God to unfold His purpose of grace. That

[1] Gal. ii.–iv. ; Rom. iv.–vii.

purpose was to be realised through a special and chosen
people. So He called Abraham to be the father and
founder of it. He gave assurances to him of blessing
and protection, and the promise of a numerous posterity,
to whom the divine favour would be continued, and
thus through him all the families of the earth would
be blessed. Abraham believed God, in spite of adverse
omens; leaned on God, as weakness leans on strength;
trusted Him to realise in and through him His own
word; and it was reckoned unto him for righteousness,
because it was an act of self-committal, reuniting him
to God. Yet, however real Abraham's surrender, it
lacked moral depth. The promise on which he rested
had very slight spiritual reference. It contained no
solution of the problem of man's sin, for the problem
was not then felt; and till the pressure of it was brought
home to the conscience, no solution was possible.

Hence the *second* stage was the *statement* of the
problem: God's revelation of His eternal character as the
Holy One, and of the laws which underlie all true
communion with Him. Man was awaked to the consciousness alike of his destiny and his tragic failure to
fulfil it. Though at first the perception of God's will
concerning him seemed to open out possibilities of
future achievement and inspired him with hope, it surely
and finally depressed and disheartened him by the
deepening recognition it brought of the endlessness of
the divine demand, and the radical feebleness of his
own moral nature. It may, indeed, be asked, Why
should the law of God have of necessity this condemnatory effect on the sinner? As made known to
the Jews, it presented an incomparably fuller view of

the divine character than that attained by Abraham. Why should it have been divorced in their thought from the present and purifying power of God Himself, and depicted as a mere external standard for human effort to reach? Why should they not have welcomed it thankfully as on its moral side a clearer manifestation of God's intention and their own duty, and while thus possessed of a profound sense of shortcoming, almost unknown to the patriarch, have still retained the patriarch's trust in God as the fulfiller of His own purpose? And was not this all the more possible, seeing that, in the symbolism of the sacrificial law, there was constantly kept before them God's acceptance of the penitent and surrendered soul?

The answer to that from Paul's standpoint is that in the case of Abraham the religious life was implicit. It had not come to self-consciousness. The unity which it attained with God through faith had no fulness of content, just because the two sides which it brought together and harmonised, the longing for God and the sense of separation from Him, were not clearly realised; and until the antagonism between the divine and the human caused by sin had received its final and emphatic expression, real and adequate reconciliation was impossible. But when, through God's further revelation of Himself, this antagonism had once been laid bare, and sin had become a conscious and ruinous fact in man's nature, there was nothing in the promise made to Abraham which met the stress of this new necessity. The sacrificial ritual, indeed, helped to relieve the burden of realised guilt, just because, though legal in form, it was in essence spiritual, teaching the penitent to find, not

in himself or his offering, but in God's mercy, the
ground of restoration.   Yet the relief was incomplete
at the best; it was the germ or hope of a deliverance
rather than its assured possession.   And frequently the
sacrifice wholly lost this uplifting and emancipating
significance, and became only an additional part of
God's imperative to man.   For, however true it may
be that the law of God and His renewing life are one
for those whose connection with Him has not been
broken, yet where this connection has been radically
impaired by sin, the soul, conscious of having lost its
inward fellowship with God, and yet impelled to relate
itself to Him in some manner, seeks to supply the void
by outward obedience.   It inevitably, and in a sense
truly, regards Him *ab extra*.   For though, as Augustine
says, God gives what He commands, yet the sinner is
unable through the perversion of his sinfulness to
recognise this, or even to receive what God gives.   The
externality of the divine law is the one condition under
which the divine can at first reveal to man the desperate
self-contradiction of his nature.   In this way alone is
he led to face sin as a serious problem, and to strive
after the possession of his divine heritage; and in this
way alone is the hopelessness of his quest made clear
to him, and the heart stirred to long for a higher
solution.

But this result only follows if the law, notwithstanding its legal aspect, retains for him its moral and
spiritual force.   When that is lost, then the standard
aimed at awakes no divine discontent, for it consists of
formal rules of behaviour and ritual which a scrupulous
devotion may adequately observe.   Hence, when the

law was denuded by the Pharisees of its ethical meaning, even the sacrificial part of it, which witnessed to the need of an abiding contrition of spirit, merely ministered the more to an empty self-glorying. Such a self-satis-faction was attained, not by the keeping of the law, but by the death of the moral nature. It was the last stage of spiritual incapacity, and " effectually prevented the inward communication of God." But wherever, as for Paul, the law kept its divine searching power, every new obedience led to a deeper self-condemnation, for it but discovered a further and more penetrating demand. The attempt to reach peace under these conditions defeated itself. The problem so stated was insoluble. The law was viewed as an *external* authority, yet it exacted an *inward* loyalty ; but this inward loyalty meant such surrender of the heart to God as left *no room* for mere individual or personal righteous-ness. Hence the whole legal method, whether the law were the Mosaic code or the injunction of conscience, was vitiated by an inherent contradiction.[1]

The *third* stage of God's self-revelation was there-fore the resolution of the antinomy in the only possible way, by the restoration of man to sonship, whereby he would be lifted clean over the barriers of a legal morality. Without repeating what has been already said of the objective work of Christ in redemption, and confining ourselves to the special point that is here in question, viz. the *method* by which He delivers us from the thraldom of the law, there are two considerations which have to be kept in view.

The first is that, in order to be the mediator of

[1] See Note 32, p. 444, " St. Paul's Conception of the Law."

the filial spirit to others, He had to possess it perfectly Himself. It was no more possible for Him than for anyone else to overcome the contradiction involved in a *legal* obedience to the Father's will. *He had from the first to be above the contradiction,* to breathe a spiritual atmosphere where the divine law had no reality apart from the divine life. When He says of Himself, " Even as the Father hath said unto Me, so I speak. He that sent Me is with Me ; He hath not left Me alone ; for I do always the things that are pleasing to Him,"[1] He is claiming absolute fidelity to God's will, only because He possesses in its fulness the filial quality of receptivity. For Him, therefore, as a moral subject, the law did not exist as an external authority ; it was one with the impulse and affirmation of His own soul. The second fact is that while this is true of Him personally, in the service that He offered up to God, yet there is a sense in which that law did exist for Him. Complete and final as His obedience was, it was wrought out, not under normal conditions, but " in the likeness of sinful flesh,"[2] and so was constantly tested by the moral struggle involved in a life in the flesh. And still further, in this curriculum of temptation through which He passed, He entered into such identification with those who were themselves subject to the condemning power of the law, that while retaining His own sonship that condemnation was endured by Him as their representative. This double consciousness in Christ, though it may appear paradoxical, lies, as we have seen,[3] at the root of His redemptive power. Paul, in quoting from Deuteronomy, and applying the passage to Christ,

[1] John xii. 50 ; viii. 29.　　[2] Rom. viii. 3.　　[3] See Lect. VI. pp. 238-40.

" accursed of God is everyone that is hanged on a tree,"
instinctively omits the words " of God," lest they should
convey the idea that Christ personally was the object
of God's curse.[1]   Nevertheless the curse of the law fell
upon Him in the bitterness of that death, in freely submitting to which the Sinless acknowledged the justice
of God's displeasure at human sin, and the awful moral
necessity whereby the sinner, by forfeiting the spirit
of sonship, turns the will of God into a threatening law.
Hence through this sacrifice of Himself He becomes the
destroyer of the old law for those who receive His filial
life.   The law as such not merely ceases to condemn,
it ceases to be; it is once more, as for the unfallen, the
law of the Spirit of life.

When we speak of Christ as " restoring " us to our
true relation to God, the phrase, though substantially
accurate, is apt to convey a false or exaggerated idea
of primeval man.   The Book of Genesis pictures to us
human life in a condition of childlike innocence.   The
idyllic union with God which it portrays is very different
from the position to which Christ's redemption raises
the soul, either in its implicit victory in this world, or
its final triumph in the next.   But the story of the Fall
has an eternal value, as teaching that sin is misconceived
when it is regarded either as a necessary stage in moral
development or as an evil imposed from without; that
it essentially implies a perversion of man's will, a departure from the true character of his life as the constant
recipient of the divine Spirit.[2]   In a word, it sets forth
the ideal purpose of God concerning man as His child;

---

[1] *Vid.* Lightfoot, *Comm. on Gal.* iii. 13.
[2] See Note 33, p. 450, "Evolution and the Fall."

and Christ's redemption may be called a restoration
because it brings man back to the lines along which
alone he could attain the end of his creation.

Considering the connotation which the term "works"
has for us through Paul's usage of the word, it may be
questioned whether it is not misleading to speak, as
the Confession of Faith does, of a "Covenant of Works
wherein life was promised to Adam, and in him to
his posterity, upon condition of perfect and personal
obedience"; but "man by his Fall having made
himself incapable of life by that Covenant, the Lord
was pleased to make with him a second, commonly
called the Covenant of Grace."[1] For, *ex hypothesi*, the
characteristic of Adam in his unfallen state was just the
perfectness of his *faith* in God, which made him continually responsive to the promptings of the divine
will; and it is only when this faith is lost or impaired
that any thought of *works* as a form of personal
obedience arises. Christ restores us by re-quickening
in us the lost power of faith. Faith is not a means
of salvation to which we must resort because other
means fail; it is the one condition, both for fallen and
for unfallen man, of acceptance and life. Only, it
operates differently in the two cases. In the sinless,
faith is the medium of receiving God's righteousness;
in the sinful, it "is counted for righteousness." He who,
on account of his sin, cannot render to God the full
obedience of faith, is by his faith identified with Christ,
who is the righteousness of God for sinful men, and he
receives through this identification the increasing power
of sonship. The eternal Son is the one mediator of

---

[1] Confession of Faith, chap. vii.

the divine life to the human spirit, whether fallen or
unfallen. But for the former His mediation only avails
when it is realised under a form which removes from
the spirit its burden of guilt, and contains the guarantee
of its ultimate victory over indwelling sin, and its perfect
union with God in filial fellowship. Thus it is that the
same lines which God laid down for man's life in his
creation are maintained in his redemption, and " After
Last returns the First, though a wide compass round
be fetched," [1] owing to the devastating entrance of sin.

Sometimes this unity of man's relation to God in
creation and redemption is obscured for us by the terms
in which the spiritual change in the soul is described.
The new birth, which is John's name for it, and the new
creation, which is Paul's,[2] both set forth the completeness
of the transformation, and its source in God. But, when
taken abstractly, they have too often been interpreted as
signifying that the life born of God has no affinity to
anything in man's natural character. A certain plausibility is given to this view by the emphatic antitheses in
which Paul contrasts the state of nature and the state of
grace, the old and the new man.[3] That such is not his
conception is very clear from the seventh chapter of
Romans, in which the conflict depicted, though it contains elements that are drawn from Christian experience,
is fundamentally true of man in general, wherever the
moral sense has attained any development.[4] The law of
the mind, which is opposed to the " law in the members,"

---

[1] Browning, *Apparent Failure.*

[2] Paul mentions the " new birth " only in Tit. iii. 5 : " The washing (or
laver) of regeneration."

[3] Rom. vi. 6 ; Eph. iv. 22, 24 ; Col. iii. 9, 10.

[4] Cf. Sanday and Headlam, *Comm. on Romans*, pp. 185, 186.

is the higher side of man's nature, the witness of his kinship to the divine.   But though it bears this testimony, it has no power to overcome the flesh or the law of sin, until it is brought under the influence of, and penetrated by, the Spirit of God, in whom the man is restored to himself; and it is through this higher element, call it conscience or moral sense or what you will, that the Spirit lays hold of him and convinces him of his need of renewal.[1]   Even when he is in the stage of condemnation under a menacing external law, man, though actually a slave, is potentially a son;[2] and it is this very contradiction between his state and his possibilities which causes the misery of his being, and inspires the cry for deliverance.   Christ makes the potential a real sonship, and so brings him, even amid earth's imperfection, in sight of his goal.

And just as some have misunderstood Paul as holding that the life born of the Spirit is a new creation which finds no affinity in man's natural condition, so it has been argued that he represents that life as a complete thing from the first.   The contention is, not that he found his ideal anywhere realised, but that the ideal itself which he cherished was that of a life in Christ requiring no painful process of growth for its perfection.   This view is based on the decisive terms which he employs to describe its absoluteness, its severance from the condemning past, its inward freedom and triumph.   " Ye are dead; ye are risen with Christ; your life is hid with Christ in God; ye are complete in Him."   But the finality which is here expressed is due to two causes, inseparably related to

---

[1] See Beyschlag, *N. T. Theology*, vol. ii. p. 209.

[2] Gal. iv. 1, 3 ; *vid.* Lightfoot, note on ver. 5.

each other.   First, it is inspired by the thoughts connected with what he elsewhere terms the justification
and adoption of the believer, who, in virtue of the righteousness of God which is in Christ, occupies a totally new
relation to God.   He has crossed the line which separates the condemned from the accepted; he has passed
from death unto life.   This step is decisive, final.   Then,
secondly, the life of which he has become possessor is
regarded as to its content in an ideal aspect.   It is
viewed *sub specie æternitatis*, not as it is under the
hampering conditions of time, but as a thing in reality
above time, a portion of God's immortality.   For, faint
and unevolved as it may be, it is yet the true self of the
believer : and the old nature, however practically ob-
structive, is yet a baffled and repudiated thing, external
to his essential personality.   Hence John says, with an
amazing boldness, " Whosoever is begotten of God doeth
no sin, because His seed abideth in him ; and he cannot
sin because he is begotten of God." [1]   As the higher and
the lower self are in their nature mutually exclusive, so
the lower has no significance for the man who is, in will
and inmost being, identified with the higher.   This may
be called an ideal picture, but only in the sense in which
the ideal is the finally real.   The new life which is still
in process is treated as complete, because, being rooted
in the divine, it contains within itself the guarantee of
its completion.   Therefore all possible excellences and
prerogatives are attributed to it.   This is especially
characteristic of Paul's description in Ephesians of the
privileges of believers, who are " enriched with all spiritual
blessings in the heavenlies in Christ." [2]   The Church, as he

[1] 1 John iii. 9.   [2] Eph. i. 3 ; cf. ii. 6.

sees it, has already put on her coronation robes. Her
triumph has come; the echoes of earth's struggle have
died away.

That is one side, the noumenal, the eternally sure
and perfect life of those who have gained the heritage of
Christ's peace. But there is the other side, the pheno-
menal, the often bitter and tragic experience of the
Christian soul as it journeys towards the city. And no
man ever saw that with a keener eye than Paul. His
Epistles are full of it. While his transcendental instinct,
his spiritual vision, lifts him at times far above it into
" the heavenlies," where the abiding realities are, yet he
does not forget that for man on earth it is no phantasm,
but the sternest of facts. Though the battle is won,
none the less it has to be fought out. The severe reprimands which he delivers to the Corinthians as babes in
Christ, unable to receive the strong meat of the Gospel,[1]
are not to be interpreted as indicating that he made no
allowance for any principle of growth in the Christian
life. As well as any, he knew that that life has its stages
of education, and that no small part of the education
consists of the salutary lessons learned through miscar-
riage and failure. But though this experience in a
greater or less degree is invariable, it does not entitle
us to attribute the responsibility of our failures to the
" law that is in our members." The bias to sin which
belongs to the carnal nature, only becomes actual through
the consent of the will, and therefore in no particular act
of sin are we relieved from blame. Here we touch one
of the many paradoxes of Christian experience. However
true it may be that, so long as we are environed by

[1] 1 Cor. iii. 1, 2.

earthly conditions, we cannot attain perfection, the only
language which does justice to the Christian conscience
is that which declares that we *ought* to attain to it.[1] But
it is stolid literalism to turn this language into a declaration that here and now a complete victory over sin is
the believer's privilege.[2]

Paul censures the Corinthians for their unspirituality
and carnality, because it would have been untrue to the
deepest facts of consciousness to treat their defects as
the unavoidable outcome of an incipient Christianity.
Nor in this is he at all at variance with the practice of
Christ Himself. When on one occasion Jesus says to
His disciples, " I have many things to say unto you, but
ye cannot bear them now," [3] He no doubt acknowledges
that there are limitations or imperfections which are not
blameworthy, and which necessarily belong to the earlier
stages of knowledge and experience. He applies this
principle to the disciples, more especially because it was
impossible for them to comprehend many of the truths
of His Gospel before the facts on which the truths were
based had occurred. This by no means implies, however, that their *actual* immaturity of spiritual comprehension had not been rendered greater through their own
fault, or that He acquiesces in it as a morally necessary

[1] On this antinomy see Note 33, p. 450.

[2] I cannot but think that Professor Agar Beet, *The New Life in Christ*,
Lect. XIX., overstates, in some of his expressions, the degree in which the
believer actually and practically realises the ideal victory which is his in
Christ. " A felt tendency to evil, trampled under our feet by the power of
God," if by this is meant (as the argument seems to suggest as possible, p. 178)
always trampled and suppressed, is no description of the real state of any
Christian. If the evil tendency is only *sometimes*, though increasingly, overcome, then Dr. Beet hardly brings out the essential paradox involved in universal Christian experience.

[3] John xvi. 12.

stage.[1] Did He not upbraid them for their lack of faith
when the storm arose, and for the hardened heart that
failed to perceive His meaning when He warned them
against the leaven of the Pharisees?[2]   But it would be
as reasonable on the ground of these reprimands to
charge Jesus with conceiving that the disciples' faith and
spiritual vision ought to have been complete from the
beginning, as to charge Paul with this conception of the
Christian life.

Very different views may be held as to the value of
the historical setting which Paul gives to his teaching.
It is therefore of supreme moment that we should
recognise that the Christian doctrine of redemption rests
finally, not on theories of what man was or was not in
prehistoric times, but on the indubitable realities of
experience. Whatever the primeval state of humanity,
certain facts are clear in its actual condition ; the universality of moral disorder, and the testimony of consciousness, that however this disorder may have its roots in
heredity or an organic bias in the race, it involves for
each soul personal wrong-doing and guilt. But this
condition is precisely what Paul describes as being
" under the law."   Though he writes specially in view
of the Mosaic law, where the lights and shadows are
both deepened, the same characteristics belong to the
struggle of the savage under the dim rebukes of conscience. What the apostle says in this part of his
argument is therefore not antiquarian, but of permanent
application to humanity. The return to God invariably
presents itself to man at this legal stage under the futile

---

[1] Cf. Bruce, *St. Paul's Conception of Christianity*, p. 355.
[2] Mark iv. 40 ; viii. 17.

form of doing something *for* God which will propitiate Him. But the law slays him, and there never is perfect deliverance for him until he finds in Christ the peace of forgiveness and the renewal of the filial will. These are the two ways of salvation which challenge man's choice : the false and the true. There is no other.

Here, then, both in the condemnation of the law and in the liberty of sonship, we are on the ground of experience. Both sides verify themselves. It is far otherwise with the facts concerning Adam or Abraham. They lie " in the dark backward and abysm of time." Whatever they were, they belong to a past that has no parallel in our life. The special purpose for which the apostle introduces twice so elaborate an exposition of the promise made to Abraham, is to show that the Jewish race was from the first called into a Covenant of Grace, and that therefore the law, which was given hundreds of years later, was subordinate and temporary as compared with that primary revelation.[1] This method of demonstration might carry great weight with the Jewish mind, but it is of no real moment to us. Of two forms of a divine truth or revelation, the first is not necessarily more valuable than the second. The superiority of the Gospel does not lie in the fact that it was vaguely adumbrated long before the promulgation of the law. It lies in its essential character. Certainly there is an impressive cogency in the fact that throughout Jewish history there are anticipations and suggestions, ever growing in clearness, of an inward and spiritual deliverance yet to be wrought out by God ; but to recognise this is a very different thing from staking the finality

[1] *Vid.* Sabatier, *The Apostle Paul,* p. 146.

of faith on the mere point of priority. Even if the law had preceded the promise, that would not have endowed it with higher value or greater permanence. There is all the more need to emphasise this in view of modern reconstructions of the Old Testament records. Very curiously, much recent criticism, while inverting the Jewish traditional account of the history, retains the same order which Paul traces in the stages of Hebrew religion: first the spiritual, then the legal. But the spiritual stage for it is not represented by Abraham, who becomes somewhat legendary, but partly by Moses and chiefly by the prophets of the eighth century; while the developed legalism of the Hexateuch is assigned to the subsequent time of Ezra.[1] The essential thing to remember is that no altered renderings of the Old Testament which physical science or criticism may necessitate can ever touch the abiding force of Paul's great antithesis, to which in the deepest sense the history of Israel bears witness, that they who follow after the law of righteousness do not attain to it, but that the requirement of the law is fulfilled in them who walk after the Spirit.[2]

It is worth while to note in passing, how closely allied is this, the essence of Paul's Gospel, to the teaching of Jesus Himself, which is so often represented as remote from it in spirit and method. For both, the one end is the creation in man of the filial spirit. For both, faith or receptivity is the only true attitude towards God. In the Gospels this truth comes out above all in two forms: a positive and a negative. The note which Jesus con-

---

[1] Cf. Bruce, *Apologetics*, Book II., especially p. 170 and chap. vii. See also Professor Robertson's criticism of this view, *Early Religion of Israel*.

[2] Rom. ix. 31 ; viii. 4.

18

stantly strikes in speaking to His disciples is that of
trust in God as the fundamental requisite of right conduct and inward peace; confidence in Him and openness
to the influence of His grace, because He is the Father
who knows what things we have need of before we ask
Him.[1]   The different types of character on which He
pronounces beatitudes are but diverse expressions of the
filial heart.   On the other hand, the unbroken severity
of His denunciation falls upon the Pharisees, in whom
legalism had not merely killed the filial quality, but all
desire for it, all recognition of it as highest and best.
The sympathy which astonishes some people in His
treatment of those who had fallen under the sway of
fleshly lust springs from the fact that, whatever their
faults, they had not buttressed themselves in a fancied
independence over against God; they had lost the spirit
of sonship, indeed, but they had not repudiated and
despised it.   They had still the possibilities of it in
them, through which they might be regained to penitence and fellowship.[2]

This is exactly Paul's doctrine.   Yet there is a
difference.   Though Christianity is a unity, it contains,
as Mr. Alexander Knox says, two sets of truths, which
may be denominated the ultimate and the mediatory.[3]
The former refer to God as the original and end, union
with whom is life; the latter to the Word made flesh,
through whom man attains to and realises this union.
On the imperativeness of the union, and on the spiritual
attitude in man which conditions it, Christ and Paul
speak with the same voice and emphasis.   But the

---

[1] Matt. vi. 8.   [2] Matt. xxi. 31.
[3] See the passage quoted in Principal Rainy's *Philippians*, p. 199.

mediatory truths receive a formal and explicit expression in Paul which is not found in the Gospels, for the obvious reason that the mediation was then in process. The primary truths and the mediatory were, so to speak, blended in the revelation which God gave of Himself in Christ. In the teaching of Jesus the accent was laid upon the former, and only slowly did the latter come into prominence as involved in them. Yet the full conception of what sonship meant was only reached through the completed manifestation in life and death of Christ's Sonship, which at once revealed the ideal relation of man to God, and the impossibility of man's attaining it except through the one unique Son. Hence, subsequently, in the preaching of the " good news," the mediatory side of the truth was necessarily put in the foreground, for it was by means of it, by means of what Christ was and did, that the true idea of God, and of man as God's child, was gained, as it was by means of it also that its realisation was effected.

Nor ought we to forget that Paul in his Epistles is not merely proclaiming the Gospel, but expounding it, showing the rationality of it as a method of restoring the human to the fellowship of the divine. And therefore he expends much of his force on questions regarding the conditions of both sides whereby the restoration is attained. This leads him to a terminology about justification and adoption far enough apart from the simplicity of Christ's utterance. But it is mere blindness not to see that the primary truths are ever before him as the centre and goal, that amid all his apparent divagations he is overwhelmed by the sense of the riches of the *Father's* grace. He is not to be made responsible for those falsely claiming his name and example, who, as Dr. Rainy well observes, rehearse the way of salvation "till the machinery clanks and groans," and all true perception is lost of that which makes the Gospel the power of God.

Now, as the ideal state of man would have been one of uninterrupted receptivity to the divine, so the life of sonship which is born in him through the spirit of Christ has receptivity for its permanent characteristic. As it is through faith that it is begun in the sinner, so it is through faith that it is nourished and can alone reach its perfectness. Personal merit no more attaches to the good works of the renewed life than to the faith that received Christ at the first. If it did, they would be the works of the law, and not the fruit of the filial spirit. Yet the idea of such a combination of the spiritual and the legal in Christian experience is only too common, of the *spiritual receptivity* which leads to justification and the *legal activities* of sanctification. Self-contradictory and fatal as it is, it requires no effort to see how it has arisen. We rightly feel that the initial trust in Christ as our Saviour, which brings us acceptance and peace with God, contains no element of personal desert. But progress in holiness involves a constant and arduous struggle, a putting forth of moral energy to overcome the antagonisms or resist the seductions of evil. The element of individual will and force so indubitably enters in, that we are almost unconsciously led to conceive of it as operating outside of, though along with, the divine influence. It is only when the human is passive that the divine appears fully to dominate and possess it; when it becomes active, it seems to acquire the dignity of a real and independent, though lesser, co-factor with the divine.   But the soul is *not* simply passive in the faith whereby it receives Christ.   The upturned look at the Crucified which saves, is a forthgoing of the self, an act of self-committal.   In yielding the heart to God, we enrich Him ; we give Him that which He has not already, and which He could not have but by our willing consent.   There is moral energy in that, though in an implicit or embryonic form, as truly as in the fight of faith and the resolved purpose of consecration.   Yet if the activity of the soul in the faith that justifies supplies no ground for " boasting," neither does its activity in the faith that sanctifies.   The mere fact that in the latter it is more conscious, pronounced, and continuous, consti-tutes no difference in the principle involved.   That it appears to do so, is due to the incomplete character of our union with God, the partial extent to which the spirit of sonship has permeated our being.   It is a relic of the old legalism that clings to us, even when we have repudiated it.   " The perfected spirits of the just " do not count their unwearied service to God as aught but the operation of His life in them, just because their filial receptivity is complete.   In one sense it is their high prerogative, as it is ours in Christ, to contribute *ad majorem Dei gloriam.*   But this increase of His glory through them and us is the effectual working of His Spirit.   That the agents through whom He thus works are self-conscious and spiritual, is no subtraction from the completeness of their dependence on Him.   It is only such agents that in the fullest measure realise in themselves what dependence upon God is ; it is only they who are capable of receiving and communicating His *personal* life.

II. This new life in Christ is no mere gift of God to the individual man. Having for its central note the spirit of sonship, it is a revelation to him of humanity, and of his relation to it. The blessing he has received is no isolated transaction between God and himself; it carries with it the manifestation of God's universal purpose concerning men. The consciousness of this may to some degree be latent in the act of faith's first surrender; but it is essentially involved in it, and is bound to come to clear recognition. Christ is the Saviour specially of those that believe, *because* He is Saviour of all men. He is the Lord of the Church, *because* He has redeemed mankind.

When once the spirit of sonship has been born in a man, the new sense of his relation to God becomes the dominant factor in his conception of life. To possess it is life's one felicity; to lack it, life's dismal failure. Association, therefore, with those who like himself have responded to the restoring love of God is an imperative instinct. The bond which unites him to them is not of his making: he but recognises it. Nor has he anything to do with creating the Society which is the expression of it. The Church, which is Christ's Body, is already there: he has but to make its fellowship his own. It is through it that he comes to the knowledge of the great historic facts which lie at the basis of Christian faith and hope. The New Testament, containing the record of the incarnate Life and of its significance for human redemption, is the product of the Church's earliest experience in the Spirit. And the Church which produced the record is itself its interpreter to mankind. When we speak of this interpretation we are apt to identify it very

largely with the formulation, as in the Nicene Creed, of
the central truths to be accepted, and of the continuous
witness which the Church bears to them.   Indispensable,
however, as such a formula may be, as guarding against
speculative theories which in their consequence would
pervert or undermine spiritual life, it is itself intellectual
rather than spiritual.   But the supreme function of the
Church as interpreter is to reveal the mind of the Spirit,
to unfold the meaning of the new life of which believers
partake, and make it a power in the individual soul.
And this it does through its teaching and sacraments,
through its ministries of worship, through the manifold
activities of its common life.   The Spirit of God indeed
works in universal humanity, breathing where He listeth :
but as the organ of manifesting the redeeming and risen
Lord, He uses the Church as the medium of His operation.   *Through* the Church, as the bearer of the historic
message, He arrests the ignorant and the impenitent ; *in*
the Church He communicates to the faithful the varied
gifts of Christ's fulness.

On three several occasions [1] Paul dwells on the
diversity of endowments conferred on the members of
the Church, "for the perfecting of the saints, unto the
work of the ministering, unto the edifying of the body
of Christ."   They were bestowed, not merely for the sake
of the Church, but *on* the Church, on those who fulfilled
the conditions of its fellowship, and laid themselves open
to the influences of which it is the sphere and home.
This does not mean that identification with it precedes
the gift of the Spirit's quickening grace.   Paul was
called to be an apostle while he still stood outside the

[1] Rom. xii., 1 Cor. xii., Eph. iv.

Christian communion. But the existence of such a communion of disciples was one of the chief factors in revealing Christ to him; and the illumination and spiritual power which fitted him for his apostolic office only became his because he united himself to the Christian fellowship and received its inspirations. It was not only the sphere of his labour, but the sphere of his qualification for the labour.

With the apostles baptism into the name of Christ, as the sacrament of admission into the Church, was an imperative obligation for believers. Whether they would have denied altogether the Christianity of a man who remained unattached, perhaps we can hardly say. It was a question which never arose for them. In their view it was an inconceivable thing that anyone could be the recipient of Christ's grace, and yet abstain from confessing Him, or fail to claim with joy the privilege of His people's communion. Moreover, they believed that they had the authority of Christ Himself for the necessity of baptism; and whatever critical difficulties may exist in the form of the great commission delivered to the disciples as recorded by Matthew,[1] it is most improbable, as Keim says, that baptism would have obtained universal recognition in the apostolic Church, and especially from Paul, who, as an independent apostle, ever tended to subordinate the formal to the spiritual, unless the ordinance had been known to possess this final authority.

Just because the apostles conceived of it as a direct command which could only be disobeyed by those who disowned the lordship of Christ, and as a condition of entrance into the one fellowship where the new life could

[1] Chap. xxviii. 19.

be fostered or even preserved, it is sometimes spoken of as if it were itself the means whereby the new life is born in the soul. Believers are " buried with Christ in baptism, wherein they are also raised with Him through faith in the working of God." " As many of you as were baptized into Christ did put on Christ."[1]   These and similar expressions drawn from the symbolism of the ordinance—the burial of immersion, the rising out of the water of cleansing, the putting on of the white robe[2] after baptism—have been made the basis of the doctrine of baptismal regeneration. Such a rendering is in flagrant contradiction to the rest of Paul's teaching, where faith or receptivity is the one essential method of spiritual renewal. He has completed his whole argument as to the soul's justification in the first five chapters of Romans before he even mentions baptism, and that incidentally, in the beginning of the sixth chapter ; and its force would be utterly destroyed if he meant to make any outward ceremony a condition of the validity of faith for the securing of salvation. The reason of his reference to baptism is quite clear. He is repudiating the contention of his opponents, that his doctrine leads to licence and self-indulgence. He replies that faith is no formal belief, but the profound surrender of the soul to Christ whereby it receives His Spirit ; and he reminds those who have grown up in Judaism or heathenism of the sacred ordinance that marked their transition from the old to the new life. " We who died to sin, how shall we any longer live therein ? Or are ye ignorant that all we who were

---

[1] Col. ii. 12 (cf. Rom. vi. 3, 4) ; Gal. iii. 27, cf. 26.

[2] Some thus explain the use of the word ἐνεδύσασθε. See, however, Lightfoot, *Galatians, l.c.*

baptized into Christ Jesus were baptized into His death ? "[1]   He emphasises the act that accompanied the public profession, not as the instrument of the change, but as its representation and confirmation ; just as Abraham received the sign of circumcision, the seal of the righteousness of the faith *which he had while he was in uncircumcision.*[2]

The solitary allusion in Galatians occurs in precisely the same connection. Not one word does he say of baptism when he is setting forth the very essence and heart of his Gospel. " Ye are all the sons of God through faith in Christ Jesus." Then comes the reminder, and the appeal founded on the sacrament that proclaimed and sealed their communion with Christ. " As many of you as were baptized into Christ did put on Christ."[3] But though baptism is not necessary for faith's validity, it is with the apostles necessary as the outcome and expression of faith. It is the symbol at once of the life which the individual has attained in Christ, and of his recognition that he shares that life as a member of the new humanity of which Christ is the head, and as thus built together with others into the one holy temple which is the habitation of God in the Spirit.

No one will dispute the high function assigned in the New Testament to the Church as the school and home of the Christian life. Three senses have been distinguished in Paul's use of the word—the local community of believers, as the Church in Thessalonica or Corinth ; the totality of Christians[4] throughout the world, or the

---

[1] Rom. vi. 3.   [2] Rom. iv. 11.   [3] Gal. iii. 27.

[4] The totality of Christian believers ; not, properly, of local Churches—
" The members which make up the One Ecclesia are not communities but

Church universal; and the ideal or mystical Church, of which he speaks in Colossians and Ephesians, and which is the fulness or perfected body of Christ. The first or local application, however, is a mere matter of convenience as among ourselves. The Church is of its essence Catholic, and knows no restrictions of time or place; and its character as a unity perpetually appears in Paul's Epistles even in connection with the more limited usage of the term.[1] When he speaks of it in the two latter aspects, the universal and the ideal, he does not present them in any antagonism to one another, as the Reformers did, by distinguishing the visible from the invisible Church. The contrast in the mind of the Reformers was between that which *appears* and that which *is*; between the professing Church and the real one. It was forced upon them by the breaking-up of the old outward unity, by the saintly souls who stood outside the ancient communion, by the faithlessness and corruption too manifest within it. But no such opposition exists in Paul's thought. Unquestionably we can trace a difference in his application of the word; but it is a contrast, not between a present formal Church and a present real one, but between a real Church as it at present is and as it has yet to be—between the Church in progress and the Church made perfect.

The problem, of which we are only too conscious, of the existence of the devout outside the Church and the unworthy within it, is one which does not press upon him. In the apostolic age the believer inevitably took

individual men. The One Ecclesia includes all members of all partial Ecclesiæ; but its relations to them all are direct, not mediate." Hort, *The Christian Ecclesia*, p. 168.

[1] 1 Cor. i. 2. Cf. Hort, *ibid.* pp. 102, 103, 108–122.

his place by public profession and identification with his
fellow Christians as against the prevailing heathenism ;
so that, practically, those who held aloof from baptism
were aliens at heart.   And as regards unworthy members
the apostle feels that they will either be regained by the
Spirit of the Lord ruling in the Christian community, or,
if persistently impenitent, will be separated by the same
Spirit from the outward fellowship.[1]   But these excep-
tions do not lead him to think of the Church as an
outward and imperfect representation of the one community of believers.   It is itself this community, the
body of Christ.   Whatever defects it has, do not prevent
it from being the chosen organ and sphere of His Spirit's
work.   It is this Church existent in time, in which when
purified and complete Paul beholds the bride of Christ,
the consummation of the mystery of God's will, and the
gathering to a unity of all things in heaven and on earth.[2]
He sees the ideal Church, not apart from the actual, but
in it.

On the question of the form and organisation of the
Church, not much that is decisive, except in a negative
way, can be drawn from the New Testament.   Pre-
eminent as was the authority of the apostles, it was
essentially of a spiritual rather than an ecclesiastical
character.   They did not even co-opt into their own
body a successor to Judas.   Matthias was appointed by
the assembled brethren ;[3] the seven deacons by the
multitude of disciples.[4]   The whole Church united with
the apostles and elders in designating the delegates to

[1] *Vid.* Beyschlag, *N.T. Theology*, vol. ii. p. 231.
[2] Eph. v. 25–27 ; i. 10, 22, 23.
[3] Acts i. 15, 26.   [4] Acts vi. 2–6.

Antioch.[1]   Paul writes throughout his Epistles with the consciousness of apostolic authority ; but even when he emphasises that, he repudiates lordship over the faith of others.[2]   The various functions conferred by Christ on His Church are several times mentioned,[3] but the lists vary in detail, showing that there was no definite or acknowledged order of subordination.   Moreover, the functions spoken of are far more endowments than offices ;[4] gifts of the Spirit bestowed for mutual service. That the apostles transmitted, or professed to transmit, their authority, which was due to the special illumination of the Spirit, is quite incapable of Scriptural or historical proof ; and, as has been well said, " to be not proven is, in claims of this sort, to be found not true."[5]   But even if this were proved, it does not carry with it in the least degree the sacerdotal conception of the Church.   None of the apostles lays claim to any sacerdotal function, though as Jews they were " steeped in the associations of sacerdotal worship " ; and they could hardly transmit what they did not possess.   It is in vain to argue that " as the teaching function of the whole Church does not militate against the special order of teachers, so the priestly function of the whole does not militate against a special order of priests."[6]   The words " priestly " and " priests " are here used in totally different senses.   The Church is a priesthood ; it carries on a perpetual work of intercession for mankind.   And every member of it is through Christ a priest unto God, offering himself up,

---

[1] Acts xv. 12, 22.   [2] 2 Cor. i. 24 ; cf. 1 Cor. iii. 5.
[3] Rom. xii. 4 ff. ; 1 Cor. xii. 28-30 ; Eph. iv. 11 ff.
[4] See Note 34, p. 459, " The Χαρίσματα in St. Paul's Epistles."
[5] Fairbairn, *Christ in Modern Theology*, p. 531.
[6] Lock, in *Lux Mundi*, p. 393.

through the power of the one perfect Sacrifice, in prayer and praise to God, and in service for his brethren. In that sense the minister of Christ ought to be pre-eminently a priest by bearing on his heart the people's need before God. But his priesthood is a spiritual service; and when it is made into a sacerdotal office, through which the validity of the sacraments is guaranteed, the whole argument from the general to the specialised priesthood falls to the ground. It could only apply if the word " priest " had, like the word " teaching," the same meaning for the Church and for the special order.[1]

Indeed, as to ecclesiastical administration, the New Testament supplies us neither with a definite form of polity nor with a directory of worship ; and it is only when we perceive that it was not its purpose to do so that we rise to the idea of the unity and spirituality of the Church as the apostles conceived it. Hooker [2] has demonstrated once for all the absurdity of divorcing Scripture from other sources of divine light and truth, and of treating it when so divorced as an exclusive guide. Because the Church has now organised itself more elaborately than in apostolic days, it may not be the worse but the better for that. Nor is it any proof because one section of it prefers to be governed by presbytery and another by bishops, that either the one section or the other is wrong. Diversities of administration in the Church as in nations have their roots deep

---

[1] On the causes that gave rise to the sacerdotal conception of the Church, see Lightfoot's well-known essay, in his *Philippians*, on "The Christian Ministry."

[2] *Eccles. Polity*, Book II.; *vid.* Dean Church's edition of Book I. Preface, p. 16.

down in the divergences of human character and training. And the same Spirit may work equally, through these divergent types of character, towards different forms of polity as well as towards different spheres of personal service.[1] The absence from Scripture of any prescribed order, and the varieties of administration approved by men alike submissive to Scripture authority and to the best teachings of history and experience, are the most conclusive evidence that diversity is not a mark in communities any more than in individuals of disloyalty to the Lord. The one real sin against the unity of the Church is the spirit which would exclude from its fellowship any who confess Christ as Head, and own the common brotherhood in Him.

In a true sense we may call the Church the Extension of the Incarnation, not only because it is the human body in which the divine manifests itself, but because it is the true Christopher, the bearer through the Spirit of the incarnate risen One. Christ, whose presence sanctifies and fills it, is not simply the divine Lord but the ascended Son of Man, who, by taking the manhood into God, has become the source and centre of the new humanity. This truth—that the whole Christ, human as well as divine, is communicated to the faithful—is caricatured rather than represented by Roman Catholicism in its doctrine of the Mass. It is not in the Sacrament of the Holy Supper alone that He thus imparts Himself to the believer, but in every act of the soul's surrender. But such a receptive attitude of soul depends upon a

---

[1] *Vid.* Bruce, *Kingdom of God*, p. 270 ; Fairbairn, *ibid.* : " The people are primary, the polity is secondary, and the polity which best articulates the religion for the people and best organises the people for the purposes of the religion, is for the time and place the best polity " (p. 547).

constant abiding in the communion of saints. He who
cuts himself off from that is in grave danger of losing
his heritage.

III. While, however, the Church is the home where
the spiritual life is fed and quickened, and the organ
through which it attains its corporate expression, it is
by no means the total sphere in which it realises itself.
For that life is not something apart from the ordinary
life of man, but the renewing spirit which takes possession of and transfigures the contents of universal human
experience. The revelation of God in Christ is not
meant to supplant His prior revelations of Himself in
nature and in man. It takes account of them, and is
built upon them. The materials with which it deals
are already given in the primary instincts of humanity
which have created the Family and the State; which
have bound men in innumerable bonds of social intercourse; which have impelled them to intellectual and
artistic achievement. In proportion as it disparages
any of the fundamental affections and aspirations of
man's nature, it impairs its own greatness, and abdicates
its supreme place as the one unifying and consecrating
principle which at once assigns to each its proper
function and inspires it with fresh vigour. No doubt
it subordinates the natural qualities and tendencies to
the higher truth it reveals. It will not accord to any
of them, be they emotional or intellectual, the first place,
just because it declares that they do not exist for themselves, but as parts and phases of a human life whose
first condition of blessedness is a right relation to God,
the unity of all. But though thus denying to them
a false independence and supremacy, it does not lessen

but heighten their value, by supplying them with new motives and loftier aims. What the Cavalier poet says of one natural impulse is true of all—

> " I could not love thee, dear, so much,
> Loved I not honour more."

They gain an unimagined glory from the presence of the divine into whose allegiance they have passed.

Yet all history shows how difficult it is to rise to this conception. In all ages in which the redemption of Christ has been deeply realised as a delivering and dominant power in the soul, it has tended to assert itself as much by suppressing, as by informing and transmuting, the natural. Men found that it was much easier to be loyal to Christ's claims, as they conceived them, if they surrendered certain parts of life, if they quenched impulses and turned aside from occupations which did not seem to minister directly to spiritual growth. The monastic ideal of Christian character demanded total severance from domestic ties and from the ordinary relations and engagements of society, in order to attain absolute concentration on the things of God. Protestantism, again, while refusing to allow that the higher religious life was thus only attainable under conditions impossible to the mass of mankind, and affirming the sanctities of home and public affairs, introduced an asceticism of its own. Grasping with overwhelming force the great truth of the responsibility of each soul to God, and construing all human experience in terms of moral intensity, it led to too restricted a conception of duty. Its most strenuous representatives, both in Great Britain and on the Continent, to whom

19

monasticism was most abhorrent, carried into the
world which they claimed for God the monastic temper.
Their bent by nature was towards the energetic rather
than the meditative; and to the energetic side of character
they gave free play.   They told with incomparable
effect in war, in statesmanship, in social reform.   Filled
with the consciousness of God, they were driven forward
to make His will prevail on earth.   They fought the
battles of the Lord; they laboured to build up a theocratic commonwealth; they threw themselves into great
philanthropic causes.   The same indomitable vigour made
them pioneers in trade and commerce.   But in this
sphere the Puritan was constantly haunted with an
uneasy sense that he was giving too much time and toil
to what had no reference to his own divine calling.
The work he was doing seemed too worldly, and yet
he was borne into it by an irresistible practical instinct.
So he strove to reconcile himself to it, either by using
the wealth thus acquired for spiritual ends, or by a
frequent and rigid observance of the acts of Christian
worship and fellowship.   The lighter and more genial
qualities of social intercourse, its amenities and amusements, were frowned upon as frivolous.   They could
not live in that severe air.   He condemned or disparaged the speculative and æsthetic interests of
humanity.   The philosopher, the artist, the poet, were
in nine cases out of ten but spending their strength for
naught, and diverting the thoughts of men from the
true aim of human life.   The vivacious epigram of
Matthew Arnold, that the English middle-class " entered
the prison of Puritanism " in the seventeenth century,
"and had the key turned on its spirit there for two hundred

years," [1] has certainly an element of exaggeration. It
is written from the outsider's point of view. None the
less it contains an abiding truth. The Puritan had,
indeed, deep sources of joy of which the world knew
nothing. His existence was *not* passed under an oppression of gloom. But his religion did violence to human
nature as God made it, by evicting impulses and aspirations
which it ought to have assimilated and utilised for God.

The error of the monastic and Puritan ideals alike, is
that they regard *that* alone as having a religious value
which has an immediate religious reference. They do
not recognise that the Christian life is fostered by everything that tends to enrich the character. But character
is not moulded merely by the conscious heroisms of
supreme moments when the forces of good and evil are
openly marshalled for conflict; it is created perhaps
more by the smaller fidelities which every hour demands,
by the inevitable trials to constancy and unselfishness
which befall men

> " In the very world which is the world
>   Of all of us." [2]

When the prodigal awakes once more to his sonship, and
returns to the Father's house, he returns to all the duties
of his restored relationship ; and it is through these that
his sonship is perfected. The filial feeling which has

---

[1] *Essays in Criticism*, First Series, p. 176.
[2] Wordsworth, *Prelude*, Book XI.
> Cf. " One place performs, like any other place,
>   The proper service every place on earth
>   Was framed to furnish man with ; serves alike
>   To give him note, that through the place he sees
>   A place is signified he never saw."

been requickened in him is not a substitute for them, maintaining an isolated existence of its own, or expressing itself merely or chiefly in direct acts of realised fellowship with God.   So far as it strives to be so, it becomes limited and overstrained.   As surely as in metaphysical language, " conceptions without perceptions are empty," so surely the spiritual life has to go outside of itself for its content, to lay hold of the activities and relations of earth for its self-realisation.   And the more widely it appropriates these, the more predominant and victorious it is.

Manifestly, the completest Christian character would be that which did justice to the natural instincts for business, for recreation, for friendship, for thought ; which did not require the suppression of any of them, in order to keep its divine sonship, but used them all as organs for its fuller expression.   This does not imply that our relation to God is always *consciously* present.   The work which we are doing may so absorb us as practically to exclude everything else ; and such concentration is one of the essential conditions of a fully discharged duty. Ever and anon, indeed, there must come to the sur-rendered soul pauses of self-recollection and blessed com-muning.   But its loyalty to Christ does not depend upon its continual consciousness of His nearness, but upon the doing of His will as revealed to it by the demands of its allotted place and its own fitness to meet them.[1]   Much of the best service done for Christ is of this indirect character.   Some of it may involve little reference to His name, and yet be swayed and penetrated by His living Spirit.   The very absence from it of all claim to repre-

---

[1] See Note 35, p. 460, " Unconscious actions as the sustaining power of faith."

sent Him endows it, if I may say so, with a special
religious power.   It prepares the way for His coming
in hearts that the world has secularised, by the heightening and ennoblement of common experience ; it interprets
the largeness of His fellowship to those who only conceive of it as a narrow spiritualism.   In speaking of his
Roman History, Dr. Arnold says : " My highest ambition,
and what I hope to do as far as I can, is to make it the
reverse of Gibbon in this respect, that whereas the whole
spirit of his work, from its low morality, is hostile to
religion, without speaking directly against it ; so my
greatest desire would be in my History, by its high
morals and its general tone, to be of use to the cause,
without actually bringing it forward." [1]   To act thus
seems to many to veil God ; it is much rather to reveal
Him.   For such work, whether in literature, art, or life,
carries its subtle purifying influence where the obtrusion
of religious teaching would but alienate.   It is both a
præparatio evangelica and a *confirmatio evangelica*.   And
if it has this winning and confirming power for others, it
has it also for the man himself.   He toils at his task,
loses himself in it ; and when the struggle is over, wakes
up to find that the divine is more to him than before.
The seed has sprung up, he knows not how.

> " Himself from God he could not free ;
>   He builded better than he knew." [2]

Nothing has tended more to obscure the value of
this indirect service of God than a false view of the

---

[1] *Life*, by Stanley, vol. i. p. 185.
[2] *The Problem*, by Emerson.   Cf. Wordsworth's *Ode to Duty*—
> " Glad hearts ! without reproach or blot ;
>   Who do thy work, and know it not."

example set before us in Christ's own life.   During the
two or three years of His ministry He moves through
the land unentangled by earthly affairs, with no fixed
home, never alluding to politics or trade, except to dwell
on their moral bearings; turning all His intercourse with
men into a means of expounding and establishing the
kingdom of God.   What more natural than for many
whom His message enthralled and gladdened than to
say, ' That is the type and model for us; happiest are
those who can reproduce that life, even down to its
details; the next best thing is to approximate to it as
far as may be.'   No one can deny the spiritual beauty
and the ethical strength of which this thought of a literal
following of Jesus has been the inspiration, from St.
Francis of Assisi taking Poverty as a bride, down to the
self-sacrificing souls who are jealous of every interest or
engagement that does not plainly subserve a religious use
for themselves or others.   Yet it rests upon a misconception.   It overlooks the lesson of the silent years in
Nazareth, when Jesus was to His fellow-townsmen, not
the moral reformer, but simply " the carpenter." [1]   And
still more, it fails to perceive that the form of Christ's life
in His public ministry was determined by His mission.
He had a special and unique work given Him to do—the
redemption of mankind, the revelation in His own person of
the divine life which He brought.   Everything, therefore,
He said or did necessarily converged on what was directly
spiritual.   It was not His function to teach philosophy or
science, or to take part in political movements; but to introduce a new power into human life which would restore
it to moral harmony.   His abstinence from many kinds

[1] Mark vi. 3.

of intellectual and practical activity is no more to be regarded as a condemnation of them, than His restriction of His career to one land and people is a disparagement of other countries and nations that He never knew.

A man's reception of Christ's Spirit does not of itself reveal to him what his function in the world is, the shape which his life's work should assume. That is to be determined primarily by his individual endowment, his training, his circumstances. When spiritual renewal comes to him, it interprets these for him, shows their place and meaning in the light of God's purpose; but they still remain the basis on which the judgment of duty must be formed. He who devotes himself to the proclaiming of the Christian message or to philanthropy is not necessarily more religious than the poet who, like Wordsworth, "dwells apart," that he may reveal the lessons which the soul may learn from nature and humanity by a "wise passiveness." Doubtless there is something in a life spent in missionary or beneficent toil which more immediately suggests the image of Christ, and which from its constant commerce with others' needs affords apparently nobler and fuller conditions of spiritual growth. But it may be that, in God's eye, as high a consecration attaches to those dedicated spirits who, in many a field of lonely research and artistic aspiration, strive with incessant self-denial after the perfecting of the gifts committed to them for the discovery of truth or the revelation of beauty.[1]

It is not our part to settle the order of precedence

---

[1] Cf. A. C. Benson, *Essays*, pp. 178 f. "The message that we are in need of is something that will introduce the loving simplicity of the Christian revelation into the world of beauty; for comprehensive as that revelation

among the varied servants of God; but it *is* for us to
see that Christianity is not so construed as to lose its
comprehensive quality as the reconciliation of all things.
That is the fate which befalls it when no allowance is
made for the diversities of talent and disposition; when
the piety of a child is expected to have the same sense
of sin and utter self-abasement that marks the recovered
prodigal; when the man of delicate sensibility, who loves
quiet ways and walks humbly with his God, who cannot
"trust his melting soul but in his Maker's sight,"[1] is
despised as a worthless disciple compared with his practical neighbour who prosecutes an unwearied evangelism.
There is an ever-recurring tendency in the Church, and
most of all in those periods when it revives to fresh
earnestness, to draw sharp lines between the permissible
and the forbidden in common relations or enjoyments.
The result, admirable though the motive may be which
leads to it, is almost invariably to create a forced and
unnatural kind of religion, which is not always free from
hypocrisy, and is only too frequently marred by a jealous
uncharitableness.   Happily the reaction is sure to come;
the expelled qualities reassert themselves, and claim their
right to expression.   They are saved by "the instinct
of self-preservation in humanity," which refuses to rest
finally in any revelation of God in grace which does
not presuppose His revelation in nature.

It is sometimes said with a sneer that the Church

claims to be, it is difficult to define the exact place which is reserved for
hearts haunted by the tyrannical instinct of beauty.   Such a life as Blake's is
an attempt at the reconciliation of the matter.   He seems to get nearer the
divine principle than many professed religionists; as he himself wrote, 'I
have laboured hard indeed, and been borne on angels' wings.' "

[1] *Christian Year*, Fourth Sunday in Lent.

shows a marvellous power of adapting itself to new conditions, of assimilating, and applying to its own ends, truths or facts which it repudiated or ignored as long as possible.   Under pressure from without, the critics tell us, it has been compelled to suffuse its doctrine of individual salvation with the nobler social spirit of modern times; to accord to physical science, its old enemy, a place in the revelation of God.   But the Church could have had no such capacity of appropriation if the message with which Christ entrusted it had not been really larger than was once dreamt of.   The adequacy of the Christian faith to meet the demands of the human spirit was there from the first; it was the Church's interpretation that failed.   Nor ought we to wonder that it has been so, considering the immensity of the task which the Church had to discharge.   The human conditions under which the Christian faith was first promulgated were entirely different from those to which it had to be applied.   It rose among a Semitic people, was wrought into the forms of their imaginative and emotional type of thought, and was enshrined in records that bore the stamp of Oriental moods and manners.   But, passing from its ancient home into Europe, it has had to confront races whose traditions, cast of mind, and social customs belong to another order.   What marvel if the Church found itself puzzled, in the presence of Western philosophy, science, and art, as to what position it should assume towards them, as to how far it could recognise them, in loyalty to the Gospel, of whose indispensableness it was persuaded by an indubitable inward witness?   It naturally viewed with suspicion intellectual interests and processes that threatened to alienate men's minds from the vital truth it declared. Only slowly could it come to realise that much of what it regarded as an essential part of the Gospel was but the temporary Semitic form in which it clothed itself, and from which it had to be disengaged to fulfil its purpose as the message of the Son of Man; and that it could equally assume other forms of thought and life, and mould them by its renewing power.

Of course it does not follow, though Christianity may claim to be alien to no human interest or activity, that the individual Christian may not find it necessary to surrender many inclinations in themselves natural and healthy, but which constitute for *him* a serious peril to the spiritual life. That is a personal question which each soul must answer for itself. Such self-imposed sacrifice may be the highest dictate of duty, or it may be only a cheap solution of an arduous spiritual problem, " making a solitude, and calling it peace." But however needful it may be for the *individual*, it constitutes no standard of obligation for his neighbour. In loyalty to Christ, men may have to impose on themselves many limitations, which vary according to the type of character; but Christianity is inclusive of all types.

And of this humanity so wide and varied the Church is the centre; not because it is its mission to supervise the different departments in which man's activity expresses itself,—to arbitrate, for example, in commercial disputes, any more than to provide amusements for the people or to foster research and scholarship,—but because it is the home of the unifying Spirit of Christ, who by binding men to the Father binds them to one another, and teaches them to cultivate their diverse gifts in the service of the brotherhood.

LECTURE VIII.

THE RELATION OF THE SPIRITUAL TO THE HISTORICAL IN CHRISTIAN FAITH.

SYNOPSIS.

I. The Neo-Hegelian rendering of Christianity.
Jesus as the Embodiment of the idea of a divine humanity.
Neo-Hegelianism and the Synoptic Gospels.
Its idealisation of Christ's Death and Resurrection.
Christianity not an Idealism, but an Achievement.

II. Objection to the union of the Historical with the Spiritual in Christian Faith.
Its Invalidity :
  (1) Historical belief, a constant factor in determining all our ideas of duty :
  (2) Pre-eminently necessary in the *religious* sphere.
  (3) The Historical element in Christianity capable of exceptional Verification : the reason of this.
    The Gospels, the link between the historic Jesus and the Church's interpretation of Him.
    Subjective affinity, the condition of all insight into characters or moral forces.
    The mediation of the Church necessary for the individual ; yet in a sense transcended by him.

The hypothesis that faith in Christ could have survived the loss of the Evangelical Records ; why untenable.
The return to the historical Christ is a return to a supreme Personality, of which Teaching was but one manifestation.
St. Paul not the rival of Jesus as a teacher, but an interpreter of His complete self-revelation.
The Gospels, the guarantee against the stereotyping of partial conceptions of Christ's purpose and work.

300

LECTURE VIII.

The Relation of the Spiritual to the Historical in Christian Faith.

WE have now to consider how far the view of Christianity which I have endeavoured to set forth is exposed to the objection stated in the opening Lecture, that it blends together two incongruous elements. Christian faith, it is said, is made to signify on the one hand the surrender of the soul to God, its recognition that it is He who graciously works in and with and through it to all good, and that only by dying to self does it become a possessor of the true righteousness which is of God. On the other hand, this self-surrender is declared to be based on what Jesus Christ was and did in the past. Faith in Him includes belief in His incarnation, death, and resurrection. But these are incidents of a bygone time, and their reality has to be established by the rules of historical evidence. They belong to a totally different order from the facts of the moral life. The qualities that discover truth in the one case are wholly different from those that operate in the other. "There is," says Mr. T. H. Green, "an inner contradiction in that conception of faith which makes it a state of mind involving peace with God and love towards all men, and at the same time makes its object that historical work of Christ of which our knowledge depends on evidence of uncertain origin and value." [1]

I hope to show that this contradiction is not so absolute as is here represented; that the historical and the moral, instead of being incompatible, are inseparably fused together in human life; that their fusion is one of the essential conditions of advance both for the individual and for the race; and that the problem which is raised regarding diverse kinds of evidence is less aggravated in the case of Christianity than in our commonest experience.

I. But before doing so, we have to inquire what success attends Mr. Green's own rendering of Christianity, whereby he attempts to detach its spiritual message from historical entanglements, and thus to lessen if not to surmount the supposed contradiction. Substantially that rendering is as follows :—Our whole moral life is rooted in God. It is because we are conscious of unity with Him that we are conscious of our sinfulness; conscious, that is, of our assertion of the mere particular self and its desires as against the universal self, which is our true being. Hence self-sacrifice, the dying to the particular, which is also a living to the universal, is man's one blessedness. More or less dimly this has been perceived in all ages, but in Christ it was the actual motive principle of a whole life, and found its final expression in a death voluntarily incurred in utter loyalty to the universal truth and love. In Paul's belief that *death* was followed by a *resurrection* on the third day. But these were to him not simply events; they were essentially the outward symbols of Christ's spiritual triumph, of that death

[1] *Miscellaneous Works*, vol. iii. p. 260.

unto sin in virtue of which Christ lived eternally unto God. They were but two sides of the same inward act. " God was in Christ, so that what He did, God did. A death unto life, a life out of death, must then be in some way the essence of the divine nature; must be an act which, though exhibited once for all in the crucifixion and resurrection of Christ, was yet eternal—the act of God Himself. For that very reason, however, it was one perpetually re-enacted and to be re-enacted by man." [1] Christ was not the eternal Son incarnate, but the supreme manifestation in humanity of the Spirit of God, who is Himself the perfect self-sacrifice; and in the receiving of that Spirit we know Him as a present, reconciled, and indwelling God. Therefore faith in its true character does not imply any assent to the atoning death or the resurrection of Christ as historic facts. Without the Christian tradition as to certain events in the past, it would not have been what it is; but in reality it is the faith which accredits the events, not the events the faith.[2] It may be quickened from this source or that, but when awaked it lives by its own vitality, and is justified by nothing but itself.

It is astonishing that Mr. Green should imagine that by this theory he was overcoming the contradiction of which he makes so much. While he maintains that the idea of self-sacrifice as man's true life is not confined to any nation or age, yet he acknowledges that in the providence of God it is in Christendom that this idea has

---

[1] *Miscellaneous Works*, vol. iii. p. 233.

[2] *Ibid.* pp. 262, 263. See article by Principal Rainy in *The Theological Review* for June 1889, on " Thomas Hill Green and his Religious Philosophy "; also a series of papers on the same subject by the Rev. T. B. Kilpatrick, B.D., in *The Thinker* for 1894.

become the power of a present and spiritual resurrection, not adequately or exclusively indeed, but most fully.[1] What then accounts for this characteristic of Christendom? It lies, he answers, in the Gospel history as interpreted by St. Paul.[2] It was he who read the eternal significance of Christ's life and death. But the quickening that flows from Paul's interpretation, whether we take Mr. Green's construction of it or not, involves at least two facts: the remarkable purity of Christ's life, and His crucifixion. But in affirming these we are already in the historical sphere. We are "assenting to propositions on evidence"; nor can it be said that our belief is "different in kind from the belief that Cæsar was murdered on the Ides of March."[3] This is true, so long as a single shred of historical fact is retained in our thought of Christ, and the only way we can escape from reliance on external evidence is by the preposterous assertion that Christianity would have possessed the same renewing power though the life and death of Christ were but creations of the imagination.

Passing from this, to which we shall have occasion to refer farther on: What is Mr. Green's conception of Christ's actual character? His language in unfolding the inner truth of the Pauline Christology naturally suggests that he regards Him as one who personally achieved a complete obedience to the spiritual law of dying to self; but from his distinct repudiation of what he terms "the intrusion of the supernatural within the natural"[4] we may safely conclude that he rejects the moral miracle of sinlessness. Dr. Edward Caird, who

---

[1] *Miscellaneous Works*, vol. iii. pp. 238, 239.   [2] *Ibid*. p. 262.
[3] *Ibid*. p. 259.   [4] *Ibid*. p. 265.

occupies substantially the same philosophical standpoint, evidently holds the same view. " By Him (Jesus) as by no other individual before, the pure idea of a divine humanity was apprehended and made into the great principle of life ; and consequently, in so far as that idea can be regarded as realised in an individual,—and it was a necessity of feeling and imagination that it should be regarded as so realised,—in no other could it find so pure an embodiment. Nay, we may add that, so long as it was regarded *as embodied in Him only in the same sense in which it flowed out from Him to others*, so long the *primacy* attributed to Christ could not *obscure* the truth. It only furnished it with a typical expression, whereby the movement of the feelings and the imagination were kept in harmony with that of the intelligence." [1] That is to say, it is the necessary action of human feeling and imagination that has endowed Jesus with an ideal perfection which cannot positively be affirmed of Him.

But, as I have sought to show,[2] the uniqueness of Christ's spiritual self-consciousness, His sense of unimpaired sonship, is borne home to us by overwhelming evidence as an indisputable historical reality. No critical theory which denies this can give even a plausible explanation of the Gospel story. That Christ was conscious of sin, but did not confess it ; that He confessed it, but the disciples were not present ; that

---

[1] *Evolution of Religion*, vol. ii. pp. 230, 231. The italics are mine. I cannot interpret this passage in any other way than as signifying that not only the belief in Christ's essential Deity but the belief in His sinless humanity is the product of religious emotion ; and therefore, intellectually regarded, *Aberglaube.* See Note 36, p. 461, " The historical Jesus as the Symbol or Example of the divine life in man."

[2] Lectures I. and II.

20

they heard His confessions, but forgot or suppressed
them, from an unconscious or conscious spirit of idealisation,—are hypotheses whose absurdity is about equal.
On the other hand, He uses expressions regarding Himself, and puts forth claims of supremacy over humanity
as the organ of the Father's will and love, which could
never have been uttered by one who bore a sense of
unworthiness.   To suppose that these were not His
words, but invented and ascribed to Him, involves a
tissue of impossibilities.   It seems to me that the
Church has some right to remonstrate with the Neo-
Hegelian School on their cavalier way of treating this
question.   They have done good service in emphasising
the universality of the Christian principle, in showing
that the self-sacrifice manifested by Christ is not the
condition on which the benefits of forgiveness and peace
with God are externally conferred on others, but that
it has to be reproduced as the dominant power in each
Christian life.   Nor is their construction of Christianity
lacking in a certain apparent reasonableness from the
philosophical point of view, when they go on to explain
how Christ, though not uniquely but only relatively
good, has become the embodiment of this divine life for
mankind, partly through Jewish Messianic conceptions,
partly through the tragedy of His career, and partly
through the transfiguration of human love and longing.
The Pauline system can be made by judicious manipula-
tion to accord somewhat with this rendering; but the
Synoptic records never.   And it is just the problem
which these records present that the Neo-Hegelians
persistently refuse to face.   Until they can prove that
the personality disclosed in the Gospels can be fairly

interpreted along evolutionary lines, their philosophy of
Christianity breaks itself on the facts.

For this reason the account they give of the effect
produced upon us by Christ's life and death is radically
inadequate. In their representation it is only the
supreme revelation of that law of dying to self which
applies both to Him and to us. Inspired by what He
was, we are led to appropriate it as the law of our
own being, and in thus committing ourselves to the
same power of God which wrought in Him, we have
within us the promise and pledge of moral deliverance.
But what Christ reveals to us is not simply that self-
sacrifice is the principle of all spiritual life, and therefore common to Him and to us, but that *He* realised
it, and that *we* do not. His effect upon us is not
single : it is dual. It reveals at once His identity with
us in principle, His solitariness in achievement. Deeply
convinced as we are that He was at peace because of
His unfailing loyalty to the divine purpose, and that
that peace would be ours if we could attain the loyalty,
it does not lessen the gulf that actually separates us
from God. If anything is certain, it is that we do *not*
attain deliverance by merely making the law of His
life our own, by surrendering ourselves to the same God
whose will He fulfilled. For the surrender is never
complete ; and it is Christ Himself who compels us to
feel the misery of an incomplete submission. It is He
who makes it impossible for us to treat our sense of
sin as a *négligeable quantité*. He intensifies it to the
uttermost. We may repent and long for that death
to self which is life to God, but as a matter of fact
that longing only shows that we still stand over against

God ; that we are actually *not* one with Him. If
Christ's life be only an illustration of unbroken loyalty
to good, it is an enigma in history.   As a mere example,
He is no encouragement to us, for His moral experience
has different conditions from ours.   We have to carry
a burden of self-condemnation before God, which He
never knew, which indeed He does not diminish but
increase.   His existence in our world is only rational
if His sinlessness has not merely an individual but a
universal meaning.   But this it cannot have, if He has
not dealt with our sin and so borne its condemnation
that He has acquired the power of communicating to
us the secret of His victory.   We do not surrender
ourselves to God, but to God in Christ, for in Christ
alone is the reconciliation realised.   In other words, only
from the standpoint of a sinless humanity can we reach
the peace which is the deepest necessity of our nature ;
and this sinless humanity cannot be wrought out by the
sinner, but only *for* him that it may be wrought *in* him.

It is doubtless true that Paul could not have based
the moral dying and rising again of believers on the
death and resurrection of Christ, unless the latter had
contained for him the same spiritual principle of dying
to self.[1]   But it is only a part of the truth ; for it
does no justice to the fundamental difference in the
two cases.   When Paul speaks of our " dying daily,"
he is referring to the moral struggle implied in overcoming the flesh with its affections and lusts, in putting
off the old man.   He never applies the phrase to Christ,
because there was no inward discord in His being.
" The death that He died, He died to sin once for

[1] *Vid.* Matthew Arnold, *St. Paul and Protestantism* (edit. 1889), pp. 51 ff.

all." [1] It was the death of the Sinless One to that
human sin which hung about Him and wreaked its
effects upon Him, on account of His identification of
Himself with a sinful humanity. In that one act the
pressure of sin upon Him culminated and closed, so
that His sinless life became the centre of a new
humanity. His death was indeed the supreme expression of that self-sacrifice which was the one law
and spirit of His being; but the essential point is that
His self-sacrifice led Him to undergo a death which
none other could endure, and by which the Holy One
opened out for the guilty a way into the holiest.
Christ "died to self" *always*; He "died to sin" *once*;
and the Hegelian interpretation which first casts doubts
on the historical actuality of Christ's perfect moral
surrender, and then employs the two expressions as
interchangeable, not only contradicts the facts, but takes
the dynamic power out of Christianity, and turns it into
"another Gospel, which is not another." So, again,
Christ's resurrection is the manifestation of a spiritual
rising into newness of life, but it is that in an exceptional form. It represents the completion of the risen
life of the human spirit. That completion, the assumption of the risen body, followed immediately in His
case upon death, because His spirit was perfectly pure
and self-sacrificing, was itself wholly risen, and entered
at once on its full felicity of being.[2] But with us it

---

[1] Rom. vi. 10.

[2] The resurrection indeed was only consummated at the ascension. But
in reality they are one act. The temporary separation of them, the retention
in His risen body of some physical attributes during the forty days, was only
for the purpose of verifying in a world of sense-perception the reality of the
resurrection. See Lecture IV., and Note 21, p. 412, "The Ascension."

is deferred, because, as sinful yet forgiven and renewed, we are only part of that body of Christ which He has redeemed, and whose organic perfection we await. We without those who come after us are not made perfect.[1] Just as it is because Christ died to sin once in another sense than ours that we are able through Him to die daily, so it is because His resurrection was the actual transfiguration of the earthly body that we know what must be the ultimate fulfilment of our risen life in Him.

It may seem at first as if there were a great gain in bringing Christ as near to our measure as possible, and identifying His experience with ours. But it is really a surrender of what gives Christianity its characteristic power of spiritual renewal. "Read all the books of Christian devotion," says Dr. Edward Caird, "from the earliest to the latest, and you will find that what they dwell upon, when they are not merely repeating the words of the creeds but speaking in the language of religious experience, is that Christ is divine *just because* He is the most human of men, the man in whom the universal spirit of humanity has found its fullest expression; and that, on the other hand, He is the ideal or typical man, the Son of Man who reveals what is in humanity, *just because* He is the purest revelation of God in man." Now the phrase so constantly employed by Hegelians about the unity of the human and the divine covers two meanings, and confuses them. It may mean *affinity of nature* between God and man, whereby man possesses the capacity of receiving and manifesting God's Spirit; and it may

[1] Heb. xi. 40.

mean *identity of personal life* between them.   But, however completely a man may be dominated and filled
by the divine, he is no more God than before, and
when the devout soul calls Christ divine it means that
He possesses *prerogatives which are no part of human
excellence*; nor is there any word of His which makes
a deeper appeal to its inmost conviction than the
supremacy which He claims as the one Master and the
one Mediator of the Father's redeeming grace.   It is
not because He is the best of men that it bows before
Him as the Son of God, but just because, being the
best of men, He is also *something more*, and can do
for it what none other can.   His transcendence of
human experience, alike in His life, death, and resurrection, in one way isolates Him from us.   But it is this
very transcendence which is the condition of our finally
reaching His blessedness.   Christianity is not an
idealism; it is an achievement.   It roots itself in a
great fact.   And when that fact is discarded, the Christian faith sinks into a vague aspiration after the divine,
an aspiration which will itself be discarded by the mass
of mankind as an idle dream, and which cannot save
some even of the purest hearts that cherish it from a
recurring half-despair for the future of humanity.[1]

II. This brings us to the objection that a faith resting
upon a historic fact is, however inspiring, inherently contradictory.   Religion, it is said, is a spiritual experience,
the right relation of the soul to God; and yet this right
relation is made dependent on the belief of what took
place hundreds of years ago.   Even for the most learned
men it is absurd to affirm that their acceptance of certain

[1] See Note 37, p. 463, "Fact and Ideal."

historic conclusions is indispensable to their knowledge of God. It is doubly absurd to affirm this in regard to the common people, who have neither capacity nor opportunity for investigation. Hence a historic Gospel is an inherent impossibility, because humanity as a whole could not verify it; at best, it could exist only for the few, and that which exists for the few is no " good news for all people."

There seems to be something extremely attractive in this objection, for it has commended itself in very diverse quarters. Mr. Green, Mr. F. W. Newman,[1] and Miss Cobbe[2] unite in emphasising it, but it has in reality very little point. So far as it distinguishes between two kinds of evidence, which may be called *evidence of insight* and *evidence of testimony*, as concurring to produce Christian faith, it states what no one disputes. But when it proceeds to disparage the evidence of testimony regarding past events as having no valid place among the factors that mould the religious belief even of the ordinary untutored man, it contradicts the plainest facts. His opinions and his resolves are determined very largely by the attitude which he assumes towards persons and incidents of bygone times, of whose reality he is convinced through the witness of others. Patriotism, for example, one of the elementary civic virtues, rests upon history. What are the motives that create it? A citizen's pride in his native country is not stirred by the mere fact that he has been born and bred within her territory, and that, being indebted to her for his training and career, he is bound alike by his interest and his duty to repay the obligation

[1] *Phases of Faith*, chap. vi.
[2] *Life of Frances Power Cobbe*, vol. ii. p. 44.

by loyal service.   She is the heir of long-descended memories, the arena of former conflicts, the birthplace and the grave of heroes.   The men who were thrilled by the words of Mazzini and rallied to the standard of Garibaldi heard behind them the voices of the centuries. Their resistance to intolerable misgovernment and oppression drew half its inspiration from the consciousness of the ancient greatness of Republican Rome, which was to them no mythical story, but the most certain of realities, and its glory their proudest possession.   Faith in the actuality of the past achievement underlay that long tragic struggle for Italian unity.   It fostered and deepened the convictions that are at the root of a nobler personal life.   The multitudes in every land whom such a historical belief influences, rely for its accuracy on prevailing opinion, on what seems to them competent authority, on the concurrent verdict of those who have themselves investigated the matter.   Were they not to do so, they would be practically cut off from the preceding ages of mankind, and shut up within the narrow circle of their individual emotions and experiences.   Whatever might remain on these lines would not be human nature as we know it, and as it will continue to be.

And if our whole character is thus affected by the conceptions which we form of what humanity has already been, there is also a sense in which the *religious* man pre-eminently is compelled to relate himself to former times.   For the God in whom I believe has not begun to speak when I first hear His voice.   Just because He is the Father of all men, it is of supreme moment for me to know how far what He has shown to others, and what His grace has made of them, corroborates what I take

to be His word to me. The knowledge of God is not
something we attain by purely personal intuition, it is
mediated through other lives that shine with His glory.
There are chosen spirits that appear in certain periods of
history, who are more akin to Him than their brethren,
and who reveal truths which the latter would never have
discovered for themselves, but which, when revealed, they
can recognise and verify.   " All human culture," as
Martineau says, " hangs upon the inequality of souls." [1]
The value of the revelation which they make does not
consist simply in the nobler *thoughts* of God's character
which they proclaim, but in the fact that the God of
whom they speak is the *reality in their own life* which
upholds and purifies it.   He manifests Himself *through*
them to the world, by what He does *in* them.   It is not
by ideas, but by personalities, that God illuminates and
uplifts men, and the moral function which they discharge
as outstanding witnesses to the divine is not restricted to
those in their own generation who have come in contact
with them.   Could anything be more ridiculous than to
maintain that the simple hearts whose lot has been cast
in a prosaic unspiritual society are debarred from passing
out of the ignoble present, and finding comfort and
strengthening in the saintly lives of an earlier time?
Are they forbidden to believe in history, unless they are
themselves historical students?   The inclusion, therefore,
of a historical element in Christian faith constitutes no
unheard-of problem; it is but an illustration of the
uniform method of God's education of humanity, without
which the race could not remain an organic whole.

But while in this respect Christianity only accords

[1] *Seat of Authority*, p. 319.

with the universal conditions of intellectual and moral progress, it is exceptional in the character of the *verification* which it supplies of the historical belief it demands. It does not require acceptance of the fact on bare external evidence.   The outward testimony it gives is capable of an inward corroboration.   This arises from the circumstance that *its* historical fact is not an isolated event or saying, but a personality, and a personality of an unparalleled type.   Incidents like the defeat of Darius by Alexander, or Cicero's impeachment of Verres, admit of no internal verification.   The proof of them begins and ends with external evidence.   Christianity begins there, but it does not end there.   That Jesus Christ lived more than eighteen centuries ago, that He was a supreme spiritual teacher, that He incurred the hostility of the leaders among the Jews, that He died by crucifixion under Pontius Pilate,—these are truths for which, in the first place, we are wholly dependent on testimony.   They are among the admitted certainties of history ; and, so far, the Church demands, even from the most illiterate, their acceptance as acknowledged facts, just as it demands the acceptance of the existence of Paul as an acknowledged fact.

But the Church goes further: it declares that this same Jesus Christ lived a stainless life, that He was the Son of God, that His death of shame was an atonement for the world's sin, that He rose from the dead, that He ever liveth to impart to all who surrender themselves to Him forgiveness and renewal.   Now the soul longing for deliverance and fellowship with God may say, ' Here is just the message I need.   But how can I be sure that Jesus Christ was actually such a one ? '   A link is

wanting to unite the historic Jesus and the Church's
interpretation of Him. *The Gospels are that link.* A
man feels in reading them that he is confronted by a
life that has been really lived. This conviction is not
dependent on disputed questions of date. He does not
concern himself whether the Gospels assumed their
present form forty or sixty years after Christ's death.
He takes them in their broad admitted character of
early documents purporting to record the words and
work of Jesus. The impression they produce upon him,
that he is dealing with a historic life, comes from this,
that while it is so natural and self-consistent, it blends
together, in a hundred detailed scenes, qualities which
are ordinarily fatal to self-consistency: a pervading
humility, and a constant self-assertion: the keenest
consciousness of God, and no feeling of abasement.
Had the picture presented been that of one who possessed only the noblest human characteristics in the
highest degree, it would have carried no such witness
to its truthfulness; for an idealist can easily create what
is termed a faultless figure by adhering to the ordinary
lines of human experience. But *a humanity which
transcends itself and yet remains human* is no dream
of the imagination; it is the act and revelation of God.
It is this personality which vindicates itself to the man
as a real thing, not necessarily the particular incidents
or sayings. These may be here or there inaccurate or
coloured. But no colouring could account for that which
lies behind them and shines through them. Through
the parts, indeed, he reaches the whole; but it is
emphatically the whole which accredits the parts, rather
than the parts the whole. Quite possibly he might be

unable to give any clear account of the elements in the personality which attest it to him as a historic fact. But the effect is none the less real or solid that he cannot analyse the causes. They are present to him, not consciously, but implicitly, as is so often the case with profound moral convictions. It might be a comfort to him, for instance, if he could follow Mr. Green's demonstration of human freedom as against the sensational school who would explain it away; but he does not wait breathlessly for any philosophical theory which shall vindicate his responsibility as a spiritual being. He rests on the instinctive witness of consciousness, and leaves the intellectual vindication of it to others.

It is not on the authority of the Church that he believes in the unique personality of Jesus as a fact in history: he sees it for himself. It is borne in upon him directly from the pages of the Gospels. What the Church does is to help him to understand the fact, to realise its contents. However convinced that Christ lived a life implying a special relation to God and to man, yet of himself he might not perceive what this implied. But the Church approaches him with its categories of sinlessness and divine Sonship, and says to him, ' These supply the true interpretation of the personality you are assured of. Is it not so?' This sends him back to the Gospels, and he finds that it is only in the light of these categories that Christ's life becomes intelligible. They alone account for those contrasts in it which are so surprising, and yet so irresistibly veracious. Through the fresh insight which he has thus gained into the nature of the historic personality, he recognises in the resurrection the natural and inevitable completion of the unique life. The Church preceded him in the discovery of these truths, but he no more believes them on its authority than men believe in the law of gravitation on the authority of Newton. He accepts them because they fit the facts.

This whole process of verification, while it has an intellectual side, is at heart spiritual. That which gives Christ His distinctive place is His supremacy in the moral sphere. Therefore it depends on our own ethical character what impression He makes upon us. Any man who has not utterly blunted his conscience feels the distance that separates him from Christ. But the more intensely real sin is to him as a destroying factor in his life, and the more he struggles amid many failings after a conscious union with God, so much the more he realises how far Christ in His unruffled sense of attainment transcends our experience; and the more he realises that, the more intolerable his own condition becomes to him. Now it is this very oppression, this helpless longing for God, which makes credible to him Christ's claim to our allegiance and surrender; which leads him to recognise that He is there, not for Himself, but for us, that God has in Him interposed in history for our deliverance. It is not the need which of itself creates the faith, but it is the need which enables him to see that this faith in Christ's divine Sonship and resurrection, and in the significance of His death, is the true reading of a unique fact which is there already.

There are some who argue that this subjective condition of need, instead of tending to prove the Incarnation, casts a suspicion upon its reality; for we readily believe what it is our interest to believe. The only way,

we are told, in which we can ascertain the actual truth
of past events is by relying upon objective evidence, and
eliminating the "personal equation." The speciousness
of this contention comes from its confusion of two kinds
of historical facts: what may be called bare or literal
facts, and moral facts. A man's ethical quality or gift
has nothing to do with the determination of the year of
the battle of Marathon, or the burning of the Pope's Bull
by Luther. That is true of all mere incidents: they are
equally accepted by people of every class on the ground
of testimony. They are the same for the conservative
as for the radical, for the agnostic as for the Christian.
But it is otherwise with the interpretation of a character
or a great political or social movement. Set Buckle and
Carlyle to write the life of Cromwell. The framework of
the story, the dates, the persons, the incidents, will be
alike in both accounts. But on Cromwell's *personality*
as a reality in history, the judgment of the two will
be widely apart. The life they pronounce upon is the
same; but Carlyle *sees* it, because he brings the power
of seeing it, because he has an affinity to it in his own
moral nature. So also, in the case of an immense
religious or social upheaval, like the Reformation or the
French Revolution, it is absurd to talk of eliminating
the personal equation, as if the facts could be equally
seen by any diligent investigator. " Gibbon's account of
the early Christians," says Mr. Cotter Morison, surely in
this matter a sufficiently impartial judge, "is vitiated by
his narrow and distorted conception of the emotional
side of man's nature. . . . Those emotions which have
for their object the unseen world and its centre, God,
had no meaning for him ; and he was tempted to explain

them away when he came across them, or to ascribe their origin and effects to other instincts which were more intelligible to him." [1] Gibbon brought *his* personal equation to the formation of his verdict; every man does and must; but unfortunately it was in him no adequate organon for perceiving the actual spiritual forces which were at work in Christianity.

Now the historic personality of Christ is, like Christianity itself, an indubitable fact. The only question is what kind of fact is it? The answer to that which any man gives will be in accordance with his moral insight. If he is haunted by no yearning after goodness, if he is not possessed by a keen feeling of self-condemnation, he cannot possibly know Christ as He was, or estimate His place in the spiritual history of mankind. It is only when in some measure life comes to mean for us what it meant for Christ, the doing of the Father's will, that we, bitterly conscious of our violated sonship, recognise in Him the everlasting Son of the Father, "who for us men and for our salvation was made man." Our conviction is no mere subjective or arbitrary impression. It is rendered inevitable by the facts of *God* and *sin*, which are to us the profoundest realities of our being. They are no less real and objective to us, though some treat them as illusions, just as they explain away the imperativeness of duty. We have not created them, we have only discovered or recognised them. And it is because we know *them* that we understand Christ. To say that this correspondence of the Incarnation with human necessity

---

[1] J. C. Morison, *Gibbon* (" English Men of Letters "), p. 122. Mr. Leslie Stephen passes the same verdict on Gibbon's work. " From his pages little can be learnt as to the true significance of the greatest religious convulsion that has transformed the world's history." *Quarterly Review*, No. 369, p. 28.

or longing casts suspicion on its historical reality, is a
senseless paradox. How could such an event ever be
proved on historical evidence without any reference
to its meaning for humanity? If it took place at all, it
had the most momentous significance for human life.
Were no purpose discernible in it, would any testimony
make it even faintly probable? And is it not plain that
the measure in which it relates itself to man as the
satisfaction or completion of his nature, forms an essential element in the demonstration of its historical truth?
Hence the assurance with which anyone believes it will
be proportioned, on the one hand, to his knowledge of the
necessities and contradictions of his own spiritual being,
and, on the other, to his consciousness of the degree in
which the Incarnation meets and resolves them.[1]

This moral susceptibility, which is one of the indispensable conditions of the proof, is not a quality possessed
by a man as an isolated individual. He gains it through
the fellowship of the good. We have seen that the
Church declares to him the interpretation of Christ, and
challenges his recognition of it as true. But it does
more: it quickens in him the capacity of recognition.
Literature supplies in this respect an almost exact
parallel to Christianity. A poet like Wordsworth, whose
song has a note in it never heard before, has, as the
phrase is, to create his audience. A few souls who have
an affinity with the singer perceive his greatness at once.
His message finds an echo in them. But at first the
multitude treat him with sheer indifference. Yet gradually he comes to his heritage. The finer and quicker
spirits whom he influences, in their turn influence others.

---

[1] See Note 38, p. 468, "The Verification of a Historical Revelation."

21

They act as the mediators and interpreters of the new truth whose freshness and beauty could not be directly perceived. They familiarise even the common mind with ideas and suggestions inspired by the poet, which prepare it for perceiving how much nobler is the poet's own expression of them. But for the critics and essayists, it would never have discovered him at all; but, having discovered him through them, it becomes independent even of their mediation. It admires him, not because of their word, but because it sees and knows his greatness for itself.

Just as the poet creates through his interpreters the taste by which he is appreciated, so Christ through the Church develops the moral insight through which He is recognised. We do not approach Him unmediated; we judge Him by faculties quickened by the power which He has already exercised over others. Wherever Christian civilisation has penetrated, it has aroused a new sense of moral obligation, and raised humility, gentleness, and unselfishness to the rank of virtues. Thus even outside the Christian fellowship it has compelled men to estimate human conduct by a more strenuous test. It is this intensification of the general conscience that gives potency to the preaching of Christ. And as the Church awakes in men the power of perceiving Him, so it exercises a constant influence in confirming and deepening the perception. Not only is our personal faith corroborated by the fact that others share it, thereby delivering us from the fear that it is merely subjective and idiosyncratic, but the Church brings us into communion with those whom we recognise as embodying more fully than we the type of character which we long

to possess.   Through them we learn to acknowledge the
finer demands of the Christian consciousness.   We see
that they surpass us in that self-knowledge, that moral
quality, which attains to the vision of Him; and therefore their testimony to the fulness of deliverance and
peace which He brings, however much it outruns our
personal experience, becomes to us a revelation of the
possibilities of the spiritual life.   The Church thus
environs us with the influences that go to create the
condition of Christian faith.   Whether they actually *do*
create it depends, as all moral influence does for its
effect, on the earnestness with which the individual
absorbs and appropriates them.   It is this subjective
condition which enables him to verify Christ as both
historical and spiritual, which at once attests the unique
life depicted in the Gospels as an actual fact in humanity,
and reveals that life as the present power of his own
sonship to God.   Christ's Sonship in the past is not
simply guaranteed to him by his experience of what
Christ is in him now; it is itself seen to be a historic
reality.   Faith is produced by the blending of these two
factors, the historic personality and the spiritual experience, as correlative phases of the one supreme self-
revelation of God in Christ.

Dr. Dale, in his anxiety to show that the rationality
of Christian belief is not affected by any questions that
may be raised regarding the *date* or *authorship* of the
Gospels, argues that the Gospels themselves are not
necessary for the creation or vindication of faith, and
holds that the whole stress might be laid on the
spiritual verification by the individual soul, as growing
out of, and confirmed by, the similar verification by

believers in unbroken succession since the time of Jesus. "Imagine," he says, "that by some inexplicable fatality the last three years of our Lord's earthly life had sunk into abysses of silence and oblivion as deep as those in which nearly the whole of His life from childhood till He was thirty years old have been lost; that the story of no miraculous work of mercy, the record of no word of power and comfort and grace, remained . . . imagine that we knew nothing more than this—that He was a great religious teacher, that He had been crucified, that those who had loved Him believed that He had risen from the dead. If this were all we knew of His earthly history, the loss to the thought and life, the strength and the joy of the Church would, no doubt, be immeasurable. But it would still be possible to believe in Him as the Lord and Saviour of the world, and to find in Him eternal life and blessedness. For *the experience of the Church through century after century would remain to bear witness to His power to redeem men of every country and every race and every age who trust in Him for redemption.* It would still be certain that, from the time His earthly friends had their last vision of Him to our own days, men of every description have discovered that when they speak to Christ, they do not speak into the air, but that He answers them, gives them peace of conscience, strength for suffering and for righteousness, and the immediate knowledge of God." [1]

An argument based on a hypothesis like this is valueless, because the hypothesis itself is really unthinkable. Faith in Christ would be possible for us, it is said, even though the records of His ministry had vanished,

[1] *The Living Christ and the Four Gospels*, pp. 39–41.

because it is attested by the Christian experience of all
the intervening centuries. But that experience of the
centuries was what it was, because it had in the heart of
it the indisputable conviction, conveyed by the records,
of Christ's reality as a unique person in history. Would
it have remained the same if one of the factors, to use
the mildest expression, which unquestionably helped to
produce it, were withdrawn? At what point are we to
suppose that oblivion overtook the facts? Imagine—
if we may venture, like Dr. Dale, to put an unreal
hypothesis—that someone had been brought through
the apostolic testimony to the acceptance of Christ as
Lord and Redeemer, and had found in Him forgiveness
and peace, with all the power of a new life; that, after
having thus experienced the joy of Christ's salvation, he
lost, by some "inexplicable fatality," all recollection of
the incidents and sayings of Christ's ministry, and that
he could tell nothing more of His earthly career than
that He was a great religious teacher, that He had been
crucified, and that they who had loved Him believed
that He rose from the dead. Even if we can conceive
that his own experience of Christ as the risen One
continued as vivid as before, by what means could he
persuade others that this Jesus, of whom he could tell so
little, was the Son of God? He had no direct connect-
ing link between the two sides of his faith which would
carry to them its full attestation. That link he had lost
in losing his knowledge of what the earthly Jesus was.
His own assurance, if it remained at all, was a survival
of which he could give no adequate account.

There are those who speak as if Paul were an illustration of a successful preacher of Christ who maintained

almost total indifference to the facts of Christ's earthly life. They contend that there is nothing in his epistles which implies that he knew anything of the *ministry* of Jesus or felt any interest in it, and yet he founded more churches than any of the other apostles. But a New Testament Epistle is not meant to contain a record of the evangelical facts; it is a letter of instruction or exhortation addressed to those who are already believers, and who may be presumed to be more or less acquainted with the facts. The First Epistle of Peter has no more special allusions to the words or works of Christ, apart from His sufferings, death, and resurrection, than any of the Pauline letters; but it is absolutely certain that Peter's *preaching* was of a different character, and it is tolerably certain that Paul's was also. Does anyone suppose that he gained Gentile converts, for example, by the simple proclamation of Christ crucified and risen as the one source of pardon and renewal? Doubtless the resurrection was to him both the proof of Christ's Sonship and the liberation of His redeeming and regenerating power for all; but he must inevitably have been cross-questioned by those who first heard his message regarding the character of One whose death brought life. ' How long did Jesus live upon earth? How did His sinlessness prove itself? What relations did He hold with others? How did He speak and act among men'? Did Paul reply, ' I don't know, and you don't need to know. You have to do with a risen and present Lord'? Can we suppose that he would be guilty of such disrespect and impiety towards the manifestation of God in flesh; and if we can, do we suppose that his hearers would have acquiesced in the stifling of their honest inquiries, and welcomed the faith at his word? What would it have been worth, had they done so? Would it have had any steadfastness or sanity in it?[1]

But there is another fact which renders this supposed disregard of the historic on Paul's part quite impossible. The converts whom he made entered into the communion of the one Church of Christ, and that Church was already acquainted with the apostolic traditions as to the teaching and life of Jesus. By means of deputies and fraternal letters, perpetual intercourse was maintained between the local churches in different countries. Even if Paul had desired, it was beyond his power to rule out the evangelic tradition. His followers would soon have found that Peter and John did not turn aside such historic curiosity as irrelevant; nay, that it was already satisfied by the concurrent accounts of those who were themselves direct witnesses to the sayings and work of the Lord. Had Paul deliberately set himself to disparage the story of Christ's ministry, his antagonism on so crucial a matter to the earlier apostolic teaching would have constantly reappeared, like his opposition to the Judaistic teachers. Yet there is no indication of it. By a perverted exegesis, indeed, some suggestion of this has been discovered in his depreciation of those who would " know Christ after the flesh."[2] But the contrast he draws between knowing Christ after the flesh and knowing Him after the spirit, is a contrast between the knowledge that judges Jesus by an earthly standard of greatness, and the knowledge that sees in His lowliness and crucifixion the very marks of a

[1] Cf. Sabatier, *The Apostle Paul*, pp. 76–85 ; Stanley, *Epp. to the Corinthians*, pp. 569–589.
[2] 2 Cor. v. 16.

divine Messiah.[1] It is a condemnation, not of the importance of Christ's human history, but of an unspiritual interpretation of it. He makes this plain by declaring that he henceforth knows no man after the flesh, which certainly does not mean that he averts his eyes from all the facts of a man's conduct or lot, otherwise there would be nothing left for him to judge the man by, but that he judges him by the spiritual test which a crucified Messiah has taught him to apply.[2] Very probably there is a reference in Paul's phrase to the pretensions of those who prided themselves on that outward intercourse with Jesus which he himself never enjoyed; but, so far as he censures them, it is not because they valued it, but because they overvalued it to the depreciation of the higher knowledge of Him in the spirit.

The Churches, therefore, of the apostolic age, whether Petrine or Pauline, were not destitute of the means of historic verification. In the evangelic story that circulated among them in oral or written form, they felt themselves confronted with a transcendent and self-attesting personality. It is nothing to the purpose to say, as Dr. Dale does,[3] that men believed in Christ and found God in Him before any one of the Gospels was written. That which forms the substance of our First Three Gospels was, in great part at least, as Luke's preface shows, current throughout the Church in its earliest days, and, though fragmentary, bore its own witness to the reality

---

[1] Cf. Sabatier, *The Apostle Paul*, pp. 73 ff.

[2] Essentially, therefore, the contrast describes two modes of thought which Paul himself exemplified in the two periods of his career; before and after his conversion.

[3] *The Living Christ*, p. 34.

of the life it portrayed.   The same correlation of fact
and experience has been in operation in Christian faith
throughout the centuries, and in the case of the humblest
disciple.

It sounds very heroic to affirm that that faith does
not hang upon records, upon the accident of the preservation of the Gospels; that if God's Son entered our
humanity and revealed Himself to a few souls in His
own generation, who after His death beheld Him as the
risen Lord and experienced the outpouring of His Spirit,
then that same Spirit could continually work through
regenerated men to the spiritual conversion and quickening of human souls, even though the traditions of Christ's
humanity had vanished.   But, however heroic this position may be, it is in the last degree absurd, because it is
impossible to conceive such a contingency.   A personality
great in his own age may become but a vague memory
to succeeding times, and leave hardly a trace behind.
But if, as in the case of Jesus, He produce such an overwhelming impression that His disciples believe Him to
be the Son of God and proclaim Him the Saviour of the
world, then this very faith in Him as the ever-living
Lord, so long as it exists, keeps fresh the memories of
the days when the apocalypse began before human eyes.
In order to maintain itself, it has to recur to the facts
out of which it grew.   If the knowledge of the human
life of Jesus was necessary for the first disciples, it could
never be a matter of indifference to the faith of any
subsequent generation.   One would like to know something of the conception of the living Christ that would
survive, when the knowledge which gave it its content
had vanished.

And such a position is not only absurd, it is dangerous ; for it misrepresents the character of Christian belief
as it exists here and now.   To declare to those who
assail the genuineness of the Gospels, that our faith would
remain substantially unchanged even if they succeeded
in discrediting them, is to play into their hands.   ' Precisely as we thought,' they reply.   ' Your faith is founded
on an inward experience of your own, corroborated by
the similar experience of other people ; it is a devout
imagination, partly your own, partly inherited.   But you
may as well drop out the historical element, when you
have lost all direct touch with historical proof.'   *It is
exactly this direct touch with the historical Jesus* which
the simplest Christian knows to lie at the root of his
confidence.   There are times when his own experience of
Christ's presence seems to falter, and when even the
testimony of Christian hearts and lives around him fails
to reassure him.   He is haunted by the fear that they,
like himself, may be swayed too much by moods and
fond imaginings, and he is only restored by the sense
of an indubitably real Christ speaking to him out of
the Gospels.   An apologetic which does not recognise
this as an indispensable part of the Christian evidence,
or which minimises its value, renders no permanent
service to faith.[1]

---

[1] As I have ventured on this point to criticise Dr. Dale, it is right to add
that no one could put more effectively than he does (*ibid.* chap. iii.) the argument for the *direct appeal* which the Christ of the Gospels makes to the spirit
of man.   " The history is not an ordinary history ; if it were, it would stand
or fall by the ordinary historical tests.   It is wholly exceptional.   Instead of
resting upon the demonstrated credibility of the Evangelists, it demonstrates
their credibility " (p. 51).   But just because there is an essential inter-relation
between the historic record and Christian experience, all attempts to make
experience adequate of itself must fail.

Thus the return to the Christ of history which is involved in faith is primarily a return to a dominant personality, not to this or that detail of His life, be it saying or incident, but to the unique life which bears itself in upon us from the cumulative mass of details, and which in turn accredits and illumines them. Yet this is often denied or forgotten by those who in our day demand a return to the historical. They say, 'Surely the one necessity is to reach the mind of the Master; and if so, must we not gain it from Himself rather than from any follower of His, however great?' "When anyone writes," says Dr. Watson, "as if St. Paul were, in the affair of teaching, not only the equal of Jesus, but His superior,—giving to the world more precious truth than the Gospels,—he has surely somewhat failed in reverence for the Master." "The question comes really to this: Ought we to read St. Paul in the light of Jesus, or Jesus in the light of St. Paul?" [1] For literary effectiveness nothing could be better put; but as a statement of the point at issue, it leaves something to be desired. Most certainly it is in the light of Jesus that Paul is to be read, but it is not simply in the light of His teaching. The teaching was not the ultimate thing in Christ. It formed but one part of His threefold self-revelation.[2] Even the disciples during His ministry felt that behind His words lay a personal life of which these were no full expression, and which revealed itself in act as well as speech. And it was from the increasing perception of what this life was that they gradually reconstrued His sayings. The resurrection was the final demonstration to them that His

[1] *Mind of the Master*, pp. 35, 39.
[2] See Lecture III.

personality constituted the centre and secret of His message. And it had this power for them, just because it gathered up into a unity their varied experiences of Him, and completed and confirmed the dim convictions of their hearts.

The problem which Christ presented to the apostles is the same problem that the Church has perpetually to face. Fundamentally, it is not, What did He say, but What did His existence in humanity mean? Paul's Epistles give his answer to that. Those who cry, ' Back to the teaching of the Gospels,' often give no answer at all. It is no marvel that Paul's exposition should alienate them. Their commentary differs from his, because the text they comment on is different. *He* seeks to interpret Christ's total manifestation of Himself. *They* fasten on a single phase of it and distort the perspective. It would be well for them to realise his standpoint before depreciating him. Books that deal with the teaching of Jesus as if it were a complete revelation in itself, may be full of suggestive interpretations, but their importance is only too apt to be radically sectional. The part which they wrench from the whole loses its proper and deepest value. Frequently they never come within sight of the one question which underlies all others. Christ's supremacy over His followers does *not* lie in the fact that He uttered deeper truths of God than they, but that He alone manifested in His own person the eternal Sonship. Paul enters into no absurd rivalry with Him as a teacher. Christ's life was more than His teaching. Paul's teaching was higher than his life. Moreover, their teaching had a different object and character. Christ's was one of the means whereby He first revealed His Sonship to

men as a fact.   Paul's was the exposition of what that
Sonship signified for humanity.   It may be possible to
supersede the apostle's rendering, but that will not be
accomplished by eliminating some of the essential factors
of the problem.

What we find, therefore, in the Gospels is, before and
above all, the great personality.   That stands out more
surely than any of the particulars which cumulatively go
to verify it, and it supplies a new point of view for judging
the details.   But while it interprets them it is also interpreted by them.   Hence the continual return to the historical Christ is requisite, not simply to guarantee our
faith in the living and present Christ, but to regulate
and correct it.   The records which enable us to verify
the Church's declaration that He was the incarnate
Son, also enable us to test its rendering of the revelation which He gave of God and man.   The apostles
derived their conception of the mind of Christ from the
human life of Jesus as illuminated for them by the Spirit.
But however true that conception in its essential principle,
it could not possibly be adequate.   The enlightenment
of the Spirit did not raise them above the limitations of
their time, and could not therefore reveal to them the
complete significance of a personality that bore relations
to all times and conditions.   The Spirit's operation was
only one factor in their vision of Christ.   The other
factor, as real, was supplied by their receptivity, their
moral and intellectual capacity.   The earthly manifestation of the Son of God had an infinite fulness, and the
comprehension of it is necessarily a gradual discovery,
widening with the thought and experience of men.   Jesus
was not merely, as Matthew Arnold says, " above the

heads of His reporters"; [1] He remains above and beyond
every generation of His followers.   No age can pass upon
Him a final verdict.   It but makes its greater or lesser
contribution to the understanding of His mission.   We
see this very clearly in the case of His teaching.   It is
cast in Oriental form, and often adapted to the circumstances and standard of His hearers.   One of the greatest
problems is to disentangle the everlasting truth it contains
from its accidental embodiment.   Spiritual insight, however clear, does not suffice of itself for the solution.   The
very saintliest souls of one century have advocated interpretations which were an offence to the common moral
feeling of the next.   Christian faith, just because it is
the expression of a man's fundamental attitude towards
God and the world, is subject to all the influences,
intellectual or ethical, which make him what he is.
Therefore, while it is true that Christianity lies at the
root of the elevation of human character and society in
all their aspects, it is by that very elevation of mind
and heart that Christianity is in turn itself more and
more truly understood.

The Gospels are the one guarantee against the stereotyping of partial conceptions of Christ's purpose and
work.   The conception which for a past generation was
perhaps relatively the best, most expressive of, and most
conducive to, its spiritual devotion, may be in some of
its elements an obstacle to us.   The refusal of the Fathers
to admit any real limitations in Christ's knowledge, the
individualistic idea of salvation cherished by Thomas à
Kempis and the monastics, the mechanical or "dictation"
theory of Scripture inspiration so widely accepted by

[1] *Literature and Dogma*, chap. vi.

theologians both in the Early and in the Post-Reformation Church, were errors that lay close to the sources of their strength, though for us they would be a hindrance, not an aid, to faith.   Each age has its own vision of the incarnate Son, and hears His word in its own language. Its faith in Him is kept fresh and vivid by this contact with a living personality, who

> " Part by part to men reveals
>   The fulness of His face."

Thus the revelation of Christ is both one and manifold : one, because it proceeds from the *Ewigkeit-Geist*, the Lord the Spirit ; and manifold, because the eternal Spirit speaks through the ever-changing forms of the *Zeit-Geist*.

Whenever the Church has treated the historic record with indifference, it has invariably fallen either into scholasticism or mysticism.   Christianity has become a barren dogmatic system which made no appeal to the personal need of man, and contained no dynamic for his uplifting.   Faith was a formal assent to propositions, not a self-surrender to a living Redeemer.   And when this abstract intellectualism was felt to be intolerable, relief was found in the pietism which dwelt much on the mystical union of the soul with Christ, and construed that in the terms of a spiritualising imagination.   Emphasis was put on special and ecstatic revelations, in which it was hard to say where the real ended and the fanciful began.   Christianity, when scholastic, lacks inspiration ; when mystical, it lacks reality and balance. In both cases we are dealing with a conception of Christ unregulated by the divine fact, and which we are at

liberty to fill with any speculative or sentimental content
we please.   His human life, in which the foundations of
the new kingdom were laid, alone supplies the materials
whereby we can rightly interpret His living presence and
power.

LECTURE IX.

THE CONDITIONS OF THE FINAL JUDGMENT—IS FAITH IN CHRIST NECESSARILY CONSCIOUS?

SYNOPSIS.

Problem raised by the existence of a high type of character in many who reject the Historic Faith.

I. Indications of a solution in Christ's Parable, Matt. xxv. 31–46: the Judgment of the Heathen.

If receptive to the quickening of the Son in the sphere of duty, they are made partakers of the benefits of His redeeming life. Love as *unconscious* Faith.

II. Is this principle capable of application *within* the Christian world ?

Different moral connotations of the phrase, " The rejection of Christ."

What Faith is in its essence.

The New Birth and the influence of Environment.

Social and intellectual conditions of belief in the Apostolic age, different from ours.

The morally irresolute without and *within* the Church.

The redemptive power of Christ not confined to the sphere in which the *ordinary* Means of Grace operate.

This admission no disparagement of the Historic Faith.

III. The doctrine of an Intermediate State.

(1) As a *Probation.*

If for *some only*, perplexes rather than lightens the problem of Destiny.

(2) As a *Training* and *Purification.*

The difference between this doctrine and that of the immediate entrance of the soul into the glory of God, not so great as is often supposed. Neither of them corresponds with Christ's Parable.

Scripture leaves the period between Death and the Judgment in shadow : places the emphasis of moral decision within the present life. What this implies.

Conclusion.

LECTURE IX.

The Conditions of the Final Judgment—Is Faith in Christ necessarily Conscious?

It can hardly be too often repeated that the belief in Christ's centrality, alike in the religious life of the individual and in universal creation, did not arise from a speculative idealisation, inspired by human needs, of the life of Jesus, but was forced upon men by the facts of that life, and the deepening discovery of its significance. His unique moral self-consciousness, as seen in all the manifestations of His character, proved that He personally realised the ideal of *human* sonship to God; His attitude towards men before the Father showed that this sonship was not merely human, but was the expression in humanity of an eternal and incommunicable Sonship. It was because He was Son in this transcendent sense, and the one organ of the Father's creative activity, and because His Sonship attained the expression of its own freedom in man as a self-conscious and spiritual being, that the personal Incarnation of the Son, for the restoration or realisation of that human sonship which sin had impaired or perverted, was possible.

Now it may be said, ' Even if the facts of Christ's life and the experience of those who have believed in Him entitle you to hold this view, is not such a conception contradicted by the state of mankind as it has been and is?   You say that Christ has by His redeeming work obtained the power to mediate forgiveness and renewal of all men, yet that the actual bestowal of them depends in each case on man's receptivity.   But multitudes have never heard of His Incarnation.   Multitudes who have heard of it have had no true idea of what it meant, owing either to their own sad incapacity, or to the inadequacy or perversion of its presentation to them. And again, many who have heard of it and rejected it have manifested rare qualities of purity, patience, and unselfishness, which, were they found in a Christian believer, would at once be described as the fruit of the Spirit.   If the Incarnation be the recovery by the Son of a humanity which was meant to bear His image but had lost it, and if this recovery only take effect through the response of the soul, then surely it ought to be brought plainly before the mind and heart of all men, and surely the rejection of it should not be compatible with a moral character which in strength and attractiveness frequently surpasses the ordinary Christian type.'

The objection thus stated constitutes a very real difficulty to many, nor has it always been fairly faced by the Church.   The day is, it is to be hoped, nearly over, when it was possible to speak of the heathen as condemned for not believing in a Saviour of whom they had never heard,[1] or of the manifest virtues of those who

---

[1] The Primate of the English Church found it necessary, in his *Charge* for 1866, to administer a rebuke to one of his clergy, who had used it as an argument for missionary effort, that "at every ticking of the clock, in every four and twenty hours, from month to month and year to year, God sends a heathen straight to never-ending misery."   See Plumptre, *Spirits in Prison*, p. 184.

were not Christians as no better than " glittering vices."
The moral sense of humanity, its instinct of fairness, has
outgrown such verdicts.   Nor is it a sufficient answer
simply to fall back on what *we* feel to be the Christian
certainties regarding the Incarnation, and the sonship
which Christ mediates to receptive hearts, and rule out
all question as to what these involve on the negative
side.   The problem of destiny is in many of its phases
shrouded in impenetrable darkness.   But if we are
rationally to maintain our faith in redemption through a
historic fact, then we ought to be able to form some conception of the lines along which that fact has a relation
to all sorts and conditions of men.

Two points in the Church's faith are perfectly clear:
(1) That the work of Christ in redemption has an
objective value for universal mankind, inasmuch as the
life which He has thus assured for them has put them in
a new position towards God by opening to all men the
divine possibility of pardon and acceptance as God's
children.   (2) That just because the subjects of redemption are free, self-determining spirits, this objective life
in Christ can only become theirs through receptivity
on their part.   Evidently the key of the problem lies
in the nature of this receptivity.   Would it not be
rather a mockery to declare that Christ by His
sacrifice and resurrection has gained for all the possibility of eternal life, if large sections of humanity are
destitute of those conditions of knowledge and spiritual
opportunity which alone can turn the possibility into a
reality?

I. Happily we are not entirely left to a speculative
treatment of the matter.   Christ has Himself, in what is

called the Parable of the Last Judgment,[1] at least indicated the solution of the difficulty. The passage is indeed a battleground of contending exegetes. For my part, I cannot doubt that the picture it presents is not the judgment of Christians or of all mankind, but specifically of those who on earth have never heard the Gospel.[2] In Christ's vision all the nations are gathered before the Son of Man, and the natural and unstrained meaning of the word ἔθνη is the Gentile and heathen peoples. This interpretation is in distinct accord with what forms the essence or heart of the parable: first, the test or standard of judgment, character or moral disposition; and secondly, the surprise expressed by those on whom judgment is passed that their fidelity or falsity to the spirit of brotherly self-sacrifice is in reality fidelity or falsity to the Son of Man Himself. Could anything be more forced than Meyer's view, that the persons whom the Judge addresses as blessed are Christian believers who have performed services of love to the brethren for Christ's sake, but who, having never rendered them to Christ personally, " do not venture to estimate the moral value of those services according to the lofty principle of Christ's unity with His people "?[3] If devotion to Him consciously inspired them to a life of burden-bearing for others, is it not absurd to say that they did not realise His identification with a suffering humanity, when the teaching of the New Testament and even this very parable itself definitely assert it? They know *in this life* that He regards their loving service to

---

[1] Matt. xxv. 31 ff.

[2] See Bruce, *Kingdom of God*, p. 315.

[3] *Comm. on St. Matt., in loc.*

the poor or sorrowful as done to Himself. How then
can the declaration of this familiar truth fill them with
astonishment when at last they stand in the revelation
of His presence?

On the contrary, the expression of surprise exactly
represents the feeling of those who, having lived in
ignorance of the redemption of humanity, suddenly discover that they are the inheritors of its unimagined
blessing. They had in a measure welcomed and walked
by the spirit of brotherly love. They knew not Him
who inspired it, but they recognised its claim. They
learn now that this spirit was the illumination and gift
of Him who is the light that lighteth every man, and
that in following it they were unconsciously loyal to
Him; and because they were receptive to the quickening
of the Son in the sphere of moral duty, they become
partakers of the benefits of His redeeming life. It is
through the Incarnation alone that men come to know
that every pure and generous natural impulse and resolve
is the sign of a sonship to God, broken but not destroyed, which has its source and basis in the eternal Son;
and consequently the only obedience which the heathen
can render to the Son is unconscious fidelity. But their
receptivity to His life, though unrecognised by them as
such, is none the less real. His acceptance of their
service as rendered to Himself is no mere personification,
signifying that they have cherished, however faintly, the
same spirit of compassion and self-denial, of which He
as the Son of Man gave the supreme example; or that
He had so sympathetically identified Himself with mankind that He suffered in their suffering and rejoiced in
their joy. It includes these meanings, but rests upon

the deeper ground of what He, and He alone, essentially is to humanity. The Incarnation is but the manifestation in its highest form of the self-sacrifice of the Son who is the organ of the Father's love in the making and sustaining of the universe: a self-sacrifice which lies at the root of every self-sacrifice in man. Therefore they from whom that highest revelation of it in the historical Christ has been withheld are not unrelated to the Son. They hear a voice prompting them to pity and practical helpfulness, though they know not who it is that speaks to them. And when they respond to its behest, they thereby open their souls to the life of the Son, and show that receptivity which under favourable conditions would have appropriated the fuller blessing of redeemed sonship had the knowledge of it been vouchsafed to them. Their love is itself unconscious faith.

And if the central truths of the parable—the practical nature of the test, and the astonishment both of the good and of the evil at the personal reference to the King which this test involved—suggest that the heathen are the subjects of the judgment, there is nothing in any other part of the parable incompatible with this view. Meyer contends that the words of welcome to the righteous, "inherit the kingdom prepared for you from the foundation of the world," are quite inapplicable to non-Christians, and can only refer to the elect of the Messianic kingdom. But one chief lesson of the parable is just that the Messianic kingdom includes many who on earth are regarded as strangers to it, and who are ignorant of their citizenship. Yet as no one can belong to it except through the grace of God, the phrase 'prepared for you from the foundation of the world"

is meant to emphasise that the *salvation* of men
is the divine intent, in contrast to the fire of penalty
which is not God's purpose of destiny for men, but
their own wilful and desperate choice. Hence the
heathen who are saved are as much His elect as true
Christians. The idea of election is widened beyond its
normal significance, because it has to be coextensive
with the widened conception of the kingdom which the
parable teaches. So again, the immediate recognition
by both sides of the assemblage that Christ is their
rightful Judge [1] does not in the least imply that they
had already known Him as such on earth. It is part of
the discovery which the great day of unveiling brings,
whose revelations show them beyond the possibility of
challenge what *they* are and what *He* is.[2]

II. This, then, is the principle laid down by our
Lord in reference to the heathen: that their response to
the inspirations of brotherhood which He as the one true
light has quickened in their hearts and consciences, is
a real though unconscious faith in Him, and constitutes
them members of His kingdom of redeemed souls. Is
this principle capable of application *within* the Christian
world? Not a few will repudiate the idea as preposterous. "Wherever Christ is preached," they declare,

---

[1] Κύριε, vv. 37, 44.

[2] Wendt, who holds that the judgment here described is that of Christians,
argues that Christ never represents Himself as the final Judge of all men, but
*only of such as have, directly or indirectly, come in contact with Him or His
preaching* (*Teaching of Jesus*, vol. ii. pp. 279, 280). This is in flat contradiction to the teaching of the whole New Testament. The entire spirit of
Christ's references to Himself as Judge implies the universal character of His
office, though He describes it now in relation to one class, and now to another.
See Bruce, *Kingdom of God*, pp. 312-316. The apostolic view as to the
universality of Christ's judgment is abundantly clear. Acts x. 42; xvii. 31:
Rom. ii. 16: 2 Tim. iv. 1: 1 Pet. iv. 5.

"the conditions are totally altered. Men either believe
in Him or they do not. There is no third course. They
have been face to face with the great alternative and
taken their side." Let me point out, however, that the
question here is not about the great alternative. That
remains. It exists in the case of Christians and non-
Christians alike. There is but one method of salvation
for all men, and it is through Him who is the new life of
humanity. The heathen welcome or refuse Him according as they welcome or refuse the spirit of self-sacrifice,
which is His gift. The question, therefore, is simply as
to whether there may not be, even in a Christian land,
a true, though unconscious, relation of the soul to the
redeeming Lord ; or, in short, whether in some cases the
alternative may not assume such a form that an *apparent*
rejection of Christ may be in truth a *real* acceptance of
Him.

It requires very little insight into human character as
it exists around us to see that what we term the rejection
of Christ covers a great variety of meanings. Nothing
can be more hopelessly astray from the facts than to talk
as if in every instance it had the same moral connotation,
as if men had always the same Christ presented to them,
or refused to give allegiance to Him on the same grounds.
There are, first, those who deliberately refuse His call
because of the surrender which it implies of their own
self-will. They love an easy, indulgent life too much to
consent that He should reign over them. The root of
their aversion is moral selfishness, which, if persisted in
to its final issues, so saps the spiritual character that they
can have no place in the kingdom of Christ's self-sacrificing love. There are, alas ! too many whose whole spirit

is so plainly in antagonism to everything that Christ
came to accomplish for man and in man, that we are
compelled to say in fidelity to His revelation, ' Except
they repent, they must perish '; and of whose repentance
we can cherish only that faint hope which is already a
half-despair.   But these are not the only people who
stand aloof from the confession of Christ.   Who has not
known some at least who have been alienated from the
Gospel by the form in which it was set before them ?
It was no good news of a great emancipation.   Its
essential evangelical character was lost in abstract doctrinal statements about the Trinity and the Atonement,
and salvation made to depend on formal acquiescence in
their truth.   There was no appreciation of the historic
method by which Jesus first verified Himself to men as
the Son of God, through His human purity and tenderness, and His passion to save.   And as the doctrine did
not visibly arise out of great ethical facts and necessities,
it had no manifest bearing on man's ethical life.   Hence
it was often most ostentatiously accepted by those whose
conduct and temper were as little Christlike as possible,
and who were not aware of the abhorrent contradiction.
Not only so, but the most lurid pictures were drawn of
the fate in store for the great mass of mankind, just
because they did not give the required adhesion to
dogmas which were not merely in themselves mysterious,
but which came suddenly upon mankind " like the shot
out of a pistol," and the belief of which had no obvious
or necessary relation to moral nobleness.   In such
circumstances the rejection of Christ was many a time
due, not to what was lower, but to what was highest and
best in men; it was the indignant repudiation by a

loving and generous soul of a message which it felt to be a caricature of the divine; it was, though they knew it not, the appeal from Christ as preached to Christ as He really is.

It is easy to say, they had the Gospels to enlighten them as to His true character, and to correct the extravagances of the preacher or the Church. But, for long centuries, the Gospels were not in the hands of the people at all. And even when, through the Reformation, they became an open book, the laity naturally relied on the interpretation given by their appointed teachers. In every age the ideas regarding Christ of the immense majority of professing Christians are those inculcated by the ministers of the word. It cannot but be so. The fervour of the first Reformation period in the sixteenth century, the scholasticism of the seventeenth, the uninspiring moralism of the eighteenth, were but reproductions in the people of the temper and attitude of recognised leaders. We are apt to delude ourselves by thinking that the Christ whom *we* see so manifestly in the evangelical records, as approving His divine claims by the unique glory of His human life, can be as plainly seen there by any man. But it is not we individually who have discovered Him in these pages. The critical, exegetical, and theological work of the past generation, together with the uprising of a new social spirit, has brought out the perspectives of His life and thought as they never were visible before, and also created in us the capacity of perceiving them. We accredit ourselves with a spiritual insight, which is largely the product of the age whose atmosphere we breathe; and condemn for their perversity men who did not welcome a Christ whom they never saw, and perhaps could not see.

Among ourselves this rejection of the Gospel from a deplorable misconception of its gracious message is much less possible than it once was. Whatever defects there may be in the preaching of to-day, it is profoundly ethical. It proclaims a Christ who is essentially a regenerating power in the soul, and whose imperatives are but the expression of an insistent love which knows that it alone has an incomparable boon to confer, and which, therefore, in its demand for the response of obedience, knows how to wait, suffers long, and is kind. Now it cannot be denied that the alienation or antagonism to this Gospel of redeeming and uplifting love on the part of many alert and cultivated minds is not antagonism to its spiritual content, to the aims and principles which it strives to make dominant, but to the historical and intellectual affirmations which underlie it. They not merely admit, but eagerly embrace its conception of human duty, and labour to make its spirit of self-sacrifice their own. Not a few declare emphatically that they would gladly accept it in its totality were this compatible with honesty, so great an accession would it bring them of strength and comfort. But if such acceptance is to be of any moral avail, it must be above all straightforward and sincere ; and they find it absolutely impossible to assent to the miraculous basis on which historic Christianity rests. A sinless individual life as a part of an organic sinful humanity is to them simply incredible, and no amount of testimony or cumulative probabilities has any weight against a conviction approaching in their view as near to certainty as anything not axiomatic can.

Obviously, this fundamental denial of Christ's stainless-ness renders nugatory all further discussion of His personality. Others, while prepared to confess that Jesus possessed a unique moral nature, and that the refusal to acknowledge this is to contradict plain facts in *a priori* interest, are wholly unable to believe that God personally manifested Himself in humanity once for all at a certain time and place,[1] with all the antinomies or mysteries that such a manifestation involves as regards the person of Christ, and the inner life of the Godhead.

The true answer to this and similar objections, as I conceive it, has been already given. I hold that the only adequate and rational interpretation of the life of Jesus, when read in the light of human experience, is that He was God manifest in flesh, and that the presence of God in an exceptional and transcendent sense in a single personality, and consequently *at a certain time and place,* was the best and most direct method that we can conceive, of securing His indwelling in *universal* humanity. But while I maintain this, I cannot shut my eyes to the fact that many who on these grounds, insufficient as I regard them, fail to surrender themselves to Christ as a personal Saviour, are nearer to Him than they imagine. It is not only, as in the case of the heathen, the dim light of the natural revelation of the Son in heart and conscience which they have had to guide them; the higher revelations, coming from the incarnate Son through His Church, of infinite self-sacrifice as the condition and crown of blessedness for man, have dawned upon them, and they have in no small measure responded. They have suppressed their own

[1] T. H. Green, *Miscellaneous Works*, vol. iii. p. 197.

ambitions; they have counted themselves debtors to the weak and helpless; they have taken disappointments patiently; they have scorned to indulge in petty grudges and envies; they have known how to bear even with the uncharitable. Where have they learned the secret? From Him whose Spirit is abroad in the world. It may come to them in the shape of impersonal law, but it is an imperative law of good, and they give their hearts to it. That it does not speak to them of a renewing fellowship, but is only a great unquenchable yearning within them, deprives them indeed of its inspiring consolation. But to say that this loss has been incurred by their own self-will, by that pride of intellect which refuses to submit itself in a childlike spirit to God's revelation of Himself, is often quite unwarrantable. In very many instances it is not a proud self-reliance that prevents them from acknowledging the historic faith. They are at times penetrated with an almost painful sense of their own helplessness before the ultimate mysteries of the universe, and a constant longing for a clearer light. They are tender-hearted, humble. But they follow what seems to them the highest truth they know. That their human sinfulness blinds them to much which God means them to see and to rejoice in is true, as it is true of the devoutest Christian that ever lived. But it is not any special moral defect which obscures from them the vision of the personal Christ to which others attain. It is an intellectual characteristic springing partly from a natural mental bias, and partly from the influences which have moulded their thought. If every man is born a Platonist or an Aristotelian,[1] it is hopeless to expect that

[1] See Coleridge's *Table Talk*, July 2, 1830.

the most dispassionate love of truth will lead men to the same speculative expression of the supreme realities of existence, and irrational to brand those with ethical shortcoming who, with every mark of ethical sincerity, arrive at disapproved conclusions. It may be that, with the most genuine desire to retain the creed of their fathers, they are driven by their mental constitution and their scientific or philosophical training to recast its form, while conserving great part of its spiritual content.

Let us remember what precisely the problem before us is. It is through His Incarnation, His life, death, and resurrection, that the eternal Son became the centre of a new life for humanity. The normal type of Christian faith is that which yields itself to Him as a present and ever-living Redeemer. It is this conscious acceptance of Him as the mediator of pardon and righteousness which is ever set forth in the New Testament as saving faith. But here are men who, while they formally reject the Church's interpretation of His personal claims on account of speculative difficulties which are to them insuperable, frequently manifest in a high degree just those inward qualities of disposition and temper—self-denial, forbearance, love—which it was Christ's mission to quicken in human souls, and which constitute the life of His kingdom. And since, moreover, they have derived these qualities from His inspiration, from the response which they make to His redeeming spirit, operating through the society around them, may we not cherish the hope that, though they do not possess the normal type of faith, yet this response of theirs is implicit or embryo faith which is counted for righteousness? No doubt in this matter we go beyond what is plainly revealed in Scripture; and deductions, however probable, from the message once delivered to the saints, can never be placed in the same category with the message itself. But the question is not an arbitrary or needless one; it is in a sense forced upon us by two unquestionable facts, the universality of Christ's redeeming work for humanity, and the welcome given by men who repudiate its dogmatic form to the spiritual power which flows from it.

It may seem to some as if the very suggestion destroyed all that is distinctive in the Christian Gospel, by so enlarging the conception of faith as to dissipate it. What, then, is a true faith in Christ? It is not simply an intellectual assent to propositions regarding His person and work, but a receptive attitude of heart and mind to Christ Himself, a dying to self and a laying hold of the life He brings. It involves, indeed, as has been already shown,[1] an intellectual assent to certain facts and truths. The historical is embedded in the heart of the spiritual, and is at once its inspiration and guarantee. That is Christian faith in its complete form. But this conscious historical element is fundamentally a means for the production of the spiritual, which is the longing for the fellowship and likeness of Christ. And, thank God, there are thousands in our midst who draw out of every doctrine of their creed its spiritual equivalent for guidance and support. They assimilate it, as the body assimilates food: it is transmuted into a vigorous moral and devotional life. The basis of their confidence is the assured victory of Jesus in His death and resurrection, by which He

[1] Lecture VIII.

23

opened the kingdom of heaven to all believers. Yet
no words can exaggerate the intensity with which they
" follow on to know the Lord " that they may attain
to the same " mind " that was in Him. But what
multitudes of Christians there are to whom such a
description is ludicrously inapplicable. They believe
Christ to be the Saviour of the world; they trust to
be accepted at last only through His merits; they pray
to the Father in His name. But no one would say
that the desire to walk as Christ walked is the master
passion of their being. Occasionally they wake up to
a fitful consciousness that they are poor enough disciples.
But the mood passes. The sense of what they owe to
Christ does not cure their ill-temper, or stir them to
pity for the hapless and submerged. That is the
aspect at least in which they appear to others. We
are not entitled to say of them that they have no part
or lot in Christ's redemption. There may be struggles
and self-repressions of which we know nothing. But
if finally they find their place in the kingdom of the
Blessed, it will not be because they yielded an assent
to doctrines about Christ; but because there was, though
little perceptible by us on earth, some true longing in
their hearts towards Him, and the righteousness which
He mediates; because, in short, there *did* exist in them
that opening and aspiration of the soul by which alone
the divine can enter and possess the human.

It cannot be denied that unbelievers in doctrinal
truth frequently surpass such in the best qualities of
Christian character. This will be readily acknowledged
even by those who sorrowfully add that, as salvation
is only through faith in Christ and not on the ground

of human merit, it cannot be theirs. Unquestionably
by the deeds of the law no one can be justified, and it
is not on account of their good works or superior
excellence that there can be any hope of their acceptance.
But is there not at the root of their finest moral qualities
the same spirit which is the essence of conscious faith?
It is grossly untrue to affirm that their disregard of
their own comfort, their gracious considerateness of
thought and feeling, their loyalty to truth and duty,
are fostered or accompanied by the Pharisaic motive
of a personal meritoriousness. On the contrary, they
are merely striving to obey the imperatives of their
moral life, and are haunted by an abiding sense of
inadequacy and failure. If anything is clear, it is that
they are *not* trusting in themselves, *not* proud in
any petty personal way of their own attainments in
goodness, but gazing with eager eyes, it may be half-
hopelessly, at the unscaled altitudes of ideal duty.
Instead of being self-centred, they are continually setting
out on fresh pilgrimages of self-denial, just because
they are so open to any new influences of good that
beat upon their life. It is deeply to be deplored that
the best influence of all, and the fullest of consolation,
flowing from a personal Redeemer, should appeal to
them in vain on account of intellectual perplexity or
misjudgment. But surely it is at least possible that
their attitude of receptivity to the spiritual obligations
and inspirations which He has revealed to mankind
may be, to their glad surprise, acknowledged by Him
at the last as an unconscious faith in Himself.[1]

It may be urged that this receptivity is a very

[1] See Note 39, p. 468.

different thing from that radical change of heart and
character which in John's Gospel is called the new
birth, and which is involved in Paul's teaching about
justification through faith ; that it is merely the result
of the environment in which they are placed, not that
definite transformation of the inner life which conversion
or regeneration expresses.   The objection brings out
a prevalent mistake as to the relation of the right
environment to personal character, as if it were something which could be wholly abstracted, and the individual might yet remain ; whereas it is the necessary
condition for the realisation of individuality.   A man
can become a Christian, only if his surroundings are
such that the Christian message is brought to him, just
as a child requires a certain teaching and example in
order to quicken in him the personal love of goodness.
The environment is indispensable *at the beginning* for
evolving the germs of morality and religion, but when
once these have been developed in the individual he
grows in a manner independent of it, and may retain
his new convictions though transplanted to alien surroundings.   If we wish, therefore, to know how far
these good influences of environment have passed into
the soul as a part of itself, we have to ask how far
it can bear such transplantation, how far its devotion to Christ and duty enables it, when unassisted by
favouring external conditions, to resist the seductions
that now assail it.   Tried by this test, is it difficult
to conceive what would be the result in the case of
a large proportion of professing Christians?   Remove
them from the restraining influences which the Church
by its manifold agencies exercises over them, and throw

them on the resources of their own fellowship with Christ amid a debased community, and experience tells us only too decisively the probable effect. They would stand this strain to their goodness infinitely less than many whom they at present condemn for their unbelief in the Christian verity, and whose moral principles they represent as nothing but the surface reflection of their Christian environment. There are men to whom, unhappily, God and Christ are but ideal personifications, but who can hardly be tempted under any circumstances to snatch a gain at bitter cost to another; in whom purity, fidelity, compassion, are an instinct of the heart, and who go far to realise that moral wholeness and single-eyed purpose which Christ so strenuously demanded. A confirmed love of God such as theirs, is no outgrowth of the natural selfishness of man; it is, the work of the Spirit of God, "without whom nothing is strong, nothing holy." The Spirit speaks to them through the Christian society in which they dwell, and they follow His guidance. In the full Christian meaning of the word they may not be regenerate souls, but they have been converted to a new life of humility and self-sacrifice. Nor does it militate against the reality of this divine change, that they can recall no point in their experience when it began. The conception of conversion which represents it as a change occurring *consciously* at a particular time and place, is not adequate to the facts. It only describes one form of it,—that sudden transformation, by which those who, like Paul, have been directly antagonistic to Christ, pass into the joy of His communion. But some of the most devout servants of the Lord have grown up in grace. Their whole life has been but a deepening discovery and appropriation of the salvation which was theirs from the first.   That is the ideal type of conversion in a Christian land ; and it is the scandalous neglect of duty by Christian parents and by the Church which has made it less frequent than it should be.

People are apt to regard the question of the possibility of an unconscious faith in Christ as foreclosed by the language of the New Testament, because they do not realise the immense gulf that separates us in thought and experience from the days when Christianity arose.   No one who compares the ideals of Christian duty as set forth in the Gospels and the Epistles with the present character of Christian society, can fail to be struck by the glaring contrast between them.   " It seems impossible," says Dean Church, " to conceive three things more opposite at first sight to the Sermon on the Mount than War, Law, and Trade ; yet Christian society has long since made up its mind about them, and we all accept them as among the necessities or occupations of human society." [1]   Our whole modern cast of life is different.   Our political enthusiasms, our pursuit of literature or scientific research, our cultivation of artistic excellence, seem to have but little correspondence with the strenuous moral tone of the New Testament, with its spiritual withdrawal and intensity.   Yet we to-day do not maintain the legitimacy of these varied spheres of human thought and action because we have disowned the Gospel, but because we believe that the Gospel, rightly understood, claims them for its own.   It is quite possible that " the austere maxims of privation and

[1] *Gifts of Civilisation*, p. 34.

separation from secular things," which accompanied the
first proclamation of Christianity, were the only means
by which the manifestation of the eternal Son in flesh
and its immeasurable significance for humanity could
have been set forth to the world. If such a revelation
was received at all, it could not but imply a shock to the
existing view of human life. It was a transformation
whose inward greatness demanded for the time a total
break with the established framework of society. The
disparagement of ordinary relationships and common
occupations was a temporary necessity.[1] But gradually
men came to see that the social activities and interests
which they had forsworn were a part of God's intended
order of the world; that Christ came not to destroy but
to fulfil them. This result was not due to the attenua-
tion of Christian truth, but to the recognition of its wider
and profounder meanings for the race.[2] It was the
teaching of God's Spirit illuminating human experience.
Not intellectual theorising, but the logic of facts taught
men to be less confident about the immediacy of Christ's
second coming, and so taught them not to undervalue
the religious import of everyday duties in the actual
world in which God placed them.

As the course of God's providence thus produced a
change in the conception of the sphere in which the
Christian life expressed itself, so it has altered the
problem presented by the non-Christian section of the
community. The Gospel came as a great renewing
force into the midst of a corrupt society. Whatever
fragments of ancient religious beliefs still survived among

---

[1] Cf. *Gifts of Civilisation*, pp. 44–47.
[2] See Note 40, p. 469.

the peoples of the Roman Empire, had ceased to exercise any ethical influence. The Greek and Roman mythologies were, from an intellectual point of view, widely discredited ; as a practical power, they were effete, where they were not actually degrading. What met the eyes of the first Christian preachers was a debased humanity in which riotous vice prevailed. The Christian Church was but a little circle of light and purity amidst surrounding darkness. Not that the natural virtues were wholly dead ; but even at the best they had nothing of the heroic in them ; they lived a struggling, depressed life, and offered the greatest possible contrast to the passion for goodness, the enthusiasm of self - sacrifice, which thrilled the followers of Jesus. Substantially for the apostles the Church and the world stood forth in absolute antagonism, not in faith merely, but in conduct. This is plain from the picture drawn by Paul of the condition of heathendom ;[1] and his emphatic summary of the works of the flesh in broad contradistinction from the fruit of the Spirit,[2] is evidently a description of the hateful and profligate character of those who refused to welcome the Christian message. In the Fourth Gospel, written at a later date, when the dual influence, attractive and repulsive, of Christianity was abundantly manifest, the same sharp antithesis is found more pronounced. There are in it hardly any half-tones or shadings of character as in the Synoptics. They who do not believe in Jesus, who are not " His own," are reprobates.[3] " We know that we are of God," says John in his First Epistle, " and the whole world lieth in the evil one."[4]

---

[1] Rom. i.   [2] Gal. v. 19–23.
[3] See Lecture II.   [4] 1 John v. 19.

It is not difficult to see that this language is coloured by the circumstances which confronted the apostles. All that was noblest in the moral life of men was found only among believers; all that was basest, among the rejecters and despisers of the faith. When John declares, "In this the children of God are manifest, and the children of the devil: whosoever doeth not righteousness is not of God, neither he that loveth not his brother," [1] he does not merely mean to affirm that the acceptance of Jesus as the Messiah, and of God's love revealed in Him, is false and hypocritical if it does not lead to love of the brethren, but that love of the brethren cannot exist unless it springs from a conscious acceptance of Him. So far as the heathen came under the sway of this brotherly affection, they passed over into the Christian fellowship. For them the moral and the doctrinal stood or fell together. If they accepted the former they welcomed the latter also, for it presented no real obstacle to belief.

But society, as it is now, shows a very different aspect. The power of Christianity is not, so to speak, coterminous with the visible Church. It has leavened and illumined social and political life; it has set up its standard of ethics even among those who repudiate its creed, and won from them often, not a reluctant, but a willing and resolved adherence. Its message of love toward man has not only been acknowledged as the highest truth, but cordially embraced as a personal duty by a great part of what John terms "the world," though for them it does not consciously draw its inspiration and motive from the prior love of God in Christ. The

[1] 1 John iii. 10.

intellectual difficulties which they feel regarding the creed of the Church did not exist for men in the first century. It was not that they were unspeculative. The Epistle to the Colossians and the Fourth Gospel are a sufficient proof of that. Speculative thought then busied itself continually about the nature and the self-revelation of God. But while Gnostic theories might require refutation or correction, they all started from the same fundamental conception, which Christianity teaches, of God as personal and self-manifesting. *It is this basal conception itself which is now so widely in dispute.* The idea of Evolution as the regulating principle of the universe, to which Hegel gave philosophic expression, and which has recently gained its confirmed hold upon men's minds by its application to the discoveries of science, has raised profound questions as to the very possibility of a monotheistic faith. The scientific investigations which increasingly disclose what may be termed the marks of an intelligent design in nature, at the same time make it more difficult for many to see any room or function for a personal God. Their blindness to Him may frequently be due to that strange misconception of His work which led Carlyle to exclaim, " He does nothing," [1] as if God had to appear visibly, and work, not *through* nature and man, but *apart* from them, in order to accredit His presence. But it is not always so ; for Neo-Hegelianism, which in spirit and purpose is intensely religious, and everywhere finds a present God, has its greatest difficulty in showing that this immanent God has any transcendent personality at all.

Of course, we who believe in Christ hold that the

---

[1] *Life in London*, vol. ii. p. 280.

moral facts regarding ourselves and God which the
Christian revelation as a whole—in the life of Christ, and
in the experience and witness of His Church—verifies to
us, have an imperative force outweighing all speculative
doubts.   But it is the Church itself which, under the
exigencies of Western logic, has entered the speculative
sphere, and it ought to recognise that the faith it proclaims presents to-day perplexing problems which were
never raised by its first promulgation.   It cannot content
itself with *merely* repeating the apostolic word that " the
whole world lieth in the evil one," but must face in some
way the existence of a Christian morality and spirit, outside the body of confessing disciples.   To speak of those
who manifest this spirit as belonging to the same class
as the Pharisees, whose conduct, in traducing Jesus and
calling good evil, led Him to warn them of the sin
against the Holy Spirit which hath no forgiveness,[1] is
simply to invert the truth, and is perhaps to incur the
danger of committing the unforgivable sin itself, in that
it is a refusal in the interest of a preconceived theory to
acknowledge the goodness to which conscience testifies.
For they bear no antipathy to Christ, but a profound
sympathy and reverence towards Him and the qualities
of character which He declared blessed.   Just as many a

---

[1] Both Matthew (xii. 24–32) and Mark (iii. 22–30) declare that it was in
reference to the Pharisees' contemptuous description of His miracles as
wrought by the devil, and the spirit of hatred to good which they thereby
showed, that Jesus spoke of the sin against the Holy Ghost.   There can be
little doubt that this is the true historical setting of the words, though Luke
(xii. 10–12) puts them in a different connection.   Godet argues, however,
that in the Third Gospel they refer, not to what immediately precedes, on
which they seem to have no direct bearing, but to the same circumstances as
Matthew and Mark relate, and which Luke records in the previous chapter
(xi. 15).   *Comm. on St. Luke, in loc.*

sincerely pious Jew might, on account of his Pharisaic education and prejudices, see in Jesus no Messiah but only a visionary enthusiast; so, under the influence of scientific conceptions carried into a spiritual sphere to which they do not apply, such may see in Him no more than the noblest of the sons of men. They may, like the Jew, though from other causes, utter "words against the Son of Man," but they do not commit the sin against the Holy Spirit by insulting and hating the goodness of which He is the inspirer in humanity. Their doubts as to a personal God will be no longer possible when the imperfect conditions and distorting atmosphere of our mortal thought have vanished, when in the light of Christ's revealed presence they "see light," and discover that all goodness in man has its source and centre in an ever-living Lord. And if it should prove that, though *here* they did not recognise Him, He recognises them *there*, would the Incarnation of the Son seem less glorious than the Church has sometimes thought it to be? And may it not be that God is seeking to teach us by the very existence of such souls among us, that the redemption of Christ has a significance of which the apostles at the beginning of the Church's career did not and could not dream?

It may be said that these are exceptional instances of nobleness, very different from the men and women of everyday life with their mixed characters of good and evil. They *are* exceptional, and I have spoken of them in particular, because they constitute a conspicuous challenge to the Church to say how it correlates the fact of their goodness with its doctrine of Christ as the one mediator of the Father's will, and the centre and consummation of all good in the universe. But the principle of judgment which governs their destiny applies to all men. If it exists at all, it is a universal law. They are but an example, " writ large," of what concerns humanity.

It is indeed to be confessed that the ultimate separation of men into righteous and wicked does not apparently correspond with the facts of human life as they exist around us. Nothing is more obvious, nor to the religious soul at times more distressing, than the prevailing colourlessness and indecisiveness of character in mankind. There are some who evidently bear the image and superscription of the King in their exceeding goodness and grace. There are others whose lives are a defiance of all moral law. But between these two extremes lies the vast territory of the morally uncertain and irresolute, whose whole conduct suggests a divided heart. This, however, is a difficulty which Christianity on any construction has to face. It is not confined to the world outside the Church. It exists, perhaps, in its most aggravated form *within* the Church. I do not refer to those of its members who, though they may avoid the gross sins which, by a most inadequate application of the word, it terms " scandalous," yet violate in conduct and temper the spirit of the Christian life, but to the immense number of well-meaning people who are " at ease in Zion." The Church charitably cherishes the hope of their final salvation. On what ground? On the supposition that there may be, notwithstanding all appearances, an inward change of heart. It may be but a feeble germ of faith, but it establishes such a relation between them and Christ as makes them the inheritors of His redeeming

life.   But if such a decisive change, which it is impossible
for human knowledge to pronounce upon, is conceivable
in their case, is it not equally conceivable in the case
of what I have called unconscious faith?   We cannot
measure the degree of receptivity to the Spirit of Christ
which is needed to give a determinate cast to character
on the side of right and truth.   Manifestly that degree
is no constant quantity.   The same amount of receptivity which in one man means a growing force of good
within him, means in another a declining moral life.
" If," says Professor Salmond, " there be at the decisive
point of life, however late it may come, the tremulous
inclination of the soul to God, the feeblest presence of
that which makes for righteousness and faith, in heathen
or in Christian, it will be recognised of the Judge, and
under the conditions of the new life it will grow to more
in the power and the blessedness of good." [1]   But such
a tremulous inclination can only, on Dr. Salmond's view
of a final separation of souls, lead to an ultimate acceptance and bliss, provided it represents a decisive movement
of the heart, or, to use Mr. Gladstone's words, " a vital
warmth which is ascending, not one which is sinking
into the abyss." [2]   Whether it is the one or the other is
only known to Him who can estimate all the cross-
currents, intellectual and moral, that have beat upon
that soul's life, and so can discern its inherent responsibility.   He who sees in the apparently careless Christian
a germ of true receptivity to good, may also see it in the
apparently equally careless life of one whom either
ignorance or intellectual perplexity has kept back from

[1] *Christian Doctrine of Immortality*, p. 672.
[2] *Studies subsidiary to Butler's Works*, p. 207.

the confession of Christ. We are here in the presence of the ultimate mysteries of the soul. "Let us fall into the hand of the Lord, for His mercies are great; and let me not fall into the hand of man." [1]

That there is a central bias or trend in every character fixing its essential quality as good or evil, is the presupposition of the whole Biblical revelation. It is involved in the very idea of a moral universe that evil shall finally be eliminated and the kingdom of good established, "where One Will alone is loved, and only One is done." [2] But it is neither according to Scripture nor to moral instinct to depict the final judgment as implying that all in whom the same set of character exists receive an equal reward or penalty. It is strange how much the doctrine of a destiny proportionate to the measure of fidelity or failure, so perpetually on our Lord's lips, has become almost "a lost theological principle." [3] It must be recovered and emphasised if we are to bring the fundamental conceptions of a final judgment and a final kingdom of righteousness into relation with the moral facts of life.

All theological thought worthy of the name recognises that the redemptive work of Christ exercises its beneficent power far beyond the sphere in which the ordin-

[1] 2 Sam. xxiv. 14.

[2] "The Christian doctrine of a final judgment is not the putting of an arbitrary term to the course of history; it is a doctrine without which history ceases to be capable of moral construction." Denney, *Studies in Theology*, p. 240. "That speculation," says Martensen, "which rests satisfied with the words of the poet, 'This world's history is its judgment too,' as an ample exposition of the 'Last Day' of Christianity, really transmutes God's righteousness itself into a Tantalus, in continual unreality, pursuing a goal which it never can reach." See the whole passage, which is admirable, *Dogmatics*, pp. 465, 466.

[3] Salmond, *ibid.* p. 670.

ary means of grace operate. While the Roman Catholic Church has consistently declared through the centuries, *extra ecclesiam nulla salus*, yet, as Cardinal Newman points out,[1] it does not follow, because there is no Church but one which has the evangelical gifts and privileges to bestow, that therefore no one can be saved without the intervention of that one Church. It is the normal appointed medium of saving grace, but He who appointed it is above His own agent, and may act through other media if it please Him. Hence the Roman Church holds along with this principle of exclusive salvation, the doctrine of " invincible ignorance," or that it is possible to belong to the soul of the Church without belonging to the body. Both dogmas are set forth authoritatively by Pope Pius IX. in the same Encyclical; and in an Allocution nine years earlier he refuses to give any definition of what invincible ignorance is.[2] " Who would be so bold as to claim that he could fix the limits of this ignorance according to the measure and variety of peoples, countries, minds, and so many other things ? "[3] The same distinction is acknowledged by Protestants when they speak of the " uncovenanted mercies of God,"[4] the

---

[1] " A Letter to His Grace the Duke of Norfolk, on occasion of Mr. Gladstone's recent Expostulation," p. 122.

[2] *Ibid.* p. 123.

[3] " Quis tantum sibi arroget, ut hujusmodi ignorantiæ designare limites queat, juxta populorum, regionum, ingeniorum, aliarumque rerum tam multarum rationem et varietatem ? "—Dec. 9, 1854.

[4] This was a favourite expression with the older type of High Churchmen. It is customary to regard it as supercilious. But it is not necessarily so. It may simply imply that, while a man is loyal to what he regards as the "faith delivered to the saints," he has the honesty to recognise the existence of moral and spiritual excellence which he cannot correlate with it. The narrowness lies with those who hold a historic and well-defined faith with no such reserve of hope.

belief in which, as extending to many outside the Church, is quite compatible with the most strenuous conviction that Christ is the only Way to the Father. The Thirty-nine Articles and the Confession of Faith equally anathematise those who hold that a man may "be saved by the law or sect which he professeth, so that he be diligent to frame his life according to that law and the light of nature."[1] Every believer in Christianity is bound to join in this repudiation of the doctrine that salvation may be merited by men, if only they perform good works according to their lights. For such a doctrine, as Dr. Hort says, "resolves God's dealings with men into a mere prize-giving and prize-refusing, in which the one uniform prize is something altogether separate from the performance which wins it, and nothing more is demanded of the prize-giver than to see fair-play."[2] The only salvation for men is that which comes from Him who by His Incarnation has won a new life for humanity; and it has to be received, not earned. The believer does not earn it because he accepts certain Christian dogmas; he becomes a partaker of it, because of his receptivity to Christ's life. And if any who hold other religious opinions are saved, it is not on the ground of these opinions or of their own good works, but solely because, as seen by God, they possess something of the same receptivity to the Spirit who proceedeth from the Father through the Son.

Some such conception of an unrealised or unconscious relation to Christ seems to me indispensable, if on the one hand we are to do justice to plain moral facts, and

---

[1] *Article XVIII.* ; cf. *Confession of Faith*, chap. x.
[2] *Life and Letters of F. J. A. Hort*, vol. ii. p. 335.

24

on the other are to give to Christ's redeeming work its central place in the deliverance and consummation of humanity. When it is omitted or denied, there inevitably grows up a feeling of disproportion between an Incarnation which cannot but have a universal bearing on the race, and the limited area of human life in which the ordinary means of conveying its grace are in any true sense effective. Indeed, the Gospel is apt in that case to lose its gracious character, which is its very heart, and to assume the aspect of a menacing challenge which subdues by fear or stings to revolt.

Nor does this idea of unconscious faith, expressed by the theories of invincible ignorance or the uncovenanted mercies of God, involve any surrender or depreciation of the historic faith in its completeness. Surely the intensity with which the Church devotes itself to foreign missions does not depend on the conviction that the heathen will perish eternally if they die without believing in a Saviour of whom they know nothing. If it does, it is likely to ebb more and more. There is much greater probability that Christians will be condemned for their remissness in not carrying the Gospel to the heathen, than that the heathen will be condemned for not fulfilling impossible conditions. The Church is irresistibly borne forward to missionary work by what it believes to be the direct command of Christ; above all, by the impulse of His Spirit who dwells in it, and fills it with His passion to save and bless. The fact that there may be unrevealed purposes of grace towards the heathen abroad who are ignorant of the Gospel, or towards many at home who apparently reject it, does not affect by an iota the Church's plain duty. It has a definite com-

mission to fulfil; it knows that there is but one Way of
salvation, and that the only faith in Christ of which
Scripture speaks is the conscious surrender to Him as
a personal Redeemer and Lord. Loyalty to Him and
compassion for all who know not the blessedness of this
faith, alike compel it to set forth His claims upon human
hearts in all their absoluteness and graciousness. It sees
that, however it may be with some elect spirits, the lack
of belief in a Christ who died and rose means for the
great mass of men the loss of the one guarantee and
inspiration for a pure and self-sacrificing character, and
of all real hold on the awful solemnities of human destiny.
And even the life of these elect spirits, who have almost
an instinct for goodness, is without the inward resources
of strength and consolation which spring from fellowship with a living Lord who has triumphed over sin and
death, and which upbear the soul amid its direst distress
and endow it with a confident hope for the future of the
race. The old word is still true: " This is the victory
that overcometh the world, even our faith,"[1] and it is
the very tenacity with which the Church maintains and
manifests this assured historic faith, which communicates
much of its own spiritual quickening to those who witness
it from without.

III. Very many who have felt the pressure of the
problem we have discussed, have sought its solution, not
in a deeper conception of what faith *here and now* in its
essence is, but in the theory of an Intermediate State
between death and the judgment, in which those who on
earth have welcomed the Gospel shall be purified of their
imperfections, and prepared for the final kingdom of

[1] 1 John v. 4.

blessedness; and in which all, whether in heathen or Christian lands, who have had no true probation here, shall have the offer of God's mercy in Christ made known to them. I am not insensible to the high motives that have led some men to this belief. It is usually called a "pious opinion," and one must admit that the name is frequently not inappropriate, as what are termed pious opinions have not seldom more piety in them than the formal creed that patronises them.

First of all, then, this doctrine has not arisen from any clear declaration in Scripture. The two passages in the First Epistle of Peter[1] which its advocates chiefly rely upon, are the most enigmatical utterances of the apostolic writings. After a minute and dispassionate examination of all the factors that enter into a right exegesis, Professor Salmond asserts that "in both paragraphs the interpretation which leaves most unaccounted for, and does least justice to the best understood terms, is that which finds in them the disclosure of a ministry of grace in Hades."[2] It is in any case rather ridiculous to rest a doctrine of such significance on phrases that are no better than conundrums, and to which Augustine's words regarding Paul's reference to the "Man of Sin" are even more appropriate than in their original application: "I confess that I am entirely ignorant what the apostle meant."[3] But perhaps it would be too much to expect some modern exegetes to make so humiliating an admission. Neither Christ nor Paul affords us any definite conception of the condition of souls in the

---

[1] Chaps. iii. 19; iv. 6.
[2] *Christian Doctrine of Immortality*, p. 485.
[3] " Ego prorsus quid dixerit fateor me ignorare."

interval between death and the judgment. Rather does their thought overleap the intervening period.[1] They speak of the blessed dead as in sleep; but the term is used "for purposes of hope and comfort, not to indicate a space of unconsciousness." This vagueness constitutes a remarkable contrast to the insistence with which the Church has striven to pierce the mystery.

The theory of an intermediate state draws its real support, not from exegetical considerations, though these are often put in the forefront, but from certain broad moral necessities which it appears to satisfy. It commends itself to those who hold that there is no acceptance or rejection of Christ except that which is conscious and made under the plain offer of the Gospel; and who, since the requisite condition of knowledge does not exist in the present life in the case either of the heathen or of multitudes in Christendom, find in an intermediate state of probation for such the only solution compatible with the justice of the final judgment. It is urged, secondly, that when we consider the soiled lives which even

---

[1] The *apparent* exception to this, in Paul's case, is 2 Cor. v. 1–8. But to suppose that he there teaches the assumption by the soul at death of a temporary (spiritual) body, to be worn in the intermediate state till the resurrection, is simply literalistic exegesis run mad. Cf. Salmond (*supra*, pp. 562–568), who endorses Dean Plumptre's saying, that it is a "manifest fact that the intermediate state occupied but a subordinate position in St. Paul's thoughts. . . . He did not speculate accordingly about that state, but was content to rest in the belief that, when absent from the body, he would in some more immediate sense be present with the Lord." Dr. Bruce's remark may be added: "It is better to hold that the apostle had no clear light on the subject of the intermediate state, no dogma to teach, but was simply groping his way like the rest of us, and that what we are to find in 2 Cor. v. is not the expression of a definite opinion, far less the revelation of a truth to be received as an item in the creed, as to the life beyond, but the utterance of a wish or hope." *St. Paul's Conception of Christianity*, p. 385. On the meaning of the word "Paradise" in Christ's promise to the dying thief, see Salmond, *supra*, pp. 349, 350.

believers carry with them into the unseen, it is unreasonable to suppose that in a moment they are miraculously transformed into spotless goodness.   Surely advance in holiness implies *there* as *here* a gradual moral process by purifying chastisements.   And the intervening period between death and the judgment, being essentially transitional, as the disembodiment of the spirit shows, precisely answers to the conception of a preparatory state previous to the final kingdom of bliss.   Though the soul be adjudged righteous, it does not enter on its full felicity till the consummation of all things.   Nor indeed can it;—" they without us shall not be made perfect."

1. While I am not prepared to affirm that the Scripture usage which always represents the judgment as based on the " deeds done in the body," [1] absolutely negates the idea of a *probationary* intermediate state, it certainly directs all our thoughts away from it.   It is easy to argue that the earthly life is still judged, though the judgment may extend also beyond its limits; but the argument pretty well empties the phrase of its solemn meaning.   Nor can it be maintained that the words have a primary and normal reference to those who live in the Christian dispensation, and do not take account of what may be termed exceptional cases.   For the great parable in Matthew xxv. shows that it is on the basis of their earthly record that the heathen are judged.   So far as Scripture teaching goes, there is no indication that any man, or class of men, is judged on any other basis.

But further, the extension of probation beyond death *for some only*, introduces confusion into the whole char-

[1] Cf., *e.g.*, Matt. xxv. 31–46 ; 2 Cor. v. 10 ; Rev. xx. 12, 13.

acter of the judgment. "When we think," says Dean
Luckock, "of the conditions of the other world, and
especially the absence of all those carnal temptations
which are such a hindrance to every effort for the
renewal of man in the image of God, we cannot but go
on and say that it may be, yea, it must be, easier in
the spiritual sphere to yield the obedience which the
Almighty Sovereign claims." [1] But this hypothesis of
compensating opportunities in the other world which
are to counterbalance the disadvantages of this, does
not so much resolve as perplex the problem. Those
carnal temptations which no longer distress the soul
whose probation is postponed to the future state, are the
occasion of many a man's fall and condemnation whose
opportunity of grace is exhausted on earth. If he too
had been delivered from their thrall, he might have kept
his loyalty to God. To say that *we* are no judges of
the measure of responsibility, and that God, whose it is
alone to judge, is able to secure equal justice for all, is
not relevant to the point; for this applies to His judgment, whether human opportunity be confined to this
life or extend beyond it. The question is, how far such
extension enables *us* to see a justice in God's judgment
of men which we cannot perceive in that judgment if it is
based wholly on the present life. Granted that, on any
theory, inequalities of spiritual opportunity will remain;
on *this* theory they are aggravated to the last degree, in
that the contrast is no longer between different conditions in the same state of being, but between two
different states of existence. If we are to allow *our* idea
of justice to influence us, we would surely say that it

[1] *The Intermediate State*, p. 192.

would be desirable for all men to have their period of probation carried into a world where the seductions of the flesh exist no more.[1]

We delude ourselves if we imagine that by any hypothesis as to the future we can redress the inequalities of earth, and secure what *we* would call a fair and equal opportunity to all men.   Even though you postulate an environment after death wholly free from the thousand evil influences that here have degraded a soul, yet that soul bears its degradation with it into the life to come. It does not start under its new conditions where many others start.   But if there be still that germ of good in it remaining from its earthly life, which is capable of development into a true faith in Christ, then God, " in whom is no before," does not need to await its development after death to adjudge to the soul its true destiny.

2. But, leaving aside the question of probation, is there not need of an intermediate state for the *training and purifying* of the soul, so that it may be prepared for the fellowship of the saints and the vision of God?   Is not the statement of the Shorter Catechism, that " the souls of believers are at their death made perfect in holiness, and do immediately pass into glory," [2] a direct contradiction of all that we know of the processes of the moral life? But the suddenness of the transformation which is here objected to, is involved, it appears to me, in any view which

---

[1] In the view of some, the intermediate state *is* a continuation for all, whether righteous or unrighteous, of the probationary character of the present life.   It is little to say that this conception of it is not supported by a single indisputable verse of Scripture ; what is of more importance is that it is extremely difficult, if not impossible, to reconcile it with the whole tone and presupposition of New Testament teaching.

[2] Question 37.   Cf. *Confession of Faith*, chap. xxxii. ; *Larger Catechism*, Question 86.

affirms a second coming of the Lord, and the establishment of an undefiled kingdom.   If the disembodied soul
is to retain the essential characteristics which belong
to it in its earthly experience, if the innate tendency to
evil which so plainly marks it *here*, and which we term
original sin, is to exist *there* too as an element in its
spiritual struggle, then no degree of growth that we can
conceive will bring it to perfect goodness.   The elimination of that tendency can never come by development,
but only by miracle or sudden renewal of the inner being;
and the miracle would not be less in the case of advanced
than of immature goodness.

The same idea of a special supernatural act underlies the apostolic conception of a regenerated universe,
a transfigured environment of souls, at the revelation of
Jesus Christ.   It is not the instantaneousness of the
soul's renewal which constitutes any difficulty for those
who believe in Christ, but the unwarranted notion so
often bound up with it, that the perfection of the soul
implies that it is henceforth beyond the need of growth,
—a notion that has no ground in Scripture or reason.
From the ultimate kingdom of the Most High evil is
shut out ; but there, as truly as on earth, the finite soul,
if it is to live, cannot cease to develop.   Its perfection
simply means its freedom from sin ; it does *not* mean the
equalising of all capacities, or the abolition of the law of
progress.   The difference, then, between the doctrine
which affirms the immediate entrance of the faithful at
death into the light of God's presence, and that of an
intermediate state of purification,[1] is simply this, that

---

[1] Dr. Hort says, " The idea of purgation, of cleansing as by fire, seems to
me inseparable from what the Bible teaches us of the divine chastisements ; and

while both declare that the righteous enter into a condition where they grow in goodness, the former doctrine places the growth after God has spoken His transforming word eliminating the soul's sinfulness, and the latter conceives of this growth as a continuation, though under happier opportunities, of the soul's earthly struggle, and as thus endowing it with a greater relative fitness for undergoing the renewal of the great day, and for beholding at last the Beatific Vision.

Neither the one doctrine nor the other is free from grave perplexity. Neither can be made to correspond with the view of the future judgment in Christ's parable. For, whether souls are at death assigned to their final destiny or pass through a temporary period of training and cleansing, they must in either case, ere the day of judgment, know the standard by which they shall be tried. There is no room, certainly none on the former theory, for the surprise expressed both by the righteous and the wicked, according to Christ's picture, at the verdicts of the Judge. Yet the surprise belongs to the essential teaching of the parable. The truth is, that the whole period between death and the judgment is left by Scripture in shadow. It may be questioned whether our Protestant Confessions, in speaking so confidently about

though little is directly said respecting the future state, it seems to me incredible that the divine chastisements should in this respect change their character when this visible life is ended. . . . I do not believe that God's purposes of love can ever cease towards us in any stage of our existence, or that they can accomplish themselves by our purification and perfection without painful processes." *Life and Letters,* vol. ii. p. 336. Such a conception of purification through pain may be tenable regarding the intermediate state, just because it is in that case a transitional experience. But is Dr. Hort's idea of its continuance so long as the soul exists compatible with the Biblical representation of the condition of the righteous after the Last Judgment and of the sinless character of the final kingdom?

it, do not go beyond their brief. But they are undoubtedly true to the strain of Scripture as a whole, so
far as they insist on placing the emphasis of moral
decision within the present life. And if that be so, we
are driven to reconsider whether the traditional idea of
the nature of that decision, the idea, *i.e.*, of faith in Christ
as necessarily conscious, is adequate to the facts.

I have thus sought in these Lectures to show the
reasonableness of that faith which sees in a historic
personality the Incarnation of the Eternal Son, an Incarnation which is at once the revelation of the divine
ground underlying the human sonship that sin has
marred, and also the supreme act by which human sonship is restored and realised. But just because it is the
special interposition of the Eternal in time, not merely
for the emancipation and perfection of humanity, but for
the consummation of God's entire purpose in creation, it
is much more likely that human thought tends to limit
than to exaggerate its beneficent power, and the conditions under which that power operates *even in time*.
" Now we see in a mirror darkly : but then face to face."

NOTES TO THE LECTURES.

LECTURE I.

NOTE 1.   See p. 10.

The Greek and Christian Ideals of Conduct.

It has been said that the difficulty for the critic of the life and thought of the Greeks is " to seize exactly that which is Hellenic — enduring and common to the race, not transient and due to individuals—in their religion and their ethics." There are, certainly, great divergences between the thought of the Homeric period and that of the dramatists and philosophers of the fifth and fourth centuries B.C.   But even with the inevitable discrediting of the earlier polytheism and the emergence of deeper ethical conceptions, the æsthetic tendency of the Greek mind remained its dominant characteristic.   Fresh elements came into view as involved in the ideal of conduct ; but the ideal itself was still that of harmony, proportion, balance. The key-word was πέρας, limit or measure, which was the mark of the highest reason and the highest moral good.   The ἄπειρον, the unlimited, the immeasurable, was the symbol of evil, of misery.

" Beauty to the Greeks was one aspect of the universal synthesis, commensurate with all that is fair in manners and comely in morals.   It was the harmony of man with nature in a well-balanced and complete humanity, the bloom of health upon a conscious being, satisfied, as the flowers and beasts and stars are satisfied, with the conditions of temporal existence.   It was the joy-note of the whole world, and echoed by the sole being who could comprehend it—Man. . . . When we arrive at Aristotle, who yields the abstract of all that previously existed in the Greek mind, we see that the scientific spirit has achieved a perfect triumph.   His science is the correlative in the region of pure thought to the Art which in Sculpture had pursued an un-interrupted course of natural evolution."—J. A. Symonds, *The Greek Poets*, 3rd ed., vol. ii. pp. 377–382.

Now Christianity has rendered impossible this artistic con-ception of human action, by its revelation of the infinite element involved in all conduct, the incalculable character of the positive obligations inherent in every relation of life.   It has thus created a dualism in man's moral consciousness which from the nature of the case can never on earth be brought to unity.   Whether men accept the Christian solution of the ethical problem or not, whereby an implicit harmony attained here is to be followed by an explicit harmony hereafter, the problem itself, in the complex character which Christianity has given it, remains a permanent one for progressive human experience.

"We are practically agreed," says Aubrey Moore, "as to the moral standard.   Cynic and Cyrenaic, Stoic and Epicurean lived different lives, and justified the difference by their moral theories.   For us one type of character has won its way to security, the Christian type, the morality of the Gospel.   So far as men differ about the moral standard now, they differ rather in their views of the history of morals, how the present type came to be what it is, whether it can be accounted for by a progressive natural evolution, or whether the Christian ideal was not a revelation, and a new departure, prepared for, indeed, but not the product of previous development.   As we take the Christian type, so Aristotle took the Greek type ; but he did not concern himself as to how it had come to be what it was, or why it was the fullest known expression of reason.   We claim the Christian standard as a standard for man as man, and criticise the moral standard of the *Ethics* as local and national, and therefore transient.   This is felt directly we attempt to transfer the virtues of the *Ethics* to modern life.   We feel the μονοκωλία of Greek ethics, as Aristotle felt the μονοκωλία of the Spartan type of character."—*Essays Scientific and Philosophical*, pp. 154, 155.

The same transformation through the awakened sense of the infinite is seen in the domain of Art itself. As Sculpture with its exactness of line and severe proportions is the representative art of the Greeks, so Music, which is, as it were, the attempt to express the unutterable in feeling and aspiration, is the representative art of modern thought. Cf. Symonds, *ibid.* chap. xxv.

———

NOTE 2. See p. 17.

The Consequence of divorcing Duty from Immortality.

The inevitable alternatives resulting from such a divorce— viz. that Duty either (1) becomes a sadness and an oppression ; or (2) is gradually emptied of its essential imperativeness—are well illustrated in the two following passages.

(1) " ' It is conceivable,' she (George Eliot) says, ' that in some minds the deep pathos lying in the thought of human mortality—that we are here for a little while and then vanish away, that this earthly life is all that is given to our loved ones and to our many suffering fellow-men—lies nearer the fountains of moral emotion than the conception of extended existence.'

" It was, indeed, above all things, this sadness with which she contemplated the lot of dying men which gave to her convictions an air of reality far more impressive than the rhetorical satisfaction which is sometimes expressed at the prospect of individual annihilation. George Eliot recognised the terrible probability that, for creatures with no future to look to, advance in spirituality may oftenest be but advance in pain ; she saw the sombre reasonableness of that grim plan which suggests that the world's life-long struggle might best be ended—not, indeed, by individual desertions, but by the moving off of the whole great army from the field of its unequal war—by the simultaneous suicide of all the race of man. But since this could not be ; since that race was a united army only in metaphor—was, in truth, a never-ending host

> ' Whose rear lay wrapt in night, while breaking dawn
> Roused the broad front, and called the battle on,'

she held that it befits us neither to praise the sum of things nor to rebel in vain, but to take care only that our brothers' lot may be less grievous to them in that we have lived.   Even so, to borrow a simile from M. Renan, the emperor who summed up his view of life in the words *Nil expedit*, gave none the less to his legions as his last night's watchword, *Laboremus.*"—F. W. H. Myers, *Essays : Modern*, pp. 267, 268.

(2) " When the supernatural does not come in to overwhelm the natural and turn life upside down, when it is admitted that religion deals in the first instance with the known and the natural, then we may well begin to doubt whether the known and the natural can suffice for human life.   No sooner do we try to think so than pessimism raises its head.   The more our thoughts widen and deepen as the Universe grows upon us and we become accustomed to boundless space and time, the more petrifying is the contrast of our own insignificance, the more contemptible become the pettiness, shortness, fragility of the individual life.   A moral paralysis creeps upon us.   For a while we comfort ourselves with the notion of self-sacrifice ; we say, What matter if I pass, let me think of others !   But the *other* has become contemptible no less than the self ; all human griefs alike seem little worth assuaging, human happiness too paltry at the best to be worth increasing. The whole moral world is reduced to a point ; the spiritual city, ' the goal of all the saints,' dwindles to the ' least of little stars ' ; good and evil, right and wrong, become infinitesimal, ephemeral matters, while eternity and infinity remain attributes of that only which is outside the realm of morality.   Life becomes more in-tolerable the more we know and discover, so long as everything widens and deepens except our own duration, and that remains as pitiful as ever.   The affections die away in a world where everything great and enduring is cold ; they die of their own conscious feebleness and bootlessness."—Seeley, *Natural Religion*, pp. 251, 252.

NOTE 3.   See p. 27.
The Prayers of Christ.

The portion of the Lecture dealing with this subject is sub-stantially a reproduction of an article entitled, "Did our Lord unite in prayer with His disciples?" contributed by me to *The Thinker* for October 1893. Strange as it may appear, considering the unbroken silence of the Gospels regarding any occasion on which Jesus took part in common prayer, the question of His abstention has not, so far as I know, been argued anywhere in detail. The general attitude has evidently been to take for granted that in this respect He was "like unto His brethren."

Dr. Stalker, in his *Imago Christi*, states with emphasis the same view as Dr. Bruce. "The Twelve were a kind of family to Him, and He assiduously cultivated family worship" (p. 133).

Finding, however, that Dr. Dale in his last volume, *Christian Doctrine* (pp. 105, 106), pronounced with equal emphasis for the "solitariness" of Christ's prayers, I took the liberty of sending him my article and asking if he was aware of any book in which the position he took was examined and maintained. In the reply with which he favoured me, he said that he was unable to recall any such discussion, but that he had himself held that position as long as he could remember, and was surprised to find in a recently-published volume of great merit a different opinion expressed. That theologians of equal eminence should thus propound opposite views on a phase of Christ's conduct surely not unimportant, without feeling called upon to enter into an argument in vindication, shows how very little the subject has been directly faced.

Bishop Chadwick in his Donnellan Lectures, *Christ bearing Witness to Himself*, declares decisively for the view advocated in the text. " Although He (Jesus) says, 'Watch and pray,' although He says, 'Could ye not watch with Me one hour?' He says not, Pray with Me. Observe how St. Paul implores his Churches to help him with their prayers, and mark how deep the chasm between the two. Why then does it never occur to anyone that

Paul thought more of human prayers than Jesus thought, except that everyone, however unconsciously, is sensible of the higher plane of existence on which Jesus moves?" (p. 105). It would perhaps be truer to say that the problem presented by the contrast between the prayers of Jesus and those of Paul, instead of being solved in this way, has, in nine cases out of ten, not been realised as existing.

NOTE 4. See p. 30.

The "*Morbidity*" of Self-examination.

Mr. R. L. Stevenson (*Across the Plains*, 303, 305) says, "The idealism of serious people in this age of ours is of a noble charac-ter. It never seems to them that they have served enough ; they have a fine impatience of their virtues. . . . If we require so much of ourselves, shall we not require much of others ? If we do not genially judge our own deficiencies, is it not to be feared that we shall be even stern to the trespasses of others ? And he who (looking back upon his own life) can see no more than that he has been unconscionably long a-dying, will he not be tempted to think his neighbour unconscionably long of getting hanged ? It is probable that nearly all who think of conduct at all, think of it too much ; it is certain that we all think too much of sin. We are not damned for doing wrong, but for not doing right. Christ would never hear of negative morality ; *thou shalt* was ever His word with which He superseded *thou shalt not.*"

The truth contained in these words is apt to obscure the fallacy that underlies them. They are a valiant protest against the morbidness of mere introspection. The defects of our character are certainly not to be overcome by brooding over them, but by turning to the immediate duties that lie before us, and fixing our thoughts on the ideals of excellence for which our nature craves, till they animate us with passion and hope. It is through the positiveness of love and achievement that we are saved from the negation of failure. But, on the other hand, it is the very keenness of our sense of shortcoming that drives us out of ourselves for deliverance. Disregard of moral faults, as if they were of no moment or simply steps in an onward movement, is to a genuine soul impossible, and even if possible, ruinous to ethical advance. It is impossible, because it cannot so shut its eyes to the facts of its own life and its inherent responsibility. The plain recognition of its sin as bound up with its personality is involved in fidelity to its true self : and without such fidelity virtue is but a name. And, secondly, the constant realisation of our defects is a necessary factor in the process whereby we rise above them. It is more than the diagnosis that precedes the cure—it is the means by which the beauty and joy of goodness are afresh revealed to us through the bitter experience of its loss, and preserves in us that spirit of humility and self-mistrust which is receptive of the divine. Even when the faith in a personal Lord who fulfils Himself in us is lost, the imperative obligation of this inner veracity remains for all strenuous spirits. They still keep judging themselves and following on to know and gain the highest ; though in their case introspection, just because they do not lose themselves in Another, tends to frequent depression and weariness. But the Christian is relieved from this depression, because for him the *subjective* is balanced by the *objective* : they are complementary, and form two sides of the same spiritual experience. The gradual disclosure of his subjective need is met by the fuller revelation of a redeeming and indwelling Power. Self-examination, instead of paralysing his energy, re-quickens it, by increasing his receptivity and surrender to the Spirit of the conquering One.

It is a strange misconception to fancy, as Mr. Stevenson does, that unless we are genial in judging our own deficiencies, we shall be tempted to apply a stern measure to others. There is no parallel in the two cases : and the best souls feel that there is none. We cannot fully estimate, on the side of omission, our own blameworthiness : but we know it as we do *not* know the blameworthiness of our neighbours. "Gentle towards others : severe towards oneself" is the instinct of all ethical sincerity. The self-judgment which issues in censoriousness is a caricature of the reality, which lives only in an atmosphere of humility and love.

NOTE 5. See p. 38.

Christ and Evolution.

Professor Le Conte (*Evolution ; its Nature, its Evidences, and its Relation to Religious Thought*, 2nd ed., pp. 360–364) holds that, " as organic evolution reached its goal and completion in *man*, so human evolution must reach its goal and completion in the *ideal man—i.e.* the Christ " ; and he strives to show that the appearance of the Christ as the goal and ideal *during the process of the evolution*, and not at its close, constitutes no objection to this view. For, " in addition to all the factors of organic evolution, in human progress there is a new and higher factor added, which immediately takes precedence of all others. This factor is *the conscious voluntary co-operation of the human spirit in the work of its own evolution.* The method of this new factor consists essentially in the formation, and especially in the *voluntary pursuit, of ideals.* In organic evolution *species* are transformed by the *environment.* In human evolution *character* is transformed by *its own ideal.* Organic evolution is by necessary law—human evolution is by voluntary effort, *i.e.* by free law. Organic evolution is *pushed* onward and upward from behind and below. Human evolution is *drawn* upward and forward from above and in front by the attractive force of ideals. Thus the ideal of organic evolution cannot appear until the end ; while the attractive ideals of human evolution *must* come—whether only in the imagination or realised in the flesh—but must come somehow *in the course.* The most powerfully attractive ideal ever presented to the human mind, and therefore the most potent agent in the evolution of human character, is *the Christ.* This ideal must come —whether in the imagination or in the flesh, I say not, but— must come somehow in the course and not at the end. At the end the whole human race, drawn upward by this ideal, must reach the fulness of the stature of the Christ."

The hopelessly ineffective character of this solution is manifest from Professor Le Conte's inability to pronounce whether his human ideal is to be conceived as actual or only imaginative : for it makes the greatest of all differences whether we regard it as the one or the other. (1) A Christ who is merely the imaginative ideal of human excellence, is *not* the goal, but only the conception of the goal. The two, as we shall see, are necessarily related : but to treat them as identical in value is to confuse the problem. (2) Professor Le Conte does nothing to establish his assertion that even the absolute imaginative ideal must come in the course of the development. Experience teaches just the reverse, viz. that the progress of humanity is secured by the *gradual and successive* supersession of lower by higher and fuller conceptions of excellence. Nor is this law affected by the fact that the forward movement is largely due to the voluntary and self-determining action of man's spirit. That the race should at an early or intermediate period in its history strike out the final ideal of duty ; that subsequent generations should make no further positive contributions, and should be occupied simply in attempting to grasp what has already been proclaimed, is contrary to all probability on any evolutionary theory. (3) This conclusion is further confirmed, when we consider that the ideal in question is a *final* one. (See Iverach, *Evolution and Christianity*, pp. 199, 200.) For character is the condition of moral insight. The pure in heart see God. Increasing purity alone brings increased vision ; but the increase is merely relative. Absolute insight implies absolute inner harmony of nature. If Christ then saw and declared the final and comprehensive ideal of man's relation to God and to his fellows, it was because this ideal lived within Him as a practical experience. Hence the absolute ideal of imagination, though distinct in thought from the realisation of it in a historic personality, is essentially inseparable from it, and grows out of it.

If, again, Professor Le Conte acknowledges that "the Christ" has come in the flesh, what proof can he give that in the course of its development humanity *must* embody its ideal in a particular personality? To say that human character is transformed, not chiefly by its environment, but by the ideals of its own creating, does not help us one whit to understand how, amid the myriads of free spirits constituting the race, One alone was able to exercise His freedom so as to retain an unbroken loyalty to the good. What factors existed in Him rendering the mysterious exception possible?

The truth is that Professor Le Conte finds that the ideal of humanity *has* arisen in connection with the historic Jesus; and because it has arisen in the course of the evolution, he says it could not have been otherwise; it must have appeared. No doubt there existed such a necessity, or it would have found no place in God's revelation of Himself to men. But he begs the question when he implies that the conditions of the necessity existed within the normal experience of humanity as it is, and the forces in operation there. The necessity lay not there, but further back, in the spiritual world of which man's life is but a part. Professor Le Conte might have been led to recognise this, had he addressed himself to the historic problem involved. It is in vain to talk of the Christ as the "ideal man," unless we face the question of the *actual origin* of the conception in the life of Jesus. When we do this, it is quite obvious that there are two respects in which the term "ideal man" fails to bring out the full truth. (1) Just because Jesus starts where no one else does, from the standpoint of an inner unity with God, He possesses a type of consciousness for ever impossible even to redeemed humanity. The attainment by men of the measure of the stature of the fulness of Christ will not obliterate the distinction. (2) Closely allied to this is the fact that Christ asserts for Himself an incommunicable centrality and sovereignty relative to mankind, and thus manifests qualities not belonging to the ideal character which He sets before us, and in our case incompatible with it (Lect. II.). In a word, He is not only the Ideal of Humanity, but the Lord of it; and this double characteristic is possible only to One who, as regards the race, is both within it and above it.

LECTURE II.

NOTE 6. See p. 58.

Dean Stanley on Christ's Self-suppression.

"Other teachers, other founders of religions, have cared that their names should be honoured and remembered. *He cared not for this*, if only Himself, His spirit, His works, survived; if to the poor, the suffering, the good everywhere, were paid the tenderness, the honour due to Him. In their happiness He is blessed, in their honour He is honoured, in their reception He is received. It is the last triumph of divine unselfishness, and it is its last and greatest reward."—*Christian Institutions*, p. 48.

Nothing, surely, could well be less adequate than this, as a description of the distinctive attitude of Christ; and it is the more remarkable that the passage occurs as a comment on the significance of the Last Supper. Undoubtedly Christ's one aim was the quickening in men of His own spirit of self-sacrifice; and every manifestation of it, whether springing from a conscious thought of Him or not, was regarded by Him as a mark of that divine kingdom of which He was the head. (See Lecture IX.) But to say that He was indifferent to their recognition of Him *personally*, is precisely the opposite of the fact. The complete self-abnegation, the all-inclusive love, which constituted the blessedness of human sonship and brotherhood, was realised in Him, and could only be realised in others through Him, through a knowledge of what He had shown Himself to be. If they ceased consciously to honour Him with their homage, there was no possibility of their attaining "His Spirit" in its fulness. He was not one among many means by which they could reach the end: He was the Way. And for this reason *He so acted* that, as Professor Seeley says, "the Law and Law-Giver together" were enshrined in the hearts of His disciples "for inseparable veneration" (*Ecce Homo*, p. 49).

NOTE 7.   See p. 80.

The Authorship of the Fourth Gospel.

"The extreme views of the Tübingen school as to the late origin of the Gospel are now virtually antiquated, though still finding representatives in such writers as Pfleiderer and Martineau. By various lines of evidence the date has been steadily pushed back to a time which brings apostolic authorship within the range of possibility.   The alternatives now may be said to lie between the Apostle John and a disciple of the apostle, belonging to the Ephesian school, acquainted with the traditions of his teaching and under his inspiring influence.   The difference between these two hypotheses in the view of some is still serious, while to others it appears trivial; but it is beyond all question that the theory of Johannine inspiration, as distinct from authorship, advocated by such a weighty writer as Weizsäcker, can be regarded with equanimity by even the most conservative, in comparison with a theory which relegates the Gospel to the middle of the second century, remote from apostolic influence, and regards it as the product of new religious tendencies, and the child of an alien world."—Bruce, *Apologetics,* pp. 470, 471.

The reasons which cumulatively make the Johannine authorship highly probable, are stated with more or less fulness by Luthardt, Godet, and Westcott in the Introductions to their Commentaries on the Fourth Gospel; by Sanday, *Authorship and Historical Character of the Fourth Gospel* (cf. also his articles in the *Expositor* for 1891–92) ; Salmon, *Introd. to N.T.*; Lightfoot, *op. cit.*; and Watkins, *Bampton Lectures* for 1890.

———

NOTE 8.   See p. 80.

Harnack on the Prologue of the Fourth Gospel.

"The prologue of the Gospel is not the key to its comprehension.   It begins with a well-known great object, the Logos, re-adopts and transforms it—implicitly opposing false Christologies—in order to substitute for it Jesus Christ, the μονογενὴς Θεός, or in order to unveil it as this Jesus Christ. The idea of the Logos is allowed to fall from the moment that this takes place. The author continues to narrate of Jesus only with the view of establishing the belief that He is the Messiah, the Son of God. This faith has for its main article the recognition that Jesus is descended from God and from heaven; but the author is far from endeavouring to work out this recognition from cosmological, philosophical considerations. According to the Evangelist, Jesus proves Himself to be the Messiah, the Son of God, in virtue of His self-testimony, and because He has brought a full knowledge of God and of life—purely supernatural divine blessings."—*History of Dogma*, vol. i. p. 97 *n*.

But it is just because the prologue is so utterly different from the Gospel itself, that it is the key to it. In the Gospel the author keeps close to the historical point of view, and sets forth the facts which attested Jesus as the well-beloved Son. Before proceeding, however, to the historical account, he tells us what he regards as involved in this human revelation of a transcendent Sonship. *The Word became flesh.* "This great sentence," as Dr. Denney says in his *Studies in Theology*, p. 61, "not only puts Christ in an essential relation to God, it puts Him in essential relation to all through which God is revealed, —to creation, to human reason, to prophecy and providence in Israel." John prefaces the Gospel with it: but he does not interweave the cosmical conception of Christ with his narrative of Christ's historic appearance, for the simple reason that the latter is the problem to be solved and the former is the solution of it.

———

NOTE 9. See p. 84.

The Baptist's Designation of Jesus as the "Lamb of God."

Some have supposed that the words of the Baptist, as recorded in the Fourth Gospel, "Behold the Lamb of God, which taketh away the sin of the world" (i. 29), are, to say the least, coloured by the Evangelist's own experience. How, they ask, are we to explain so distinct an allusion at that date to Christ's sacrifice, considering the views which the Baptist afterwards cherished of the Messiahship as an external triumph (Matt. xi. 2–6 ; Luke vii. 18–23) ? Whatever difficulty exists is not to be removed by the "time-honoured exegetical tradition that John sent the messengers to resolve, not his own doubts, but theirs (see refs. in Meyer, *Matt., l.c.*). Nor is it possible to eliminate the sacrificial idea from John's early designation of Jesus, by supposing that he merely termed Him the "Lamb of God" (cf. ver. 36) as a type of innocence and meekness, and that the subsequent words were added by the Fourth Evangelist. Even if the phrase "Lamb of God" were alone used, it cannot but have carried in the Baptist's own mind a reference to the "lamb led to the slaughter" in Isaiah liii., or to the Paschal lamb whose blood shielded from the destroying angel (Godet, *Comm. on St. John, in loc.*).

If the later doubts in the Machærus prison are to be regarded as casting suspicion on these words, they practically discredit the whole account as given, not only in the Fourth Gospel, but in the Synoptics, of John's testimony to Jesus, which implies a special illumination granted to him for his unique function as Forerunner. Unless to those who are possessed by a naturalistic bias, there is nothing inconceivable in the idea that in his fulfilment of this function he should have attained at that supreme point the prophetic perception that the suffering and death of the Messiah were the necessary means of His people's deliverance. Nor, on the other hand, is it at all strange, but rather quite in accordance with experience, that this insight might vanish or grow dim, when the demands of his mission were over, and especially when his spirit was thrown back upon itself in the depression of a lonely imprisonment. Such high visions are not permanent endowments, or constant quantities. When they have served their hour, they pass.

NOTE 10.   See p. 85.

The Fatherhood of God in the Synoptics and in St. John.

When Jesus, in the Sermon on the Mount, designates God as " your Father," both Matthew (v. 1, 2) and Luke (vi. 20) mention that He was addressing " His disciples." It has there-fore been maintained by some that He does not regard God as the Father of all men, but only of such as have already welcomed the filial spirit.   But the word disciples includes all who for a longer or shorter time had attached themselves to Him as hearers. (See Meyer and Alford, *in loc.*).   Many who at the earlier stages of His ministry were drawn into the train of His followers, afterwards went back and walked no more with Him (John vi. 66).   Consequently we cannot infer from this phrase that all here addressed had in them even the *beginnings* of that spiritual experience which makes men in the full sense the sons of God.

Moreover, though the ' Sermon ' was primarily spoken to disciples, using the word in its wider meaning, yet we are distinctly told that it was addressed also to ' the multitudes ' (Matt. vii. 28 ; Luke vii. 1) ' who pressed forward to hear.'   " He spoke to all the people," says Godet (*Comm. on Luke, in loc.*), " but regarding them as the representatives of the new order of things which He was about to institute.   In Matthew, αὐτούς, ver. 2 (He taught *them*), comprises *both the people and the disciples*, ver. 1."   The attempt to show that on this or any other occasion when Jesus speaks of ' your Father,' He confines the reference to one class possessed of a certain spiritual quality, utterly breaks down. Quite naturally His addresses are described as delivered to " His disciples," because they stood nearest to Him at the time, and because His instructions were spoken specially to those who had acquired some fitness to receive them.   But they were intended for all ; and there can be no doubt that the joy and astonishment of the multitudes at His words sprang from the new truth He declared of God's fatherly relation to them as individuals.

The same truth is involved in His conduct towards the outcast and unworthy, as that of One searching for lost treasure.

The three parables in the fifteenth chapter of Luke are at once a vindication of His own course of action, and a revelation of the Father to men. When He sought the wandering or outcast, it was not to raise them into a state in which God *could* love them ; it was the manifestation of the love of the Father who had sent Him, and whose love devised means whereby His banished ones might be brought back. It is the recognition by the disobedient of God's fatherly tenderness towards them that *awakes* in them the repentant and filial spirit. Wendt puts the Synoptic view in one epigrammatic phrase : " God does not *become* the Father, but *is* the Heavenly Father even of those who *become* His sons " (*Teaching of Jesus*, vol. i. p. 193).

The Johannine teaching has unquestionably a different tone. It is not that it is restrictive in its view of God's redeeming love. On this point the Fourth Gospel is pronouncedly universalist (*e.g.* The Prologue, iii. 16, etc.). But as regards the *Fatherhood*, its representation does not strike the same note as the Synoptics. It is impossible to deny that a deep significance attaches to the fact that with one exception (and that after His resurrection) Jesus never employs the Synoptic phrase 'your Father.'[1] On the other hand, while He frequently speaks of God as 'the Father,' in a large proportion of instances He expressly correlates the term with the allusion to Himself as the Son (v. 19–27, and *passim*). It contains within it in such cases the same meaning as the more specific term 'My Father,' which also frequently occurs in John ; and indicates a Fatherhood of God to men founded on the knowledge and acceptance of Himself as the Son. As this correlation of Father and Son is so characteristic of the Gospel, analogy would suggest that in those passages where it is not stated it may be implied (cf. iv. 21–26), especially in the total absence of the distinctive Synoptic expression.

It is true that when we think out what is involved in the Johannine idea of the full sonship which belongs to the believer, we see that it has for its presupposition the Synoptic conception

---

[1] In the one exceptional instance (xx. 17) it occurs in a connection—'My Father and your Father '—which brings out emphatically the central thought of the Fourth Gospel.

of God's fatherly attitude towards him previous to his faith, and in order to his attaining it; that, in short, such a view of the universality and intensity of God's love *to the world* as is given in John iii. 16, *implies* what the Synoptics *teach*. Therefore the contrast which the Fourth Gospel presents is not in the way of contradiction, but of supplement. Yet the contrast is great, alike in what it omits and what it includes.

LECTURE III.

NOTE 11. See p. 97.

The Attestation of Sonship at the Baptism and the Transfiguration.

Matthew (iii. 17) represents the voice from heaven as addressed to the Baptist, "This is My beloved Son, in whom I am well pleased"; while in Mark's account (i. 11) the words are spoken to Jesus Himself, "Thou art My beloved Son; in Thee I am well pleased." Much needless controversy has taken place as to which is the original version. The dove and the voice, even if they were sensuously visible and audible, were only the outward signs of an invisible grace, of a spiritual assurance borne in upon the soul regarding the call of Jesus to His Messianic mission. The assurance naturally expressed itself in forms drawn from prophetic utterances (see Weiss, *Life of Christ*, vol. i. pp. 324, 325). But to argue that because Mark records the words at the Baptism as a direct personal address, while he gives the similar words at the Transfiguration (ix. 7) in an indirect form, he therefore means that the Baptism was the point where the Messianic conviction first awoke in Jesus, and the Transfiguration only the occasion of its confirmation or its proclamation to others, is, even apart from the fact that Matthew uses the same phrase in the two cases (iii. 17, xvii. 5), the very extravagance of literalistic exegesis. The psychological reasons against this view are, as I have shown in the lecture, overwhelming. An expression which belongs to the realm of spiritual intuition is not to be interpreted like a clause in a legal document.

NOTE 12. See p. 106.

The true Glory of Christ's earthly Life.

La distance infinie des corps aux esprits figure la distance infiniment, plus infinie des esprits à la charité, car elle est sur-naturelle.

Tout l'éclat des grandeurs n'a point de lustre pour les gens qui sont dans les recherches de l'esprit. La grandeur des gens d'esprit est invisible aux riches, aux rois, aux capitaines, à tous ces grands de chair. La grandeur de la sagesse, qui n'est nulle part sinon en Dieu, est invisible aux charnels et aux gens d'esprit. Ce sont trois ordres différents en genres. . . .

Jésus-Christ, sans bien et sans aucune production au dehors de science, est dans son ordre de sainteté. *Il n'a point donné d'invention,* il n'a point régné : mais il a été humble, patient, saint, saint, saint à Dieu, terrible aux démons, sans aucun péché. O qu'il est venu en grande pompe et en une prodigieuse magnifi-cence aux yeux du cœur et qui voient la sagesse !

Il eût été inutile à Archimède de faire le prince dans ses livres de géométrie, quoiqu'il le fût. Il eût été inutile à Notre-Seigneur Jésus-Christ, pour éclater dans son règne de sainteté, de venir en roi : *mais il est bien venu avec l'éclat de son ordre.*

Pascal, Pensées, ed. Garnier, pp. 122, 123.

NOTE 13. See p. 106.

The Limitations of our Lord's Knowledge.

(1) As regards the *scientific* knowledge of nature or history, "I repeat, then," says Bishop Moorhouse, "and I repeat it emphatically, the question of the age or the authorship of any passage in the Old Testament was never either started by our

Lord Himself or raised by His opponents. . . . When, however, we affirm our Lord's human ignorance of natural science, historical criticism, and the like, we are not to be understood as denying the possibility of the miraculous communication of such knowledge ; but only the affirmation so constantly made, that the union of our Lord's humanity with His divinity necessarily implies the possession of such knowledge. He might be without it. We know that in one case He was without it. He never claimed to possess it, nor did His mission require that He should possess it" (*The Teaching of Christ*, pp. 42–44). It is needless to raise the question of the *possibility* of Christ's possessing scientific knowledge : the one point that really concerns us is, whether we have any grounds for believing that He *actually* possessed it. And when we see, on the one hand, that He not only gives no indication of it in His utterances, but that the whole of His self-revelation suggests the opposite ; and when, on the other hand, we recognise that essentially His specific work for humanity belongs to a different order,—then the conclusion, if we are to be guided by the evidence and not by an arbitrary hypothesis, is not doubtful.

(2) As regards the knowledge of ordinary facts and events. This raises a more difficult problem, because the facts of the Gospels do not all point one way. There are two or three occasions where Christ's acquaintance with incidents seems to imply supernatural illumination (Matt. xvii. 27 ; Mark xiv. 13–16 ; John iv. 18). A very good example of the diverse views on this subject occurs in connection with the parable of the feeding of the Five Thousand. Canon Gore (*Dissertations*, p. 82) holds that the question addressed to Philip, "Whence are we to buy bread that these may eat ? " (John vi. 5), was not put by Christ for the sake of information ; for the Evangelist adds, " This He said to prove him, for He Himself knew what He would do." Dr. Dale (*Christian Doctrine*, pp. 61, 62) pronounces strongly for the other view. " Yes—our Lord knew *what He Himself intended to do* : but to suppose that He knew before He was told how much bread the disciples had, or that there was a lad with them who had 'five barley loaves and two fishes,' is to destroy the

reality of the narratives, and even to suggest that the story of our Lord may be full of illusions." But instances of this description, which either imply supernatural illumination or at least admit of such an interpretation, are few compared with those where Christ's questions and His exclamations of surprise distinctly and naturally convey the impression of limited knowledge. To say that the surprise was feigned, or that His questions did not signify ignorance on His part, but were merely the means He employed to draw forth the confidence of others or to relieve the tension of minds distracted by sorrow, as in the case of the father of the demoniac or the mourners at Bethany, is to run the risk of casting suspicion on the veraciousness of Christ's entire manifestation of Himself. It is but another form of the biassed Patristic exegesis of His reference to the End.

(3) It is in the moral and spiritual sphere alone that no limits can be discovered in the range or accuracy of Christ's knowledge. The question has been raised whether we are to regard His intuitive perception of character as the proof of a nature truly divine, or only as the intensification of the prophetic quality of insight. Now, while there is a true analogy between the insight of our Lord and that of the prophets, yet the difference of degree between them may almost be said to constitute a difference in kind. The latter was partial, occasional ; the former, universal in its range and immediate in its action. And this contrast takes us further back ; for the insight of any soul depends on its moral condition. A prophet's vision was variable and uncertain, came in flashes of inspiration, because his inner life was a complex struggle of good and evil, and only at times was he true to his best self. In these moments he saw God, and therefore in a measure saw men. But Jesus had the single eye of the pure heart, and so His insight remained constant.

We are not able to say whether a sinless humanity, from the mere fact of its sinlessness, its unbroken fellowship with God, would not possess the power of reading individual human lives with perfect sureness. But we can say that mere sinlessness would not entitle a man to take up the attitude of sovereignty over others which Jesus assumed, and assert for himself the right to be the one mediator between them and the Father. If we confine our thoughts merely to Christ's *knowledge*, unerring though that be in the spiritual sphere, it may not be possible to affirm that it involves His Deity: but then His knowledge was indissolubly conjoined with other characteristics that *do* involve it; and so we are driven to ask ourselves whether the existence of an absolutely stainless life, of the pure heart to which alone full spiritual knowledge is given, does not prove that it is no mere part of organic humanity, but implies a transcendent being. We have no data which would warrant us in holding that Christ's unique Sonship, the consciousness of which lay at the root of all His relations to men, and alone accounts for His tone of unshared authority as disposing of them now and judging them hereafter, contributed nothing to His unique insight into their needs, and that His knowledge was but the prophetic human gift raised to its highest power. All that we can say on this point is that, so far as we can judge, His divine insight acted not absolutely, but along what we call prophetic lines (see Gore, *Dissertations*, pp. 80–88).

An interesting discussion on the influence of Christ's surroundings on His view of the unseen world, will be found in Bishop Moorhouse's *Teaching of Christ*, pp. 113–145.

NOTE 14.   See p. 118.

The Duration of Christ's Intercourse with the Twelve.

We do not possess the materials for determining with certainty the length of our Lord's ministry. A prevalent view in the Early Church was that it lasted only about a year; but, in spite of the ingenious advocacy of Mr. Browne in his *Ordo Sæclorum* (pp. 342 ff.), it now finds little support. The Fourth Evangelist mentions three, possibly four, Passovers; and although, as both Lightfoot and Westcott remind us (*Biblical Essays*, p. 58, note 2; *Gospel of St. John*, Introduction, p. 81), we have no guarantee that he gives a complete list, there is a presumption that no

26

omission of that kind would be made by a writer who is excep-
tionally careful in his chronological references, and in his record
of the Jewish feasts. Practically, the choice lies between a two
years' and a three years' ministry ; but anything more bewildering
than the conflict of opinion on the chronology of the question,
turning upon the interpretation of the unnamed Feast in John v. 1,
is hardly to be found in literature. It is not my intention to
enter into the details, but merely to mark the broad lines of the
discussion.

Three main views may be distinguished :—

1. The Feast referred to was the Passover, and consequently
the ministry extended to three years and a quarter, from January
A.D. 27 to April A.D. 30. This may be called the traditional
view, and is well represented by Andrews in his *Life of our Lord.*
He holds that the early Judæan ministry (John iii. 22) lasted
eight months, that Jesus passed northward through Samaria in
December A.D. 27 (*ibid.* pp. 182, 183), and that the Galilean
period began two whole years before the Crucifixion.

2. The supporters of the two years' ministry may be sub-
divided into two classes—

(1) Those who, like Wieseler and Ellicott (*Chron. Synops.* ;
and *Hulsean Lectures* for 1859), believe that the Feast was Purim,
March A.D. 29. They agree with the preceding theory as to the
eight months spent in Judæa and the journey through Samaria
in December ; but they differ from it in regarding this first year
as A.D. 28, not A.D. 27, and so compress into the three weeks
between the Purim and Passover of 29, the events which, according to the former view, occupied a whole year, from the Passover
of 28 to the Passover of 29.

(2) Those who hold that our Lord's sojourn in Judæa lasted
only a month, and that He passed through Samaria in May
A.D. 28. They usually place the unnamed Feast in September of
that year, Caspari holding it to be the Day of Atonement, and
Latham and others the Feast of Tabernacles. This hypothesis,
by greatly lengthening the Galilean period, escapes the objection
urged with considerable force by Andrews (*ibid.* pp. 194, 195)
against Ellicott, that he crowds into the short space of three

weeks two-thirds of all that is recorded of Christ's work in Galilee. Much will depend on the length of time we assign to the "circuits" (Luke viii. 1 ; Mark vi. 6) which Jesus made through the surrounding towns and villages. (See Ellicott, *ibid.* pp. 169, note 3 ; 185, note 1).

How, then, does the case stand as regards the duration of Christ's *intercourse with the Twelve?* Though five[1] of the disciples were, according to the Fourth Gospel (John i. 35–51), called by Jesus apparently soon after His Baptism, yet there is no reason to suppose that they then continued with Him. They did not become His constant companions till the second call had been addressed to them at the Sea of Galilee, as related by the Synoptics (Matt. iv. 18–22). In the case of some of the Twelve, we have no assurance that they knew Him at all during the Judæan period. But on Wieseler's and Ellicott's view, which it would be presumptuous to pronounce untenable, there would remain only fifteen months after the departure from Judæa. I have therefore sought to avoid any possible over-statement by speaking of the impressions of Jesus which the disciples had at the close of the ministry, as based on *at least* a year's continuous intimacy, though personally I believe that either of the other views, which both assign a longer term, is more probable.

Caspari's *Chronological and Geographical Introduction to the Life of Christ* is a valuable contribution to the whole question ; but it is rather confusing in its method and its superabundance of detail. Latham's Chronological Appendix in his *Pastor Pastorum*, pp. 473–490, will be found useful for its shortness and lucidity.

For the *three stages* of the disciples' fellowship with Jesus and their special characteristics, see Bruce, *Training of the Twelve*, pp. 11, 12.

[1] John, Andrew, Peter, Nathanael or Bartholomew, and Philip. While there is no mention of James the brother of John, yet there is every probability that either then or soon after, he was "brought," like Peter, to Jesus (John i. 42).

NOTE 15.   See p. 122.

Christ's Self-restraint in His Miracles.

Nowhere is this aspect of them, especially as regards the *impression* they produced, stated with more freshness and force than in *Ecce Homo.*

"He imposed upon himself a strict restraint in [the use of his supernatural powers. He adopted the principle that he was not sent to destroy men's lives but to save them, and rigidly abstained in practice from inflicting any kind of damage or harm. In this course he persevered so steadily that it became generally understood. Everyone knew that this *king*, whose royal pretensions were so prominent, had an absolutely unlimited patience, and that he would endure the keenest criticism, the bitterest and most malignant personal attacks. Men's mouths were opened to discuss his claims and character with entire freedom; so far from regarding him with that excessive fear, which might have prevented them from receiving his doctrine intelligently, they learnt gradually to treat him, even while they acknowledged his extraordinary power, with a reckless animosity, which they would have been afraid to show towards an ordinary enemy. With curious inconsistency, they openly charged him with being leagued with the devil; in other words, they acknowledged that he was capable of boundless mischief, and yet they were so little afraid of him that they were ready to provoke him to use his whole power against themselves. The truth was, that they believed him to be disarmed by his own deliberate resolution, and they judged rightly. He punished their malice only by verbal reproofs, and they gradually gathered courage to attack the life of one whose miraculous powers they did not question. . . .

"It was neither for his miracles nor for the beauty of his doctrine that Christ was worshipped. Nor was it for his winning personal character, nor for the persecutions he endured, nor for his martyrdom. It was for the inimitable unity which all these things made when taken together. In other words, it was for this, that he whose power and greatness as shown in his miracles were overwhelming, denied himself the use of his power, treated it as a slight thing, walked among men as though he were one of them, relieved them in distress, taught them to love each other, bore with undisturbed patience a perpetual hailstorm of calumny; and when his enemies grew fiercer, continued still to endure their attacks in silence, until, petrified and bewildered with astonishment, men saw him arrested and put to death with torture, refusing steadfastly to use in his own behalf the power he conceived he held for the benefit of others. It was the combination of greatness and self-sacrifice which won their hearts, the mighty powers held under a mighty control, the unspeakable condescension, the *Cross* of *Christ*."—Pp. 43–46.

NOTE 16.   See p. 123.

Miracle and Natural Revelation.

The Greek Fathers, especially, have as a fundamental thought the correlation of Christianity to all other revelations of God. Nature itself implied for them that which was above nature; and they argued, as Canon Gore says, that "no one who believes that God is living and manifesting Himself in the world, can reasonably repudiate His intensified presence in Christ." The miraculous in Christ's person and work was to them a revelation of God, which accentuated and made clear the natural revelation that of itself did not suffice for those whose vision of the divine was darkened by sin.

Athanasius and Augustine expressly say "that the miracles or exceptional actions of God are to be accounted for by man's blindness to Him in His normal method."—Gore, *Incarnation of tho Son of God*, p. 246.   For detailed references, see *ibid.* p. 245; Trench, *Miracles*, chap. ii.

NOTE 17. See p. 123.

Miracle as belonging to a disorganised World.

Professor A. C. Fraser has an admirable criticism of the Spinozistic view of miracle in his Second Series of Gifford Lectures, *Philosophy of Theism.* " Spinoza's argument for the absolute impossibility of physical miracles may be taken as expressing, in a philosophical way, the common scientific difficulty. The infinite system of God or Nature, it is by implication argued, if it is Divine, must be perfect. . . . Miraculous suspension of the perfect reason, perfectly expressed in whatever is by nature, must mean irrationality in natural law thus dispensed with ; it implies inconstancy or caprice, not the absolute perfection in which there can be no room for second or amended thoughts. . . . To interpose occasional physical miracles in the physical system would be to make it other than the perfectly rational system which natural science presupposes that it must be. And so we are asked, on these premisses, to conclude that the miraculous entrance into existence of any visible event, or of any invisible inspired experience of which no natural account can be given, is absolutely impossible, and not merely a physically uninterpretable fact.

" This might perhaps be a sufficient argument, if the universe were a wholly natural or non-moral universe—if it consisted of non-moral *things* only, and not also, and this too in its highest known aspect, of good and bad *persons.* Then the only sort of science possible would be found in the sciences commonly called ' natural,' which search for the caused causes, or natural signs, of events. It might be an argument, if men at their highest, according to the true ideal of man, were only conscious automata, who could have no more than a physically scientific interest in themselves or in anything else—if this were a world in the experience of which man could have no final moral trust, and in which he could not be responsible for what he was or did, because he could not, in any degree, make or unmake his own character. But is this the sort of universe in which man actually finds himself ? Is this not a world in which *men can and do act immorally*, and in which, accordingly, without unreason, omnipotent goodness may be revealed in a larger reason than that measured in terms of the causal connections visible in nature, yet not inconsistent with this natural evolution? The existence of individual persons—moral forces—may make reasonable an unfolding of divine Purpose larger than that which appears in physical causation measured by sensuous intelligence. It seems not inconsistent with reason that physical order and method of procedure should not be the only, or the highest, form which omnipotence reveals, and that, in the final rationale of the universe, the customary order of events should have a subordinate place, in an incompletely understood yet intellectually possible harmony. . . .

" ' I hold,' says Leibniz, ' that when God works miracles He does it not in order to supply the wants of *nature*, but those of *grace ;* and whoever thinks otherwise must have a very mean notion of the wisdom and power of God.' Miracles are in that case divine or rational acts, proper to a universe that includes persons under moral relations ; while they would be out of place in a universe of things wholly under physical or mechanical relations."—(Pp. 234–237.)

Professor Fraser goes on to say (p. 238): " But if, in the progressive development of the human mind, man's conceptions of what is natural could become so enlarged as that the whole Christian revelation of God should be seen to be a development of the ordinary course of nature—theistic faith, the most deeply Christian, would then be discovered to be the most natural religion of all, but surely would not on that account be undivine. It would rather be seen as the culmination of the normal self-manifestation of God." It may be questioned whether such language does not give rise to confusion. The rationale of physical miracle does not rest merely on the fact that the universe includes *persons* as well as *things.* If *persons* were as true as *things* to the respective laws imposed upon them, that rationale would disappear ; for it rests finally on the moral disorder in which the persons have freely involved themselves. In the highest meaning of the word, it is *natural, i.e.* according to the nature of God, who is the life of the universe, that in the exercise of His restorative grace He should, as Leibniz says, manifest Himself in ways that imply a modification of the laws of that physical sphere which we commonly call Nature. But to suggest that if our conceptions were only sufficiently enlarged, we should see in this modification but the culmination of the *normal* self-manifestation of God, conveys the idea that sin, which is the pre-condition of the miracle, is as much an expression as 'the *ordinary* course of nature' is, of the ultimate divine purpose and will. The protest of the moral consciousness on this point cannot be set aside, however difficult it may be to overcome the metaphysical and scientific argument for the necessary existence of moral evil. See Note 33, p. 450, "Evolution and the Fall." For other criticisms of Spinoza's view, *vid.* Trench, *Notes on the Miracles,* pp. 15 ff. ; and Mozley, *Miracles,* pp. 19, 215 ff.

NOTE 18. See p. 125.

The false View of Miracle.

" I remarked on the absurdity of founding religion on histories of miracles. 'Ah, les miracles !' exclaimed D'Azeglio, 'je n'en crois rien. Ce sont de coups d'état célestes.' Could the strongest argument against them have been more neatly packed in one simile ? A *coup d'état* is a practical confession that the regular and orderly methods of government have failed in the hands of the Governor, and that He is driven to irregular and lawless methods to compass His ends and vindicate His sovereignty. A *coup d'état* is like the act of an impatient chess-player, who, finding himself losing the game while playing fairly, sweeps some pieces from the board to recover his advantage. Is this to be believed of Divine rule of the universe ? " (*Life of Frances Power Cobbe,* vol. ii. p. 6).

Nothing could be better than D'Azeglio's epigram or Miss Cobbe's comment as an example of the false idea of miracle. They have underlying them exactly the same fallacy that vitiates Emerson's phrase that 'miracle is monster.' The natural order is treated as displaying *all* the rules of the game, *all* the methods of regular government. But this is precisely what is rendered unlikely by the *moral* problem which the world presents.

NOTE 19. See p. 131.

Dr. Martineau on Peter's Confession of Jesus' Messiahship.

The futility of Dr. Martineau's attempt, in his *Seat of Authority in Religion*, to prove that the title of Messiah was never accepted by Jesus, but only ascribed to Him and read into His words by the apostles after His death, is exemplified in his rendering of Jesus' reply to Peter's confession. He treats it as a repudiation of the Messiahship. " The impetuous apostle breaks out, 'Thou art the Messiah.' Does Jesus accept the part? His answer is peremptory. 'Silence! to not a creature are you to say such a thing again!' and He instantly adds that at Jerusalem He expects the cross and not the crown. . . . The state of mind implied in both the speakers of this dialogue is exactly what would exist if the one had heard and the other inwardly seen nothing beyond the tragic issue at Jerusalem. If Peter had just been told not only of the cross but of the resurrection, could he have deprecated the death and taken no notice of the immortal glory to which it was but the prelude and condition? His remonstrance is plainly occupied with a humiliation pure and simple, and relieved by no reversal. And if Jesus knew and had just said that He should ' lay down His life that He might take it again,' if, having explained that this was the divine gateway to the Messiahship, He was going to Jerusalem on purpose to pass through it, how is it possible that He should meet the apostle's suggestion as an alternative, and thrust it away as a temptation? It is only in the deep darkness of the soul, where nothing is clear but the nearest duty and its instant anguish, and the issue is shut out by the midnight between, that any Satan can slink in with pleas of ease and evasion.' —(Pp. 349, 350.)

1. Even if we confine ourselves to Mark's account (chap. viii.), where the subsequent benediction on Peter involving the clear

acceptance of the title is not given, the prohibition ("He charged them that they should tell no man of Him"), standing where it does, will not bear this interpretation. It was Jesus Himself who led up to the subject, who, after hearing the different verdicts passed on Him by the people, asked the disciples pointedly for theirs. How could He possibly have abjured Peter's reply in the terms suggested, "Silence! to not a creature are you to say such a thing again!" without going on to tell them who He was and what they were to think regarding Him? Would He have put an inquiry, and, finding them in total darkness or gross error, have left them there? The key to the prohibition lies in the transformation which He introduced into the conception of the Messiahship. In that new sense alone He assumed the name. The disciples had not fully grasped it, but the beginning of it had been laid in their thought through their intimate association with Him; and they had come to have such confidence in His leadership that He could now venture to acknowledge to them what, if promulgated generally to the multitudes who had undergone no such preparation, would give rise to unavoidable and perilous misconstruction. Nothing can be plainer than that Jesus was only forbidding them to make the declaration openly, not because it was untrue, but because the time had not come for making it.

2. To say that, if Jesus believed, as the record asserts, that death was but the gateway to resurrection and triumph, Peter's suggestion of escape from it would have constituted no temptation for Him, is psychologically false. True though it was that it behoved Him to suffer these things, and enter into His glory, yet the assurance of final victory did not eliminate the agony of the intervening trial. For the conflict with sin in which He was engaged had an element in it of unimaginable bitterness; and the death in which it culminated hung over His thought like a black cloud, and filled Him months beforehand with a sense of oppression and horror. (See Lecture VI.) It was the specific and unparalleled quality of the suffering through which He had to pass, and the natural shrinking with which He anticipated it, that made Peter's remonstrance so painful to him; because that

remonstrance not only awaked in Him feelings which He had strenuously put aside and overcome as disloyal, but it brought vividly before Him the disappointment and sorrow which His resolve would cause to the hearts He loved, who amid difficulty and misgiving would follow Him to the end.

3. Dr. Martineau ridicules what he calls the strange statement, that "they questioned among themselves what the rising from the dead should mean," by asking whether the rising from the dead was not the most familiar of thoughts to the Israelite of that day, the very matter in dispute between Pharisee and Sadducee, and as such discussed before these very disciples by Jesus Himself. But surely the explanation is not far to seek. The difficulty of the disciples was not in believing in a resurrection, but in conceiving what possible connection it could have with the Messiahship of Jesus as they understood it, or in what way it would further His work.

LECTURE IV.

NOTE 20.   See p. 150.

Christ's Resurrection as a " Process."

Dr. Newman Smyth (*Old Faiths in New Light*, pp. 156, 157) holds that during the forty days the body of Jesus was undergoing a "process of resurrection," and that the earthly element which still in part belonged to it when He rose out of the tomb, was gradually attenuated or dissipated till its final disappearance at the ascension, when the body became purely spiritual. His endeavour to show that the successive appearances recorded indicate such a gradual transformation seems to me quite ineffectual. To say that Christ's aspect to Mary Magdalene when at first she mistook Him for the gardener, and then the next moment saw in Him something withdrawn and unearthly, was of a more human character than that in which He appeared to the disciples later in the day and partook of food before them

(John xx. 11–23 ; Luke xxiv. 36–43), is surely the reverse of the fact. Dr. Smyth makes much of the circumstance that in the later Galilean manifestation the seven disciples did not know Him as He stood on the beach (John xxi. 4) ; but, immediately after (vers. 12–22), the Evangelist gives us the most realistic account of the meal which Jesus provided for them, and of His conversation with Peter. It is possible, of course, by "picking and choosing" certain incidents out of the accounts to make a plausible theory. But, taking the record as a whole, there is as much plausibility in the view that it is the earlier rather than the later manifestations that contain more of the unearthly element. Matthew's declaration (xxviii. 17) that at the appearance to the Eleven on the mountain in Galilee, "some doubted," though they had already seen Him several times before, does not really point the other way ; for it seems probable that on each occasion of His manifestation they had at first their misgivings regarding Him, which He subsequently removed by plain proofs of His presence. If some of the Eleven doubted for a time, they soon ceased to doubt. The idea that Christ's resurrection, or assumption of the resurrection body, was a process slowly realising itself till it was practically completed at the point of His ascension, is an arbitrary supposition, which is contradicted rather than supported by the evidence.

NOTE 21. See p. 152.

The Ascension and the Forty Days.

As textual criticism regards as doubtful both the verse in Mark which refers to the ascension, and the phrase καὶ ἀνεφέρετο εἰς τὸν οὐρανόν in Luke xxiv. 51, some hold that no account of the ascension is given us in the Gospels, and that Acts (i. 9–11) is our only authority. But Luke's expression (xxiv. 51), διέστη ἀπ' αὐτῶν, the genuineness of which is not disputed, certainly means not merely a withdrawal, as after the previous appearances, but a final separation. Vers. 52, 53 (μετὰ χαρᾶς μεγάλης) not only show that the separation was final, but that it occurred under circumstances that demonstrated to the disciples their Master's completed triumph.[1] Dr. Gould (*International Comm. St. Mark*, p. 309) says that even if the doubtful words ἀνεφέρετο in Luke, and ἀνελήμφθη in Mark, be taken into account, they do not of themselves imply a visible ascent. But the subsequent joy of the disciples distinctly points to some such manifestation. The nature of Christ's risen appearances, with their dual characteristic, essentially implied their temporariness. As they were themselves necessary as the objective signs of His continued and trans-figured life, it was natural that they should culminate in a visible representation of the beginning of His supreme power and reign. Cf. Weiss, *Life of Christ*, vol. iii. 407–409.

The book of Acts is our only source for the statement that forty days intervened between the resurrection and the ascen-sion. From the Gospel of Luke it might be inferred that both events took place on one day; and the same interpretation might be put on the disputed passage in Mark (Gould, *ibid.* p. 308). It has been often suggested that Luke gained his information on the point after his Gospel had been completed. Was then the period of forty days, mentioned by him in Acts, not known to Christian disciples generally, even thirty or forty years after the ascension, when the Third Gospel was written ; and if known generally, could it have been unknown to one who claims to have "traced the course of all things accurately from the first"? (Luke i. 3). The Fourth Gospel, in its account of the appear-ances, speaks of a week, and in the appendix points to a longer term. Nor does the Third Gospel *necessarily* imply any contra-diction of the statement in Acts. It names no specific time ; and the fact that the words admit of the inference as to a single day may be due to that indifference to chronological exactness which is so manifest throughout Luke's Gospel. Cf. Bp. Light-foot, *Biblical Essays*, p. 180.

[1] It is quite possible, as Dr. Plummer (*Intern. Comm. St. Luke*, p. 565) argues, that Luke, when he declares in Acts i. 1, 2, that he had already written the life of Jesus ἄχρι ἧς ἡμέρας . . . ἀνελήμφθη, "considered that he had recorded the ascension in his Gospel."

NOTE 22. See p. 164.

Harnack and Martineau on the Significance of the Christophanies for subsequent Ages.

"However firm," says Harnack (*History of Dogma*, vol. i. p. 86, *n.*), "may have been the faith of the disciples in the Appearances of Jesus in their midst, and it was firm, to believe in appearances which others have had is a frivolity which is always avenged by rising doubts." To the same effect Martineau declares in his *Seat of Authority* that these visions cannot serve "as objective proofs of His immortal life. As psychological facts in the consciousness of others, their validity is simply for the persons to whom they were present; and to us the only thing they attest is the intense power of His spirit over the springs of veneration and trust in them" (p. 376). But this has no more than a superficial reasonableness. Why am I entitled to accept these appearances on the testimony of others? Because the conviction which I have of the character of Jesus, of His dominance and centrality for mankind, drawn from what He was during His ministry, would have been turned into an enigma, as that of the disciples was, by His death. His crucifixion, had it been the close of all, would have been as unnatural to me as it was to them; and nothing but such appearances, which testified both to the continuity and the transfiguration of His earthly life, would have resolved the enigma, and restored my inmost experiences of Him to harmony. The mere circumstance that I did not myself live at the time when the revelation was in process, *does not disable me from seeing the congruity and necessary interdependence of its different parts.* I can judge of the truth of the disciples' witness regarding what I have no direct means of perceiving, from its relation to what I do perceive, and what I actually know of Him. Nor is there any inconsistency in saying that His appearances to unbelievers would have been futile, and yet that the Church should preach the resurrection to all men as a part of the Christian Faith. For the Church can never preach it effectively except to those whom it first subjects to the discipline of intercourse with Jesus which the apostles underwent; *i.e.* to those in whom this *præparatio* produces the same fitness for seeing in the risen Christ alike the crown and the interpretation of His previous life on earth.

NOTE 23. See p. 167.

Herrmann's Conception of the Exalted Christ.

Professor J. S. Candlish, in reviewing Herrmann's *Communion with God* (*Critical Review*, April 1896, p. 123) says: "While he contemplates almost exclusively the earthly life of Jesus, he avoids the fatal error of a merely humanitarian view, that of making our Saviour a mere departed man. He believes that He is living now, able to help and bless us. Only, he insists that we should always look at Him through His earthly life, because as to His present activity we have only general statements, and those actions of His that reveal His character and will, all belong to His life on earth." This seems to me hardly to bring out what is really involved in Herrmann's position. He certainly affirms that, when God touches us and reveals Himself to us in the historical Jesus, we cannot but believe that Jesus is taking part now in our struggles "with all His human sympathy and power." But as he asserts quite as strenuously that this belief is only a thought or doctrine arising from and expressing faith in our redemption, that there is no actual fact known to us which could produce this belief by its undoubted reality, and that there is nothing in experience which warrants our speaking of a communion with the Exalted Christ (*Communion with God*, p. 223), he practically empties the belief in Christ's present help of all rational content. The Christian consciousness from the first has declared that so far as any fact of experience attests communion with the Father, it equally attests communion with Him through whom alone the Father is truly known. They form parts of one indivisible whole (see Lecture IV. p. 166). Herrmann, indeed, appears to agree with this, when he quotes with approval Luther's saying that "the recognition wherein He (Christ) and the Father are recognised is one recognition," though he immediately proceeds with his usual confused combination of opposites to evacuate the declaration of its obvious meaning. Luther meant just what John meant when he wrote, " Our fellowship is with the Father and with His Son Jesus Christ " (1 John i. 3). To speak of a present communion with the Father through a Christ who is *not* present with us and in us, or who does not verify His presence, is something like a contradiction in terms. Moreover, as it is merely " *human* sympathy and power " which Herrmann ascribes to the Exalted Christ, it is folly to think of these qualities as possessing an unlimited value for all souls : and if limited, *how far* are we entitled to draw comfort from the thought of Him ? Anyone who maintains, as Herrmann is said to have done at a recent Conference at Eisenach, that " all speculations concerning the pre-existence of Christ must be declined with a heart as cold as ice," ought to see that in that case all speculations concerning the nature of Christ's *present existence* and the extent to which He intervenes to aid us are fundamentally nugatory, and the religious comfort based upon them a superstitious emotionalism.

LECTURE V.

NOTE 24.   See p. 172.

The Universalism of Christ.

Though it was only gradually that the full significance of Christ's divine Sonship was realised, yet the recognition of His cosmic function involved no conflict of opinion among believers. It was simply the inevitable statement for thought of what their belief implied.

But on another vital point the Church had to pass through a prolonged struggle before reaching unanimity, namely, the question of the universalist or particularist reference of Christ's teaching and work.   How are we to account for Paul's controversy with the Judaist section? Was it due to a mis-understanding by the original apostles of Christ's universalism? Or was Christ's own view particularist and Jewish? "Jesus," says Weiss, "had appeared in Israel, and on principle laboured for Israel exclusively. He wished to realise the kingdom of God, according to promise, among the chosen race, who were to participate in its salvation to the greatest extent. It is true that when the people became more and more hopelessly hardened, He had spoken of the passing over of salvation to other peoples, and of the destruction of Jerusalem and the temple; but this prophetic threat might remain for ever un-fulfilled, if the nation as such were to turn and be converted" (*Introduction to the New Testament*, vol. i. p. 166).

1. It is perfectly obvious that in one sense the ministry of Jesus had a particularist aspect. He was not only a Jew by birth, by training, by all the surroundings of His life, but He was loyal to His Jewish inheritance. He had the deepest reverence for the older revelation; and His own teaching had for its pre-supposition the acquaintance of His hearers with the law and the prophets. But all this does not prove His thought particularist *in essence.* Just because He was speaking to Jews, He bade them be true Jews, and enjoined the faithful observance of their national worship. Only thus could they discharge the function which was theirs in the order of Pro-vidence : for, as Burke finely puts it, "the situation of man is the preceptor of his duty." But the real question is, What did Jesus emphasise as primary and fundamental? Was it not what was ethical, spiritual, what belonged to man as man and to his essential relation to God? Can we point to anything in His message concerning the kingdom of God—its nature and the conditions of entrance into it—which made that kingdom characteristically Jewish as opposed to Gentile? Jesus did not openly repudiate the distinction between Jew and Gentile, as Paul afterwards did; but He *undermined* it. The grounds on which He broke down the barriers within Judaism between Pharisees and sinners, between the scribes and the common people, implied the breaking down of all barriers between

27

Judaism and what lay outside of it. Speaking broadly, therefore, we may say that, from first to last, His teaching was implicitly universal. That He Himself did not see that it was so, is wholly incredible. We cannot tell, indeed, what knowledge Jesus possessed of the nations beyond; but that does not affect the fact that He must have recognised that the demands which He made for the true service of God could be fulfilled by any earnest soul of whatever land or race.

It is specially needful to insist on this point, that universalism was a necessary *implication* of His thought, because with regard to the explicit utterances of it attributed to Him, attempts have been made to throw doubt on their authenticity, or to explain away their importance as merely forced from Him by the exigencies of His later position. If, however, it be embedded in His whole view of man's relation to God, then the occasional expression of it becomes in every way probable. Even in the very flood-tide of His Galilean ministry, He declared that many should come from the East and the West, and should sit down with Abraham, Isaac, and Jacob in the kingdom of Heaven, while the sons of the kingdom should be cast out.[1] But it was only natural that these intimations should chiefly belong, as represented in the records,[2] to the closing period of His life, not because the idea only then dawned upon Him, but because the circumstances made its utterance appropriate or indispensable. As was remarked regarding His foresight of His own death, no blunder could be greater than to "judge of *His* knowledge of His mission at any point by the degree in which He communicated it to others."[3]

Jesus felt Himself called of God to a lot within the chosen people, because He was Himself the culmination of the revelation made to them in the past. As that revelation had been through a special nation, so it had to complete itself there. That He Himself lived within the limits of Judaism was not a confession that He was merely the crown of a national or racial faith,

---

[1] Matt. viii. 11, 12.
[2] Matt. xxi. 43, xxiv. 14; Mark xiii. 10; Luke xiii. 29; John xii. 20–32.
[3] See *ante*, p. 100.

but rather the vindication of the older religion as an inherent part of a world-revelation. It was not the lowering of His message to the particularism of the Jewish religion, but the elevation of the latter into a universal significance first fully revealed in Him.

The problem which Jesus had to solve was not the destruction of Judaism, but its consummation, the liberation of its spiritual content from the restrictions of its form. That under such circumstances as those depicted to us by Luke (iv. 16–31) He should have, even at the opening of His ministry, indicated the supersession of Jewish privilege, is not at all unlikely; but manifestly this could not be His usual or characteristic tone, if He were to implant in Jewish minds the germs of His wider faith. Had He perpetually employed language which seemed to them to disparage their most sacred traditions (as would have been the case had He, like Paul, reduced Jew and Gentile to the same level before God), He would have arrested His mission at the outset. He had largely to put Himself in their place, and work through the forms of their thought. Primarily, therefore, His universalism *had* to be implicit. He did not so much give them new religious terms, as fill the old terms with a new meaning and reference. Hence it was only after He had at least partly accomplished this in the case of a chosen circle of followers, and attached them unalterably to Himself, that He spoke openly and frequently of the larger issues of His Gospel, and the ingathering of the "nations" ($\tau\grave{\alpha}$ $\check{\epsilon}\theta\nu\eta$). Weiss's remark that these declarations about the passing over of salvation to other peoples, and the destruction of Jerusalem, are to be regarded merely as "prophetic threats," may be left to take care of itself.

2. We can see, then, how unavoidable it was that a conflict should take place in the Apostolic Church regarding this question of universality. Jesus saw that if He were to conserve the eternal element in the Jewish religion, He must work within its lines. He broke, indeed, with the existing authorities, but only because He maintained that they misrepresented it. The principle on which He acted, as regards both the teaching of His ministry and the subsequent development of His Church, was to sow

germinal truths which could only come to maturity through the
reaction of individual thought and the enlarging of experience
(see *ante*, pp. 110–114).   Therefore, while He did not leave the
disciples wholly without plain announcements of the universality
of His mission, He did not so emphasise this as to impair their
confidence in the unity and continuity of the old and the new
faiths.   Nor, while thus including the "nations" in His outlook,
did He give any instructions as to the conditions of their admission, though He could not but perceive that this was a point
which would cause difficulty even to a liberal Jewish Christian.

The consequence was that, after His resurrection and ascension, the Apostolic Church held in its heart a complex revelation,
one which, while essentially spiritual and universal, was specialist
in form and in many of its associations.   For a time the particularist element determined and conditioned the other.   That
Christ was the full and final revelation of God, summing up all
that God had previously disclosed of Himself, was the unalterable
conviction of the apostles ; and they felt that in Him was centred
all blessing for mankind.   But that did not lead them to suppose that the Gentiles could share the blessing, except by passing
through the gateway of Judaism.[1]   For not merely was Christ
the Fulfiller of promises vouchsafed only to the Jews, but His
apparent example in confining Himself to His own people, and
the absence of any definite injunction from Him regarding the
equality of men before God, combined to confirm them in holding the Jewish condition indispensable.   Though this was the
undoubted attitude of the Church as a whole, there is every
probability that Weizsäcker is right in seeing in such men as

[1] It may be asked, If they believed this — *i.e.* that the Gospel, even
with this limitation, applied to Gentiles—why did not the first apostles
organise a mission to gain Gentile converts?   Simply because their primary
duty was to their own countrymen, the *direct* heirs of the promises.   The
Reformers of the sixteenth century believed absolutely in the commission to
preach the Gospel to every creature, that it was meant as much for the heathen
or for Mohammedans as for Germans and Scotsmen.   But they did practically
nothing for what we call "foreign missions," because they were wholly absorbed in saving the home Church, and making the truth prevail within their
own borders.

Stephen and Barnabas a tendency to wider views on the part of some of its members. There can be little doubt that Peter himself was sympathetic towards the larger reference; as is implied, indeed, by the whole character of Paul's remonstrance with him at Antioch (Gal. ii. 11 ff.). The Church must sooner or later, from the mere working of the spiritual principle within it, have been compelled to face openly the question of the relation of Jew and Gentile under the Gospel. That the crisis arrived as soon as it did, and that the recognition of the direct appeal of Christ to humanity as such was so speedily accorded, was due, under God, to one man.

The extraordinary insight with which Paul grasped the essential significance of Christ for the race was rendered possible by the very circumstances which at first sight might appear unfavourable to it. He speaks of himself as "one born out of due time," because it had not been his lot to be a witness of the ministry of Jesus. But it was this very fact which enabled him to perceive what was hidden from the first disciples. They could not "see the wood for the trees"; their recollections of their Lord perpetually recalled to them the Jewish and limiting conditions under which "the Life was manifested." The accidental was in their memory so bound up with the essential, that it appeared equally significant and permanent. But when Paul was confronted with the revelation of God in Christ, that revelation was already complete. In the mind of Paul the Pharisee, the story of Jesus called up immediately both the humiliation of the death and the glory of the resurrection. The two together formed one whole; and he abhorred it. But when the hour of illumination came, when it pleased God to reveal His Son in him, he saw the whole manifestation *at once* in the light of its culmination. He thus approached the earthly through the risen Christ. But this recognition of the Crucified as the Risen One meant simply that the revelation of God, which hitherto had been the privilege of Israel, had passed beyond Jewish limits; for, as it was on behalf of the law that Paul had been a persecutor, so, as Weizsäcker says, from the moment he adopted his faith in Jesus he ceased to believe in the permanence of the law. The salvation which he now rejoiced in did not come to him through Judaism, but in spite of it. His conversion to Christ was therefore his conversion to a world-wide faith.

It was not, however, by argument alone, but by *action*, that he forced the problem of Gentile rights to the front. During the fourteen years spent by him in "the regions of Syria and Cilicia" (Gal. i. 21–ii. 1), far removed as he was from the hampering influences of the Judæan Church, he followed the dictates of his own conviction, and preached to Gentiles as well as to Jews. The Church in Antioch, which he largely moulded, contained both sections. When this state of matters was challenged by the Judaisers from Jerusalem, and an appeal made to the mother Church, Paul was able to point to a Gentile Christian community who manifested in their life "the fruit of the Spirit" as plainly as any Jewish believers. And it was the actual existence of such a body of Christians which enabled Paul to contend that, if Christ had granted them the power and joy of His salvation, *He* could not mean it to be conditioned by Jewish antecedents. The essence of the faith in Jew and Gentile was alike. Paul triumphed, not merely because his reasoning was right, but because it was reinforced by facts.

When once the initial ceremony of circumcision was acknowledged not to be essential for Gentiles, the beginning of the end had come. For a period, minor restrictions might be laid upon them : for a further period, the Christian Jews might retain their Jewish observances. But henceforth the universalism of the Gospel practically stood confessed as "the mind of Christ."

Cf. Weizsäcker, *Apostolic Age*, vol. i. pp. 92–101; Harnack, *History of Dogma*, vol. i. pp. 88–91; Bruce, *Apologetics*, pp. 430–447.

NOTE 25. See p. 183.

The apparent Antagonism between Nature and the Moral Life—Sin and Death.

I. The material world, just because it is an intelligible world, presupposes spirit. The regularity of its laws, the adaptations of its several parts, and the progressive forms of beauty which are gradually evolved, show that the same rational power is at work there which expresses itself in man's consciousness. Creation is a process in which the beginning is only understood in the light of the end : but if the end interprets the beginning, it is because it is already present *in* the beginning.

There would be no difficulty in this conception of the relation between matter and spirit, if man found in nature only the manifestations of a wisdom and goodness akin to, though surpassing, his own. But he sees also much that is in direct contradiction to his ideas of justice and mercy. How is he to correlate the paroxysms that sweep over the earth, carrying suffering and destruction to large masses of sentient beings, or the appalling ferocity of beasts of prey, with the manifold marks of beneficence elsewhere visible in the physical universe? How can it be said that the same Logos operates and expresses His will in both?

It is not unusual for those who wish to argue for "the unfathomable injustice of the nature of things,"[1] to make a catalogue of the destructive acts and tendencies of the material or animal world, and then exclaim, 'Is not all this the work of a demon rather than a God?' But there is not much force in a condemnatory verdict which carefully excludes from view the gracious and healing ministries of nature, and dwells with microscopic precision on what seems disastrous or brutal in her operations. The greatest fact of all—the recognition of which lies at the basis of all fair judgment—is that nature is a unity, and that no part of her system can be seen aright unless in relation to the whole. If scientific research has demonstrated anything, it is that what we regard as alien or maleficent in physical processes is indissolubly bound up with all that conditions life and health and happiness, and that it is the latter, not the former, which is the *normal central tendency of things.* The early frost that kills the budding fruit, the whirlwinds and floods and

---

[1] *Vid.* Huxley, *Romanes Lecture : Evolution and Ethics.* A suggestive criticism of Prof. Huxley's position is given by Prof. Henry Jones in his Inaugural Lecture, *Is the Order of Nature opposed to the Moral Life?*

avalanches that destroy human habitations, are the inevitable result of laws whose constant operation makes the beauty and gladness of the world. "The same rules which are death-dealing for an hour or a day are life-giving for ever."[1] The optimism which averts its eye from the occasional catastrophe is not a tenth part so shallow as the pessimism which, seeing nothing but the catastrophe, is blind to the general beneficence of nature and her ultimate issues. Pessimism of this kind reminds one of the man who, because he was suffering from a bad toothache, declared that there could be no God.

Probably the most painful aspect of nature from the moral point of view is that presented by a vast section of the animal world, in which one race by instinct preys upon another. We shrink with natural horror from the thought of the owl swooping down upon the field mouse, or the panther tracking out and bringing down the reindeer. Yet the revulsion with which we contemplate these is partly exaggerated by the attribution of our feelings to the suffering animal. In the first place, the end, shocking as it is, comes swiftly : a sudden spring, and all is over. Or, if the hunted deer perceives the enemy afar, it is often paralysed by fear ere the fatal blow is struck. Secondly, it suffers nothing from imaginative anticipation of death. When it escapes for the time, it forgets the peril, and is in no dread of its recurrence. The pleasure it experiences from feeding and roaming, and from association with its kind, is out of all proportion to the final pain. The instinctive clinging to life common to all animals may be scorned by the pessimist as a "mad passion, working irrespectively of the individual interests, for the greatest conservation of vitality in nature"; but it is in reality the best vindication of the "good of living," and finds its indorsement in man's *rational* affirmation of it. Thirdly, hateful as the function of the carnivora seems to us, it has to be viewed, like all the destructive forces of nature, in relation to her whole economy. Through them she relieves the earth of those dead bodies which, were they left to the ordinary processes of putrefaction, would fill the streams and the atmosphere with

[1] Martineau, *Idea of Religion*, vol. ii. p. 91.

poisonous germs. The elimination of predaceous tribes would require a total and unimaginable reconstruction of the physical universe.[1]

It may be contended that whatever alleviations exist in the struggles of the animal world, do not alter the fact that it is dominated throughout by the principle of self-assertion and rivalry, which is the very antithesis of goodness as we know it in man and believe it in God. This, however, is not an adequate description of the life of the animal creation. Cosmic nature is *not* simply "the headquarters of the enemy of ethical nature": it has in it, as Professor Drummond and others have shown, the altruistic as well as the egoistic tendency. Were it not so, the latter would speedily work out its own destruction. The instincts which are the physiological basis of human self-assertion and self-sacrifice [2] are both present in the animal sphere. But the whole objection proceeds on the false assumption that you can apply a moral standard to the lower animals. Neither good nor evil has any meaning for them. These exist only where there are self-determination and ethical motives. But animals as such have no personality. The question, therefore, whether their existence is vindicable in a world governed by God is to be determined by the test, not of their morality, but of their happiness. If it could be shown that the creation of any single race involved a preponderance of pain over pleasure either in their case or that of other races, it might be difficult to reconcile it with a beneficent Providence.[3] But, so far as we can judge, the

[1] See Martineau, *ut supra*, pp. 78–97 ; Wallace, *Darwinism*, pp. 36 ff.

[2] Self-sacrifice is not, as is often represented, absolutely destructive of all self-regard. "According to the normal constitution of man," says Prof. Harris, "the two principles, sometimes designated the altruistic and the egoistic, are complemental, not antagonistic and reciprocally exclusive. They are both included in the Christian law, Thou shalt love the Lord thy God with all thy heart, and thy neighbour as thyself. . . . Man must obey the Christian law of universal love in its large, roundabout comprehensiveness, uniting the egoism and the altruism as complemental manifestations of right character in subordination to supreme love to God" (*God the Creator and Lord of All*, vol. ii. pp. 24, 25).

[3] Even then it may be doubted whether we would be entitled to declare the two incompatible, inasmuch as we have no calculus for fixing, in a universe

preponderance is all the other way in the realms of sentient existence around us.   And if the essential meaning and tendency of the universe be good, we are in no position to draw up an indictment against it on the ground of what we term defects, yet which even *we* can see to be in some measure inextricably involved in the production of the general beneficent result.   We may, indeed, amuse ourselves by imagining schemes of a physical life in which enjoyment would be unintermittent, and the capacity of pleasure would not imply susceptibility to pain ; but it will ordinarily be found that we have endowed our material Utopia with attributes belonging only to the spiritual and the abiding.

There are those who, like Hugh Miller and Dorner, believe that the constitution of nature had from the first a teleological relation to sin : that the entire mundane creation has thus been perverted in its development.   Dr. Bushnell accounts for the horrible monsters, the death, prey, and abortion belonging to the geologic eras long prior to the appearance of man, as the "anticipative consequences" of human sin.   "Whoever plants a state erects a prison, or makes the prison to be a necessary part of his plan ; which prison, though it be erected before any case of felony occurs, is just as truly a consequence of the felonies to be, as if it were erected afterward, or were a natural result of such felonies." . . . "What now does this strange process of deformity, chronicled in the rocks of the world, signify ?   What but that God is preparing the field for its occupant ; setting it with types of obliquity that shall match, and faithfully figure to man, the obliquity and deformity of his sin" (*Nature and the Supernatural*, pp. 135, 142).

I confess that this theory raises, to my mind, more perplexities than it removes.   For (1) the signs of animal monstrosity and cruelty in primeval times do not convey obviously or necessarily to man the sense that his wrong-doing is the root of the evil, nor can it be proved that it actually is so.   (2) The

governed by the mysterious principles of evolution and solidarity, the precise limit of suffering which ought to be endured by an individual or a single species, as a means towards attaining the final end of good.

fact that the cruelty existed before he appeared on the scene, instead of leading him to regard the world as shaped by the divine forethought "to the mould of his fortunes," *i.e.* to his moral perversity, rather suggests to him the very distinction which Professor Huxley makes between the cosmic order and the ethical nature that humanity has slowly and laboriously acquired. (3) It need hardly be pointed out that, though it may be natural to erect a prison beforehand in view of the felonious tendency *actually existing* in humanity, it is not quite the same thing to erect a prison, place man in it, and then give him a choice whether he will develop the evil intent or not. Such a method does not seem very favourable for producing the right decision. It may be difficult to conceive, on any view which faces the facts, how man could be originally capable of preserving perfect loyalty to God; but this idea of a " preparation of the field " for the moral transgressor, however admirable as a vindication of the divine foresight and unity of plan, practically means that every precaution is taken that man *shall* fall.

The problem of animal suffering is one of which no perfect solution seems possible under the conditions of human thought. It would perhaps be too strong to say that there is no truth in the conception of sin as entailing on the animal world not only direct, but "anticipative," consequences; but I believe that the most real alleviation of the problem comes not from any hypothesis of this kind, which, even if it were more helpful than it is, cannot be verified, but from such considerations as have already been adduced concerning the facts and character of animal life and its relation to the whole economy of nature.

II. It is in man that the creative process finds its goal. Not that that process, to our eyes at least, is continuous in its development. As there seems to be one new departure at the first appearance of life on the earth, so there seems to be another at the dawn of self-consciousness. None the less these stages, though separated by a hiatus which our knowledge does not enable us to fill up, are correlated to each other. The inorganic prepares the way for the organic, and the organic for the rational. Man is at once the last term in the evolution of nature, and *different* from nature, because transcending it as a spiritual being. Seeing, then, that in him creation, so to speak, first attains to self-consciousness and freedom, are we entitled to say that the spiritual part of his nature, being his essential characteristic as man, was ideally meant to react upon and transform the physical, so that his fidelity as a moral agent to God's purpose would have raised him above those laws by which, throughout the material world, life and growth are invariably followed by decay and death? It is argued by many, that as man was made for immortality, so, had he remained true to God, there would have been no severance between body and soul at any point : the body — being as much a part of his nature as the soul, and "its energies replenished from vital forces from within"—would either have been exempt from decay, or would have only decayed when "a new and more spiritual tenement for the soul had been prepared." [1]   It was sin that broke "the fair companionship," and brought man under the dominion of mortality to which as a spiritual being he was not meant to be subject.

This view unquestionably labours under enormous difficulties.

1. The conditions of organic life which now prevail were in operation long before the creation of man. His sin certainly did not *at the time of its occurrence* introduce death into the vegetable and animal world, and, as Dr. Orr says, there is not a word in Scripture to this effect. This is practically admitted by all.[2]   Are we to suppose, then, that his body, through its union with an immortal spirit, would have been enabled to resist those forces that make universally for the dissolution of animal organisms? Would it have been rendered impervious to the

---

[1] Orr, *Christian View of God and the World*, p. 232. "That the body of the first man," says Prof. Laidlaw, "could not be immortal by its constitution is implied, if not expressed, in the narrative. 'Dust thou art, and to dust thou shalt return.' That is to say, the curse assumes the form of a prediction, that in consequence of sin the law of organised matter should be allowed to have its way, even in the case of man. . . . Man's constitution, even in innocence, implied, to use the language of the theological schools, not an *impossibility of dying*, but only a conditional *potentiality of not dying*" (*Bible Doctrine of Man*, new edit., pp. 240, 241. Cf. Denney, *Studies in Theology*, pp. 97–99).

[2] See Laidlaw, *ibid.* p. 239.

chill of bitter winds and the poisonous germs that rise from fetid swamps? If it breathed the same air as the animals, and was subject to the same atmospheric and meteorological laws, how could it be secured against the lightning-stroke, or the destructive hurricane, or the thousand accidents that violently terminate animal existence? It is easy to imagine exemption from these mischances, and from the discomforts of hunger and thirst and weariness, if the body were itself transformed and spiritualised; but it would then require a fitting environment. To retain it in its earthly environment, and then to affirm that it was enabled to extract from it only what was life-giving and beneficial, is a most improbable hypothesis. This is not simply to assert that man is spiritual : it is to deny that he is in any sense natural, or correlated to a material world. Of course, if any one is prepared to carry the "teleological" theory above referred to so far as to maintain that in a sinless universe there would have been no physical death either for man or animals, he cuts the knot. But a physical world in which there is no dissolution of organisms is at best an unknown quantity, if it be not indeed a self-contradiction.

2. While it is held that there would be something incongruous in subjecting man as a sinless being to physical pain and death, he is still left, on this view, surrounded by the signs of mortality. The woods decay and fall, the birds die of cold, the crops which promised so well are nipped by the frost. Those whom he loves best pass into the Unseen. But if his sinlessness would not exempt him from these disappointments and bereavements, why should it be incompatible with physical mischances or sufferings? The same consciousness of God's fellowship which sustained him under the former, would support him under the latter. And it has ever to be remembered that the elimination of sin would remove nine-tenths of the "ills that flesh is heir to." There would still remain the possibility of sudden catastrophe from without; but death would ordinarily come as the inevitable result of failing strength, and an old age "serene and bright" would usher in the end. It might have been, as Canon Gore says, a physical dissolution, but it would have been a moral

victory. It would certainly not have been what men have known as death, " the overshadowing fear, the horrible gulf, the black destruction." In all that constitutes its horror and gives it its sting (1 Cor. xv. 56), in all that makes it really death for us, it entered the world through sin.[1]

The attempt to make the immortality of man guarantee his immunity from physical death necessarily involves a mystical transformation of his physical nature. It postulates a permanence and continuity of life which the material world in every part of it denies. " The things which are seen are temporal "; and a human body is none the less temporal that it is united to a spirit charged with immortality. When we speak of it as " replenished from vital forces from within," we are worlds apart from the only flesh and blood existence which we know anything of, and which is always correlated to, and conditioned by, its physical environment. It then ceases to be a natural, and yet it is not a spiritual, body. Why should we thus seek to obliterate the distinction which God has clearly made between the two spheres to which man on earth belongs? They have, by His ordinance, their own definite and separate tendencies and qualities. The Bible, as Dr. Laidlaw remarks, " consistently represents man from the first as more than animal—as a personal, responsible, and God-related creature ";[2] but this does not in the remotest degree imply that the rational factor alters, or can alter, the essential processes of the animal factor in his being.

The miracles of Christ, *e.g.*, were an illustration and a proof of the *dominance* of the spiritual over the material world : they arrested or reversed the operation of the lower physical law by the introduction of a higher and spiritual. But they did not make the processes of the lower sphere *in themselves* other than they were. He healed the sick, but He did not render the body which He restored to health incapable of subsequent suffering.

---

[1] Athanasius and Augustine both distinguish between mortality as the law of man's physical being and the " death " caused by sin. See the refs. in *Lux Mundi*, p. 536. On the Pauline view of the relation between sin and death, *vid.* Jowett's note on Romans v. 12.

[2] *Ibid.* p. 245.

He raised Lazarus, but the body of Lazarus was afterwards just as subject to dissolution as before. The only instance in which there was a real transformation of the physical organism, or an interpenetration of it by spiritual qualities, was that of our Lord's resurrection-body. But He did not then belong properly to this world. He was in a transition state, in which He appeared only for a unique purpose of revelation.[1] Is it at all credible that a similar, though lesser, transformation of the physical nature, neutralising its inherent tendencies to exhaustion and decay, would have been the *ordinary* experience of sinless man? And as to his transition from the earthly life, is it not idle to speak of a change analogous to that which Christians expect at the coming of Christ?[2] For it is one thing to believe in the ultimate transfiguration of men at the restitution of all things, when the present material order has itself ceased, and quite another to believe in such a transfiguration as the normal close of each human life during the continuance of that order.

The final problem as regards man and nature consists in the union in humanity of a soul that belongs to eternity with a physical organism which is a creature of time and change. The material world, of which man is the consummation, supplies the basis on which his spiritual life is built. Why the moral should thus rise out of the background of a vanishing non-moral universe; why God did not give to the human spirit from the first a spiritual environment, are questions beyond our power to answer. Yet *there* lies the root of the entire difficulty. But it is not to be solved by mingling or confusing things that differ.

The whole creation, says the apostle, groaneth and travaileth in pain, longing for the new birth of God (Rom. viii. 19–22). It is a great poetic word. It assuredly does not mean that the material universe awaits a period when, while still remaining material in our sense of the term, it will realise its every promise of good, but that the material leans forward ($\dot{a}\pi o\kappa a\rho a\delta o\kappa\acute{\iota}a$ $\tau\hat{\eta}s$ $\kappa\tau\acute{\iota}\sigma\epsilon\omega s$) towards the spiritual as its crown and vindication, con-

---

[1] See Lecture IV.

[2] For different views of this "transition" of sinless man, see Laidlaw, *ibid.* p. 241.

tent to lose itself in order to find itself, when the better and eternal world of spirits and spiritual environment is born.   It strives towards its fulfilment in the new heavens and the new earth, as the acorn may be said to long for its perfection in the full-grown oak.   Christianity declares that the whole man, body and soul, will yet be emancipated and made perfect ; but it assigns that victory to a state in which the body being spiritual will be a fit companion of the spirit.   To ante-date, even in part, that serene time, is to land ourselves in something of the inextricable confusion involved in all dreams of an earthly millennium.

———

NOTE 26.   See p. 183.

Human Sonship grounded in the Filial Love which is eternally in God.

Cf. R. H. Hutton, *Essays, Theological,* 2nd ed., pp. 235, 239 : "' I believe that the revelation of God through an Eternal Son would realise to us, if it can be adequately believed, that the relation of God to us is only the manifestation of His life in itself, as it was or would be without us—' before all worlds,' as the theologians say ; that ' before all worlds ' He was essentially the Father, essentially Love, essentially something infinitely more than Knowledge or Power, essentially communicating and receiving a living affection, essentially all that the heart can desire.   This is not, then, relative truth for us only, but the truth as it is in itself, the reality of Infinite Being.   It is first proclaimed to us, indeed, to save us from sin, strengthen us in frailty, and lift us above ourselves ; but it could not do this as it does, did we not know that God was, and His love was, and His Fatherly Life was, apart from man, and that it is a reality infinitely deeper and vaster than the existence of His human children. . . .

" I do not think that, as a matter of fact, the faith in an Eternal Father can either be adequately realised, as I have before said, without the faith in an Eternal Son, or that, even if it could, it would fully answer the conscious wants of our hearts.   We need the inspiration and present help of a perfect filial will. We cannot conceive the Father as sharing in that dependent attitude of spirit which is our principal spiritual want. It is a Father's perfection to originate—a Son's to receive. We crave sympathy and aid in this *receptive* life. We need the will to be good *as sons*, and to this the vivid faith in the help of a true Son is, I think, essential. Such a revelation alone makes humility divine, rather than human ; eternal, instead of temporary and finite ; such a revelation alone refers the origin of self-sacrifice to heaven rather than earth. And to make humility and self-sacrifice of essentially human birth is false to our own moral experience. We feel, we *know*, that those highest human virtues, humility and self-sacrifice, are not original and indigenous in man, but are grafted on him from above. This faith, that from the life of the Son of God is derived all the health and true perfection of humanity, is the one teaching which robs Stoicism, Asceticism, Unitarian, and Roman Catholic good works, and the rest, of their unhealthy element of pride, by teaching us that, in some real sense, every pure feeling in man, everything really noble, even self-sacrifice itself, comes from above ; that God's virtue is the root of all man's virtue ; that even the humility of the child of God is lent us by Him who lived eternally in the Father's will before He took upon Himself our human life."

NOTE 27. See p. 187.

On the expression 'God's Plan of the World.'

When we use the phrase, the *modification* of God's plan, we are speaking obviously *secundum hominem*. Professor Orr rightly says that it is an ' abstract ' way of thinking which leads us to talk " as if God had first one plan of creation—complete and rounded off in itself—in which sin was to have no place ; then, when it was foreseen that sin would enter, another plan was introduced which vitally altered and enlarged the former " (*Christian View of God and the World*, p. 322). But abstract though it be, it is our only way, if we are to speak of God's plan at all, of

28

representing to ourselves a real distinction in God's relations to the world. That distinction is that, while all that happens is included in His government of creation, some events are the expression of His will, and others are the contravention of it. Both classes of events are overruled and made subservient to His ultimate purpose ; but He is not related to both in the same way. Certainly the existence of sin did not come to Him as a surprise, causing Him to rearrange the lines along which creation was to realise itself. But as certainly He did not will it, did not *will* that His will should be contravened ; He willed that created spirits should have the power to contravene it, and foreseeing their contravention prepared in redemption for its removal.

If, then, we mean by the 'plan of the world' the detailed course of history, we may say that much of it, like the massacre of St. Bartholomew, is not His plan at all, though it is mysteriously incorporated with the action of His Spirit and subordinated to His end. Indeed, the phrase 'God's plan' is manifestly inappropriate for expressing the relation which He holds to a world of self-determining beings. For it suggests God's will or intention, and just because it is *God's* plan, it cannot but be fulfilled, thus making no allowance for the fact that, within certain limits, He has cleared a space for human freedom to operate.[1] It may be a suitable enough phrase on the lips of a hyper-Calvinist like Toplady, who says, "If God had not willed the Fall, He could and no doubt would have prevented it ; but He did not prevent it, *ergo* He willed it ; and if He willed it, He certainly decreed it" (*Works*, vol. v. p. 242). But such an argument, founded as it is on the attribute of the divine Power,

[1] Many thinkers, such as Martensen and Rothe, have maintained that there exists a divine world-plan only in a modified sense ; that as regards the ultimate end, the realisation of a kingdom of love, it is unalterably fixed ; but that as regards the persons who can only be incorporated into this kingdom by means of free agency beyond the reach of foresight, the divine world-plan is still indefinite. So also Martineau (*A Study of Religion*, vol. ii. pp. 278–280). This view is compassed by difficulties as great at least as those which attach to God's foresight of man's free activity. See Dorner's criticism of it, *System of Christian Doctrine*, vol. ii. pp. 60, 61. Cf. the discussion in Harris, *God the Creator and Lord of All*, vol. i. pp. 136–145.

is itself fundamentally 'abstract' or partial. (Cf. Mozley, *Augustinian Doctrine of Predestination*, p. 343.) If, however, we are warranted in using the inadequate word 'plan' at all in this connection, we are compelled, in order to correct its false impression, to employ a further inadequate phrase, and speak of the modification of God's plan.

NOTE 28.   See p. 194.

The Christological Formulæ of the Church Councils negative rather than positive.

It is interesting to note the consensus of opinion on this point among men representing different schools of thought.

" We ought to remember that such an attempt " (to define the Person of Christ) " did not originate with the great body of orthodox believers, but was, on the contrary, forced upon them, in a manner, by the speculations of those who differed from them. And when it is further considered that the decisions of the ancient Church, as substantially embodied in our own Confession of Faith, as well as in the Articles of other Reformed Churches, are, as to this subject, altogether *negative* ; and that no such thing as a positive explanation of the hypostatical union is contained in them,—we can see no cause for bringing against them those charges of dogmatism and presumption with which they have sometimes been assailed.   They do not intrude into things that are unrevealed, or affect a wisdom above that which is written. They simply apply to the dogmas which they negative, those statements of Scripture with which they hold them to be inconsistent."—T. J. Crawford, *The Fatherhood of God*, pp. 184, 185.

" Now these decisions do, it is contended, simply express in a new form, without substantial addition, the apostolic teaching as it is represented in the New Testament.   They express it in a new form for protective purposes, as a legal enactment protects a moral principle. . . . The language of these " (New Testament) " writings is such that I say, not only that there is nothing in the decrees of the Councils that is not adequately, if untechnic-

ally, represented there ; but that also, whereas the decrees of the
Council are of the nature of safeguards, and are rather repudiations
of error than sources of positive teaching, the apostolic language
is a mine from which, first taught and guided by the creed of the
Church, we can draw a continual and inexhaustible wealth of
positive teaching.   The decrees are but the hedge, the New
Testament is the pasture-ground."—Gore, *Incarnation of the Son
of God*, pp. 96, 97.

" Whatever opinion the reader may entertain of the decisions
at which the Church arrived on the doctrine of the Trinity, it is
at least clear that they were not in the nature of explanations.
They were, in fact, precisely the reverse.   They were the negation
of explanations.   The various heresies which it combated were,
broadly speaking, all endeavours to bring the mystery as far as
possible into harmony with contemporary speculations, Gnostic,
Neo-platonic, or Rationalising, to relieve it from this or that
difficulty ; in short, to do something towards 'explaining' it.
The Church held that all such explanations or partial explanations
inflicted irremediable impoverishment on the idea of the Godhead
which was essentially involved in the Christian revelation.   They
insisted on preserving that idea in all its inexplicable fulness ; and
so it has come about that, while such simplifications as those of
the Arians, for example, are so alien and impossible to modern
modes of thought that if they had been incorporated with Christianity they must have destroyed it, the doctrine of Christ's Divinity
still gives reality and life to the worship of millions of pious souls,
who are wholly ignorant both of the controversy to which they
owe its preservation, and of the technicalities which its discussion
has involved."—A. J. Balfour, *Foundations of Belief*, p. 279.

<hr />

NOTE 29.   See p. 211.

The Personality of God.

Whatever categories we employ to describe the Being of
God cannot fail to be inadequate ; but this does not in the

least imply that they are not substantially true. Man is more akin to God, comes nearer to Him, on the ethical than on the intellectual side of his nature. Goodness in man is of the same essence and quality as goodness in God ; but the forms of human thought are not those of the divine. Hence the terms which best enable us to realise what God is, are those which have most of ethical content, and are least speculative and abstract.

When we say, 'God is love,' that commends itself to us as a real and worthy expression of His essential Being. It suggests to us what is positive and satisfying. But when we speak of God as *personal*, we seem to call up an idea that is as much negative as positive. Yet whatever limitations are involved in personality are equally involved in love : for love implies personality, has simply no meaning apart from it, and is with reason and will one of its three constituent elements. Love is called out in a finite spirit by the sense of its incompleteness, just as its personality is only realised through the consciousness of difference from something external to itself. When, then, we apply either the one term or the other to God, we apply it by the method of eminence (*via eminentiæ*)—"the method, that is, which considers God as possessing, in transcendent perfection, the same attributes which are imperfectly possessed by man " (Illingworth). Though it appears otherwise, there is in such a case no more real reference to the limits implied in human personality than to those implied in human love. It is the positive content of the idea that is alone retained and regarded as ideally fulfilled; so that as a matter of fact human personality is no more perfect personality than human love is perfect love (*vid.* Lotze's masterly discussion of the problem of personality, *Microcosmus*, Book IX. chap. iv.).

Nothing in theological literature is more amazingly futile than Matthew Arnold's gay polemic[1] against the phrase ' a personal God.' Had it not been for that lack of metaphysical gift, which he humorously rejoiced in as giving him an advan-

---

[1] See *Lit. and Dogma.*

tage over the 'dogmatism' of the Bishops of Winchester and Gloucester, he would have seen that to deny personality to God is essentially to deny to the "Eternal, not ourselves," any moral qualities whatever. This is clearly put by Professor Fraser. "The conception of the final Power as Personal is alleged to involve a contradiction in terms. . . . Those who allege this objection to the finally ethical or theistic interpretation of existence seem to include as necessary to their idea of personality what I should exclude as irrelevant, even when the term is applied to human beings, still more to the supreme moral Power. Does not the faith on which life reposes—the faith that the universe is finally trustworthy, and that I am morally free—put one who experiences this faith in a consciously *ethical* relation to the reality that is operative in all his experience? Now, if the term 'person,' as distinguished from 'thing,' is taken as the one term which especially signalises moral relation among beings, and which implies moral order as distinguished from merely mechanical or physical order ; and if the universe of reality, in its final principle, must be treated as an object of moral trust, when we live in obedience to its conditions, does not this mean that it is virtually personal, or revelation of a person rather than a thing—an infinite Person, not an infinite Thing? If our deepest relation to it must be ethical trust in perfect wisdom and goodness or love at the heart of it—trust in its harmonious adaptation to all who are willing to be physically and morally adapted to it—this is just to say that our deepest or final relation to reality is ethical rather than physical ; that *personality* instead of *thingness* is the highest form under which *man* at any rate can conceive of God." [1] Professor Fraser, however, hardly brings out the full truth in saying that personality is the highest form under which man can *conceive* of God. For it is not only man's highest idea, it is, so far as it goes, a *true* idea : *i.e.* if we could think of God *sub specie æternitatis*, we should find that all that is positive in our human conception of personality existed in Him, however much it was transcended. And this is so, because, to use Mr. Illingworth's

[1] *Philosophy of Theism* : Gifford Lectures, Second Series, pp. 149, 150.

words, "our anthropomorphic language follows from our theo-morphic minds." [1]

Now the Christian conception of God as a 'society in Himself,'—as not a simple unity, but a unity that includes difference,—mysterious though it may be, answers to these ultimate forms, personality and love. God's life contains within itself the conditions which lie at the root of both, and which in human experience imply mutually exclusive individualities. It is in many ways unfortunate that the word Person, which we derive from the Latin Church, should be employed to designate those distinctions within the Godhead which the Scripture describes as Father, Son, and Spirit. It does justice to the distinctions, but not to the unity in which alone they subsist. " *Dictum est tamen tres personæ,*" says Augustine, " *non ut illud diceretur, sed ne taceretur.*" [2] If, however, we are to use abstract terms at all, no better word can be suggested. "But we are nearer reality if we conceive God in the terms of the Gospels, than if we define Him in the categories of the schools." (Fairbairn, *Christ in Modern Theology,* p. 400.)

Cf. Illingworth, *op. cit.* chaps. ii.–iv. and pp. 243–246 ; Orr, *Christian View of God and the World,* pp. 111, 112, 308, 309 ; Iverach, *Is God Knowable ?* pp. 208–233 ; T. B. Strong, *Manual of Theology,* chap. iv.

LECTURE VI.

NOTE 30. See p. 240.

The indefinable Element in Christ's Suffering.

"The statements of Scripture, in speaking of Christ's suffer-ings, are characterised by a dignified sobriety. . . . The writer of the Epistle to the Hebrews, when he would commend Jesus as the pattern of patience, says of Him simply, 'that He endured

[1] *Personality Human and Divine,* p. 214.
[2] Augustine, *De Trin.* v. 9.

the cross, despising the shame.' Paul, when he would exhibit the humility of Christ in its utmost depth of self-abasement, indicates the limit of descent by the phrase, 'obedient unto death, even the death of the cross.' It did not occur to him to say, 'even death spiritual,' or 'even death eternal,' or 'even the death of the damned.' It may safely be concluded that such extreme phrases are not required for a correct statement of the true doctrine, and that it will suffice to say in general terms that Christ suffered in body and soul all that it was possible for a holy Being to suffer. This general statement leaves the question open, whether the personal holiness of Christ did not fix a limit beyond which His experience of suffering could not go, even as it set bounds to His experience of temptation. That it did fix such a limit seems beyond question. To speak of the Holy One of God as enduring spiritual and eternal death, is surely a gross and mischievous abuse of terms! Instead of following the example of Protestant scholastic theologians in the use of such expressions, we ought rather to regard such use as an instructive illustration of the danger to which the dogmatic spirit exposes us of wresting Scripture, and manufacturing facts in support of a preconceived theory" (Bruce, *Humiliation of Christ*, pp. 344, 345: cf. the passage quoted from Jonathan Edwards, *ibid.* pp. 445, 446).

NOTE 31.   See p. 246.

'*Justitia imputata*' and '*Justitia infusa.*'

The controversy regarding the meaning of δικαιοῦν in Romans is now as good as closed. It means "to pronounce righteous" or "to treat as righteous," never "to make righteous." It describes simply the acceptance as righteous before God of the man "that hath faith in Jesus" (chap. iii. 26), and *in itself* contains no reference to his real character or actual righteousness. That is the precise exegetical signification of the word. But this *objective* vindication or acceptance only applies to those who have the *subjective* condition of faith ; and it is the subjective condition which is the living nexus between acceptance and progressive sanctification. In the first five chapters of Romans Paul treats of the objective vindication of the believer, considered in itself; and in the next three chapters proceeds to unfold the implications of the subjective condition which has led up to that vindication. The distinction, therefore, between *justitia imputata* and *justitia infusa*, which the Reformed theologians so emphasised, belongs essentially to the apostle's thought and has a supreme religious value; but it is at best a relative distinction, inasmuch as the two sides have no existence except as mutually related.

"There is an organic unity in the Christian life. Its different parts and functions are no more really separable than the different parts and functions of the human body. And in this respect there is a true analogy between body and soul. When Dr. Liddon concludes his note (p. 18) by saying, 'Justification and sanctification may be distinguished by the student, as are the arterial and nervous systems in the human body; but in the living soul they are coincident and inseparable,' we may cordially agree. The distinction between Justification and Sanctification, or between the subjects of chaps. i. 16–v. and chaps. vi.–viii., is analogous to that between the arterial and nervous systems; it holds good as much and no more—no more, but as much" (Sanday and Headlam, *Romans*, p. 38). But when theology deals with Christian truths or experiences as abstract conceptions, not as concrete realities in "the living soul," it but "murders to dissect."

"Theologians," says Professor Stearns (*Evidence of Christian Experience*, p. 150), "have been wont to describe justification in forensic terms, as a declarative act of God by which a new legal status is effected; and unquestionably their *meaning* is correct. But if we derive our theology not from scholastic treatises, but from the experience of the Christian read in the light of the Bible, we see that this mode of statement fails to do justice to the fact. The believer does not find himself merely in the presence of a Judge who has withdrawn the charges of the law against him; he stands before a Father who has given back His favour and confidence. . . . The forgiveness or justification of which the Christian consciousness testifies in the first hours of faith is a personal matter. In it God comes near to us, and we, who were far off from God, are brought near to Him. It is not so much a matter of the divine government as of God's personal love. . . . It looks forward so unambiguously to a holy life, is so clearly not an end in itself, but a means to a higher end, namely, our complete redemption, that it is impossible to regard it as unethical. The prodigal is brought back into the Father's house, the Father's kiss of forgiveness is bestowed upon him, the ring is put upon his finger and the shoes upon his feet, the fatted calf is killed for him, there is music and dancing and great rejoicing—and all that a new life may be possible, with new love to the Father, new obedience and service." When Dr. Stearns speaks of the new life as something which this consciousness of forgiveness *renders possible,* or to which it points forward, his ' meaning' is right, but the expression rather lacks precision. The new life in its development as an actual fact lies still in the future, but in essence it is there already "in the first hours of faith." Dr. Stearns makes this perfectly clear elsewhere. " In the experience of the new life the believer receives the forgiveness of sin, and knows by the witness of the Spirit that he receives it. . . . This boon comes to him through Christ as a part of *his union with Christ*" (p. 148, cf. pp. 127–130).

What is true of δικαιοῦν is true also of υἱοθεσία as used by St. Paul (Rom. viii. 15 ; Gal. iv. 5). It denotes not sonship, but the status or adoption of sonship. And yet this status is no mere external relation to God ; it is rendered possible for the believer only because he has undergone the ethical change involved in repentance and faith. I cannot follow Professor Bruce when he says that the status and the spirit of sonship "are not only distinguishable but separable. All who are justified, all who believe in Jesus, however weak their faith, are in the Pauline sense sons of God, have received the adoption. But not all who believe in Christ have the spirit of sonship. On the contrary, the fewest have it, the fewest realise their privilege, and live up to it." (*St. Paul's Conception of Christianity*, p. 191.)

Certainly no man perfectly *realises* the filial spirit, else he would
be sinless, entirely obedient to the Father's will in every detail of
his life. But the surrender to God in Christ, which is implied in
the weakest faith, has in it the germ of the filial spirit. It
signifies a response of the soul which identifies it with the one
perfect Son. If it be not this, what is it? "As many as are led
by the Spirit of God, these are sons of God" (Rom. viii. 14).
Would Paul have admitted that there might be some who had
obtained the υἱοθεσία, and who yet in no sense possessed the
Spirit or were led by it? Dr. Bruce has some admirable remarks
on the different meanings which υἱοθεσία bears in Paul and in
dogmatic theology (pp. 190, 191).

The ethical significance of "Imputation" is well stated by
Canon Gore. "In this truth of the inward Christ, let us see the
explanation of a doctrine which often bewilders us, the imputation of Christ's merits. To impute the merits of one person to
another, external to him and independent of him, would always
be an arbitrary and immoral act. . . . Now, by new birth and
spiritual union, our life is of the same piece with the life of Jesus.
Thus He, our Elder Brother, stands behind us, His people, as a
prophecy of all good. Thus God accepts us, deals with us, '*in*
the Beloved': rating us at something of His value, imputing to
us His merits, because in fact, except we be reprobates, He
Himself is the most powerful and real force at work in us. . . .
For consider, God, who is truth, deals with us according to
reality. He must deal with things at the last resort as they are.
He cannot reckon what does belong to us, as if it did not. Thus
at the last He can only 'not impute' our sins to us, if they no
longer belong to our transformed characters ; as Saul the persecutor's 'kicking against the pricks' belongs no longer to Paul the
apostle, 'the slave of Jesus Christ.' We can be absolved then,
at the last great acquittal, only because by discipline in this
world or beyond it, we have actually had our sins purged out of
us. Here in this world, in order at any moment to be the
subjects of forgiveness, we must really repent, which means that
we really abjure our sins, and separate ourselves from them in
will and intention. Not the best of us, however, can hope to be

completely freed from sin except very slowly and gradually.   But God deals with us—this is the great truth—by anticipation, by anticipation of all that is to come about in us, 'non quales sumus, sed quales futuri sumus'; accepting us *in Christ,* forgiving us *in Christ,* and thus setting us free from the burden of our past sins, as often as, being really members of Christ, we do really, in the sincerity of a good will, unite ourselves to Him, and claim to be His servants" (*Bampton Lectures,* pp. 224–226).

On the general subject, see Weizsäcker, *Apostolic Age,* vol. i. pp. 166–169; Sanday, *ibid. passim,* where both the exegetical and the theological aspects are fully discussed: Bruce, *ibid.* pp. 157–160, and *passim,* especially chap. xi., in which he accounts for the two phases of Paul's doctrine of righteousness by the apostle's " psychological history."

LECTURE VII.

NOTE 32.   See p. 262.

St. Paul's Conception of the Law.

I. At first sight it seems hard to harmonise the different expressions which the apostle applies to the law.   But the difficulty arises not from any real contradiction, but from the dual character which in his view attaches to it, and which he regards now from one side, now from the other.   The law was for him the will of God conceived as an external authority, and expressing itself in positive precepts.   It demanded everything; it gave nothing.   Hence under its exactions man was prostrated in helplessness.   But even when most oppressed by his failure to obey, he had to recognise that obedience was due from him, that the injunctions imposed upon him were just, and in accordance with his true nature, with what he ought to be.   Thus the law had to be both *abolished* and *conserved*; abolished as a method, but conserved in its ethical significance and content.   To abrogate it in the latter respect was inconceivable and impossible, for it was essentially the expression of the divine will; to preserve it in the former was to retain an impassable gulf between God and man. But the fulfilment of both necessities was Christ, who was the end of the law unto righteousness to everyone that believeth (Rom. x. 4), but through whom also the law was established (Rom. iii. 31).

Paul unquestionably believed in this spiritual and permanent value of the law as regards its inner purport. Dr. Matheson argues that in the apostle's view "the law was never meant to be a guide to moral life. It was only designed to be a line of boundary between the moral and the immoral, to constitute a regiment of police which should prevent the passions of men from breaking forth into deeds of crime. . . . He certainly regarded the keeping of it as a very easy thing, so easy that, to his mind, the achievement did not indicate any great amount of righteousness at all. He says that he himself was, 'touching the righteousness which is in the law, blameless'" (*Spiritual Development of St. Paul*, pp. 96, 97). No doubt Paul conceived that the law was intended, as all law is, to check transgressions; but inasmuch as it was a *moral* law, bearing on the right relation of man to God, it was, however definite or limited in its form, infinite in its implication. When he affirms in Philippians that, "as touching the righteousness which is in the law," he was "blameless," he is speaking of the law from the ritual point of view. He had been a Pharisee of the "straitest sect," and had omitted none of the observances imposed, however trivial. But even in the days of his Pharisaism he did not regard this conception of the law as exhausting its meaning.[1] At the very time when he was 'blameless' in his performance of the prescribed ritual of duty, he was filled with a haunting sense of restlessness, because he felt that the demand of the law penetrated far beyond such specific acts. He is again speaking of the law from the Pharisaic standpoint when he describes the reversion of the Galatians to it as a return to "weak and beggarly rudiments" (Gal. iv. 9). It is not that he is thinking of the ceremonial as distinguished from the moral law, for this distinction was not

[1] See Sanday and Headlam, *Romans*, p. 186.

made by the Jews as by us, but he is regarding the entire law in its ritual aspect. It is the same law which he himself kept so blamelessly. And yet the other and deeper side of it is present in this very Epistle, when he goes on to say that "the whole law is fulfilled in one word, even in this, Thou shalt love thy neighbour as thyself" (v. 14). How could the apostle ever have spoken thus, if, as Dr. Matheson says, his view of the law was *merely* that of a code for the repression of crime? He evidently thought it something very searching and spiritual; the keeping of which, had it been possible (which it was not in the legal spirit), would have brought true blessedness. Therefore, while he emphatically declares that, if righteousness is through the law, then Christ died in vain (Gal. ii. 21), he also declares that Christ died, so that the ordinance of the law might be fulfilled in us who walk after the Spirit (Rom. viii. 4). See the same contrast in Rom. x. 4, xiii. 10.

It is almost certain that Paul did not intend by the elliptical phrase, "It was added because of transgressions" (Gal. iii. 19), merely to assert the commonplace, that the law was given to *repress* transgressions. He was suggesting the much deeper truth, which he develops so incomparably in the seventh chapter of Romans, that it revealed, and even provoked or created them.[1] And the law had this terrible power for him, by reason of the double character which he attributed to it. Just because, while it expressed itself in definite external commands, it was itself infinite, there was no end to its progressive imperatives (cf. Jowett, *Thessalonians, Galatians, and Romans*, ed. 1894, vol. ii. pp. 256, 279, 280).

When the apostle dwells on the contrast between law and grace, the immediate reference is to the Pentateuch. Bishop Lightfoot indeed maintains that νόμος without the article never means the Mosaic law, which, he says, is always ὁ νόμος (see his note on Gal. ii. 19). The context in many passages makes this doubtful (*vid. Grimm's N.T. Lexicon*, ed. by Thayer). Yet, however the precise exegesis may stand, the fact that Paul employs the anarthrous form so frequently shows that while the

[1] Cf. Lightfoot, *in loc.*

Mosaic law may be specially in his thought, he takes it simply as the highest type of law in general, *i.e.* of a system of mere commands, whether these are embodied in a code, or are the unwritten dictates of conscience (*vid.* Lightfoot, *Galatians,* iv. 11 ; Sanday and Headlam, *Romans,* iii. 31).

II. The question naturally arises, How is it possible to accept Paul's description of the law as an authority pressing down upon the soul with its inexorable demands, when, as is obvious from the Psalms (*e.g.* ciii., cxix.), there were Jews for whom there was no such absolute divorce as he expresses between the law and the quickening life of God; who delighted in the law and made it their meditation day and night? Could the law, if it were divinely given, be intended to have a purely outward threatening character, active only in its exactions, and powerless to give or to inspire?

In the first place, it is quite clear that the apostle's view is largely coloured by his Pharisaic antecedents. Dr. Bruce says, "When Saul the Pharisee began to see into the spiritual inwardness of the law, through the contact of his conscience with such a precept as 'Thou shalt not covet,' he knew that there was no hope for him save in the mercy of God, and he drew the conclusion : By the law at its best, as a spiritual code of duty, comes not righteousness as I have hitherto been seeking it, *i.e.* as a righteousness with which I can go into the presence of a merely just God and demand a verdict of approval. By the law comes rather the consciousness of sin, and through that a clear perception that the only attitude it becomes me to take up is that of one who prays, 'God be merciful to me.' The apostle's doctrine concerning the law must be read in the light of this experience. When he says, righteousness comes not by the law, he means righteousness such as I sought when a Pharisee, the approval of God *as pharisaically conceived.* This doctrine was an axiom to the man who wrote Psalm cxxx."[1] How, then, did the author of this Psalm regard the law? Not as a dead inert thing interposing between him and God, but as the expression of the will of One who was really on his side, and not against him ; who loved

[1] *St. Paul's Conception of Christianity,* p. 300.

to pardon and restore the penitent transgressor. He had no thought of a righteousness which he could present to God as the ground of acceptance. The righteousness which he longed for was *in* God, not apart from Him. Are we to say, therefore, that the law could not have for such a one the condemning character which it bore for Paul; that, having no existence apart from the grace which was equally the expression of God's essential nature, it created no barrier which that grace could not remove? Was Paul's view of it simply the Pharisaic misconception, which he retained and made subservient to Christian faith?

Now a distinction has to be made when we speak of the Pharisaic idea of man's relation to God. That idea implies not only that a man feels that as a moral individuality he has obligations under which he lies to God, that he *owes* God something, but that he can by his own acts discharge the debt and create a claim to the divine favour. He can, as it were, build up a fabric of good works which endows the soul with merit before the Infinite One. But a law, obedience to which involves a personal title to reward, could not be the law as given by God, inasmuch as even its "blameless" observance would in no degree bring a man into the fellowship of Him who is *All in all.* For the prophets and the writers of the penitential Psalms, at least in their best moments, this was indeed an "axiom." Their loyalty to God's commandments was simply joy in God, the response of loving service to the Source of all good.

But what effect had the consciousness of sin upon them, the sense of their failure to maintain the right relation to Him? It did not create in them the Pharisaic notion of re-establishing this relation from the outside, from a merely human standpoint. It led them to abase themselves before Him; but to abase themselves in hope, because He was the All-good. That is, so far as they stood fast, they ascribed it to His gracious presence; and when they fell, they recognised that only by the action of the divine love could the disharmony be removed. *They threw upon God the burden of solving the problem of their sin,* by His forgiveness and requickening. "Hide Thy face from my sins; and uphold me with Thy free spirit" (Ps. li. 9, 12). But though they felt thus in their higher moods, they never attained to that confirmed sense of sonship, that perfect peace with God, which is the heritage of Christian faith.   They knew that the problem of their disobedience could only be solved by God, and they believed that it *was* in some way solved by Him; but that did not prevent them from feeling that *on the side of humanity* there was still a service unrendered, and a debt still due.   One can hardly express what that feeling was, except in terms of legalism; but it was not legalistic.   It was at bottom moral and spiritual; a dim *suggestion* of the revelation given in the incarnate Son, that while God is the one redeemer and reconciler, yet the reconciliation has finally to be wrought out in humanity, in a human life. It could not be more than a suggestion.   Only through Christ was the full significance of sin realised, not only as a personal demerit, but in its organic character as a dissolvent of God's moral government of the universe.   It was the satisfaction of the need that first revealed what the need was in its extremest form. None the less there is wrapped up in the moral nature of man, and there was involved in the prophetic thought, an adumbration of the truth which in the Christian redemption alone is made manifest, that salvation implies in a deep sense an offering of the human to the divine, an offering which is ours and yet not *of us.*

Thus for the noblest souls of the Old Testament the law had two sides.   On the one hand, it was not simply a code of threatening ordinances, but a law or revelation of God's will which restored the soul, and in the keeping of which there was great reward (Ps. xix. 7, 11).   On the other hand, being conscious that they had failed to preserve this spirit of hearty loving obedience to God's commandments which brought blessedness, His law *had* for them a depressing, threatening aspect, which was only partially relieved by their confidence in His forgiving love. In both aspects, positive and negative, it was a "tutor" preparing men for Christ (Gal. iii. 24).   On the positive side, it trained them in those good dispositions towards God, which, though but intermittently cherished, revealed to them the joy of His service and led them to long for the full liberty of the children of God, only to be reached through the one perfect Son.

29

On the negative side, by reminding them of a broken covenant of love, and of omitted services, it filled them with an oppression which only a completed deliverance in humanity and for humanity could wholly remove. In this double way it disciplined them for the fulness of the time (Gal. iv. 4), when men should serve not after the law of a carnal commandment, but after the power of an endless life (Heb. vii. 16). They had their happy hours of childlike surrender and their ecstatic moments of conscious pardon and restoration; but still they remained haunted by an ever-recurrent fear, children of hope rather than of achievement—

"Tendebantque manus ripæ ulterioris amore." [1]

But such a description only applies to the more spiritual souls of the Older Dispensation. The mass of the nation in Paul's day construed the law in its legalistic sense. Quite naturally, therefore, in his great controversy he dwells far more on the negative than on the positive, spiritual side. The latter had no meaning for a generation who thought that obedience to God meant human merit. Consequently the apostle takes the prevailing conception of the law and proves that it ends in a hopeless self-contradiction. But the positive aspect, though not emphasised by him, is not on that account to be regarded as denied. It is even implied in his elaborate comparison of the Jewish nation to the heir who is under guardians and stewards till he arrive at full age (cf. Lightfoot, *Galatians*, iv. 1–7 ; Bruce, *ibid.* pp. 308, 309).

NOTE 33. See p. 264.

Evolution and the Fall.

The essential truth contained in the doctrine of the Fall of man does not rest on the story of the temptation in the Garden, but on the nature and condition of man, as shown in experience and history, and especially as made manifest through the life and teaching of Christ. The narrative in Genesis does not touch the

[1] Virgil, *Aen.* vi. 314.

question of the origin of sin itself; it merely gives a representation, in picturesque forms natural to the early stages of human thought, of the entrance of sin into humanity. That the details of the account are symbolic, is obvious to all; the one point worth discussing is whether the state of innocence depicted is itself to be regarded as historically real, or only as the symbol of the ideal truth of man's nature and destiny.

Scientific discovery, and still more the theories founded upon it, seem to rule out the historical interpretation as impossible. On this, two things have to be said :—1. It is not likely that any advance of scientific knowledge proper, as distinguished from scientific speculation, will ever be able to *disprove* that man may have stood at first in an exceptional relation of happy fellowship with God. 2. The value of the speculative inferences drawn from that knowledge will ultimately depend on the degree in which they account for the present realities of man's ethical life.

I. The Fall in the Christian sense means the free choice by man of one course of action *when it was in his power, and would have been for his good*, to choose another. It can therefore find no place in the view of those who regard sin as a necessary condition of man's self-realisation. No matter how wrong disobedience may be in itself, yet if it be, as Hegel [1] maintains, the *only* means whereby the human spirit could finally arrive at conscious freedom, then it is only relatively bad, and is metaphysically vindicated as part of a whole of good. For it is God's will that man's state should not be always that of mere innocence, of unconscious goodness, but that he should advance to a condition of conscious and resolved obedience. If, then, the latter condition cannot be reached except by passing through the negative stage ; if man can only come to full moral self-consciousness through opposing his will to that of God, what is termed a Fall is quite as truly a Rise. It is as plain as can be that such a view is totally incompatible with the Christian idea of God. The very act by which His authority is defied is represented as *indispensable* to the fulfilment of His purpose. Everyone, indeed, can see that moral evil is made in the order of His Providence to subserve

[1] See Wallace's *Logic of Hegel*, Translation, pp. 54–6.

high ends of good. But our thought becomes a mere confusion when we say that these ends of good would have been otherwise unattainable. In that case we affirm and deny sin in the same breath ; and the unavoidable consequence is that it is the *affirmation* of it which is gradually emptied of all meaning. It is impossible for the human soul to retain its instinctive horror of evil, or the sharpness of its penitence, if once it is penetrated with the conviction that without the disruption of disobedience, the fuller and conscious unity could not be. To maintain this, however, is quite consistent with the frankest acknowledgment that sin has been the occasion of the manifestation of goodness in forms impossible in a sinless world. Where the Father's love is not rejected or thwarted by His children, it cannot reveal itself to them in the tenderness of redeeming grace. But though this aspect of love be to us, just because we are sinners, the most resplendent manifestation of it, we are not entitled to say that it is absolutely a higher form of it than that which love takes for souls that maintain the steadfastness of their communion. To say this is to contradict the revelation of the eternal Fatherhood and Sonship in the Godhead. For the perfect love of the Father is only known to the Son who is the *perfect* organ of the Father's will. Paul's consciousness of his past perverseness and of the unmerited mercy that had visited him gave to his devotion its last intensity ; but it is against all moral reason to affirm that his sense of fellowship with God was deeper than that which would exist in one who, like Christ, ' did always the things that pleased the Father.' Christ's life with its curriculum of temptation (see Lecture I.) is the final proof that sin is not the necessary result of finitude ; nor the necessary condition of the best knowledge and service of God.

Further, even in those cases where sin has been the means of educing good in ourselves or others, its own essential character remains unchanged. It is still sin for us as much as before it was committed, *i.e.* the thing *which ought not to be.* A wicked or selfish act is not itself made less hateful because it is repented of, or because in the rush of shame and humiliation which followed it we have welcomed the arresting and cleansing mercy

of the Father.   Many a man has thanked God for the imperfection or misfortune which taught him courage or patience;
but no one who retained his moral sanity has ever blessed God
for the vice which was the occasion of bringing him the tenderest
revelation of human or divine pity.   How then can *that* be an
inherent and inevitable part of man's experience as God meant
him to be, for which (even when it has brought the most blessed
indirect consequences) he cannot either in this world or the
world to come give God thanks ?

II. The moral consciousness thus pronounces with final
authority that sin is in no sense the expression of God's will,
however it may be controlled by Him and made to contribute to
the furtherance of His kingdom.   It lays the responsibility of it on
the man himself, and charges him with a perversion of his free will.

But just here a strange antinomy declares itself.   Take any
individual transgression, a lie or meanness.   Be the temptations
to it what they may, the man who commits it can never acquit
himself of the blame.   It is *his* act, because he voluntarily
identified himself with the evil suggestion.   That is the first
instinctive verdict that conscience passes; but the more the
meaning of the act and of subsequent similar acts comes home
to him, the more he recognises that each of them was not merely
an individual sin, but the outcome and evidence of a sinful
nature, of a deranged state of soul.   Doubtless this deranged
state has been aggravated by his past sins, but it was not created
by them.   It was implicit in him at the very beginning of life.
And if this be so, *he did not approach even his first temptation
unbiassed*; he did not possess the *temperamentum æquale*, the
perfect balance of nature, which would belong to one who was
passing out of the stage of unconscious innocence into that of
moral struggle.   While, however, this natural bias to evil impaired
the action of his will, it did not destroy its freedom.   His moral
obligation remained.   Thus we are forced to acknowledge the
existence of two elements which yet we can never bring to a
unity.   The universal experience of the race, testifying as it does
to this ' depraved ' tendency in humanity, declares that it is not
possible for any man wholly to avoid sin, that the perverted

nature will sooner or later assert itself ; yet the moral consciousness refuses to allow sin *in any instance* to be necessary.   Hence
it appears as if *that* were pronounced at least in some form or
degree inevitable, which yet in every form is morally prohibited.

Now it has to be observed that not merely the evil deed he
has been guilty of, but the deep-rooted *bias* itself—which he has
not created but received, and of which in part the deed is the expression—is felt by him to be *sinful.*   It is not a mere physical
defect which somehow or other predisposes him to act wrongly;
it is a moral taint.   But a moral taint in the nature springs, and
can only spring, from the perverted action of a free personality,
and as this taint is universal in mankind it seems impossible to
account for it, compatibly with the moral consciousness, unless
on the hypothesis that there was a time when this tendency
did not exist in man, when in the exercise of a freedom which
was then unimpaired, he by a ' sin of will ' caused this deflection
of nature.   Such a view proceeds, of course, on the assumption
of the unity of the human race, and the transmission of moral
tendencies from one generation to another.   If it be objected
that God is thus made responsible for imposing on the race a
law of solidarity under which it becomes subject to a *damnosa
hereditas*, it is sufficient to say that solidarity and heredity are in
themselves, properly speaking, neither good nor evil, that they
are simply the conditions under which alone humanity could be
a moral organism ; that they are necessary for the realisation of
the highest good, which they are intended normally to subserve,
and therefore render possible, in the case of free spirits, the
greatest evil.

"All I imagine that Christianity is interested in affirming,"
says Canon Gore, " is that when the animal organism became
the dwelling place of the human spirit, that human spirit might
have taken one of two courses.   It might have followed the path
of the Divine Will ; and in that case human development would
have represented a steady and gradual spiritualising of the animal
nature, reaching on unto perfection.   It might have taken, on
the other hand, and did in fact take (more or less) the line of
wilful disobedience.   And the moral effects of this wilfulness and

disobedience from the beginning onwards have been felt from parent to son."[1] It may be questioned, however, whether Canon Gore, in speaking of a "germ of spiritual consciousness" breathed into the anthropoid animal,[2] quite brings out the modification thus necessitated in the purely evolutionary theory of man's physical descent. For if the human spirit was really free to choose either course, that surely implied that the animal organism into which it was breathed was in some manner prepared for its reception. The physical passions as previously existing in the animal must have been modified and regulated, or the "germ of spiritual consciousness" would hardly have been likely to cope with their violence. Miss E. M. Caillard frankly accounts for the Fall by saying that the self-conscious will in man was "newly born and feeble," while other parts of his "complex nature, the animal appetites and impulses, were stronger in proportion, and the will succumbed before them, becoming their slave, instead of their master."[3] If these were the conditions of his life, was not the issue a foregone conclusion? Power to choose the right was no more than a name. Such a picture of man's primeval freedom reminds one of Dr. Johnson's definition of a *congé d'élire*: "it is such a recommendation, as if I should throw you out of a two-pair-of-stairs window, and recommend to you to fall soft."[4] If that freedom was a reality, it certainly involved the *temperamentum æquale* or equipoise of flesh and spirit.

But is this equipose an irrational supposition? God's creative purpose reached in man a wholly new stage—self-conscious being —which was the crown and completion of the preceding natural development. But the turbulent and savage passage of the non-moral animal becomes a wholly different thing when the animal is endowed with moral perception. Instead of being any longer the means whereby the end of its existence is realised, it becomes an obstacle to progress, and needs repression. The conditions of happiness are entirely altered. That which in the lower physical stage fostered the life, is the very thing which in the

[1] *The Guardian*, Feb. 17, 1897.   [2] *Ibid.*
[3] *Progressive Revelation*, p. 77.
[4] Boswell's *Life of Johnson* (ed. by Napier), vol. iv. p. 237.

higher spiritual sphere poisons and perverts it. " While every other living thing is striving for its own good, man alone is found choosing what he knows to be for his hurt." Can we believe it to have been according to God's will that man should carry over into association with his newly-given rational consciousness the wild impulses which, though formerly the means of development in the mere animal, would be the sure cause of his degradation and misery; that that which was normal before, should be re-tained when it became abnormal ? Just as natural history shows that each species of the lower creation has conditions appointed for it that enable it to live a normal *physical* life, so analogy would suggest that the human species was at first placed under such conditions as would have enabled it, subject to temptation, to live a normal *moral* life.[1]

It ought not to be necessary to say that the idea of a primitive state of innocence is not to be charged with attributing to man at the beginning of his history advanced intellectual qualities. There is not a word in Scripture which gives colour or support to the well-known saying of South, that "an Aristotle was but the rubbish of an Adam, and Athens but the rudiments of a Paradise." Whether sinful or sinless, man could only gradually come into possession of his powers. The effect which sin has had is not that of obliterating intellectual attainments formerly his, or of *making* development the condition of his life ; but of rendering the development, which under any circumstances must have taken place, devoid of the completeness and harmony which would otherwise have belonged to it. " A child who is obedient and teachable and willing to learn, who trusts his father or his teacher, may be in actual knowledge as inferior as he is in size and strength to the full-grown man, though the man may be wayward and wilful and self-assertive. And yet, for all that, the child is in a higher moral condition, and capable of a fuller and truer intellectual development ; for he is in a right relation to truth, while wilfulness and self-assertion are antagonistic to truth and impede knowledge." [2]

[1] See article by Principal Simon in the *Bibliotheca Sacra* for Jan. 1897.
[2] Aubrey L. Moore, *Essays, Scientific and Philosophical*, p. 63.

On *the moral side* also man's perfection could only be of an implicit character. It might appropriately enough be described as childlike, so long as we remember that the basis to evil which underlies what we term the unconscious innocence of the child, and which will certainly in some form express itself, did not *ex hypothesi* in his case exist. If we are to represent his perfection to ourselves at all, it can only be as that of a nature morally whole, with an instinctive love of good and horror of evil. It is utterly false to say that, on that view, surrender to temptation would not imply plain and wilful misdoing. For the rightness or wrongness of an act does not depend on clear intellectual conceptions, but on the immediate verdict of the moral consciousness. The breaking down of the *instinctive* aversion to disobedience really signifies a perversion of the *will*.

That great difficulties attach to the conception of an original state of human innocence, I have not sought to deny. Some of the most devout Christian thinkers have felt themselves unable to accept it. Dr. Hort says, referring to the ninth Article of the Church of England, "The authors of this Article doubtless assumed the strictly historical character of the account of the Fall in Genesis. This assumption is now, in my belief, no longer reasonable. But the early chapters of Genesis remain a divinely appointed parable or apologue setting forth important practical truths on subjects which, as matter of history, lie outside our present ken. Whether or not the corrupted state of human nature was preceded in temporal sequence by an incorrupt state, this is the most vivid and natural way of exhibiting the truth that in God's primary purpose man was incorrupt, so that the evil in him should be regarded as having a secondary or adventitious character. Ideal antecedence is, as it were, pictured in temporal antecedence."[1] One who takes this position may say: 'I cannot see, in view of man's relation to the physical world and of the embryo condition of his moral nature, how it was possible for him to avoid sin. But that only means that I find *the same antinomy* in his earliest experience as in his latest: namely, that what in some form seems inevitable yet is in every form pro-

[1] *Life and Letters*, vol. ii. p. 329.

hibited.   He could no more with the consent of his moral sense lay the blame of his *first* sin upon circumstances, than of any subsequent one.'   This attitude is quite compatible with Christian faith, provided we realise that it is a confession of the *insolubility* of the problem of the origin of man's sin.   It is hopeless on this basis to attempt a solution.   No doubt it has been argued that if on the principle of the solidarity of the race we can account for the depraved tendency in men as due to the sin of their progenitor, it is just as conceivable that in the mysterious purpose of God the principle of solidarity may cover a wider area, and that man's fate is so linked with that of the universe that he suffers the entail of his physical descent.   But surely it is obvious that in the former case the sinful bias is attributed to an adequate (that is, a moral) cause, to an act of will, while in the latter it is attributed to a physical or non-moral cause, which could not possibly explain the consciousness of human depravity.   The postulate of an original untainted freedom belonging to humanity which has now been lost, is—whatever mysteries it may involve—the only one which even helps to interpret the facts of moral experience.

One is entitled to hold, if he prefer, that no solution can be given of the problem.   "The plain truth," says Dr. Denney, "and we have no reason to hide it, is that we do not know the beginnings of man's life, of his history, of his sin: we do not know them historically, on historical evidence." [1]   Christianity is not so much interested in insisting on the acceptance of the traditional solution as in withstanding the denial that there is any problem to be solved, and in opposing pretended solutions which really abolish sin, as it exists for man's consciousness.   As Mr. Aubrey Moore reminds us, "We are here on ground where natural science can help us little.   Moral facts cannot be put under the microscope."   Could any advance of scientific discovery tell us what the *spiritual* possibilities of humanity originally were?   The facts and verdicts of the moral consciousness are what they are, whatever were the conditions under which they arose.   But if we are to construe these conditions to our-

[1] *Studies in Theology*, p. 79.

selves, our construction must be such as to render possible the *actual result*, as we know it to be.

When Mr. Goldwin Smith says [1] that with disbelief in the doctrine of a historical Fall disbelief in the Atonement must follow, he shows that he simply does not comprehend the real Christian position. Christianity is absolutely committed to the view that sin is not the only means whereby man could have intellectually and morally developed; that, on the contrary, it has impaired and perverted his development. All Christians hold that man is fallen; that every sin is a fall, not a rise. Nor is their persuasion that man needs redemption and renewal, and that in Christ alone is he able to rise, in the least degree affected by the fact that they may have no satisfactory conception of how it was possible for him originally to stand.

NOTE 34. See p. 285.

The Χαρίσματα in St. Paul's Epistles: Functions, not Offices.

Speaking of the two lists of "gifts" in I Cor. xii. and Eph. iv., Dr. Hort says: "All this variation of enumeration, and also the variation in the form of description (persons and, so to speak, things being terms of a single series), becomes intelligible and natural when we understand clearly that St. Paul is not speaking at all of formal offices or posts in the Ecclesia, much less enumerating them. The chief reason why he *seems* to do this is because apostles stand at the head in the two chief lists, and the apostolate of the Twelve and St. Paul was in an important sense a definite and permanent office. But it was part of St. Paul's purpose to show that the service which they were intended to render to the Ecclesia of that age was on the one hand, as in the other cases, the service of members to a body to which they themselves belonged, and, on the other, was too peculiar to be included under any other head. What is common in substance to all the terms of the series is that they are so many kinds of partial ser-

[1] *Guesses at the Riddle of Existence*, p. 50.

vice, and from this point of view it was immaterial whether there were or were not definite offices corresponding to any or all of these kinds of service; or, again, whether two or more kinds of service were or were not, as a matter of fact, ever performed by the same persons. Hence these passages give us practically no evidence respecting the formal arrangements of the Ecclesiæ of that age, though they tell us much of the forms of activity that were at work within them, and above all illustrate vividly St. Paul's conception of an Ecclesia and of the Ecclesia."—*The Christian Ecclesia*, p. 160.

NOTE 35.   See p. 292.

Unconscious Actions as the Sustaining Power of Faith.

Cf. R. H. Hutton, *Essays, Theological*, 2nd ed., p. 372 ff. : "The Lutheran assertion, that a living trust in the Christ within man is the only pure fountain of action,—that this alone can produce a holiness unstained by human pride,—had relapsed into a confidence in the terms of a technical agreement, in which Christ and men are the contracting parties. This was the result of laying too much stress on the *consciousness* of the act of faith, the effect of putting a strain on the inward attitude of the heart which it cannot in most men bear, and which produces artificial reaction. It cannot be wondered at, then, that a large party looked eagerly for a more comprehensive church which should nourish the unconscious life of man, and recur to action as the school of faith, instead of looking on conscious faith as the only holy spring of action. This is the strength, I believe, of that Puseyite reaction towards the sacramental system of grace by outward ordinances. . . .

"I believe the true safeguard against Puseyism on the one hand, as against Calvinism on the other, is to preach what may be termed the sacramental power of common everyday duty—to preach that a real Eucharistic grace goes forth from the unconscious action to the spirit—unless that influence is destroyed by 'receiving it unworthily,' *i.e.* by a conscious self-trust.

"Luther was wrong in saying that all pure life goes forth out of conscious faith. Rome and the Puseyites are right in affirming that unconscious actions are often the sustaining power of faith, and that God may feed us with Himself through common bread and wine taken in humble thankfulness for His incarnation. Common minds, and English minds especially, are not equal to a constant strain on their conscious relation to God. Many can do their duty who cannot do it out of a life of faith, *i.e.* out of conscious and living dependence. But Luther was right in asserting that all conscious trust in *ourselves* is tainted with sin, that all conscious attitudes of our moral nature must be attitudes of trust in One higher and purer than ourselves."

LECTURE VIII.

NOTE 36. See p. 305.

The historical Jesus as the Symbol or Example of the Divine Life in Man.

In his *Philosophy of Religion*, vol. iv. pp. 120, 121, Pfleiderer gives an interesting summary of different forms in which this conception has been worked out.

"Nothing, according to Spinoza, is essentially necessary for salvation but the knowledge of the Eternal Son of God, *i.e.* of divine wisdom ; the knowledge of the historical Christ is not absolutely necessary, though it is helpful, because divine wisdom, though revealed in the human mind in general, has revealed itself in Christ Jesus more than in any other.

"According to Kant, the only essential object of saving faith is the ideal Christ, *i.e.* the ideal of God-pleasing humanity. The origin and the authentication of this idea lie in human reason itself ; but a visible form has been given to it in a historical personality like Jesus, whose moral power so victoriously asserted itself against all opposition, that we may regard him as an example of the idea of moral perfection ; it matters little whether he corresponds accurately with that ideal or not, and nothing certain can ever be said on this point.

"A sharper line is drawn between the religious ideal and the historical reality by Jacobi. 'We quite understand,' he writes to Claudius, 'how everything man can see of the divine, everything that can awaken him, as he beholds it, to a divine life, represents itself to you under the image and with the name of Christ. In so far as what you reverence in him is that which is essentially good and divine, your soul keeps itself upright, you do not humble, by the worship of an idol, the reason and morality that are in you. What Christ may have been outside of you, for himself, whether the reality of him corresponded to your notion or not, or whether he ever really existed at all, all this can make no difference to the essential truth of your idea, nor to the value of the dispositions which spring from it. What he is in you is the only important matter; and in you he is a truly divine being; through him you see the Deity, so far as you are capable of seeing the Deity at all, and when you rise *with* him to the highest ideas, you fancy, and it is an innocent error, that you can only rise to them *in* him.'

"Fichte draws a distinction in the theology of the Church between two propositions of very different value: the metaphysical one, which contains the perception of the unity of human existence with the divine life; and the historical one, which amounts to the statement that this unity first came to man's consciousness in Jesus of Nazareth. 'It is only the metaphysical element, by no means the historical one, that saves; the latter only informs. If a man is really united with God and entered into Him, it makes little difference by what road he reached that point, and it would be a very useless and perverse proceeding to be always going back upon the idea of the way, instead of living in the thing.' 'The one means of blessedness is the death of self-ness, death *with* Jesus, regeneration; but to know the history of the instruction to this point contributes nothing whatever to salvation.'"

The criticism passed in the Lecture on the Neo-Hegelian view applies substantially to all statements like the above which affirm—(1) that it is impossible for us now to verify the actuality of Christ's moral victory; and (2) that the actuality is not of the essence of the question.

It is often very difficult to say what those who take this position regard as the historical truth about Jesus. Fichte, for instance, affirms that He is, " in a wholly peculiar manner attributable to no one but Him, the only-begotten and firstborn Son of God, and that all ages which are capable of understanding Him at all must recognise Him in this character" (*The Way towards the Blessed Life*, Lect. vi.). This reverential attitude towards Jesus is usually declared by such to be indispensable to the highest spiritual life; but to what extent, in their conception, it rests upon fact, or is due to the glorifying of the fact through religious emotion, it is almost impossible to discover.

NOTE 37. See p. 311.

Fact and Ideal.

Since the days of the *Aufklärung* in last century there has been a tendency in many quarters, both philosophical and popular, to disparage what are called 'literal facts' in comparison with 'ideal truth.' The extreme form of it found epigrammatic expression in the famous saying of Lessing, "Contingent historical truths can never become the proof of necessary rational truths."[1] The vogue which this saying obtained was largely due to the now exploded conception of a 'natural religion,' which each individual could attain for himself by according with the laws of nature and reason. The course of human experience in the past was a thing of no moment for his apprehension of religious truth. The first thing he had to do was to rid himself of the degrading conventions which society as an artificial product had imposed upon him; and then to let his real nature have free play. On this view history lost all its meaning. Why

[1] Cf. Pünjer, *History of the Christian Philosophy of Religion*, p. 576 ff.; Harnack, *Das Christentum und die Geschichte*, p. 4.

trouble about it, if I am able of myself to discover what is essential for morality and the knowledge of God?

No one holds such a position nowadays. Science and philosophy alike have made it impossible, by showing that humanity is an organism, and that, like every organism, it has growth as the law of its life. A spiritual being, such as man, cannot be a mere individual : he realises his individuality just in proportion as he serves himself heir to the inheritance which lies open to him not only in his present environment, but in the bygone experiences and achievements of the race. It is strange that Lessing, whose best work consisted in superseding the shallow conceptions of the *Aufklärung,* and who has shown in his *Education of the Human Race* the true view of history as a development, should have described historical truth as merely 'contingent.' Human history is not an accidental succession of events ; it is the gradual unfolding of ultimate intellectual and spiritual forces. And the manner and form of this unfolding are of immense import for the individual. For the development of humanity is not that of an inevitable natural process, but a spiritual movement working through free personalities. Just because these constitute new centres of action, and differ in their power and quality, the later are not necessarily higher or better than the earlier. And as a personality may be much greater than anything which it immediately effects, it has often to be rediscovered in subsequent times, if a valuable contribution to human development is not to be lost. Individuals and nations are elected to special functions of service for mankind ; and if their message is to be fully absorbed, there must be a continual return to them. This is true in the intellectual sphere ; but it has a double force in the moral world, where the problem is the *personal actualising* of ideals. No man can afford to be indifferent, in his own struggle, to the degree in which ethical standards have been previously realised.

Yet it is just this personal element which is sometimes depreciated even by those who have most emphasised the evolutionary character of human history. Take, for example, Mr. Wallace's account of Hegel's attitude to Christianity. " The greatness of a philosophy is its power of comprehending facts. The most characteristic fact of modern times is Christianity. The general thought and action of the civilised world has been alternately fascinated and repelled, but always influenced, and to a high degree permeated, by the Christian theory of life, and still more by the faithful vision of that life displayed in the Son of Man. To pass that great cloud of witness and leave it on the other side, is to admit that your system is no key to the secret of the world—even if we add, as some will prefer, of the world as it is and has been. And therefore the Hegelian system, if it is to be a philosophy at all, must be in this sense Christian. But it is neither a critic nor an apologist of historical Christianity. The voice of philosophy is as that of the Jewish doctor of the law: 'If this counsel or this work be of men, it will come to nought: but if it be of God, ye cannot overthrow it.'[1] Philosophy examines what is, and not what, according to some opinions, ought to be. Such a point of view requires no discussion of the 'how' or the 'why' of Christianity. It involves no inquiry into historical documents, or into the belief in miracles; for to it Christianity rests only incidentally on the evidence of history; and miracles, as vulgarly explained, can find no reception in a philosophical system. For it Christianity is 'absolute religion'; religion, *i.e.*, which has fully become and realised all that religion meant to be. That religion has, of course, its historical side: it appeared at a definite epoch in the annals of our race: it revealed itself in a unique personality in a remarkable nation. . . . But in the light of philosophy this historical side shrivels up as comparatively unimportant. Not the personality, but the 'revelation of reason' through man's spirit: not the annals of a life once spent in serving God and men, but the words of the 'Eternal Gospel,' are henceforth the essence of Christianity."[2]

But if the greatness of a philosophy is its power of comprehending facts, this is surely a curious way of comprehending

---

[1] Most people will be inclined to think that Hegelianism, instead of assuming this impartial attitude, has proved itself, by its essential metaphysic, the most powerful critic yet known of historical Christianity.

[2] *The Logic of Hegel*, Prolegomena, pp. 32, 33.

30

them—by exclusion. If Christianity is anything, it is a historical religion : and if you treat its history with indifference (whatever view you may take of that) you are not explaining *it*, when you select certain of its principles and show their place in the spiritual evolution of humanity. The fundamental fact in Christianity is not the truths taught by Christ about God and man, but the *embodiment* which they found in Him, the supreme and solitary character of His personal life. Without the acknowledgment of this as a reality in history, the Gospel records are inexplicable : and the belief of it lies at the basis of all that Christianity has been to men. If in our view the historical side of it shrivels up as comparatively unimportant, and we don't even trouble to inquire into historical documents, what are we doing but passing by the 'great cloud of witness,' and really admitting that our philosophy is no key to the secret? It may perhaps explain what we conceive Christianity ought to have been, but hardly what it has been and is.

For the interpretation of history there are, as Harnack says, two conceptions necessary : evolution and personality. And the latter is as important as the former, above all in the religious sphere. " Ein Christ erzieht den andern, an einem Gemüt ent-zündet sich das andere, und die Kraft, das zu wollen, was man billigt, entspringt aus der geheimnissvollen Macht, durch die ein Leben das andere erweckt. Am Ende dieser Reihe von Boten und Kräften Gottes steht Jesus Christus. Auf ihn weisen sie zurück ; von ihm ist das Leben ausgeströmt, das sie jetzt als ihr Leben in sich tragen. Verschieden ist das Mass der bewussten Beziehung auf ihn—wer könnte das leugnen !—aber sie alle leben von ihm und durch ihn. *Hier stellt sich eine Thatsache dar, die dieser Person, in der Geschichte fortwirkend, einen unvergleichlichen Wert verleiht.* . . . Achtzehn Jahrhunderte trennen uns von dieser Geschichte, aber wenn wir uns ernstlich fragen, was giebt uns den Mut zu glauben, dass Gott in der Geschichte waltet, nicht nur durch Lehren und Erkenntnisse, sondern mitten in ihr stehend, was giebt uns den Mut an ein ewiges Leben zu glauben, so antworten wir : wir wagen es auf Christus hin. 'Jesus lebt, mit ihm auch ich.' Er ist der Erstgeborene unter vielen Brüdern : er verbürgt uns die Wirklichkeit der zukünftigen Welt." [1]

Er verbürgt. A past achievement, which is the guarantee of a present spiritual power in humanity, redeeming and renewing it—that is the differential characteristic of Christianity ; and no speculative rendering of the Christian faith can ever be adequate which either denies or minimises it.

Matthew Arnold, who was anxious not to be philosophical, and succeeded, tells us in his emphatic way : "Our religion has materialised itself in the fact, in the supposed fact ; it has attached its emotion to the fact, and now the fact is failing it. But for poetry the idea is everything ; the rest is a world of illusion, of divine illusion. Poetry attaches its emotion to the idea ; the idea *is* the fact. The strongest part of our religion to-day is its unconscious poetry." [2] It may be that for poetry the idea is everything, but it is certainly not everything for religion. And if the sinlessness of Christ and the Incarnation be indeed poetry, they are at any rate *unconscious* poetry ; and the strength which they now impart will be gone, when we all become Illuminati like Mr. Arnold, and recognise them to *be* poetry.

The special work of philosophy, says Mr. Wallace, is "to comprehend the world, not try to make it better" ; and therefore it may be quite beside the mark to ask whether, when philosophy has disparaged the possibility of a divine "achievement" in history, it can provide mankind with a substitute from the sphere of the Ideal. But we may fairly ask that, if it cannot create the 'ought to be,' it should at least do justice to what 'is.' The nature and the need of humanity make it perfectly plain that such a unique manifestation of God in personality would supply a spiritual dynamic which cannot otherwise be found. On the other hand, the evangelical records *interpreted merely as historic documents*, and the unbroken experience of the Christian Church, alike affirm that this manifestation is no dream, but an actuality. When, then, the very idea of it is scouted as philosophically impossible, we are entitled to say with Professor

[1] Harnack, *Das Christentum und die Geschichte*, pp. 12, 14.
[2] *Essays in Criticism*, Second Series, pp. 1, 2.

James, that "a rule of thinking which would absolutely prevent me from acknowledging certain kinds of truth, if those kinds of truth were really there," is "an irrational rule."[1]

Cf. Iverach, *Is God Knowable?* chap. ii. ; Gordon, *The Christ of To-day*, pp. 283–295.

―――――

NOTE 38. See p. 321.

The Verification of a Historical Revelation.

Cf. R. H. Hutton, *Essays, Theological* : "The best testimony we can get for very simple *physical facts* of any kind is, so to say, *accidental* testimony—the testimony of men who have no theory, and no wish to have a theory. But what is a true and important criterion of the value of testimony in reference to very simple physical facts that come within the range of eye, ear, and touch, can never be legitimately generalised into a criterion of the general *evidence* of a complex, spiritual, moral, and physical event. Were we as a rule to mistrust the testimony of persons to events which could be proved to have been expected, feared, or hoped for by them beforehand, we should, in fact, often doubt events *because* they were probable."

See his whole discussion of the question (2nd ed., pp. 223–229), which is a fine example of penetrative analysis.

―――――

LECTURE IX.

NOTE 39. See p. 355.

Unconscious Faith.

Dr. Hort's biography contains an interesting series of letters which he wrote to an Oxford undergraduate who had asked for help in difficulties suggested by the Thirty-nine Articles.

"In Article XIII.," he writes, "nothing is said about

[1] *The Will to Believe*, by William James, M.D., LL.D., Harvard.

'conscious' faith in Jesus Christ, and I do not see why we may not read the Article in the light of such passages as Matt. xxv. 34-40; Rom. ii. 14-16. What is fully true in the case of conscious and explicit faith may well be true in lesser degrees for lower forms of faith. . . .

"The principle underlying Article XIII. seems to me to be this, that there are not two totally different modes of access to God for men: faith for Christians, meritorious performance for non-Christians. There is but one mode of access, faith; and but one perfect, and, as it were, normal faith, that which rests on the revelation in the person of Jesus Christ. But faith itself, not being an intellectual assent to propositions, but an attitude of heart and mind, is present in a more or less rudimentary state in every upward effort and aspiration of men. Doubtless the faith of non-Christians (and much of the faith of Christians, for that matter) is not in the strict sense 'faith in Jesus Christ'; and therefore I wish the Article were otherwise worded. But such faith, when ripened, grows into the faith of Jesus Christ; as also it finds its rational justification in the revelation made through Him. Practically the principle of the Article teaches us to regard all the good there is in the world as what one may call *imperfect Christianity*, not as something essentially different, requiring, so to speak, to be dealt with by God in a wholly different manner. Of course I take for granted that acceptance of the Christian creed is not identical with Christian faith, but only the necessary condition of its existence in the highest or strictly Christian form."—*Life and Letters of F. J. A. Hort*, pp. 332, 337.

NOTE 40. See p. 359.

Contrast of Christian Society as it now is, with the Life of the New Testament.

No one has stated this contrast, or brought out its real significance, with deeper insight than Dean Church, *Gifts of Civilisation.*

"Christianity has been not only an eminently social religion, but a liberal religion. It has been so, not merely from slack indifference, but with its eyes open, and with deliberate reason given to itself for what it did. It has made large allowance for the varieties of character. It has naturalised and adopted in the boldest way (I say this, looking at the general result of what has come to pass, and not forgetting either narrow fears and jealousies, or very terrible abuses and mischiefs), art, literature, science. It has claimed to have a charm which could take the sting out of them. We educate by the classics, and are not afraid of Shakespeare. We may say, and say truly, that where there is society, these things must be; but Christian society began in the life of the New Testament, and they are not there. In all directions we see instances of the necessities of things enforcing an enlarged interpretation of its language; and we believe that the common-sense and instinct of Christians have, on the whole, caught its true meaning. . . . The Sermon on the Mount was once taken very literally: it is easy to say, take it literally still, with the Poor Men of Lyons or the Moravians; only then you sacrifice society. . . .

"Is then the history of Christian society the history of a great evasion? We Christians of this day believe that in its earlier and later forms it is one and the same; that the later has not forfeited the mind and the hopes of the earlier. Unless we are apostates without knowing it and meaning it, we accept the difference as being, in spite of enormous and manifest faults, the result of natural and intended changes. Are we mistaken? . . .

"If we have anything to guide us as to God's will in the facts of the world,—if we see His providence in the tendencies and conditions amid which we live, and believe that in them He is our teacher and interpreter, we must believe that social order, with its elementary laws, its necessary incidents and pursuits, is God's will for this present world. He meant us to live in this world. And for this world,—unless there is nothing more to be done than to wait for its ending,—what we call society, the rule of law, the employments of business, the cultivation of our infinite resources, the embodiment of public force and power, the increase of wealth, the continued improvement of social arrangements—all this is indispensable. There is no standing still in these matters; the only other alternative is drifting back into confusion and violence. If the necessities of our condition, with all the light thrown on them by long experience, are no evidence of God's purposes, we are indeed in darkness; if they are, it is plain that man, both the individual and the race, has a *career* here, that he has been furnished for it, I need not say how amply, and was meant to fulfil it. It is God's plan that in spite of the vanity and shortness of life, which is no Christian discovery (it was a matter for irony or despair long before Christianity), and in spite of that disproportionateness to eternity which the Gospel has disclosed to us, men should yet have to show what they are, and what is in them to do; should develop and cultivate their wonderful powers ; should become something proportionate to their endowments for this life, and push to their full limit the employments which come to their hand. The Church by its practice, its greatest writers by their philosophy and theories, have sanctioned this view of the use and divine appointment of the present life. This natural order of things was once interrupted. It was when Christ came to begin society anew. But as soon as the first great shock was over, which accompanied a Gospel of which the centre was the Cross and Resurrection, it became plain that the mission of the Church was not to remain outside of and apart from society, but to absorb it and act on it in endless ways; that Christianity was calculated and intended for even a wider purpose than had been prominently disclosed at first."—Pp. 34–39.

INDEX.

Sonship, human: grounded in the eternal Sonship in God, 432–3.

Spinoza, 461.

Stalker, Dr. J.: on the prayers of Christ, 385.

Stanley, Dean: on Christ's self-suppression, 391.

Stanton, Prof. V. H.: on the Jewish Messianic Hope, 70–2.

Stearns, Prof. L. F.: on justification, 441–2.

Stephen, Leslie, 320.

Stevenson, R. L.: on morbid introspection, 386–7.

Strauss: on Paulus's view of Christ's resurrection, 139.

Strong, T. B.: on the origin of the Logos-doctrine in John, 180; on Christ's sacrifice, 245.

Suffering, Christ's, 238–40; the indefinable element in, 439.

Symonds, J. A.: on the Greek ideal of life, 381–2.

TEACHING of Jesus, the: its authoritative character, 45–6; one means of His self-manifestation, 108–14; the order and method of, 108–9; dealt first with the Fatherhood of God, 109–10; His supreme purpose in it, to mould character, 110–1; not didactic, but germinal, 111–2, and therefore the more authoritative, 112–4.

Thomson, Dr. J. E. H.: on name 'Son of Man,' 65.

Toplady, A. M.: on the Fall, 434.

Trinity, the: a Christian conception, 208; in what sense adumbrated in the Old Testament, 208–9; speculative renderings of, 209–10; essentially a historical revelation, 211.

Twelve, the: influence of Jesus' personal presence on, 127–9, 131; a school, but a school in the world, 130–1; His acknowledgment of His Messiahship to, 131; effects of this on His subsequent intercourse with them, 131–3; potency of His indirect method of dealing with them, 134; duration of His intercourse with them, 401–3.

UNCONSCIOUS faith: in the case of the heathen, 341–5; within the Christian world, 345–71; in the light of N.T. teaching, 358–64; possibility of, no disparagement of the historic Faith, 370–1; Dr. Hort on, 468–9.

Universalism of Christ, 110, 416–22.

VISION hypothesis: fails to account for the Christophanies, 139–46.

WATSON, Dr. J. : on the teaching of Jesus and of Paul, 331.

Weiss, B.: on the prayers of Christ, 23; on Jesus' claim to be Messiah, 93; on the birth-time of Jesus' Messianic consciousness, 98; on Jesus' view of His mission as particularist, 417.

Weizsäcker, Carl v.: on discourses in Fourth Gospel, 83; on the Christophanies, 149–50.

Wendt, H. H.: on Christ's pre-existence, 77; on discourses in Fourth Gospel, 80, 81; on the birth-time of Jesus' Messianic consciousness, 94; on Jesus' anticipation of His death, 99; on Christ's claim to be the final Judge, 345.

Westcott, Bishop B. F.: on the appearances of the risen Christ, 156; on an Incarnation apart from sin, 188; on propitiation, 221; on the Passovers in the Fourth Gospel, 401,–2.

Westcott and Hort, 19, 20, 146, 235.

Wieseler, K.: on the duration of Jesus' ministry, 402–3.

Wordsworth, 57, 291, 293.

PRINTED BY
MORRISON AND GIBB LIMITED, EDINBURGH.

𝕶𝖊𝖗𝖗 𝕷𝖊𝖈𝖙𝖚𝖗𝖊𝖘—𝕾𝖊𝖈𝖔𝖓𝖉 𝕾𝖊𝖗𝖎𝖊𝖘.

In demy 8vo, price 10s. 6d.,

MORALITY AND RELIGION.

BY

Rev. JAMES KIDD, D.D.,

MINISTER OF ERSKINE CHURCH, GLASGOW.

'We are not acquainted with any other book that has so clearly shown the vital unity between religion and morality. . . . It is a strong book by a strong man.'—*Methodist Times.*

'We know of no original writer in English who, with such mastery of the points at issue, and such philosophical method in their handling, has united a devout evangelical and orthodox view of Christian doctrine. . . . It is the work of a master of psychological analysis.'—*Record.*

'Dr. Kidd has written a remarkable volume, able, learned, closely reasoned, thoughtful, and clearly and eloquently expressed. . . . We had not read much before we found ourselves in the grasp of a man who can think and can vividly express his thoughts. The old, old theme on which a hundred generations have thought and written, became new in his hands, and we found ourselves taking part in a fresh and vigorous discussion.'—Professor J. IVERACH, D.D.

'The ranks of theology are not often recruited by a thinker so cautious, sagacious, and independent. Marked by quite extraordinary analytical power, combined with great constructive skill, the book is one of the ablest contributions made in recent years to our theological literature.'—*Glasgow Herald.*

'Its grasp of the subject reveals a wide-read student of religion and philosophy. Its penetrating and fearless criticism of the masters therein reveals an acute thinker.'— *Expository Times.*

EDINBURGH: T. & T. CLARK, 38 GEORGE STREET.

Messrs. T. & T. CLARK'S NEW PUBLICATIONS.

———◆———

Now ready, in crown 4to (pp. 1040), price 26s. net;
in half-morocco, 31s. 6d. net,

A CONCORDANCE

TO THE

GREEK TESTAMENT.

According to the Texts of WESTCOTT and HORT, TISCHENDORF, and the ENGLISH REVISERS.

Edited by W. F. MOULTON, D.D., and A. S. GEDEN, M.A.

*** *It will be generally allowed that a new Concordance to the Greek Testament is much needed in the interests of sacred scholarship. This work adopts a new principle, and aims at providing a full and complete Concordance to the text of the Greek Testament as it is set forth in the editions of Westcott and Hort, Tischendorf (VIIIth), and the English Revisers. The first-named has throughout been taken as the standard, and the marginal readings have been included. Thus the student with any one of these three editions in his hands will find himself in possession of a complete Concordance to the actual text on which he is engaged; while the method employed, it may fairly be claimed, precludes the omission of any word or phrase which, by even a remote probability, might be regarded as forming part of the true text of the New Testament. On the other hand, passages disappear, as to the spuriousness of which there is practical unanimity among scholars.*

Professor W. SANDAY, D.D., LL.D., Oxford, writes: 'There can be no question as to the value of the new "Concordance." It is the only scientific Concordance to the Greek Testament, and the only one that can be safely used for scientific purposes.'

'*It would be difficult to overpraise this invaluable addition to biblical study. . . . For all English students of the Greek Testament this great work is indispensable.*'—BRITISH WEEKLY.

Prospectus, with Specimen Page, free on application.

The Ancient Faith in Modern Light: A Series of Essays. By Principal T. V. TYMMS, Rawdon College ; Professor MEDLEY, Regent's Park College ; Principal A. CAVE, D.D., Hackney College ; SAMUEL G. GREEN, D.D., London ; Principal R. VAUGHAN PRYCE, New College ; S. NEWTH, D.D. (late Principal), New College ; JOSEPH PARKER, D.D., City Temple, London ; Rev. W. BROCK, Hampstead ; J. GUINNESS ROGERS, D.D., Clapham ; H. R. REYNOLDS, D.D. (late Principal of Cheshunt College). In demy 8vo, price 10s. 6d.

' These writers have passed their storms and found anchorage. They are the men who do the world's best work ; healing work it often is, and will be here ; saving work it will even be, for there is no dulness or dissipation that would weary the youngest reader. There is the living mind, fearless in face of the living problems of to-day; and the young minds who come to this volume will find rest to their souls, for they will come to the mind of the Master Himself.'—*The Expository Times.*

Life after Death, and the Future of the Kingdom of God. By Bishop LARS NIELSEN DAHLE, Knight of St. Olaf. Translated by Rev. JOHN BEVERIDGE, M.A. In demy 8vo, price 10s. 6d.

Rev. C. A. BERRY, D.D., writes : ' Messrs. T. & T. Clark have enriched modern theological literature by the publication of this book. The volume is a careful, scholarly, and evangelical treatment of the doctrine of " Last Things," and bears evidence on every page, not only of close and prolonged study, but of the profound piety and charming spirit of the writer.'

EDINBURGH : T. & T. CLARK, 38 GEORGE STREET.
LONDON : SIMPKIN, MARSHALL, HAMILTON, KENT, & CO. LTD.

God the Creator and Lord of All. By SAMUEL HARRIS, D.D., LL.D., Professor of Systematic Theology in Yale University, Author of 'The Self-Revelation of God,' 'The Philosophical Basis of Theism,' etc. In Two Vols. post 8vo, price 16s.

⁎ *In this work Professor Harris develops the principle that the idea of God is not attained by mere subjective thinking, but that God is known through His action revealing Himself in the constitution and evolution of the universe, and in the constitution and history of man issuing in Christ, and in the Holy Spirit bringing gracious Divine influence on men.*

SUMMARY OF CONTENTS : PART I. GOD THE ONE ONLY ABSOLUTE SPIRIT.— PART II. GOD THE CREATOR.—PART III. GOD THE LORD OF ALL IN PROVIDENTIAL GOVERNMENT.—PART IV. GOD THE LORD OF ALL IN MORAL GOVERNMENT.—INDEX.

'Professor Harris is in touch with the most progressive, active, enterprising theology of to-day. But he has not lost his hold of yesterday. He knows what the youngest Ritschlian is saying; he has not forgotten what Augustine said before him. The whole field of the history of theology is in his sight, and long labour has given him possession of it. Yet he is as independent as if he had not read a book; his clear, rapid, forcible writing is a constant and most agreeable witness to his independence.' —*The Expository Times.*

Recently Discovered Manuscripts, AND ORIGEN'S COM-MENTARIES ON MATTHEW AND JOHN. Being an Additional Volume to the 'Ante-Nicene Christian Library.' Edited by Professor ALLAN MENZIES, D.D., St. Andrews University. Containing : GOSPEL OF PETER (By Professor ARMITAGE ROBINSON)— DIATESSARON OF TATIAN—APOCALYPSE OF PETER—VISIO PAULI— APOCALYPSES OF THE VIRGIN AND SEDRACH—TESTAMENT OF ABRAHAM—ACTS OF XANTHIPPE AND POLYXENA—NARRATIVE OF ZOSIMUS—APOLOGY OF ARISTIDES—EPISTLES OF CLEMENT (Complete Text)—ORIGEN'S COMMENTARIES ON MATTHEW AND JOHN, etc. In One Volume, 4to (pp. 540), price 12s. 6d. net.

' It was a happy idea which occurred to the publishers of the "Ante-Nicene Library" to supplement that series with a volume containing translations of the more important discoveries of recent years. A judicious arrangement has been observed in grouping the recovered treasures. . . . It has been compiled with great care, and the Introductions are short and to the point.'—*The Record.*

The Prophecies of Jesus Christ, relating to His Death, Resurrection, and Second Coming, and their Fulfilment. By Dr. P. SCHWARTZKOPFF. Authorised Translation. In crown 8vo, price 5s.

' Deserves ample recognition as an honest, reverential, and able attempt to solve one of the most difficult problems connected with the Person and Work of Christ. . . . He has produced a book blossoming on every page with suggestions, and worthy of the most serious study of theologians.'—Professor MARCUS DODS in *The Critical Review.*

NEW BIBLE-CLASS PRIMERS.

Paper covers, 6d. ; cloth covers, 8d.,

The Exile and the Restoration. With Map and Plan. By Professor A. B. DAVIDSON, D.D., LL.D., Edinburgh.

Christian Conduct. By Rev. T. B. KILPATRICK, B.D.

The Miracles of our Lord. By Professor J. LAIDLAW, D.D.

NEW BIBLE-CLASS HANDBOOKS.

The Times of Jesus Christ. By Rev. L. A. MUIRHEAD, B.D. With Map. Crown 8vo, 2s.

Foundation Truths of Scripture as to Sin and Salvation. By Professor J. LAIDLAW, D.D. Crown 8vo, 1s. 6d.

EDINBURGH : T. & T. CLARK, 38 GEORGE STREET.
LONDON : SIMPKIN, MARSHALL, HAMILTON, KENT, & CO. LTD.

'By a bright, attractive appearance, by a very comfortable typography, by the participation of dignified scholars and experienced writers, this series is likely to enjoy a deserved popularity.'—*The New World.*

Eras of the Christian Church.

EDITED BY

JOHN FULTON, D.D., LL.D.

MESSRS. T. & T. CLARK have pleasure in announcing the Serial Publication of 'ERAS OF THE CHRISTIAN CHURCH.'

Christians of all denominations have begun to understand that many of the existing divisions of Christendom had their origin partly in misapprehensions, and partly in causes which have long since passed away, and that the cause of unity will be most surely promoted by a calm and impartial study of the Church in its long and varied experience under the guidance of the Holy Spirit.

It is impossible, however, for persons of ordinary leisure and opportunity to make a profound study of ecclesiastical history. It has therefore been suggested that a series of popular monographs, giving, so to speak, a bird's-eye view of the most important epochs in the life of the Church, would supply a real want, and this series is intended to furnish such monographs.

THE SERIES WILL BE COMPLETED IN TEN VOLUMES.

Five Volumes are now ready, price 6s. each,

The Age of Hildebrand. By Professor M. R. VINCENT, D.D. 6s.

The Age of the Great Western Schism. By CLINTON LOCKE, D.D. 6s.

The Age of the Crusades. By JAMES M. LUDLOW, D.D. 6s.

The Ecumenical Councils. By Professor W. P. DU BOSE, D.D.

The Age of the Renascence. By HENRY VAN DYKE, D.D. and PAUL VAN DYKE. 6s.

'These "ERAS" are histories that will be enjoyably read and easily remembered. . . . Professor Vincent had a great subject allotted to him, and "The Age of Hildebrand" is an altogether worthy treatment of it. . . . In "The Age of the Crusades" we have the prose version of a story familiar to most of us in the trappings of romance. Dr. Ludlow holds the attention of his readers. . . . "The Age of the Great Western Schism" is a bright and popular résumé.'—*The Literary World.*

The following Volumes are in preparation :—

The Apostolic Age. By J. VERNON BARTLET, M.A., Oxford.

The Post-Apostolic Age. By the Right Rev. H. C. POTTER, D.D., LL.D., Bishop of New York.

The Age of Charlemagne. By Professor CHARLES L. WELLS.

The Protestant Reformation. By Professor W. WALKER, Ph.D., D.D., Hartford.

The Anglican Reformation. By Professor W. R. CLARK, LL.D., D.C.L., Trinity College, Toronto.

EDINBURGH : T. & T. CLARK, 38 GEORGE STREET.
LONDON : SIMPKIN, MARSHALL, HAMILTON, KENT, & CO. LTD.

DR. PLUMMER ON ST. LUKE'S GOSPEL.

A Critical and Exegetical Commentary on the Gospel according to St. Luke. By Rev. ALFRED PLUMMER, M.A., D.D., Master of University College, Durham. In post 8vo (pp. 678), price 12s.

** *Being the Fifth Volume of 'THE INTERNATIONAL CRITICAL COMMENTARY.'*

' Dr. Plummer's work is, it need hardly be said, admirably done, both in the Introduction and in the Commentary. Readers will peruse with pleasure his treatment of the leading characteristics of the Gospel. The linguistic analysis leaves nothing to be desired.'—*The Record.*

' We feel heartily that it will bring credit to English scholarship ; and that in its carefulness, its sobriety of tone, its thoughtfulness, its reverence, it will contribute to a stronger faith in the essential trustworthiness of the Gospel record.'—*The Guardian.*

The Mohammedan Controversy, Biographies of Mohammed, Sprenger on Tradition, the Indian Liturgy, the Psalter. By Sir WILLIAM MUIR, K.C.S.I., D.C.L., LL.D., Principal of the University of Edinburgh. Just published, 8vo, price 7s. 6d.

' Sir William Muir, Principal of Edinburgh University, and author of the standard life of Mohammed, is undoubtedly the highest authority on Mohammedanism that is to be found in this country. . . . Sir William Muir is doubtless right in declaring that Mohammedanism is the most formidable antagonist that Christianity possesses, and that, while from all the varieties of heathen religion Christianity has nothing to fear, in Islam it has an active and powerful enemy. . . . Sir William Muir knows India well, having spent there forty years of his life, while as a lifelong student of Moham-medanism he is able to gauge correctly the currents of thought and feeling that are to be found within it. . . . Sir William Muir has rendered important service, alike in defining the issues and in pointing out the sources where the Christian controversialist may furnish himself with material for the struggle.'—*The Glasgow Herald.*

The Right of Systematic Theology. By Professor B. B. WARFIELD, D.D., Princeton University. With an Introduction by Professor J. ORR, D.D., Edinburgh. Crown 8vo, price 2s.

Contemporary Theology and Theism. By Professor R. M. WENLEY, M.A., D.PHIL., D.Sc., University of Michigan. Crown 8vo, price 4s. 6d.

Christian Life in Germany: As seen in the State and the Church. By EDWARD F. WILLIAMS, D.D. Post 8vo, price 4s.

' The number of English-speaking youth in the Universities and Technical Schools in Germany is increasing every year. It is interesting to know what kind of religious influences are within their reach even if in their student life they do not yield to these influences. Great Britain and America owe a debt of gratitude to Germany for the literature she has furnished their people, for the contributions she has made to Christian song, and for her devotion to higher Christian learning. . . . The purpose of this book is to set forth, in as few words as possible, the real condition of the Protestant Churches in Germany, to describe their present spiritual condition, and to furnish data on which to form an opinion of their probable future.'—Extract from the PREFACE.

The Hope of Israel : A Review of the Argument from Prophecy. By the Rev. F. H. WOODS, B.D., late Fellow of St. John's College, Oxford. In crown 8vo, price 3s. 6d.

' The book is a convenient and attractive one. And the subject being the keenest controverted in our day, being, indeed, the one subject which has passed into feverish interest and unrest ; and Mr. Woods, being a master on both sides of it, this volume should have a wide and thankful welcome.'—*The Expository Times.*

EDINBURGH : T. & T. CLARK, 38 GEORGE STREET.
LONDON : SIMPKIN, MARSHALL, HAMILTON, KENT, & CO. LTD.

The International Critical Commentary.

UNDER THE EDITORSHIP OF

The Rev. S. R. DRIVER, D.D., Oxford; the Rev. A. PLUMMER, M.A., D.D., Durham; and the Rev. C. A. BRIGGS, D.D., New York.

The time has come, in the judgment of the projectors of this enterprise, when it is practicable to combine British and American scholars in the production of a critical, comprehensive Commentary that will be abreast of modern biblical scholarship, and in a measure lead its van. The Commentaries will be international and inter-confessional, and will be free from polemical and ecclesiastical bias. They will be based upon a thorough critical study of the original texts of the Bible, and upon critical methods of interpretation.

'The publication of this series marks an epoch in English exegesis.'—*British Weekly.*

The First Seven Volumes are now ready, viz. :—

Deuteronomy. By S. R. DRIVER, D.D., Regius Professor of Hebrew, and Canon of Christ Church, Oxford; formerly Fellow of New College, Oxford. Price 12s.

Romans. By W. SANDAY, D.D., LL.D., Lady Margaret Professor of Divinity, and Canon of Christ Church, Oxford; and Rev. A. C. HEADLAM, B.D., Fellow of All Souls College, Oxford. Price 12s.

Judges. By G. F. MOORE, D.D., Professor of Hebrew in Andover Theological Seminary, Andover, Mass., U.S.A. Price 12s.

St. Mark. By E. P. GOULD, D.D., Professor of New Testament Exegesis in the P. E. Divinity School, Philadelphia. Price 10s. 6d.

St. Luke. By A. PLUMMER, D.D., Master of University College, Durham. Price 12s.

Philippians and Philemon. By MARVIN R. VINCENT, D.D., Union Theological Seminary, New York. Price 8s. 6d.

Ephesians and Colossians. By T. K. ABBOTT, D.Lit., Trinity College, Dublin. Price 10s. 6d.

(1) Of DRIVER'S 'DEUTERONOMY,' Prof. G. A. SMITH (in *The Critical Review*) says: 'The series could have had no better introduction than this volume from its Old Testament editor. . . . Dr. Driver has achieved a commentary of rare learning and still more rare candour and sobriety of judgment. . . . It is everywhere based on an independent study of the text and history. . . it has a large number of new details: its treatment of the religious value of the Book is beyond praise.'

(2) Of SANDAY'S 'ROMANS,' Principal F. H. CHASE, D.D., Cambridge, says: 'We welcome it as an epoch-making contribution to the study of St. Paul.'

(3) Of MOORE'S 'JUDGES,' Professor H. E. RYLE, D.D., says: 'I think it may safely be averred that so full and scientific a commentary upon the text and subject-matter of the Book of Judges has never been produced in the English language.'

(4) Of GOULD'S 'MARK,' *The Baptist Magazine* says: 'As luminously suggestive as it is concise and sober. The commentary proper is thoughtful, judicious, and erudite—the work of a master in hermeneutics.'

(5) Of PLUMMER'S 'LUKE,' *The Record* says: 'Dr. Plummer's work is, it need hardly be said, admirably done, both in the introduction and in the commentary. Readers will peruse with pleasure his treatment of the leading characteristics of the Gospel. The linguistic analysis leaves nothing to be desired.'

** A Prospectus giving full details of the Series, with list of Contributors, sent free on application to the Publishers, Messrs. T. & T. Clark, 38 George Street, Edinburgh.

BEYSCHLAG'S NEW TESTAMENT THEOLOGY.

New Testament Theology; or, Historical Account of the Teaching of Jesus and of Primitive Christianity according to the New Testament Sources. By Dr. WILLIBALD BEYSCHLAG, Professor of Theology at Halle. Translated by Rev. NEIL BUCHANAN. In Two Volumes, demy 8vo, Second Edition, price 18s. net.

' It is not only very able, but it is a truly valuable contribution to its subject, and no one who takes upon himself to expound the deep things of God as set forth by the New Testament writers should neglect to make an earnest study of it, and thus enrich his ministration of the word.'—Professor A. S. PEAKE, M.A.

' Dr. Beyschlag has achieved so large a measure of success as to have furnished one of the best guides to an understanding of the New Testament. . . . These pages teem with suggestions. . . . In the belief that it will stimulate thought and prove of much service to ministers and all students of the sacred text it expounds, we heartily commend it to our readers.'—*Methodist Recorder.*

' A book of much interest and importance, independent in conception and treatment ; happy in seizing and characterising the courses of thought with which he has to deal; ingenious in combination, and acute in criticism; expressing the results which he reaches, often with terseness and point, almost always with clearness and vigour. . . . The work well merits translation into English.'—Professor W. P. DICKSON, D.D., in *The Critical Review.*

WENDT'S TEACHING OF JESUS.

The Teaching of Jesus. By Professor HANS HINRICH WENDT, D.D., Jena. Translated by Rev. JOHN WILSON, M.A., Montreux. In Two Volumes, 8vo, price 21s.

'Dr. Wendt's work is of the utmost importance for the study of the Gospels, both with regard to the origin of them and to their doctrinal contents. It is a work of distinguished learning, of great originality, and of profound thought. The second part [now translated into English], which sets forth the contents of the doctrine of Jesus, is the most important contribution yet made to biblical theology, and the method and results of Dr. Wendt deserve the closest attention. . . . No greater contribution to the study of biblical theology has been made in our time. A brilliant and satisfactory exposition of the teaching of Christ.'—Professor J. IVERACH, D.D., in *The Expositor.*

'Dr. Wendt has produced a remarkably fresh and suggestive work, deserving to be ranked among the most important contributions to biblical theology. . . . There is hardly a page which is not suggestive ; and, apart from the general value of its con-clusions, there are numerous specimens of ingenious exegesis thrown out with more or less confidence as to particular passages.'—*The Critical Review.*

Dr. R. F. HORTON refers to Beyschlag's 'New Testament Theology' and Wendt's 'Teaching of Jesus' as 'two invaluable books.'

Messianic Prophecy: Its Origin, Historical Growth, and Relation to New Testament Fulfilment. By Dr. EDWARD RIEHM. New Edition, Translated by Rev. L. A. MUIRHEAD, B.D. With an Intro-duction by Prof. A. B. DAVIDSON, D.D. In post 8vo, price 7s. 6d.

' No work of the same compass could be named that contains so much that is instructive on the nature of prophecy in general, and particularly on the branch of it specially treated in the book.'—Professor A. B. DAVIDSON, D.D.

' I would venture to recommend Riehm's "Messianic Prophecy" as a summary account of prophecy both reverent and critical.'—Canon GORE in *Lux Mundi.*

SCHULTZ'S OLD TESTAMENT THEOLOGY.

Old Testament Theology. The Religion of Revelation in its Pre-Christian Stage of Development. By Professor HERMANN SCHULTZ, D.D., Göttingen. Authorised English Translation by Professor J. A. PATERSON, D.D. In Two Volumes, 8vo, Second Edition, price 18s. net.

'Professor Paterson has executed the translation with as much skill as care. . . . Readers may rely on his having given the meaning of the original with the utmost accuracy.'—*From the Author's Preface to the Translation.*

'The book will be read with pleasure, and, it need not be said, with profit, not only by professional students, but by all intelligent persons who have an interest in the Old Testament. . . . Though externally popular and of singular literary finish, the author's work within is a laborious and able study of the whole subject.'—Professor A. B. DAVIDSON, D.D.

'A standard work on this subject may be said to be indispensable to every theologian and minister. The book to get, beyond all doubt, is this one by Schultz, which Messrs. Clark have just given to us in English. It is one of the most interesting and readable books we have had in our hands for a long time.'—Professor A. B. BRUCE, D.D.

KAFTAN'S TRUTH OF THE CHRISTIAN RELIGION.

The Truth of the Christian Religion. By Professor JULIUS KAFTAN, Berlin. Translated from the German, under the Author's supervision, by G. FERRIES, D.D. With a Prefatory Note by Professor FLINT, D.D. In Two Volumes, 8vo, price 16s. net.

SUMMARY OF CONTENTS:—Division I. *Ecclesiastical Dogma*—The Origin of Dogma —Development of Theology—Orthodox Dogmatics—Breaking-up of Ecclesiastical Dogma—Judgment of History. Division II. *The Proof of Christianity* —Knowledge—The Primacy of Practical Reason—Criticism of the Traditional Speculative Method—The Proof of Christianity—Conclusion.

'Eminently a work which the times require, and will be cordially welcomed by all students of theology.'—*Scotsman.*

'Quite apart from the immediate question of obtaining a knowledge of the Ritschlian theology at first hand, these volumes are welcome. For Kaftan is no imitator, but a fertile and able writer. In the near future his view of theology, its essence and its accidents, will exercise a deep influence in our land.'—*The Expository Times.*

'One of the most important productions of the Ritschlian School of Theology, and of special interest for the way in which it treats the proof of Christianity as a something "connected in the closest manner with the whole organisation of Christian faith and life at a given time."'—*The Critical Review.*

The Apostolic and Post-Apostolic Times: Their Diversity and Unity in Life and Doctrine. By Professor G. V. LECHLER, D.D. Third Edition, thoroughly Revised and Rewritten. In Two Volumes, crown 8vo, price 16s.

'It contains a vast amount of historical information, and is replete with judicious remarks. . . . By bringing under the notice of English readers a work so favourably thought of in Germany, the translator has conferred a benefit on theology.'—*Athenæum.*

GRIMM'S LEXICON.

Greek-English Lexicon of the New Testament, Being Grimm's Wilke's Clavis Novi Testamenti. Translated, Revised, and Enlarged by JOSEPH HENRY THAYER, D.D., Bussey Professor of New Testament Criticism and Interpretation in the Divinity School of Harvard University. Now ready, Fourth Edition, demy 4to, price 36s.

'The best New Testament Greek Lexicon. . . It is a treasury of the results of exact scholarship.'—Bishop WESTCOTT.

'I regard it as a work of the greatest importance. . . . It seems to me a work showing the most patient diligence, and the most carefully arranged collection of useful and helpful references.'—THE BISHOP OF GLOUCESTER AND BRISTOL.

'An excellent book, the value of which for English students will, I feel sure, be best appreciated by those who use it most carefully.'—Professor F. J. A. HORT, D.D.

'This work has been eagerly looked for. . . . The result is an excellent book, which I do not doubt will be the best in the field for many years to come.'—Professor W. SANDAY, D.D., in *The Academy.*

'Undoubtedly the best of its kind. Beautifully printed and well translated, . . . it will be prized by students of the Christian Scriptures.'—*Athenæum.*

CREMER'S LEXICON.

Biblico - Theological Lexicon of New Testament Greek. By HERMANN CREMER, D.D., Professor of Theology in the University of Greifswald. Translated from the German of the Second Edition by WILLIAM URWICK, M.A. In demy 4to, Fourth Edition, with SUPPLEMENT, price 38s.

This Lexicon deals with words whose meaning in the Classics is modified or changed in Scripture, words which have become the bases and watchwords of Christian theology, tracing their history in their transference from the Classics into the LXX., and from the LXX. into the New Testament, and the gradual deepening and elevation of their meaning till they reach the fulness of New Testament thought.

'Dr. Cremer's work is highly and deservedly esteemed in Germany. It gives with care and thoroughness a complete history, as far as it goes, of each word and phrase that it deals with. . . . Dr. Cremer's explanations are most lucidly set out.'—*Guardian.*

'It is hardly possible to exaggerate the value of this work to the student of the Greek Testament. . . . The translation is accurate and idiomatic, and the additions to the later edition are considerable and important.'—*Church Bells.*

'We cannot find an important word in our Greek New Testament which is not discussed with a fulness and discrimination which leaves nothing to be desired.'—*Nonconformist.*

A Treatise on the Grammar of New Testament Greek, Regarded as a sure Basis for New Testament Exegesis. Translated from the German of Dr. G. B. WINER. Edited by Rev. W. F. MOULTON, D.D. With large additions and full Indices. In One large 8vo Volume, Ninth English Edition, price 15s.

'We need not say it is *the* Grammar of the New Testament. It is not only superior to all others, but *so* superior as to be by common consent the one work of reference on the subject. No other could be mentioned with it.'—*Literary Churchman.*

Greek and English Lexicon of the New Testament. By Professor EDWARD ROBINSON, D.D. In demy 8vo, price 9s.

'Excellent.'—Principal CAVE, D.D., Hackney College.

NEW PUBLICATIONS.

Now ready, in Two Vols., 8vo, price 21s.,

GENESIS

CRITICALLY AND EXEGETICALLY EXPOUNDED.

BY

DR. A. DILLMANN,

LATE PROFESSOR OF THEOLOGY IN BERLIN.

Authorised English Translation.

The Guardian (in announcing this work) said: 'We note with interest that the commentaries of the late Professor Dillmann are to be given to us in an English version. No recent scholar of the German school has a higher reputation than Dillmann.'

Just published, in demy 8vo, price 9s.,

ST. PAUL'S CONCEPTION OF CHRIST;

OR,

THE DOCTRINE OF THE SECOND ADAM.

(The Sixteenth Series of 'The Cunningham Lectures.')

BY

DAVID SOMERVILLE, M.A.,

MINISTER OF ROSEBURN FREE CHURCH, EDINBURGH.

Just published, in post 8vo, price 7s. 6d.,

HOMILETIC:

LECTURES ON PREACHING.

BY

THEODOR CHRISTLIEB, D.D.,

FORMERLY PROFESSOR OF THEOLOGY AND UNIVERSITY PREACHER AT BONN,
AUTHOR OF 'MODERN DOUBT AND CHRISTIAN BELIEF.'

Authorised English Translation.

'Valuable for fulness of learning and thoroughness of discussion and suitability for practical purposes.'—Professor JAMES ROBERTSON, D.D., in the *Critical Review.*

Just published, in crown 8vo, price 3s. 6d.,

A NEW AND CHEAPER EDITION.

THE INCARNATE SAVIOUR.

BY

W. ROBERTSON NICOLL, M.A., LL.D.,

EDITOR OF 'THE EXPOSITOR,' ETC.

The late Canon LIDDON.—'It commands my warm sympathy and admiration. rejoice in the circulation of such a book, which I trust will be the widest possible.'

EDINBURGH: T. & T. CLARK, 38 GEORGE STREET.